Modeling, Simulation and Optimization
Focus on Applications

Edited by
Shkelzen Cakaj

Modeling, Simulation and Optimization – Focus on Applications
Edited by Shkelzen Cakaj

Republished by InTech
Janeza Trdine 9, 51000 Rijeka, Croatia

Technical Editor Zeljko Debeljuh

Cover Designer Dino Smrekar

Additional hard copies can be obtained from orders@intechopen.com

Modeling, Simulation and Optimization – Focus on Applications,
Edited by Shkelzen Cakaj
p. cm.
ISBN 978-953-307-055-1

For EU product safety concerns:
IN TECH d.o.o., Prolaz Marije Krucifikse Kozulić 3, 51000 Rijeka, Croatia,
info@intechopen.com or visit our website at intechopen.com.

Meet the editor

Dr. Shkelzen Cakaj has received his BSc and MSc degrees from Prishtina University in Kosovo. Since 2003 is cooperating with Technical University in Vienna, where he has prepared his Master Thesis. He was awarded a PhD in area of satellite communications from Zagreb University, in January 2008. Later on, in 2009, as Fulbright scholar, he continued his post doctorate research at NOAA (National Oceanic and Atmospheric Administration) at Maryland, USA. He is the author of 60 papers published in worldwide conferences and journals; mostly IEEE and also engaged as a reviewer. His area of interest is the satellite ground station performance. He is lecturing satellite systems at Polytechnic University of Tirana, Albania. On 2016 he was awarded as Albanian ICT Researcher of the Year 2015.

Preface

In recent years, our life and surrounding environment are deeply influenced by new technologies making the world smaller from the globalization perspective on one hand, while increasing the complexity of technical, scientific, social, economic and political problems on the other hand. Usually, new challenges stemmed by this complexity have no simple particular solution and are not easily solved through conventional methods.

Modeling and simulation approaches are forms through which different problems can be solved more efficiently. Among traditional modeling and simulations in electrical and mechanical applications, new developing trends are promising, from areas of climatic, biomedical and health care, business and education to ethics and linguistic modeling processes. Modeling and simulation systems designers should apply proper methods and tools to satisfy the expected requirements. The eventual contradictions within these requirements and set objectives must be traded off toward the feasible solutions. Multi objective optimization is a method which relies on finding the best possible solution.

Chapters of this book provide modeling, simulation and optimization applications in the areas of medical care systems, genetics, business, ethics and linguistics, applying very sophisticated methods. Algorithms, 3-D modeling, virtual reality, multi objective optimization, finite element methods, multi agent model simulation, system dynamics simulation, hierarchical Petri Net model and two level formalism modeling are tools and methods applied on these papers.

Computer based simulations methods for teaching clinical knowledge in decision making process on health care events, a real world example of radio frequency identification tag implementation for patient traceability, simulation of brain tissue palpation enabling the surgeon to distinguish between normal and affected brain tissue, modeling the circadian rhythms, and finite element model used to determine relative micro motion of a modular hip implant related to biomedical applications. Transport routed planning optimization, research studies dedicated to multimedia, game agents application in computed games, the modeling of business processes, computing system for making autonomous ethical decisions, education quality control and optimization system for high level education quality, and finally a model applied to linguistics are a few other interesting applications.

Finally, I enjoyed reading these impressive papers which do provide new scientific research hints, each one within its specific field of study. I wish all authors successful scientific research work for a better future of nature and people worldwide.

Editor:

Dr. Sc. Shkelzen Cakaj
Post and Telecommunication of Kosovo
Satellite Communication Lecturer at Prishtina University
Fulbright Postdoctoral Researcher

Contents

1

Simulation Needs Efficient Algorithms

Marian Chudy
Millitary Univesity of Technology
Poland

1. Introduction

Many simulation systems which can be applied, for example, to solve problems in manufacturing, supply chain management, financial management and war games need procedures that have to make current decisions in limited time. It means that the procedures, mentioned above, should work efficiently and give the right or almost right solutions at the right time. The time the procedures need to prepare a solution depends on the quality of an algorithm and the "size" of the problem the algorithm solve. It leads us to the computation theory. To omit very theoretical considerations we assume that:

- the size of a problem denotes the length of the chain of its input data,
- the time complexity of an algorithm denotes the number of elementary operations it takes to solve the problem in the worst case,
- the time complexity of a problem denotes the complexity of the best possible, may be unknown yet, algorithm.

The chain of input data should be unambiguous and expressed in the shortest possible way. It is important, because the time the procedure needs to put the chain of data into a computer must be the shortest one. The more precisely definitions base on the idea of Turing machine. It is necessary to mention that there are other kinds of complexity like complexity in average sense or best behavior.

The theory of computation bases on decision problems for uniformity. The formal definition of the decision problem we can find for example in (Hromkovic, 2001). Without any losses of generality we define the decision problem as a problem which requires only a "yes" or "not" answer; some authors call such problem as a recognition problem.

There are many problems which are decision problems inherently. The Satisfiability Problem (SAT) is one of paradigmatic decision problems. It is to decide, for a given formula in the Conjunction Normal Form (CNF), whether it is satisfiable (output: "yes" = "1") or not (output: "no" = "0").

Decision problems are strongly connected with optimization problems which rely on finding the "best" solution among all solutions in some set of the feasible solutions. An objective function and the goal (min, max) determines which of the feasible solution is the best. The formal definition of an optimization problem we can find, for example, in (Hromkovic, 2001).

For every optimization problem there exists a set of decision problems which are connected with it.

Moreover, we can indicate a method that solves the optimization problem by solving the series of the decision problems from the set we mention above. The example given bellow describes the relation between optimization and decision problem.
The 0-1 optimization problem is to find

$$x^* \in S \subset B^n = \{x \in E^n : x_j \in \{0,1\}\ j = \overline{1,n}\}$$

such that

$$(c \mid x^*) = \min_{x \in S}(c \mid x) = \min_{x \in S} \sum_{j=1}^{n} c_j x_j \tag{1}$$

where

$$S = \left\{ x \in B^n : \sum_{j=1}^{n} a_{ij} x_j \le d_i \quad i = \overline{1,m} \right\} \tag{2}$$

The set of the decision problems relevant to the optimization problem (1), (2) is to decide whether exists vector $x \in B^n$ such that

$$(c \mid x) = \sum_{j=1}^{n} c_j x_j \le y, \quad x \in S \tag{3}$$

for given integers y and S defined by (2). The answer is "yes" or "no".
We observe that taking some sequence of integers y and solving relevant to them problems (3), one can obtain an optimal solution of the optimization problem (1), (2).
To refer to the previous definitions it is worth to add that
- the set of all instances of the optimization problem (1), (2) is determined by the parameters n, c, A, d.
- the set of all instances of the relevant decision problem (3) is determined by parameters n, c, A, d, y.

2. Measuring the efficiency of algorithms

The introduction given below justifies our focus on the complexity as a main measure of the algorithm efficiency.
To describe the characteristics of an algorithm time complexity more precisely one should introduce a few necessary objects and definitions.
Let us denote by
$N = \{0,1,2,...\}$ the set of all natural numbers,
R_+ - the set of non negative real numbers

and let $f : N \to R_+$ be a function and F be the set of such functions.

Definition 1 Let $g : N \to R_+$ be a function. We define

$$O(g(n)) = \{f \in F : \exists a \geq 0, n_o \in N \, such that \, \forall n \in N, n \geq n_o \, f(n) \leq a \cdot g(n)\}.$$

If $f(n) \in O(g(n))$ we say that the function f does not grow asymptotically faster than the function g.

Definition 2 Let $g : N \to R_+$ be a function. We define

$$\Omega(g(n)) = \{f \in F : \exists b \geq 0, n_1 \in N \, such \, that \, \forall n \in N, n \geq n_1 f(n) \geq b \cdot g(n)\}.$$

If $f(n) \in \Omega(g(n))$ we say that the function f grows asymptotically at least as fast as the function g.

If $f(n) \in O(g(n))$ and $f(n) \in \Omega(g(n))$ we say that f and g are asymptotically equivalent. It means that

$$f(n) \in \Theta(g(n)) = O(g(n)) \wedge \Omega(g(n)) =$$

$$= \begin{Bmatrix} t \in F : \exists c \geq 0, d \geq 0, m \in N \, such \, that \, \forall n \in N, n \geq m \\ t(n) \leq c \cdot g(n), \quad t(n) \geq d \cdot g(n) \end{Bmatrix}.$$

Let us denote by $f_\alpha(n)$ the complexity of an algorithm α, n - the size of a problem.

Definition 3 We say that an algorithm α is polynomial time one when $f_\alpha(n) \in O(p(n))$, where $p(n)$ some polynomial for $n \in N$. It means that

$$\exists c \geq 0, n_0 \in N \, such \, that \, \forall n \in N, n \geq n_0 \, f_\alpha(n) \leq c \cdot p(n),$$

in other cases the algorithm α is called exponential time algorithm.

The definition 3 allows us to describe the fundamental classes of decision problems.

The class P (polynomial) consists of all these decision problems for which a polynomial time algorithm exists, maybe unknown yet.

The class NP (non deterministic polynomial) can be define in many different but equivalent ways. It seems that more useful definition which allows to verify if a decision problem belongs to the class NP is the following one.

The class NP consists of all these decision problems for which the "yes" answer is verifiable by some procedure it takes polynomial time.

The class P is a subclass of NP $(P \subset NP)$. It comes from the definition of P and NP; every instance of P with answer "yes" is verifiable in polynomial time because it is obtained in polynomial time from definition of P. One can explore the special subclasses of NP and also search the classes of problems which contain NP class.

Let us denote by

D_Π - the set of all instances of the decision problem Π,

$x(z)$ - the input chain for $z \in D_\Pi$; the symbols of the chain $x(z)$ belongs to some defined alphabet Σ,

$N(z)$ - the size of instance $z \in D_{\Pi}$ (length of the chain $x(z)$).

There is only one $x(z)$ for given $z \in D_{\Pi}$.

Definition 4 We say that problem Π_1 transforms to problem Π_2 in polynomial time, $\Pi_1 \propto \Pi_2$, when there exists a polynomial time algorithm (function) α such that for every $z \in D_{\Pi}$ and $x(z)$, $\alpha(x(z)) = y(s), s \in D_{\Pi_2}$

where $y(s)$ - the input chain of some instance $s \in D_{\Pi_2}$.

It means that for every chain $x(z)$, we can compute in polynomial time adequate chain $\alpha(x(z)) = y(s)$ which is the input chain of some instance $s \in D_{\Pi_2}$.

The polynomial transformation is a useful tool to investigate unknown problems basing on information about related known problems.

Definition 5 A problem Π is called $NP-hard$ if, for every $\Pi' \in NP$, $\Pi' \propto \Pi$.

A problem Π is called $NP-complete$ if, $\Pi \in NP$ and Π is $NP-hard$.

The following comes from the definition above: an optimization problem does not belong to NP class, but when a related decision problem belongs to $NP-complete$ class, we call the optimization problem $NP-hard$.

From the definition of $NP-complete$ class results that if, someone found polynomial time algorithm for solving a $NP-complete$ problem, then all problems from NP class would be solved in polynomial time. This conclusion comes from the definition of $NP-complete$ class and polynomial transformation.

Summarizing our considerations we can say that efficient algorithm means algorithm with complexity bounded by some polynomial. The following table confirms this thesis by some important relations.

Time complexity function	Size of largest instances solvable in 1 hour	
	With present computer	With computer 100 times faster
n	N_1	$100N_1$
n^2	N_2	$10N_2$
n^3	N_3	$4{,}63N_3$
2^n	N_4	$N_4 + 6{,}64$
3^n	N_5	$N_5 + 4{,}19$

Table 1. Competition between efficiency of algorithms and computers

We should add that any complexity results for the decision problem also hold for the original(optimization) problem i.e. the optimization problem is not much harder than related decision problem.

To classify the efficiency of an algorithm more preciously some remarks about $\Theta(g(n))$ notation and the little-0-notation is necessary.

Property 1 The following relation holds

$$f(n) \in \Theta(g(n)) \text{ if and only if } g(n) \in \Theta(f(n)).$$

The set $\Theta(g(n))$ contains these functions which are equivalent to function $g(n)$.

The set $\Theta(g(n))$ is called the category of complexity which is represented by function $g(n)$.

Property 2 All logarithmic functions belong to one category $\Theta(\log n)$.

It means that if, $a > 1, b > 1 \text{ then } \log_a n \in \Theta(\log_b n).$

Definition 6 We say that function $f(n)$ belongs to $o(g(n))$ if

$$\forall c > 0 \ \exists N(c) \in N \ \forall n \geq N(c) \ f(n) \leq c \cdot g(n).$$

Intuitively, it means that function $g(n)$ grows much faster than function $f(n)$.

Property 3 Exponential functions do not belong to one category of complexity i.e.

$$\text{if } 0 < a < b \text{ then } a^n \in o(b^n)$$

i.e. if $0 < a < b \text{ then } \forall c > 0 \ \exists N(c) \in N \ \forall n \geq N(c) \quad a^n \leq c \cdot b^n$.

Now, we introduce nine categories of complexity:

$$c(1) = \Theta(\log_2 n), c(2) = \Theta(n), c(3) = \Theta(n \log_2 n), c(4) = \Theta(n^2),$$

$$c(5) = \Theta(n^i), c(6) = \Theta(n^j), c(7) = \Theta(a^n), c(8) = \Theta(b^n), c(9) = \Theta(n!)$$

$$\text{where} \quad j > i > 2 \text{ and } b > a > 1.$$

Property 4 If $c(r) = \Theta(g(n)) \text{ and } f(n) \in c(s) \text{ for } s < r$ then

$$f(n) \in o(g(n)).$$

It means: the lower category the better complexity.

2. Examples of the exact efficient algorithms

The set of all possible algorithms that one can use to solve a problem we divide into two parts: exact algorithms and approximation algorithms. Precise definitions of these two kind of algorithms one can find in (Hromkovic, 2001). Roughly speaking, an approximation algorithm gives a solution that is closed the optimal solution. At this part we focus our attention on exact algorithms. At the previous part of the chapter we establish the difference between the complexity of a problem and the complexity of an algorithm it solves.

From the definition, the complexity of a problem cannot be worse than the complexity of an algorithm the problem solves.
In the majority we do not know the complexity of a problem. Improving the algorithms they solve the problem we bring nearer to this unknown value.

2.1 Advanced sorting algorithms

Sorting problem is one of the most important in computer science and practice, including simulation. A sorting algorithm is an algorithm that puts elements of a list in a certain order. The most-used orders are numerical order or lexicographical one. Many algorithms, such as search and merge algorithms require sorted lists to work correctly and efficiently. So, the sorting algorithms that prepare the data to them should be also efficient. We assume that the size of sorting problem is the number of elements at list to be sorted. The piece of data actually used to determine the sorted order is called the key. Most of the algorithms in use have the complexity that belongs to $O(n^2)$ category or $O(n \log n)$; the lower bound for them is $O(n)$. It is difficult to establish only one criterion for judging sorting algorithms because many algorithms that have the same complexity do not have the same speed on the same input. Despite of this we assume that the complexity is the main criterion of the efficiency. A second (additional) criterion for judging sorting algorithm is their space (memory) requirement. Do they require extra space or can the list be sorted in place without additional memory beyond a few variables? A third (additional) criterion is stability. An algorithm is stable if it preserves the order of keys with equal values. Taking into account only the main criterion the class of advanced sorting algorithms contains these of them which have $O(n \log n)$ complexity, for example merge, quick sorts and heap. Unfortunately, the very known algorithms like bubble, insertion, selection and shell sorts belong to the class $O(n^2)$.

Quick sort (Partition Exchange Sort) algorithm is a divide and conquer algorithm which relies on a partition. To partition a list, we choose an element, called a pivot. Each round of quick sort contains the following actions:
- move all elements smaller then pivot before the pivot,
- move all elements greater then pivot after the pivot,
- recursively quick sort the values (sublist) before the pivot,
- recursively quick sort the values (sublist) after the pivot.

The most complex issue in quick sort is choosing a good pivot. Bad choices of pivot can result in drastically slower $O(n^2)$ performance. If at each step we choose the median as the pivot then quick sort works in $O(n \log n)$. Quick sort is instable and needs constant space.

Merge sort is also a divide and conquer technique. It has two phases: divide phase and conquer phase. The divide phase repeatedly divides the list into smaller sublists until the sublist is small enough to sort. The conquer phase relies on sorting simpler sublists and merging to the overall list. To realize this idea we should know: how to sort sublist (a list containing smaller number of values) and how to merge two sorted lists. The complexity of this algorithm is $O(n\log n)$. Merge sort is stable but needs additional space.

Heap sort is an efficient version of selection sort. This algorithm works in following way:
- determine the largest (smallest) element of the list and place that at the end (or beginning) of the list,
- continue this operation with the rest of the list.

These tasks are accomplished efficiently by using a data structure called a heap which is special type of binary tree. Heap sort is stable, runs in $O(n\log n)$ time and needs constant space.

Parallel computation is the most promising method to obtain real speed up in sorting. The ideal model is Parallel Random Access Machine (PRAM). To find the largest element of the table $A[1..n]$ we need $n(n-1)/2$ processors p_{ij} $i,j=\overline{1,n}$, $1\le i\le j\le n$

and additional table $T[1..n]$ with all elements $T[i]=1$, $i=\overline{1,n}$ at the start moment. We assume that processors can simultaneously read and write the same part of memory (Concurrent Read, Concurrent Write memory access). Each processor p_{ij} compares elements $A[i]$, $A[j]$ and writes in table $T[1..n]$ the following values $T[i]=0$ *if* $A[i]<A[j]$, $T[j]=0$ *if* $A[i]>A[j]$. After all comparisons we obtain one element $T[k]=1$ and number k denote the index of largest element from table $A[1..n]$. The complexity of this procedure is equal to $O(1)$. Repeating this procedure for the series of reduced tables we obtain the ordered one. This computing model is not realistic but indicates a direction of thinking (Neapolitan & Naimipour, 2004).

2.2 Polynomial time algorithm for solving linear programming problem

Linear programming (LP) is one of the most frequently used optimization method. It is used to prepare decision in the industrial, economic and military activity. It is also important that linear programming is often used as a part of more complex models in optimization, for example as a relaxed model in discreet optimization. The linear programming problem (LPP) relies on minimization (or maximization) of linear function subject to linear constrains. One of the form of the linear programming problem is

$$\max(c\mid x)=\max\sum_{j=1}^{n}c_jx_j \tag{4}$$

subject to
$$Ax\le d \tag{5}$$
$$x\ge 0 \tag{6}$$

where $A=(a_{ij})_{m\times n}$, $x\in E^n$, $c\in E^n$, $d\in E^m$.

This problem is called primal problem.

For each primal problem exists dual problem. The dual problem related to (4) – (6) is given bellow

$$\min(d \mid y) = \min \sum_{i=1}^{m} d_i y_i \tag{7}$$

subject to

$$A^T y \geq c \tag{8}$$

$$y \geq 0 \tag{9}$$

where $y \in E^m$.

There are many relations between primal (4) – (6) and dual (7) – (9) problems.
They are often applied in constructing method for solving LPP.
The most important are:
- the primal and dual LPP either have the optimal solutions or they do not have ones,
- for optimal solutions x^* and y^* the following relation holds $(c \mid x^*) = (d \mid y^*)$,
- if for some feasible solutions x, y, $(c \mid x) = (d \mid y)$ holds then $x = x^*$, $y = y^*$.

The simplex method and its many modifications are the most useful and most important methods for solving LPP yet. The essence of this method relies on searching adjacent vertices of polyhedral (5), (6) to find the vertex which is the optimal solution. Algebraic equivalent of this is to search adjacent bases and nonnegative base solutions of the linear equation system $Ax = d$. This conception results from the following theorem.

Theorem 1 If there exists an optimal solution x^* of linear programming problem (4) – (6) then there exists a vertex $\bar{x}$ of the polyhedral (5), (6) such that $(c \mid x^*) = (c \mid \bar{x})$.

It allows one to search only the vertices of the polyhedral defined by (5), (6) because the linear programming problem belongs to the class of convex problems and it means that every local minimum is equal to the global minimum of LPP. As it was shown by (Klee & Minty, 1972), the simplex method has the exponential complexity in the worst case. It is in contradiction with the practical experiences. This problem was explained by (Shamir, 1987). He obtained, for simplex method, a quadratic lower bound on the average number of pivots (steps from one basic to an adjacent one). This outcome confirms the good quality of the simplex method.

There are at least two methods which are better than the simplex method, taking into account their complexity. Older of them is the ellipsoid method developed by (Khachiyan, 1979), which is the first polynomial algorithm for solving linear programming problem. The exact description of the ellipsoid algorithm would take large space. We will present only short explanation of this algorithm. In fact the ellipsoid algorithm computes the sequence of feasible solutions of the system of strong inequalities related to LPP (4) – (6). We assume that data of the problem is integer. For given system of inequalities $Ax \le d$ the size of the problem is $L = \sum_{i=1}^{m} \sum_{j=0}^{n} \left\lceil \log_2(|a_{ij}|+1)+1 \right\rceil$, $a_{i0} = d_i, i = \overline{1,m}$

The system $Ax \le d$ has a solution if and only if the system

$$(a_i \mid x) < d_i + 2^{-L}, i = \overline{1,m} \tag{10}$$

has a solution.
The set of feasible solutions of the system (10) should be nonempty.
We start to estimate the maximum value of the objective function $(c \mid x)$ with checking the feasibility of the following system: $(c \mid x) \ge \alpha_0, \quad Ax \le d, \quad x \ge 0.$ (11)
If the set of feasible solutions is nonempty, we know that the optimum value is lesser than α_0. We may now decrease α_0 by factor 2 and check for feasibility again. If this is true, we know that $(c \mid x^*) \in [\alpha_0 / 2, \alpha_0)$. We get the optimum in a number of steps polynomial in the input size, each step being a call to feasibility checking polynomial algorithm. The feasibility checking algorithm for current value α is the main part of the ellipsoid algorithm. It relies on computing sequences of ellipsoids $E_k(x^k)$, x^k - the centre of this ellipsoid, such that $\frac{volE_{k+1}(x^{k+1})}{volE_k(x^k)} < 1.$

So, the volume of ellipsoid $E_{k+1}(x^{k+1})$ is substantially smaller than the volume of the previous ellipsoid. This is the most important point in this method because the polynomial complexity follows this property. The computing of this algorithm ends when the centre of an ellipsoid is the feasible solution of the system (11) for current value α or the set of feasible solution is empty.
It is necessary to add that the ellipsoid method can also start with the following system of inequalities: $Ax \le d, x \ge 0, A^T y \ge c, y \ge 0, (c \mid x) \ge (d \mid y).$

The iteration complexity of the ellipsoid method is $O(n^2 L)$ but computational complexity in worst case is $O(n^4 L)$.
In 1984 Narendra Karmarkar introduced a new idea for solving linear programming problem.
Let us consider the following pair of linear programming problems:

- primal problem $$\min_{x \in R_0}(c \mid x) = \min_{x \in R_0} \sum_{j=1}^{n} c_j x_j \tag{12}$$

where $$R_0 = \left\{x \in E^n : Ax = d,\ x \geq 0\right\}$$

- dual problem $$\max_{y \in Q_0}(d \mid y) = \max_{y \in Q_0} \sum_{i=1}^{m} d_i y_i \tag{13}$$

where $$Q_0 = \left\{y \in E^m : A^T y \leq c\right\}$$

We assume that $$R_0^+ = \left\{x \in E^n : Ax = d,\ x > 0\right\} \neq \phi$$ and

$$Q_0^+ = \left\{y \in E^m : A^T y < 0\right\} \neq \phi$$

Denoting by $w = c - A^T y$, $X = xI^n$, I^n - diagonal matrix
the Karush-Kuhn-Tucker (KKT) conditions are

$$Ax = d,\ x \geq 0, \quad A^T y + w = c,\ w \geq 0, \quad Xw = 0 = (o, o, \ldots, o) \tag{14}$$

For each par (x, y) which satisfies conditions (14) x is the optimal solution of primal problem (12) and y is the optimal solution of dual problem (13).
The relaxed form of KKT conditions is

$$Ax = d,\ x \geq 0, \quad A^T y + w = c,\ w \geq 0, \quad Xw = 1\mu = (\mu, \mu, \ldots, \mu) \tag{15}$$

We obtain (14) from (15) when $\mu = 0$.
Following (Sierksma,1996) we have.

Theorem 2 Let $R_0 = \left\{x \in E^n : Ax = d,\ x \geq 0\right\}$ be bounded. Then (15) has for each positive μ $(\mu > 0)$ a unique solution, denoted by $x(\mu), y(\mu), w(\mu)$.

Definition 7 The sets $\{x(\mu) : \mu > 0\}$, $\{y(\mu) : \mu > 0\}$ are called the interior path of problem (12) and (13) respectively. For shortness, we will call $x(\mu)$ the interior path of primal problem and $y(\mu)$ the interior path of dual problem. The parameter μ is called interior path parameter.

Theorem 3 For each interior path parameter μ, the duality gap satisfies

$$(c \mid x(\mu)) - (d \mid y(\mu)) = n\mu \tag{16}$$

Basing on these properties we can form the general steps of the algorithm. Let x^k be the current interior point of the feasible region (x^k is not the point of interior path but only corresponds to the point $x(\mu^k)$), and μ^k be the current interior path parameter. The algorithm determines next interior point x^{k+1} which is closer to interior path than x^k. This new point is given by the following expression

$$x^{k+1} = x^k + s(x^k, \mu^k)$$

where $s(x^k, \mu^k)$ is the search direction which causes x^{k+1} to be closer the interior path than x^k. Next, the algorithm decreases the interior parameter according to formula bellow

$$\mu^{k+1} = \eta\mu^k, \quad \eta \in (0,1)$$

The procedure is repeated for pair (x^{k+1}, μ^{k+1}), until a pair (x^+, μ^+) has been reached for which the stop criteria $n\mu^+ \leq \varepsilon$ is satisfied. Since $\mu^+ \approx 0$, and $n\mu^+$ is approximately equal to the duality gap $(c \mid x^+) - (d \mid y^+)$ then vectors $x^+ \; and \; y^+$ approximate optimal solutions of primal and dual problems respectively; $x^+ \approx x^*, y^+ \approx y^*$. We omit the explanation of this part of algorithm that deal with the search direction $s(x^k, \mu^k)$. This needs large space to describe it. We also omit the problem of searching start point and the prove of polynomiality of the interior path method. The complexity of the first interior algorithm (Karmarkar, 1984) is:

- iteration complexity - $O(nL)$,

- computation complexity - $O(n^3L)$, where L denotes the length of input chain. The Karmarkar's idea has been improved and extended. Now, there are many new interior point methods with better complexity. For example, an infeasible-interior- point algorithm (Anstreicher at al., 1999), applied to random linear programs generated according to a model of Todd gives an exact solution in expected number of iterations $O(n \log n)$.

2.3 Efficient algorithms in graph theory

The graph theory is one of the most important tools for modeling and solving problems. The area of its applications is very broad. To refer to the title of the chapter we will give only short presentation dealing with selected but important problems and algorithms. An efficient algorithm can be obtained using greedy approach. A greedy algorithm iteratively makes one greedy choice (local optimum) after another, reducing each given problem into a smaller one, and never reconsider its choices. A suitable structure of the problem guarantees the efficiency of the greedy algorithm. For many other problems (with improper structure), greedy algorithms fail to produce the optimal solutions. They sometime produce the unique worst possible solutions. Despite this, greedy algorithm is often used because it is faster than other methods in many cases.

The minimum spanning tree (MST) belongs to the class of problems that have suitable structure to use greedy approach. This problem is formulated as follows:

for given connected graph $G=(V,E)$ with weighted edges, find the tree $T=(V,F),\ F\subset E,$ such that the graph T is connected and the sum of the weighs of edges in T is as small as possible.

Telephone companies are interested in minimum spanning tree, because the minimum spanning tree of set sites determine the wiring scheme that connects the sites using minimum wire. The greedy algorithms of Prim and Kruskal solve this problem efficiently (Neapolitan & Naimipour, 2004).

Prim's algorithm continuously increases the size of a tree starting with a single arbitrary vertex until it spans all the vertices:

1. take an arbitrary vertex $v_1 \in V$, $V^T=\{v_1\}$, $F=\phi$

2. chose edge $(v_1,v^*)\in E$ such that $w(v_1,v^*)=\min\limits_{(v_1,v)\in E} w(v_1,v)$, (greedy step)

   where $w(v_1,v)$ denotes the weight of edge (v_1,v),

3. set $F=\{(v_1,v^*)\}$ and $V^T=\{v_1,v^*\}$

4. repeat steps 2 and 3 for actual values F and V^T until $V^T=V$.

The complexity of this algorithm is $O(|V|^2)=O(n^2)$.

Kruskal's algorithm starts with a graph $T=(V,F), F=\phi$ and the ordered set E_o containing all edges from E in the order of increasing weights. We assume that each vertex is connected component and each component is a tree.

For $k=1,\ k\le n-1$ with step equals one do: select the next smallest weight edge (greedy step) and if the edge connects two different connected components then add the edge to F. The complexity of this algorithm is $O(n^2\log n)$.

One has observed that for sparse graph Kruskal's algorithm is better than Prim's but for dense graph Prim's algorithm is better than Kruskal's one.

The single-source shortest path problem arises in transportation and communications. For given connected graph $G=(V,E)$ with weighted edges, which is a model of structure of a transportation or communications system, the important problem is to find the shortest paths from given vertex (source) to a destination or to all the others. This problem is related to the spanning tree problem because the graph representing all the paths from given vertex to all the others must be a spanning tree. Dijkstra's algorithm (greedy approach) solves this problem in polynomial time.

The running time of this algorithm is estimated by expression $O(n^2)$.
Greedy approach can be effectively used to solve the problem of data compression. This problem relies on finding the minimum length bit string which can be used to encode a string of symbols. For example, the problem of text compression is: what is the smallest number of bits one can use to store a piece of text. The Huffman's algorithm (greedy approach) generates optimal code of symbols by related binary tree. The complexity of the Huffman's algorithm is $O(n \log n)$, where n denotes the number of different symbols in a file.

3. Approaches to solving NP-hard problems

The common opinion is that the majority of practical problems belong to the $NP-hard$ class. It means, from the definition that for any such problem does not exist a polynomial algorithm that solves it. This obliges us to search special approaches to these problems that give acceptable, from the practical point of view, results. We will present only a few such approaches.
Denote by D_Π the set of all instances of given $NP-hard$ problem Π.

The first approach relies on exploring the set D_Π to find some subset $D_{\Pi_s} \subset D_\Pi$ of "easy" instances and designing an efficient algorithm for solving special problem Π_s for which the set of instances is equal to D_{Π_s}. To explain this approach we will consider $NP-hard$ problem Π, which is the linear integer programming problem (LIPP):

$$(c \mid x^*) = \max_{x \in S}(c \mid x) = \max_{x \in S} \sum_{j=1}^{n} c_j x_j \tag{17}$$

where $$S = \{x \in E^n : Ax \le d,\ x \ge 0,\ x - \text{int}.\} \tag{18}$$

and the relaxation of the problem (17), (18), which is the linear programming problem (LP):

$$(c \mid x^o) = \max_{x \in T}(c \mid x) = \max_{x \in T} \sum_{j=1}^{n} c_j x_j \tag{19}$$

where $$T = \{x \in E^n : Ax \le d,\ x \ge 0\} \tag{20}$$

The special problem Π_s can be obtained by selecting special properties of constraint matrix A or special properties of the objective function $(c \mid x)$.
An excellent example for the first case is integer linear programming problem with totally unimodular matrix A.

Definition 8 An integer matrix A is totally unimodular (TUM) if every square submatrix of A has determinant either 0, 1, or -1.

Theorem 4 Let A be totally unimodular matrix. For each integer vector d the polyhedron (20) has only integer vertices. The proof one can find in (Sierksma, 1996).

Theorem 5 If A is totally unimodular and d is an integer vector, then optimal solution x^o of LP is also optimal solution of ILPP i.e. $x^o = x^*$. The proof results from theorem 1, 4 and relation $S \subset T$.

So, we can solve special integer linear programming problem (17), (18) with totally unimodular matrix A by solving its polynomial relaxation (19), (20).

Another special problem Π'_S, one can obtain from general problem (17), (18) taking into account an original property of the objective function $(c \mid x)$.

The sequence (c_j) is called superincreasing

when
$$\sum_{i=1}^{j-1} c_i < c_j \quad for \quad j=2,3,... \tag{21}$$

We will consider sequences containing n elements only and assume that for $n = 1$ a sequence is a superincreasing one.

Theorem 6 If the problem (17)-(18) satisfies the following assumptions:

- a sequence (c_j) is the superincreasing and non negative one,
- elements a_{ij} are non negative($a_{ij} \geq 0$),

then the optimal solution of the problem (17)-(18) is given by the following procedure

$$x_j^* = \begin{cases} 1 & when \quad a_j \leq d - \sum_{k \in N_j^+} a_k \\ 0 & otherwise \end{cases} \qquad j = n, n-1, \ldots, 1 \tag{22}$$

where

a_j - the j-th column of the constraint matrix A,

$$d = (d_1, d_2, \ldots, d_m)^T, \quad N_n^+ = \phi$$

$$N_j^+ = \left\{ k : x_k^* = 1, \quad k \in \{n, n-1, \ldots, j+1\} \right\}.$$

The proof results from (21) and assumptions.

The complexity of the procedure (22) is equal to $O(n^3)$, (Chudy, 2007).

Theorem 6 allows us to solve special case of optimization problem (17), (18) in polynomial time, when the assumptions it needs are satisfied.

The second approach relies on designing exponential algorithm which belongs to the lower category than the algorithms known at present. Promising results base on new concept of complexity which is called parameterized complexity. The theory of parameterized complexity was developed by Rod Downey and Michael Fellows. An introduction to the new field was presented in the monograph (Downey& Fellows, 1999). This is two-dimensional complexity theory where complexity is measured in terms of input size and some parameter of a problem. The concept of the parameterized complexity is motivated by the observation that there exist several hard problems that require exponential time of computing when the complexity is measured in terms of the input size only, but they are computable in polynomial time in the input size and exponential in a selected one parameter of the problem. It worth to note (Hromkovic, 2001) that the concept of parameterized complexity includes the concept of pseudo-polynomial complexity.
The interesting version of parameterized algorithm we find in (Reed at al, 2004). For given graph $G=(V,E)$ with m edges and n vertices the algorithm settles either a set $V_1 \subset V$ of at most k vertices which intersects every odd cycle, or the information that no such set exists. The running time is $O(4^k kmn)$.
The third approach bases on designing an approximation algorithm that gives reasonable feasible solution of the given problem. The formal definition of the approximation algorithm and its properties is presented in (Hromkovic, 2001). The book by Vazirani, (Vazirani, 2003) contains many precisely selected problems and approximation algorithms that provide solutions whose quality are good enough.
We will consider the problem (17), (18) and try to find an approximation algorithm using the superincreasing sequence (21) renumbering, if necessary, all variables of this problem and assume that the sequence (c_j) is nonnegative and none decreasing. To obtain upper-bound of optimal objective function value, we will introduce new objects (Chudy, 2007).
Let us denote by

H^n - set of all finite superincreasing integer sequences (h_j), $j=\overline{1,n}$,

$A^n = \{h \in H: \;\; h_j \geq c_j, \;\; j=\overline{1,n}\}$ - the set of finite superincreasing sequences with integer elements no smaller than suitable elements of the sequence (c_j).

Remembering that (c_j) is non decreasing we form the following definition.

Definition 9 A superincreasing sequence $h^* = (h_j^*)$ is called the nearest up to the sequence (c_j) when $h^* \in A^n$, $\left\|c-h^*\right\| = \min_{h\in A^n} \|c-h\| = \min_{h\in A^n} \sum_{j=1}^{n} \left|c_j - h_j\right|$.

The complexity of the procedure that compute this sequence is equal to $O(n^2)$.

The upper-bound
$$\sum_{j=1}^{n} h_j^* x_j \geq \sum_{j=1}^{n} c_j x_j^* \tag{23}$$
of optimal objective function value for the problem (17), (18) is given by (23)

where $x = (x_j),\ j = \overline{1,n}$ denotes a feasible solution computed by procedure (22)

when we set the sequence (h_j^*) instead of the sequence (c_j) in (17), (18) and

$x^* = (x_j^*),\ j = \overline{1,n}$ denotes an optimal solution of the problem (17), (18),

under assumption $a_{ij} \geq 0,\ c_j \geq 0$. The assessment (23) we obtain in polynomial time. The presented approaches can be combine to obtain more efficient method that give optimal or almost optimal solution of the hard problem. It is necessary to say that we have omitted in our considerations such important methods like randomized algorithms, evolutionary algorithms, quantum computing and parallel computing.

4. Conclusion

We must repeat that high quality of simulation system needs efficient algorithms. The algorithms we have described above deal with only part of the areas we are interested in. The presented short review indicates that almost all problems including hard ones can be solved efficiently enough. The designer of a simulation system should posses a set of tools that support him in selecting proper methods which could satisfy the requirements.

5. References

Anstreicher, K.; Ji, J. & Potra, F. (1999). Probabilistic Analysis of An Infeasible-Interior-Point Algorithm for Linear Programming. *Mathematics of Operations Reseach,* Vol.24, No.1, (January 1999), page numbers (176-192), ISSN 0364-765X

Chudy, M. (2007). Remarks on 0-1 optimization problems with superincreasing and superdecreasing objective functions, BOOK OF ABSTRACTS 23rd IFIP TC7 Conference on System Modelling and Optimization, pp.392-393, ISBN978-83-88309-0, Cracow, Poland, July 2007, University of Science and Technology, Cracow

Downey, R. & Fellows, M. (1999) *Parameterized Complexity,* Springer-Verlag, ISBN 978-0-387-94883-6, Berlin

Hromkovic, J. (2001). *Algorithmics for Hard Problems. Introduction to Combinatorial Optimization, Randomizattion, Approximation, and Heuristics,* Springer-Verlag, ISBN 3-540-66860-8, Berlin

Karmarkar, N. (1984). A new polynomial-time algorithm for linear programming. *Combinatorica,* Vol.4, No. 4, (1984), page numbers (373-395), ISSN 0209-9683

Khachiyan, L. (1979). A polynomial algorithm in linear programming. *Soviet Mathematics Doklady,* vol. 20, No.1, (1979), page numbers (191-194), ISSN 0197-6788

Klee, V. & Minty, G. (1972). How good is the simplex algorithm, In: *Inequalities, III,* Sisha, O. page numbers (159-175), Academic Press, ISBN 0125641141, New York

Neapolitan, R. & Naimipour, K. (2004). *Foundations of Algorithms. Using C++ Pseudocode* Jones and Bartlett Publishers, Inc, ISBN 07637-23878, Boston

Reed, B.; Smith, K. & Vetta, A. (2004) Finding Odd Cycle Transversals. *Operations Reseach Letters,* Vol. 32, No. 4, July 2004, page numbers (299-301), ISSN 0167-6377

Shamir, R. (1987). The Efficiency of the Simplex Method: A Survey. *Management Science,* Vol. 33, No. 3, (March 1987), page numbers (301-334), ISSN 0025-1909

Sierksma, G. (1996). *LINEAR AND INTEGER PROGRAMMING Theory and Practice,* Marcel Dekker, Inc. ISBN 0-8247-9695-0, New York

Vazirani, V., V. (2003). *Approximation Algorithms,* Springer-Verlag, ISBN 3-540-65367-8, Berlin

2

MODEL-DRIVEN ENGINEERING FOR HIGH-PERFORMANCE COMPUTING APPLICATIONS

David Lugato*, Jean-Michel Bruel**, Ileana Ober** and Benjamin Venelle*

**CEA-CESTA, **IRIT/Université de Toulouse*
France

1. Abstract

The main three specific features of high performance scientific simulation consist of obtaining optimal performance levels, sustainability of the codes and models and the use of dedicated architectures. The construction of codes and of the physical phenomena to be simulated requires substantial investments both in terms of human resources and of the experiments required to validate the models. The need for increasingly refined modeling leads to optimization of the performance levels of the codes to obtain simulation results within acceptable calculation times. Finally, the necessary recourse to highly specialized hardware resources adds further constraints to the programming of such software, especially when the lifetime of the codes, often close to 20 years, is compared to that of super computers, in the order of just 4 years.

The MDA approach (Model Driven Architecture), standardized by the OMG (Object Management Group) and based on UML 2.0, provides among things a generic method for obtaining a runnable code from a UML (Unified Modeling Language) model describing a system on several levels of modeling. Its various abstraction mechanisms should make it possible to increase the lifetime of our codes by facilitating the porting operations while at the same time improving performance thanks to the capitalization of good programming practices. MDA technologies have already proved their value in other fields of the computer industry. The sector of real time systems, for example, is based on UML to define a profile specific to their programming constraints (size on the on-board code, limited resources, rapidity of upgrades, etc.).

By analogy to these other sectors of the computer industry, we have therefore chosen to adopt the definition of a UML profile specific to the constraints for the development of high performance scientific simulation. We also choose to complete this profile with a DSL (Design Specific Language) in order to fit physicians and developers needs. This approach is explained in this chapter which addresses in turn the following points: definition of a meta-model for high performance simulation, the use of proven technologies (e.g., Topcased, Acceleo) for the automatic transformation of models with in particular the automatic generation of a Fortran code, and finally an overall illustration of an implementation of this profile.

2. Introduction

2.1. Preamble

The developer of a high performance simulation code has to take into account a set of multiple constraints. As if the algorithms required for modeling physical phenomena were not sufficiently complex, the ever-increasing needs of calculation precision and performance also have to be integrated. This has naturally meant turning to programming languages enabling such levels of performance to be met (e.g. Fortran) and to increasingly fine and sensitive optimizations of the code (Metcalf, 1982). Not only have the codes developed very rapidly become dependent on the target hardware architectures but also the developer has had to acquire new skills in hardware knowledge. Finally, the latest current constraint is that due account must be taken of the short lifetime of the hardware of such architectures while at the same time ensuring the long lifetime of the codes developed. As an example, the CEA considers that the simulation models and numerical analysis methods associated with our professional problems have a lifetime in the order of 20 to 30 years and must therefore be maintained over that period. In order to meet the constantly increasing demands in terms of precision and performance, the CEA, in agreement with Moore's law (Moore, 1965) on hardware, has decided to change its main super computer every 4 years through the Tera program (Gonnord et al., 2006).

Over the last few years, Object oriented technologies have evidenced their good properties in terms of productivity and sustainability. Unified Modeling Language (UML), as the prime example of an object modeling language, makes it possible to effectively describe a system leaving aside all superfluous details (Pilone & Pitman, 2006). Standardized by the *Object Management Group* in 1997, its use has since been extended to many fields even if it was originally designed as object oriented software. The first advantage of UML is that to understand the notation there is no need to manipulate a development tool or to have any knowledge of programming or even to have a computer. This extremely powerful and widely adopted notation therefore greatly facilitates the modeling, design and creation of software. Another asset of the UML notation is that it provides support to all those involved throughout the various phases of the genesis of software (expression of the need, analysis, design, implementation, validation and maintenance) around one and the same formalism.

As a natural development of UML, the MDA method (OMG, 2005) introduces a new approach in computer development. Its main advantage is that it describes an application leaving aside all the details of implementation. MDA is based on the concepts of a Platform Independent Model (PIM) and a Platform Specific Model (PSM). That results in a better independence from technological upgrades and an increased lifetime of the codes as only the models need to be maintained.

2.2. State of the art

MDA philosophy has significantly gained ground since its standardization. One of the main reasons lies in the possibilities of UML adaptation and extension through the notion of profile for optimal integration of the constraints of specific development to a given field of application.

The current fervor for increasingly reduced systems offering multiple services has made the development of real time applications extremely complex. UML-RT (Douglass, 2004), or *UML profile for Real Time*, enables the rapid design of onboard systems taking account of the problem of simple user interfaces, of the high level of dependence of the system on its external environment (sensors, triggers, motors, etc.) and of the real time management of the processes involved. This UML profile also provides solutions for reducing costs and strategic development lead times in industries such as aeronautics, the automotive industry or mobile telephones. An example of good UML/SysML profile is MARTE (Modeling and Analysis of Real-time and Embedded Systems). This profile adds capabilities to UML for model-driven development of Real Time and Embedded Systems. It provides support for specification, design, and verification/validation stages and is intended to replace the existing UML Profile for Schedulability, Performance and Time.

2.3. Approach adopted

The above examples together with the numerous other UML profiles clearly show the advantages of using a UML profile for the integration and specialization of UML in line with its own development constraints. We chose to develop UML-HPC, or *UML Profile for High Performance Computing,* in order to integrate the constraints specific to our field of application: high performance, specific hardware architectures and long life. After a brief recapitulation of the development cycle used in the CEA/CESTA to enable us to define the place of UML-HPC, we shall explain the concepts present in this meta-model and detail its main operational principles. We shall then present the services revolving around the meta-model required for future users and therefore developers of scientific computing applications. Finally, we shall propose the technical solution that we have adopted for its software implementation and justify our preferences. The conclusion will report on the current state of progress and on the future prospects envisioned.

One interesting approach in this context is based on the use of Domain Specific Languages (DSL)s. Domain specific languages (DSL)s are languages specific to a domain or to a family of applications. They offer the correct level of abstraction over their domain, together with accessibility for domain experts unfamiliar with programming. DSLs focus on doing a specific task well and on being accessible for domain experts, often less competent in programming. DSLs come together with variable complexity development environments. The obvious main advantage of using a DSL is that it provides the right vocabulary and abstraction level for a given problem. As a result they can be used by engineers without particular programming skills or training. The price of this is a Tower of Babel and the risk to have costly and less powerful development environments.

Similarly, domain specific modeling (DSM) allows modeling at a higher level of abstraction by using a vocabulary tailored to a specific business domain. Domain specific languages are not only dependent on their application domain, but also their usage is often tailored on an enterprise's culture, personal programming, or modeling style. As a result a domain is often represented by family of (modeling) languages.

3. UML-HPC

3.1. Development process

In a « V » like development cycle, the sequence « design → production → unit tests » can become iterative. At each iteration, the developer integrates additional functionalities described in the specification. This incremental approach in development produces productivity gains and the assurance that each requirement in the specification will be integrated.

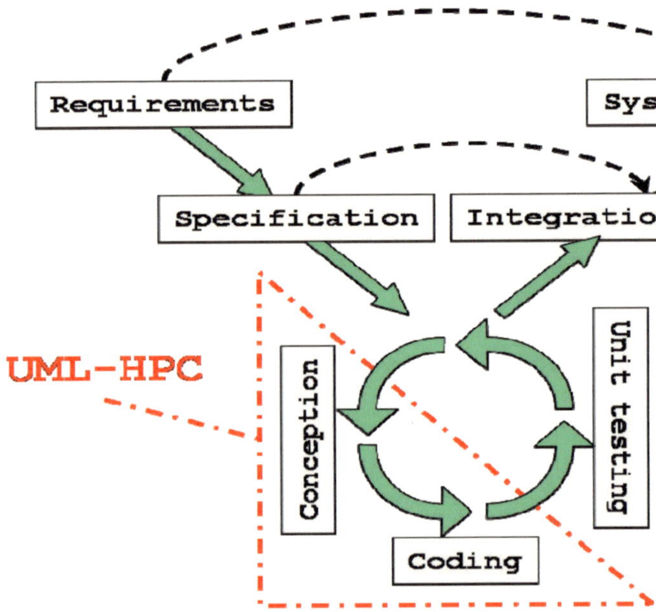

Fig. 1. Integration of UML-HPC in a "V" like development cycle.

Our meta-model currently falls within a hybrid development cycle as shown in Fig. 1. UML-HPC supports automation of the transition between the design phase and the production phase through the modeling of all the elements required for the generation and optimization of the generated source code.

The user can call upon one or several types of diagram (class, state-transition and activities) to model the design of his application. In addition, the final IDE (*Integrated Development Environment*) offers solutions of model checking, optimization and metrics of the various models designed by the developer. Once the model has been completed, verified and validated, it is left to the user to choose the language(s) and the target architecture(s) to obtain his high performance code(s). The iterative approach also applies to UML-HPC because in the future we want to help in the automation between other development phases, with a meta-model of the requirements expression, a specification meta-model, the automatic generation of tests, etc.

3.2. Structuring of the design models

From the user viewpoint, UML-HPC structures the design of a scientific computing software package with the help of the following concepts: modules (HPCModule), methods (HPCMethod). These concepts are deliberately close to those currently envisioned by designers with Fortran language. With UML-HPC, we wanted to raise the level of abstraction in the design phase without radically changing the habits of developers. UML-HPC makes the distinction between the manipulated objects (HPCStaticElement) and the manipulating objects (HPCDynamicElement).

However the meta-model leaves the possibility of defining manually the source code to be integrated through a specific class, HPCCode, or the annotations to be included (HPCComment). In particular, such annotations can be specialized to describe the design with comments or even to provide information on the theoretic level of performance of a method. All the data contained in the HPCComment can be post-processed for the automatic generation of documentation, for example.

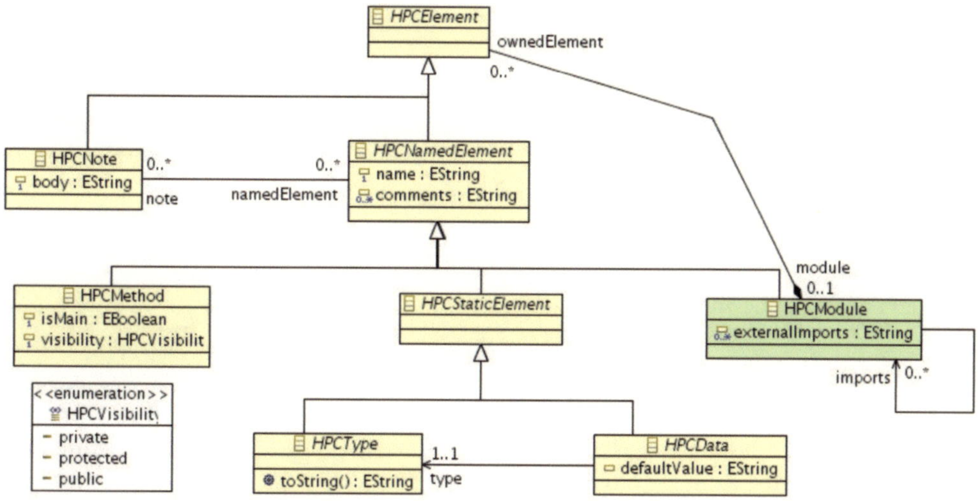

Fig. 2. Structures in UML-HPC.

3.3. Data typing

To obtain optimal performance of the codes to be produced, the designer of scientific applications must be able to have full control over the data structures he wants to manipulate. Each data item, each parameter (HPCParameter) or each attribute (HPCAttribute) is used by a processing object and must therefore be typed to maintain control over the execution semantics of the model.

In this meta-model we choose to include all the types usually employed in scientific computing. The designer has the possibility of using standard, primitive types (HPCPrimitiveType) or of building structured types (HPCStructuredType). The latter may consist of several attribute fields (HPCComposedType) or be derived from types conventionally used in scientific calculation (HPCDerivedType).

The definition of the types using UML-HPC must make it possible to meet the need of designers to model mathematic structures such as matrices, complex numbers, vectors, etc. UML-HPC also makes it possible to associate a set of specific processes with a given type, as for example the concatenation of chains of characters or the calculation of Eigen vectors.

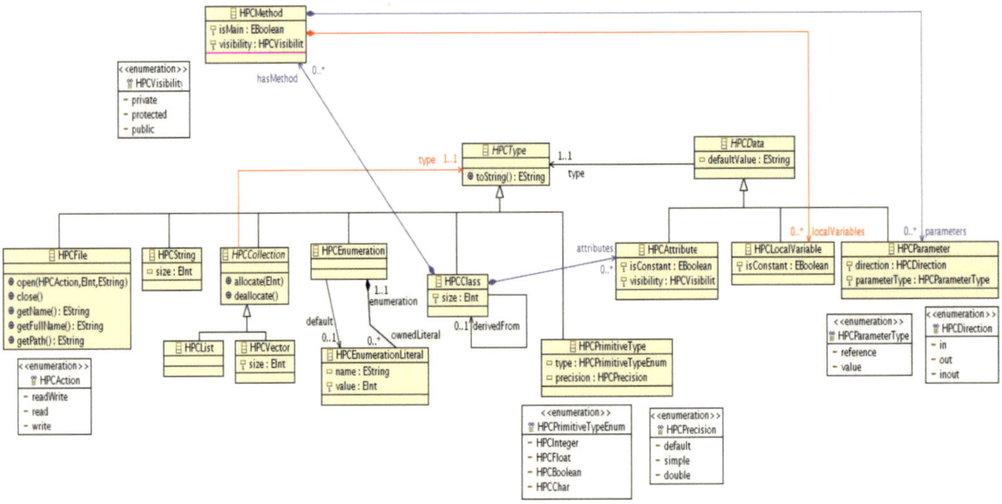

Fig. 3. Data typing in UML-HPC.

3.4. Data processing

Outside of the « hands-on » definition of the body of processing of a method or a program using the HPCCode, the definition of an algorithm essentially involves the modeling of an activities diagram (HPCActivityDiagram).

These activities diagrams are very similar to those of UML. The designer can thus model a succession of states that can contain strings of instructions or ranked activities diagrams and each transition will contain a boolean condition or communication between the various processes. These conditions must include at least one initial state (initialization of the variables) and a final state (release of the memory) with a pathway between the two.

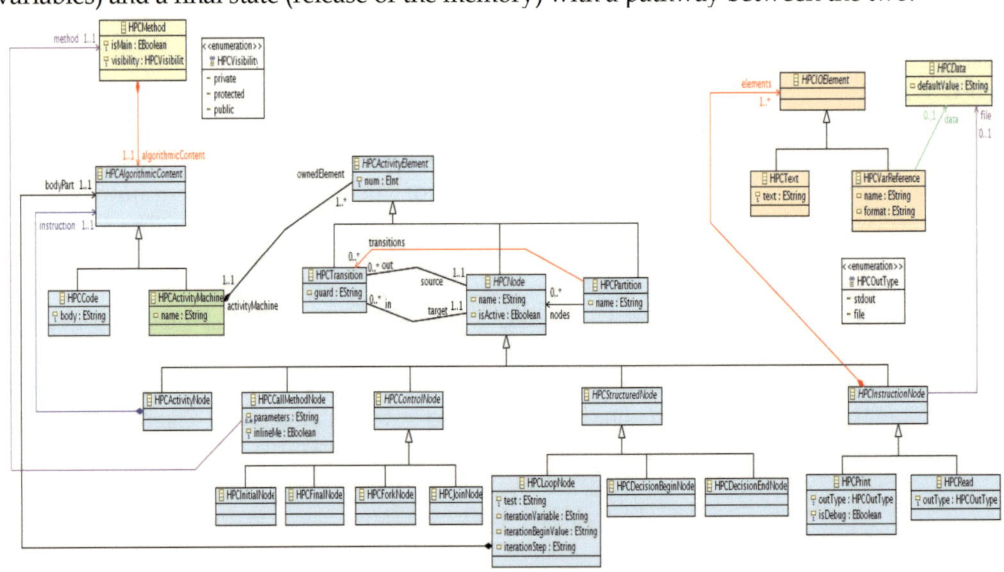

Fig. 4. Data processing in UML-HPC.

4. The UML-HPC services

The UML-HPC meta-model is not sufficient for the easier design of scientific computing applications. In this section, we therefore present a few additional, necessary services for the construction of a complete software engineering workshop.

4.1. Model-checking

The first essential service for a designer is the capability of checking the validity of the model he has designed. Without being exhaustive, a few basic rules included are given below:

- Respect of the UML-HPC meta-model in an MDA approach.
- Checking of the type and the assignment of attributes, data typing or checking the types of the procedure of function call parameters.
- A HPCDynamicElement must always be specialized either by a HPCCode or by a HPCActivityMachine so that the model does not contain any totally abstract processing and for the code generation to be complete.
- An activities diagram must contain at least one initial node with all the declarations and initializations of local variables and a final node with all the necessary memory releases plus a pathway between the two nodes.
- Application of design patterns and tracing of anti-patterns.

4.2. Optimization

The UML-HPC meta-model has no completely hard and fast optimization rules, mainly because optimizations may depend on the target language, on the hardware architecture or even on the experience of the designer. The goal of the meta-model is to assist designers in creating an efficient and effective code. In particular, the complexity of the target architectures (number of processors, level and rapidity of the cache memories, etc.) will become accessible through high level abstract functions.

Nevertheless, numerous choices depend on the designer and his experience, for example the decision to arrange variables contiguously in the memory. UML-HPC contains constructions to facilitate this type of design. Another avenue of thought for such problems of optimization relates to the activities diagrams. Each diagram may be considered as a string of instructions. The classic optimizations used in scientific calculation (unfolding of loops, in-lining, etc. cf. (Metcalf, 1982)) can therefore be applied. Subsequently, on a set of activities diagrams, the parallelism can be optimized (the relationship between the number and the size of the communications with the periods dedicated to calculation) thanks to basic algorithms of graph theory (cf. Cogis & Robert, 2003).

4.3. Software metrics and profiling

Thanks to all the information contained in a model, the theoretic performance levels of the future application can be analyzed. It is in fact possible to deduce from all the activities diagrams a product automaton structure from which in particular the McCabe number (cyclomatic complexity), the Halstead metrics (maintainability complexity) or even the Amdahl speed-up coefficient (theoretic gain in performance dependent upon the parallel code percentage) can be estimated.

We also want to extend this concept of generation of call and dependence graphs to take account of the target architectures. The objective is to obtain a theoretic profiling taking account of the time required for the performance of each instruction. That requires associating a performance time with each atomic instruction (addition, saving in the memory, etc.) in order to deduce an estimate of the performance time of certain algorithms.

4.4. Automatic code generation

Automatic code generation must be based on all the data given in the model in order to produce an effective code. We have currently chosen to generate a majority of Fortran code but we envisage in the future a multi-source code generation in order to choose the most appropriate language according to the parts of the code to be produced (calculation, IHM, inputs/outputs, etc.).

Over and beyond the data contained in the model, the code generator must also be based on the optimization techniques mentioned above to know, for example: what are the so-called « in-line » methods, to what extent the loops can be unfolded, on what module such or such a procedure depends, and so on.

Similarly, it can be based on the possibilities of the target language to generate optimized constructions. Above all, automatic code generation must be based on the target architecture as the majority of the optimizations are based on the hardware potential (use of various levels of cache memory, shared memory or distributed memory type parallelisms, etc.). Compilers can also become a parameter in code generation insofar as each compiler has its own optimization algorithms depending on the instructions employed.

Finally, we have the possibility of parameterizing the level of traces contained in the code. The designer can thus generate either an optimized code for the production of calculations or an instrumented code to be able to debug it and measure it in comfort.

5. Technical Solutions

5.1. Needs

The aim of this study is to facilitate the work of future developers of high performance computing applications. Our first need is therefore to provide them with an IDE offering all the services outlined above. The use of a portable and upgradeable software development environment but also a medium for the meta-model therefore becomes essential.

The MDA approach adopted is strongly based on graphic modeling techniques. We therefore need a sufficiently open UML modeler to adapt to the formalism of our meta-model.

Finally, there must be the capability of transcribing the models produces into Fortran source files. For that transformation of models, we needed a model interpreter offering functionalities of automatic code generation respecting a pre-defined meta-model. Given the specific features that we want to give to the Fortran code developed, the interpreter must be parameterable and transparent for future developers.

5.2. Integrated Development Environment

Microsoft Visual Studio, Windev, and Eclipse are some of the most remarkable IDEs. The initial choice of the Eclipse developers was to provide a complete and interoperable software development platform to an open-source community. The advantages of that tool include the integration of code compilation/edition tools, extensibility through a system of frameworks and a vast choice of plug-ins for various applications. The open source aspect of the tool, its modularity and the wide, dynamic community rapidly led us to adopt Eclipse as the medium for our study[1].

5.3. UML modeler

In a similar open-source approach, the CNRT Aeronautics and Space supplies Topcased. This modeling tool, that can be integrated into Eclipse, aims to meet the industrial constraints of long term software maintenance, of reducing production costs, of capitalizing on knowledge and the transparent integration of technological changes. Outside of the UML, EMF, SysML and AADL modelers supplied by default, Topcased proposes the generation of modelers specific to the meta-models of the user.

The integration into Eclipse, its openness and an active community encouraged us to adopt Topcased[2] over other open-source or commercial UML modelers that we have tested for our study such as Papyrus, Omondo, Rational Rose or Objecteering.

5.4. Code generator

In term of tools, actual transformation environment are mature. The AtlanMod team for example provides several solutions that have been worked out as open-source components contributed to Eclipse.org. One of them is the ATL (Atlanmod Transformation Language), a declarative, rule-based, model-to-model transformation system including a virtual machine, a compiler, a wide library of reusable transformations and a corresponding development environment[3]. Among the other solutions available under Eclipse, AMW (AtlanMod Model Weaving) allows to express, compute and use abstract correspondences between models (http://www.eclipse.org/gmt/amw) while AM3 (AtlanMod Megamodel Management) is a scalable solution for global model management.

The code generation candidates were Open Architecture Ware, AndroMDA and Acceleo. The French editor, Obeo, supplies the Acceleo plug-in to anyone wishing to benefit from the advantages of MDA and, by extension, to improve the productivity of their software development. With its proprietary scripts, the tool makes it possible to generate files from UML, MOF, EMF and other models. These exchange files, serialized in the SMI format, are compatible with the majority of the current modelers.

We therefore adopted the Acceleo solution[4] for its advanced functionalities such an incremental generation, debugging or the deployment of generation scripts in the form of plug-in Eclipse.

[1] cf. http://www.eclipse.org/org

[2] cf. http://www.topcased.org

[3] cf. http://www.eclipse.org/m2m/

[4] cf. http://acceleo.org/pages/presentation-generale/fr

6. Application software: Archi-MDE

The CEA/CESTA has initiated the implementation of UML-HPC together with various services described in this article, in an integrated software environment called Archi-MDE. Whilst it is still in the development stage with its initial implementations, its architecture (cf. Fig. 5) is entirely based on the Eclipse open source platform and on some of its extensions described in Section 3. The current use of UML-HPC in Archi-MDE integrates certain services intrinsic to its use (cf. Section 4).

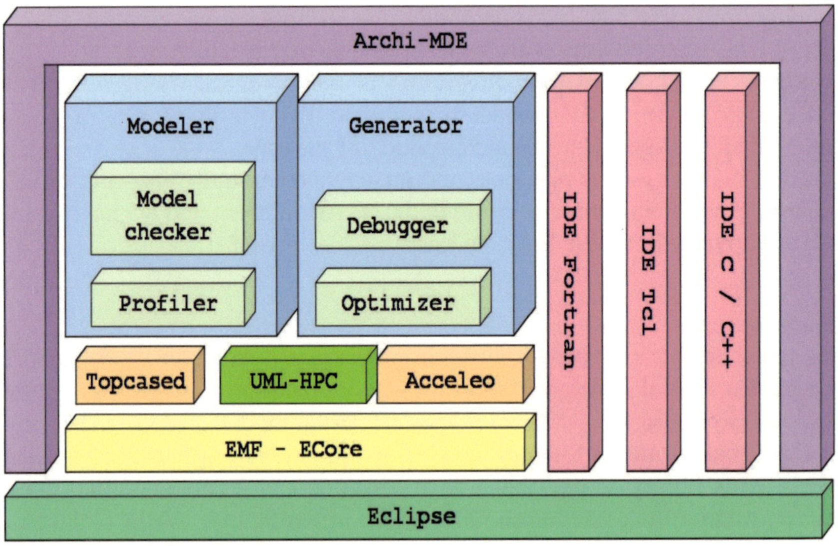

Fig. 5. Architecture of the plug-in Archi-MDE.

Archi-MDE has three main components. The first is a modeler specific to UML-HPC based on the Topcased workshop. This integrates the model-checking and profiling services in a graphic modeling environment. It is this part of Archi-MDE which will enable the user to build his models of applications designed for scientific computing.

The second component is the generation service based on Acceleo. This can be configured with in particular options for optimization (generation and compilation) and for debugging. Synchronization between the modeler and this generator is controlled by an XMI standard exchange file. The unit, which is transparent for the user, will authorize a transformation of the models into compatible and/or runnable Fortran code on the basis of a library of generation scripts.

The final, key component of Archi-MDE is the editors set of source files supplied by the Eclipse community. With these plug-ins, Archi-MDE is capable of editing in standard languages such as Fortran[5], C or C++[6], and Tcl[7]. Naturally, the modularity of Eclipse enables the user to add other development environments to Archi-MDE depending on the needs and languages managed by the generator.

---

[5] http://www.eclipse.org/photran

[6] http://www.eclipse.org/cdt

[7] http://www.eclipse.org/dltk

7. Conclusion and prospects

Whilst implementation of techniques presented in this paper will be finished in the future months, the CEA/CESTA regarding first initial studies believe in all the potential of these technologies not only in terms of cost and production lead time for new high performance scientific computing codes but also in terms of the maintenance aspects resulting from such codes. In this article, we have presented the first building bricks of UML-HPC. As illustrated in Fig. 1, we have to date focused on the Design and Code aspects. In the near future, we hope to reassemble the V cycle to integrate all the requirements definition and thus automate a new part of the design process.

Similarly, the services presented in the article have yet to be finalized but will rapidly become inescapable in an industrial use of Archi-MDE. We shall initially focus on the optimization aspects before progressively integrating more model-checking and the implementation of a multi-source code generator.

8. References

Michael Metcalf (1982). Fortran Optimization, Academic Press.

Moore, Gordon E. (1965). Cramming more components onto integrated circuits. *Electronics Magazine*. 4. Retrieved on 2006-11-11.

Jean Gonnord, Pierre Leca & François Robin (2006). Au-delà de 50 mille milliards d'opérations par seconde, *La Recherche* n°393.

Dan Pilone & Neil Pitman (2006). *UML 2 en concentré*, O'Reilly.

Object Management Group (2005). *Model Driven Architecture*. http://www.omg.org/mda/.

Bruce Powel Douglass (2004). *Real Time UML : Advances in the UML for real time systems*, Addison-Wesley Professional.

Olivier Cogis & Claudine Robert (2003). *Théorie des graphes*, Vuibert.

Grace A. Lewis, B. Craig Meyers, Kurt Wallnau, *Workshop on Model-Driven Architecture and Program Generation,* TECHNICAL NOTE CMU/SEI-2006-TN-031August 2006.

3

Designing and Integrating Clinical and Computer-based Simulations in Health Informatics: From Real-World to Virtual Reality

Elizabeth Borycki, Andre Kushniruk, James Anderson, Marilyn Anderson

1. Introduction and Motivation

Simulations were first used in health care over 40 years ago when Denson and Abrahamson (1969) developed and used a simulator (i.e., Sim One) to train medical residents to perform two medical procedures (endotracheal intubation and anesthesia induction) and demonstrated the usefulness of the simulator in teaching medical students how to perform these medical procedures. Although innovative at the time, simulation was not readily adopted as a methodology for training health care professionals and students until the 1980's. In the mid 1980's there was a resurgence of interest in using simulation to train health professionals with improvements in the availability of computers. Computer-based simulations were identified as a method for teaching health professional students clinical knowledge that could be used in decision-making involving patient care. Computer-based simulations were found by researchers to be helpful as an aid in educating physicians and other health professionals about the anatomy and physiology of the human body and its pharmacologic treatment. Unfortunately, these computer-based simulations did not provide health professional students with sufficient opportunities to develop both the practical knowledge and the technical skills that were needed in real-world clinical situations involving patients. Computer-based simulations could not adequately mimic real-world, patient health care events characteristic of those found in physician office, clinical and hospital environments (Byrick & Wylands, 2009).

In the mid to late 1980's Gaba (1988) developed a simulator that allowed medical students to learn how to manage real-world, life threatening patient health events. Gaba's simulator involved the use of patient mannequins that could be programmed to mimic a wide variety of human responses (from periods of health to end-stage disease). Gaba's computer controlled mannequins were able to mimic real-life patient illness and disease and thereby improved the quality of medical students' training - providing opportunities to use knowledge gained in the classroom setting in situations representative of the real-world. Gaba's simulator was used to train medical students on a range of real world procedures from the simple to the complex in a range of situations representative of real-world patient health situations. The simulator afforded medical students the opportunity to experience real-world critical events in a safe environment that would allow them to improve their knowledge while at the same time having the opportunity to practice their skills. As a consequence, students when confronted with similar situations in a real-world setting (e.g., a patient in an operating room) were better able to respond to the situation, having practiced it with a computer controlled mannequin or simulator.

Today, computer-based simulation continues to be used by health professionals to improve clinical knowledge. In addition, physical simulators (i.e., computer controlled mannequins) are also being used to teach differing health professionals (e.g., physicians, nurses, pharmacists, respiratory therapists) additional knowledge and skills that can be used in the care of patients. Both these technologies continue to be used to teach health professional students. As well, both these technologies are being used to teach health care practitioners about new and emergent medical procedures, therapies, treatments and the role of differing types of medical interventions in the spread and progression of disease (as in the case of computer-based simulation use in public health surveillance) (Byrick & Wynands, 2009).

The use of computer-based simulations and simulators is not limited to teaching health professionals. Computer-based simulations and simulators have been used in the field of biomedical engineering to prototype, test and determine the impact of new medical devices before their being used in health care settings such as hospitals. More recently, clinical simulations (i.e. simulations involving observation of health professionals interacting with systems in carrying out simulated clinical activities) are being extended for use to the field of health informatics (i.e., the study of health information systems and their use in health care settings) (Borycki et al., 2009a; Borycki et al., 2009b; Kushniruk et. al., 2005). In health informatics simulations are being used to prototype, test and evaluate health information systems (i.e., to determine the safety of these systems and their ability to support physician, nurse and other health professional information seeking and decision-making) (e.g., Kushniruk et. al., 2005; Borycki et. al., 2009). As well, simulations are being used to evaluate the organizational impacts of implementing differing health information systems and their associated devices in physician office, clinic and hospital settings (Kushniruk et al., 2005; Kushniruk et al., 2006). Such use of simulations is necessary to support health administrator decision-making involving the procurement, customization and implementation of health care software and devices in the clinical settings (Borycki et al., 2009c; Kushniruk et al., 2009). This is a new area of research in health informatics that has shown considerable promise in improving the safety of health information systems and their associated devices as well as their fit with the clinical environment before an implementation has occurred (Borycki & Kushniruk, 2005). In this book chapter we will present an overview of a new and emerging area of research that examines the role of clinical and computer-based simulation in assessing the safety and task-technology fit of health information systems software and devices that are to be implemented in health care settings. More specifically, the authors of this book chapter will begin by presenting their work in this area of health informatics. We will describe how clinical simulation and computer-based simulation have been used in health informatics and how these two types of simulation can be integrated to support the decision-making of health professionals and health administrators when procuring, selecting and implementing such systems for use in real-world clinical settings. Lastly, the authors will discuss future directions for the use of clinical, computer-based and hybrid simulations in health informatics and the potential role of computer programmed mannequins in future research.

2. Clinical Simulations

2.1 Introduction

Clinical simulations are increasingly being used by health care organizations (e.g., hospitals and home care agencies) to evaluate health information systems (i.e., software applications) and their associated devices (e.g., computer workstations, hand held devices and wireless carts). Such simulations typically involve the observation and recording (i.e., audio and video) of human subjects (e.g., healthcare professionals) as they interact with real or simulated patients using information technology and healthcare devices, under realistic conditions (Borycki & Kushniruk, 2005; Kushniruk & Borycki, 2005). Clinical simulations can help organizations to evaluate software applications or devices prior to their real-world implementation in a hospital, physician office or home care setting (Borycki et al., 2009).

In using clinical simulations health care organizations and vendors can identify potential issues arising from software applications, devices and software/device integrations prior to their use in real-world settings. More specifically, clinical simulations offer vendors and health care organizations the opportunity to evaluate the real-world impacts of a technology(ies) upon health professional work processes (e.g., workflow) and patient outcomes (e.g., medical errors, adverse events, and vaccination rates) prior to their real-world use (Borycki et. al., 2009c; Kushniruk et al., 2009).

Clinical simulations have emerged as a new form of evaluation in the field of health informatics. They are unlike traditional evaluations (e.g., randomized clinical control trials or pre-test post-test quasi-experimental studies that have been used to evaluate systems) which typically take place after a technology(ies) has been implemented (Anderson et al., 2005; Friedman & Wyatt, 2008). Clinical simulations can lead to significant cost savings as they allow for modification of the software application and/or device prior to an organization wide implementation (Patton, 2001). If the software application and/or device is modified prior to a system wide implementation, the costs associated with re-implementing the application and re-training users could be avoided or significantly reduced if the application/devices workflows and impact upon patient outcomes can be improved or optimized (Borycki et al., 2009b).

Therefore, clinical simulations allow the vendor or healthcare organization to identify those intended and unintended consequences arising from a software application and/or device that influence health professional's work processes and outcomes to be addressed before it affects the organization and its health professionals and patients. For example, there have been several studies published in the medical and health informatics literature that have reported that electronic health record applications such as physician order entry can facilitate medical errors (i.e., inadvertently cause technology-induced errors) (e.g., Ash et al., 2007; Borycki & Kushniruk, 2005; Koppel et al., 2005; Kushniruk et al., 2005). In most cases these studies have reported upon the role of the technology in increasing some types of errors only after the software application and/or device has been implemented (e.g., Ash et al., 2007; Campbell et al., 2006). In some cases these errors were "new" types of errors as they did not exist in the paper patient record environment that has characterized most hospitals in North America (Borycki & Kushniruk, 2008; Shulman et al., 2005). These publications led some researchers to call for the development of evaluative approaches that could be used to identify such error facilitating aspects (i.e., features and functions of software applications and/devices before their implementation in real-world health care settings). Clinical simulations were developed by a group of researchers in an effort to identify these types of unintended consequences prior to real-world implementation so that these error facilitating aspects of the software application and/or device could be addressed before being used in a hospital (Kushniruk et al., 2005).

Such knowledge early in the software development lifecycle (SDLC) prior to organizational implementation can prevent the occurrence of unintended consequences that may affect health professionals and patients (i.e., elimination of the unintended error facilitating aspects of applications/devices or technology-induced errors that may lead to harm). Such apriori knowledge allows organizational decision makers to consider the impact of changes to health professional work arising from such changes resulting from the introduction of an application or a device and take into account process and outcome changes arising from those changes involving technology. Organizations can in response make proactive decisions about whether to redesign or modify an application and/or device. Alternatively, organizations can better customize the application/device to the local organizational context (i.e., improve task-technology fit) or provide interventions that would prevent the occurrence of such events (e.g., additional training and support during the period when the application/device is being implemented) (Borycki & Kushniruk, 2008; Borycki et al., 2009b).

2.2 Development of Clinical Simulations

The construction of clinical simulations involves several phases: the design of a representative environment (e.g., a clinic or a hospital room), the development of a representative situation (the healthcare scenario or task) and the selection of representative users (e.g., physicians or nurses). The development of a representative environment involves identifying a location in an organization that is representative of the real-world. The organizational location should include the equipment that is typically used by individuals in that organization. For example, a hospital that is implementing a new software application and devices that could be used by a physician in managing a patient's care could use an empty room in a hospital that has a hospital bed, bedside table and computer workstation that a physician or nurse would use when reviewing patient data or documenting patient information. The development of a representative situation involves identifying the conditions and positions that health professionals would find themselves in when using the software application/device. Here, representatives of the organization would identify those scenarios where the physician or nurse would interact with the application/device. For example, a nurse may interact with a medication administration system and a wireless cart while giving patient medications. Organizational representatives may then identify those tasks that would be part of that scenario. Using our example of a nurse using a medication administration system and wireless cart to give a patient medication, the tasks involved in administering a medication may include such tasks as verifying the patient's identity, verifying that the correct medication is being given, giving the medication and documenting that the medication has been given using the software application (Borycki et al., 2009b; Kushniruk et al., 1997).

2.2.1 Data Collection

Data collection during the clinical simulation takes three forms: (1) video data of the user interacting with the software application and/or device and the surrounding organizational environment, (2) audio data of the user(s) while interacting with the applications and devices in an organizational environment, and (3) screen recordings of the users' interaction with the software application under study. Video and audio data can be collected using a video camcorder. Screen recordings of the software application can be collected using a software screen recording program such as Hypercam® (See Kushniruk and Borycki, 2005 for more detail). In many studies subjects may be audio recorded as they interact with systems and may be asked to "think aloud" or verbalize their thoughts. Other audio recordings may be of the subject (e.g., physician) interacting with a patient or someone playing the role of a patient - i.e., a "simulated patient") while using a health information system. For example in Figure 1 we have a picture of a health professional interacting with a workstation while "thinking aloud". As can be seen in the figure a video camcorder is recording both video and audio data. On the workstation a screen recording program is recording all interactions the health professional is having with the software application (resulting in a digital movie of the computer screens and audio track). Once the video, audio and screen recording data is captured, the audio data needs to be transcribed. Transcriptions are then annotated with data collected from the screen recordings and descriptions of interactions between the health professional, software application, device and the organizational environment (see Borycki & Kushniurk, 2005). Interesting or problematic user interactions with the system under study can be annotated. Data can also be coded using a predefined coding scheme. For example, pre-defined codes may include categories for identifying errors and human-computer interaction issues such as problems with system navigation, display visibility or consistency of interface design. New codes are added if the existing codes do not adequately describe the audio, video or screen recording data. Audio, video and screen recording data can be triangulated. The transcript and annotations provide both qualitative and quantitative data. Qualitative codes provide insights into how the software application and device perform in a given organizational environment during specific scenarios and during specific work tasks. Qualitative codes can also be quantified. Quantification of qualitative data provides frequencies of occurrence for specific types of events such as errors or the occurrence of specific types of cumbersome workflows. Here, the evaluator can determine the cumbersome workflows and errors that occur most frequently and then attempt to modify the software application or they can select a device that prevents the cumbersome workflow or error from occurring. In addition to this the evaluator can recommend that the implementers of the software application and device provide specific types of education or training for users that would reduce the effects of the application/devices changes on workflow and error rates (Borycki et al., 2009a).

Fig. 1. A Health Professional Being Video Recorded as He Interacts With a Health Information System in a Clinical Simulation

2.2.2 Application

The authors have used clinical simulations to identify the features and functions of software applications that may facilitate medical errors. They have conducted a study where they examined the relationship between usability and medical error and found that specific types of usability problems were related to specific device and interface features. For example, in one study it was found that device size affected display visibility and there was a relationship between medical errors rates and display visibility. They also found that interface design features such as default menu options provided by a system (for medications, dosages etc.) were related to medical error, when health professionals would choose such defaults when they were inappropriate (Kushniruk et al., 2005). In another study the researchers used clinical simulation to identify cumbersome workflows resulting from the introduction of a medication administration system that included a wireless cart and a medication administration system application. In the study the researchers asked health professionals (i.e., physicians and nurses) to administer medications. Participants in the study were asked to administer several differing types of medications to a simulated patient (i.e., a mannequin was brought in to serve as the patient). From the simulation the researchers found that the software application and device (i.e. wireless medication administration cart) could seriously affect the sequence of workflow activities, could increase the complexity of work activity, could lock out the user from some activities and could impose a specific order of tasks upon clinical work. Such information was then used to inform software application design or re-design and organizational implementation of the software application and device (i.e., customization of software applications to the local organizational environment, selection of devices for the organization, training of users, and implementation approaches for the system in a healthcare organization) (Kushniruk et al., 2009).

2.3. Advantages of Clinical Simulation

Clinical simulations have a number of advantages associated with their use. For example, clinical simulations allow one to determine the impact of a software application in conjunction with a software device or constellation of devices upon patient care processes (i.e., health professional workflows involving patients) and patient outcomes (i.e. quality of the patient's health care) (Borycki et al., 2009a; Kushniruk et al., 2006). Clinical simulations allow one to test software applications and equipment in a safe environment (outside of the hospital or physician office) so that the "unintended consequences" that may arise from introducing a new software application and/or device into a hospital or clinic do not affect health professional work or patient health care significantly. For example, a clinical simulation could be used to predict potential changes in workflow, information seeking behaviors and medical error rates prior to system implementation (Borycki et. al., 2009a; Kushniruk et al., 2005). This would reduce the already high rate of adoption failures in health care - it is estimated that 65% of all health information systems fail to be adopted by health professionals (Rabinowitz et. al., 1999). In addition to this clinical simulations reduce organizational risks - reducing the need for re-implementation. When an application or device fails to be adopted by health professionals or it is adopted in such a way that the full functionality of the application/device is not used to improve patient care, the organization will need to re-implement the application/device (Ash et. al., 2007; Granlien et al., 2008). There are significant costs associated with re-implementation such as further customization of the application, switching costs associated with identifying a new device to implement and re-training of staff who will be using the device. Clinical simulations allow one to make software application and device changes based on observed evidence that the application/device work with the given health care environment, the situations health professionals encounter and the tasks they perform. Such use of clinical simulations would reduce the need for re-implementation (Borycki & Kushniruk, 2005).

Clinical simulations allow organizations to determine if applications and/or devices introduce "new errors". In the health informatics literature there has been significant research that has shown that technology can introduce new types of errors - technology-induced errors. Clinical simulations allow an organization to assess the potential for these new types of errors occurring and by identifying their cause prevent them. This is important as a clinical simulation may be used to assess the safety of a application and/or device. Clinical simulations allow for such evaluation activities to take place and avoid the use of "live" patients and patient data (Kushniruk et al., 2005). In addition to this health professionals avoid exposure to situations that may cause "real life" errors to occur.

Such knowledge would be extremely useful if taken into account during the procurement of a software application or device. Information from the clinical simulations could be used to determine the level of task-technology fit between an application, device and the organizational context where it will be deployed. Lastly, clinical simulations have the potential to inform organizational decisions during procurement and implementation.

Organizations typically implement differing constellations of software applications and devices. Clinical simulations may help organization to select applications and devices that best meet organizational needs (Borycki et al., 2009c).

Clinical simulations can also be used to inform organizational decisions involving the type of implementation that will be undertaken (i.e., should the application and software be implemented organization wide or in a single department). They also have the ability to inform the type of approach taken during training. For example, an organization may choose to train users using a "hands on approach" involving the device and the software application versus a pure lecture format if the clinical simulation demonstrates there is a need to directly work with the application and device (Borycki et. al., 2009). In summary, clinical simulation involving software applications and/or devices offer organizations the opportunity to assess task-technology fit with the organizational environment. As a result, the impact of the application and device upon health professional work processes and outcomes is learned. This allows the organization to make modifications to the software application and device prior to its implementation in a real-world setting. Such knowledge is a key to preventing technology adoption failures and future modification and training costs associated with reimplementation after the software application and device has failed.

3. Computer-Based Simulations

3.1. Introduction

Many health informatics applications cannot be evaluated with traditional experimental methods involving human subjects. In these instances computer simulation provides a flexible approach to evaluation. The construction of a computer simulation model involves the development of a model that represents important aspects of the system under evaluation. Once validated, the model can be used to study the effects of variation in system inputs, differences in initial conditions and changes in the structure of the system (Anderson, 2002a,b). In addition, as will be described in a subsequent section, the outputs of clinical simulations (described in the previous section) can be used as inputs into computer-based simulations.

3.2. The Modeling Process

3.2.1 Systems Analysis

Construction of a computer simulation model begins with the identification of the elements of the system and the functional relationships among the elements. A systems diagram is used to depict subsystems and components and relationships among them (Anderson, 2003). The diagram should also show critical inputs and outputs, parameters of the system, any accumulations and exchanges or flows of resources, personnel, information, and system performance measures. Relationships may be specified analytically, numerically, graphically, or logically and may vary over time.

Many information technology applications that are to be evaluated are multifaceted. Subsystems and components are interrelated in complex ways and may be difficult to completely understand. Model development requires the investigator to abstract the important features of the system that generate the underlying processes. This requires familiarity with the system that is being evaluated and its expected performance.

3.2.2 Data Collection

Qualitative and quantitative information are required in order to adequately represent the system. Qualitative research methods are useful in defining the system under investigation. Quantitative data are necessary in order to estimate system parameters such as arrival and service distributions, conversion and processing rates, error rates, and resource levels. Data may be obtained from system logs and files, interviews, expert judgment, questionnaires, work sampling, etc. Data may be cross-sectional and/or time series.

3.2.3 Model Formulation

In general, there are two types of simulation models, discrete-event and continuous. Swain (1997) reviews 46 simulation software packages and provides a directory of vendors. The example below uses a continuous simulation model to describe a medication error reporting system.

Discrete-event models are made up of components or elements each of which perform a specific function (Banks & Carson, 1984). The characteristic behavior of each element in the model is designed to be similar to the real behavior of the unit or operation that it represents in the real world. Systems are conceptualized as a network of connected components. Items flow through the network from one component to the next. Each component performs a function before the item can move on to the next component. Arrival rates, processing times and other characteristics of the process being modeled usually are random and follow a probability distribution. Each component has a finite capacity and may require resources to process an item. As a result, items may be held in a queue before being processed. Each input event to the system is processed as a discrete transaction. For discrete-event models, the primary objective is to study the behavior of the system and to determine its capacity, to assess the average time it takes to process items, to identify rate-limiting components, and to estimate costs. Simulation involves keeping track of where each item is in the process at any given time, moving items from component to component or from a queue to a component, and timing the process that occurs at each component. The results of a simulation are a set of statistics that describe the behavior of the simulated system over a given time period. A simulation run where a number of discrete inputs to the system are processed over time represents a sampling experiment. Applications of discrete event simulation are provided in Anderson (2002a).

Continuous simulation models are used when the system under investigation consists of a continuous flow of information, material, resources, or individuals. The system under investigation is characterized in terms of state variables and control variables (Hannon & Ruth, 1994). State variables indicate the status of important characteristics of the system at each point in time. These variables include people, other resources, information, etc. An example of a state variable is the cumulative number of medication orders that have been written on a hospital unit at any time during the simulation. Control variables are rates of change and update the value of state variables in each time period. An example of a control variable is the number of new medication orders written per time period. Components of the system interact with each other and may involve positive and negative feedback processes. Since many of these relationships are nonlinear, the system may exhibit complex, dynamic behavior over time.

The mathematical model that underlies the simulation usually consists of a set of differential or finite difference equations. Numerical solutions of the equations that make up the model allow investigators to construct and test models that cannot be solved analytically (Hargrove, 1998).

3.2.4 Model Validation

Once an initial model is constructed it should be validated to ensure that it adequately represents the system and underlying processes under investigation. One useful test of the model is to choose a model state variable with a known pattern of variation over some time period. The model is then run to see if it accurately generates the reference behavior. If the simulated behavior and the observed behavior of the system correspond well, it can be concluded that the computer model reasonably represents the system. If not, revisions are made until a valid model is developed (Law & Kelton, 1991; Oreskes, Schrader-Froechette & Belitz, 1994). The behavior of the model when it is manipulated frequently provides a much better understanding of the system. This process has been termed postulational modeling (Katzper, 1995).

Sensitivity analyses also should be performed on the model. Frequently, the behavior of important outcome variables is relatively insensitive to large changes in many of the model's parameters. However, a few model parameters may be sensitive. A change in the value of these parameters may result in major changes in the behavior pattern exhibited by the system. It is not only important to accurately estimate these parameters but they may represent important means to change the performance of the overall system.

3.3. Application

In this section we describe an example of a computer simulation model that can be used to explore organizational changes that are required to improve patient safety based on a medication error reporting system. (Anderson, Ramanujam, Hensel & Anderson, 2005). The model is used to illustrate the fact that patient safety initiatives require more than clinical initiatives. In order to be successful, these initiatives must be designed and implemented through organizational support structures and institutionalized through enhanced education, training, and implementation of information technology that improves work force capabilities (Anderson, 2004).

In an effort to determine whether hospitals working collectively to report medical errors can improve patient safety, a coalition was formed consisting of 40 hospitals. These hospitals implemented a voluntary retrospective reporting system. The MEDMARX system was implemented to report medication errors. Data from these hospitals were used to validate the model.

A computer simulation model was constructed in order to model medication error reporting systems and organizational changes needed to improve patient safety. STELLA was used to create the model represented in Figure 2. The model consists of three stages. In stage 1, medication errors are generated and a certain proportion of these errors are reported. Medication errors are of two types: errors that do not harm patients (Categories A-D) and errors that harm the patient (Categories E-I). Next, the model includes communication about the errors that are reported. Information about the errors may be shared with the staff who made the error, with the caregivers more generally and with the patient. Medication errors may also result in qualitative changes to the communication process

The third stage of the model involves organizational actions taken in response to medication errors. These organizational changes may involve changes in policies, technology, personnel and organizational culture. Changes in goals involve policy and procedure modification in response to medication errors. Technological changes may involve changes in the hospital's formulary and/or modifications to the computer software used in the medication process.

The model was used to simulate medication error reporting in a typical hospital over twelve quarters. The model predicts the number of medication errors reported by type and organizational actions taken as a result of reported errors. Figure 3 shows the results over the 12 quarters. As can be seen from the graph, the number of errors reported increases over time. This suggests that, as a hospital gains experience with the error reporting system, health care providers report a greater proportion of errors that occur.

In order to validate the model, the model predictions for the first five quarters were compared to actual data from a regional coalition of 40 ewhospitals. Predicted values are quite close to the actual number of reported errors, especially for first three quarters. Model predictions are a little high for quarters 4 and 5.

3.4. Advantages of Simulation

Simulation provides a powerful methodology that can be used to evaluate medical informatics applications. Modifications to the system or process improvements can be tested. Once a model is created, investigators can experiment with it by making changes and observing the effects of these changes on the system's behavior. Also, once the model is validated, it can be used to predict the system's future behavior. In this way, the investigator can realize many of the benefits of system experimentation without disrupting the practice setting in which the system is implemented. Moreover, the modeling process frequently raises important additional questions about the system and its behavior. In summary, computer-based simulations provide organizations with opportunities to develop models that represent actual systems or systems that are under evaluation. As a result, they allow organizations to study the effects of variation upon system inputs and changes in system conditions and structures upon system behaviors.

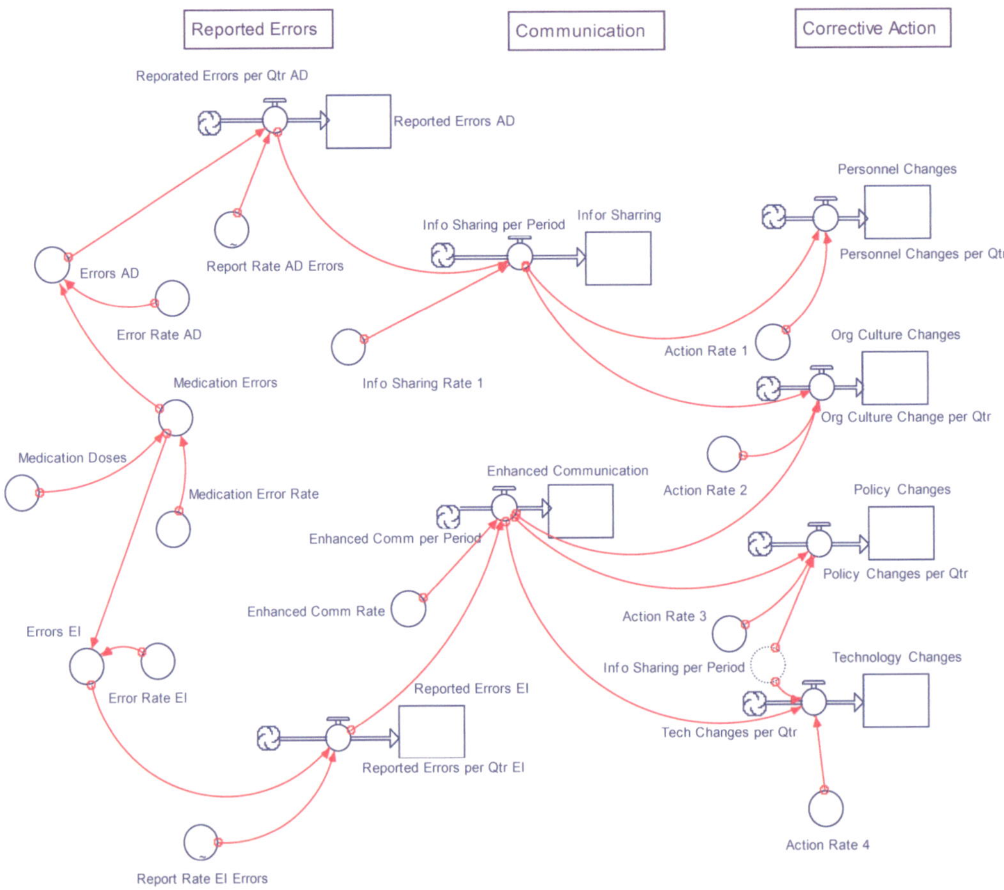

Fig. 2. Hospital Medication Error Reporting System

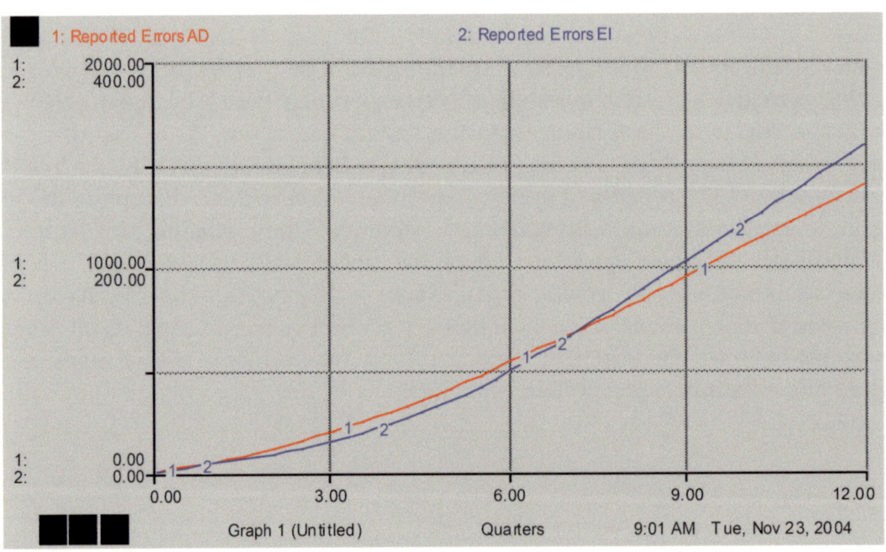

Fig. 3. Medication Errors Over Twelve Quarters

4. Hybrid Simulations: Combining Clinical Simulation with Computer-Based Simulation

4.1. Introduction

As noted above, in order to develop computer-based simulations (e.g., of healthcare processes or errors) the researcher needs to input starting parameters (e.g., number of patients, number of errors etc.) into the simulation and underlying mathematical model. Such information may be obtained from analysis of system logs and files, interviews, expert judgment, questionnaires, work sampling, etc. Also such starting data may be obtained from values published in the scientific literature and previous empirical studies where applicable. In addition, data used for computer simulations (as described above) may be obtained directly from the running of clinical simulations (targeted at obtaining baseline data on things like medication error rates and usability problems). Such studies, which combine results from clinical simulations (involving study of human subjects interacting with systems, as described above) with computer-based simulations (providing baseline data to be used by the computer-based simulation) can be termed "hybrid simulations". We will illustrate this hybrid approach with an example from our work in the analysis, detection and forecasting of technology facilitated error in health informatics.

4.2 Application

In this section we describe an example of use of hybrid simulations that connect work from clinical simulations with computer-based simulations to predict impact of a new handheld prescription writing application (that allows physicians to record medications in a PDA, a personal digital assistant). The initial part of this work (Phase 1) involved conducting a clinical simulation where physicians were asked to "think aloud" while entering prescriptions (given to them on a piece of paper) as accurately as possible into a handheld PDA application (Kushniruk et al., 2005). The physician subjects were also asked to interact with the system while interviewing a research collaborator who played the part of a patient (i.e., a "simulated patient"). Subjects consisted of ten physicians who were familiar with PDA applications but had never used the one under study before. The procedure consisted of recording all subject interactions with the application, specifically all of the screens of the application were video recorded (by projecting the PDA display on to a projection screen using a data projector and video recording the projections using a video camera) while subject's verbalizations were audio recorded as they carried out medication order entry tasks. Medication order entry tasks included entering medication orders into the PDA application from a list of medications on a piece of paper that was provided to subjects. The resultant data consisted of video and audio recordings of the subjects' entering medications into the application.

The analysis of the data resulting from the clinical simulation in Phase 1 consisted of coding the video and audio data for the occurrence of the following: (a) usability problems involving aspects of interface design and (b) medication errors. The following specific categories of user interface and usability problems were identified when the transcripts were annotated by a researcher with a background in human-computer interaction: (1) data entry problems; (2) display visibility problems; (3) navigation problems; (4) locating problems; (5) procedure problems; (6) printing problems; (7) speed problems; and (8) attention problems. In addition, problems regarding content of the information displayed were also noted, including the following: (1) database content problems; (2) inappropriate default problems, and (3) training manual deficient problems. Thus, the main categories of usability problems could be considered to be a result of specific issues with the application's user interface and the content of information displayed by the system. The same video data (of user interactions) was also independently coded for inaccurate or errors in the entry of medications, which were divided into: (a) Slips - which were mistakes caught by the subject before finalizing their data entry (e.g., a typo that was corrected) and (b) Mistakes - errors that were made in the medication entry (e.g., wrong dose) which were not caught by the subject and were recorded in the health information system. In the final phase of the analysis the investigators explored the relationship between usability problems and errors in medication entry. For each medical error identified, the record of coded usability problems was examined to determine if the usability problem had been associated with an actual data entry error. For example, the presence of a "display visibility" problem was highly associated with occurrence of a medication error (84% of coded display visibility were associated with an error). Overall 37% of coded usability problems were associated with one or more medication errors made by the physician subjects. The intent of this analysis was to determine the relationship between specific usability problems and the occurrence of slips and mistakes (to determine base rates for number of errors and their statistical relationship to specific usability problems).

In the second part of this work (Phase 2), in order to extend the findings from phase 1 to provide input into development of computer-based mathematical models (to predict the occurrence of technology-induced error in populations of users in large real-world organizations), the output of Phase 1 (i.e. the base rates of error associated with each category of usability problem) was used as data to serve as the base rate parameters for a computer-based mathematical simulation of medication error rates. Initially, a computer simulation model was constructed in order to represent how health information technologies may increase the incidence of certain types of medical errors using base rates from Phase 1. The simulation software package STELLA was used to create the model. Based on the results of the Phase 1 clinical simulation, usability problems may arise because of the nature of the interface with the technology or because the content of the medication database is incomplete. Each of these problems can result in error (the simulation models error rates that occur when new prescriptions are entered that have usability problems associated with them as described in Phase 1 above). In the initial STELLA model (based on Phase 1 findings) overall 41% of usability problems related to the PDA application's interface resulted in errors; while 16.7% of the content problems resulted in errors. Several simulation runs were created, to assess over time the impact of removing specific user interface features, as well as to simulate the impact of the learning curve of users over time on total number of medication errors. For example, see Figure 4 showing four successive runs of the STELLA simulation (the lines labeled 1 to 4 in the graph) showing a decrease in mistakes over time as specific user interface problems are fixed in each of the simulation runs. This information can be used for assessing potential impact of systems (as well as specific user interface features and their impact on error rates).

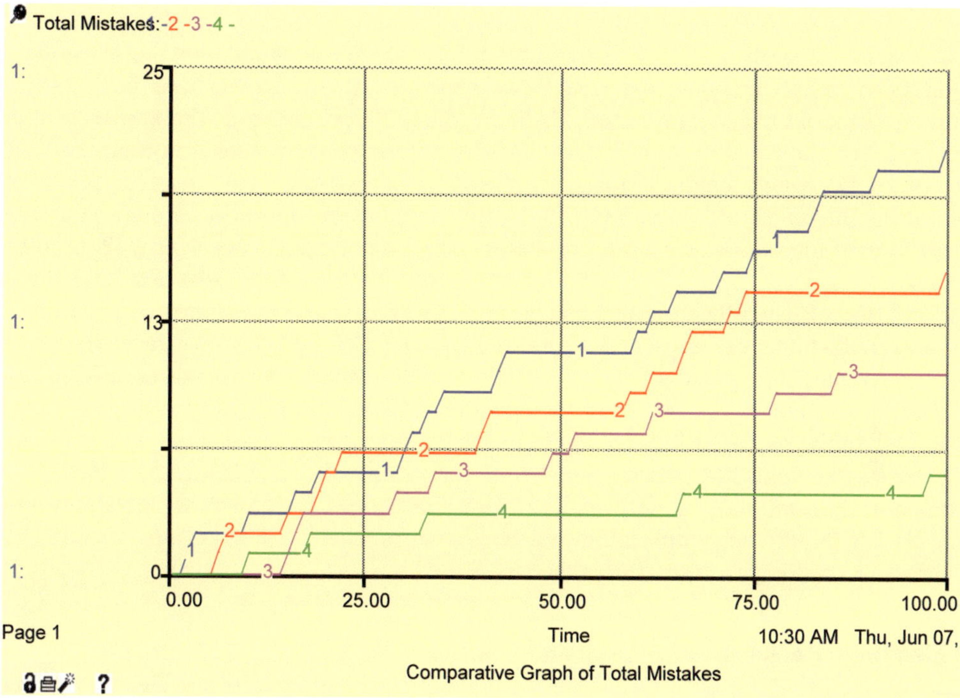

Fig. 4. Graph of Total Mistakes Over Four Simulation Runs

5. Future Research

5.1 Health Informatics and Simulation

The authors of this book chapter have highlighted three areas of work at the intersection of the fields of health informatics and simulation research, namely: (a) the use of clinical simulations to evaluate health care software applications and their associated devices, (b) the use of computer-based simulations to evaluate the effects of health care system level changes (such as introducing a new health information system upon system inputs, throughputs and outputs), and (c) the integration of both (i.e., hybrid approaches) by using data collected from clinical simulations as the basis for computer-based models of introducing new software applications/devices upon a systems outputs (i.e., number of technology-induced errors). The use of this full range of simulations in health informatics for testing systems is a relatively new phenomenon. Early work in this area by Anderson (2005) proved that health care systems (e.g., physician offices, emergency rooms) could be modeled and the effects of implementing a health information system could be observed before a software application was introduced to a hospital or clinic environment. Work by Borycki, Kushniruk and Kuwata (2009b) demonstrated that clinical simulations could be used to evaluate the effects of software application/device constellations upon health professional work. Both these approaches have been integrated in a hybrid model of simulation (one where clinical simulations provide inputs for computer-based models) drawing on the advantages of using both approaches.

5.2 Computer Controlled Mannequins, Health Information Systems and Devices

Research at the intersection of health informatics and simulation continues to advance. Our most recent research involves using computer controlled simulation mannequins to prototype, test and evaluate new health information system applications (e.g., personal health records, electronic patient records, electronic medical records). The use of computer controlled simulation mannequins allows health information systems and their associated devices to be tested using a range of health professionals (e.g., nurses, physicians, respiratory therapists etc.) involving the a full continuum of health care situations and events (where the patient is healthy or experiencing a critical life event as well as routine and atypical or rare patient situations involving rare illnesses/diseases) and over the full course of the software development lifecycle (i.e., from design, development, customization to the organization, implementation, evaluation, operation to maintenance of the system and its associated devices). Our research will be further extended to include computer-based simulations to forecast the effects of the software and hardware upon health professional work. Our initial experience suggests that such an approach would serve as a significant decision support and risk management tool for health care administrators. Health care administrators could use the information from simulations to reduce organizational risks associated with software application and hardware procurement, selection, customization and implementation processes (Borycki et. al., 2009c).

5.3 Electronic Health Record Portal and Electronic Health Record Simulators

Other research that we are conducting includes the development of an Electronic Health Record portal that provides health professional students with access to several differing types of electronic health records. The portal is essentially an electronic health record simulator. At present there are few opportunities for medical, nursing and other health professional students to learn how to use an electronic health record in the safe environment (where there is no live patient data) in the context of a university or college setting under the supervision of an educator. Such use of electronic health record simulators allows students to develop skills around documentation, use of differing communication and decision support tools. Presently, most health professional students learn how to use electronic health records using real patient data in the context of real health care organizations. There is a need to provide students with opportunities to learn how to manage patient illness and disease processes as well as learn how to use differing types of electronic health records and their decision support tools (as they often must learn to work with more than one electronic health record application at the same time or across the course of their professional career).

These electronic health records are pre-populated with representative, artificial patient information representing a wide range of patient states of health and illness. The electronic health record simulator allows health professional students to learn about how to review patient information, document and utilize decision support tools (such as alerts, reminders, checklists and electronic dashboards) in the management of patients in a "safe" environment (i.e. students can access the "simulated" patient data contained in the electronic health records remotely over the WWW). The students have used our electronic health record simulator to evaluate the strengths and weaknesses of differing electronic health record features, functions, designs and workflows in the classroom and from their homes as part of classroom assignments.

One of the portal's simulated electronic health records has been used by medical school faculty to present patient cases to medical students learning about the management of patient health and disease using the electronic health record. Nursing school faculty have used the electronic health record simulator to teach nursing students about the features and functions of the electronic health record that support their practice. Health informatics faculty have used the electronic health record simulator to teach health informatics students about the design, development, testing and evaluation of health information systems. The portal's simulated electronic health records are providing differing types of health professional students with significant learning opportunities while at the same time supporting the instruction of key aspects of health professional curricula by faculty from the health disciplines.

The portal simulation environment we have created will ultimately be used both for health professional education (by providing health professional students with access to representative systems remotely) and also as a test-bed for conducting analyses of impact of a range of electronic health record systems, as the systems available on-line through the portal can be tested within any clinical environment (e.g., accessed within a clinician's office in the simulation study of impact of electronic health records on workflow) (Armstrong et al., 2009; Borycki et. al., 2009d).

We are also extending our work to the professional community (i.e., those physicians, nurses, other health professionals, policy makers and health services administrators) who are considering purchasing an electronic health record. The electronic health record portal provides access to varying electronic health records with differing design metaphors and embedded workflows. Policy makers and health services administrators have used the portal to learn about the types of systems that are available and how they might be viewed on differing devices across the continuum of care (from hospital to community). Such knowledge provides policy makers with the requisite knowledge to craft organizational policies that would promote adoption and appropriation of technology by health professionals. Health services administrators have accessed the portal also. Health service administrators have used the portal to better understand how such a technology and its devices could be deployed in a health care setting (i.e., hospital, physician office, or patient's home) to improve the quality and safety of patient care as well as improve patient health outcomes. Lastly, for those health professionals who are purchasing systems the portal and the electronic health record simulators allow professionals to view an electronic record in their own organizational context and to make decisions about how to select and deploy a system to improve their work. As in the example, of a physician who would like to purchase an electronic health record, the portal and the electronic health record simulator allows the physician to access differing electronic health records over the WWW in their office and their exam room on a wireless laptop and to identify those parts of the office and the examination room where the record and device can be placed to provide support and to be enhance rather than be disruptive to office work flow.

We are also currently exploring the integration of simulated electronic health records with computer controlled mannequin simulations. Historically, computer controlled mannequins have been used to prototype and test differing types of medical devices for their utility and safety. In our work we are integrating two types of simulators: (1) computer controlled mannequins simulators and (2) electronic health record simulators and exploring their effects upon health professional information seeking and decision making across a range of patient health situations from critical life events to routine medical or nursing care of patients. This work is important as computer controlled mannequin simulators are increasingly being used to educate health professionals. The computer controlled mannequins are taking the place of patients. Much of the work involving computer controlled mannequin simulations to date and to our knowledge has not integrated differing electronic health records (with differing design metaphors) into the health care situations that are being used to train students. Such work is necessary so that students and student health professional teams learn how to integrate information from the patient (i.e. computer controlled mannequin), the devices that are being used to provide life support (e.g., intravenous pumps, ventilators etc.) and the electronic health record via a workstation or wireless device such as a Palm device.

5.4 Virtual Reality and the Simulation of Virtual Worlds

Recent advances in the field of virtual reality and simulation of virtual worlds will also extend this research. Increasingly, we are moving towards developing virtual representations of patients and we are simulating virtual worlds (including physician offices, clinics and hospitals). National Library of Medicine initiatives including The Visible Human Project® (National Library of Medicine, 2009) now provide image data that has been used to develop computer-based prototypes of the anatomy and physiology of the human body. In our future work with these software applications we plan to provide such information during student learning involving computer controlled mannequins in an environment that also provides access to the electronic health record. As well we believe that this work will be a prelude to complementing computer controlled mannequins that currently simulate real-life patient health events for health professional students (used to prototype, test and evaluate health information system software applications and devices) with the use of virtual reality computer controlled patient simulators located in virtual environments where there is an electronic health record simulator available.

An extension to this is to use of virtual world simulations such as Second Life® to test applications within the context of a simulated health care environment that is representative of the real-world and to be able to visualize the implications of software and device changes upon virtual physicians, nurses, other health professionals and patients. In addition, this approach allows for extending these changes to computer-based models that can help health care decision makers to understand the long term effects of these types of changes upon health care organizational inputs, throughputs and outputs and visualize their impact in a virtual hospital or clinic environment. Organizations such as the Center for Disease Control and the National Library of Medicine are already providing health care consumers with access to virtual worlds where virtual conferences, meeting and interactions with other health professionals are already taking place to educate individuals about health care (i.e. Second Life) (Maged, Boulos, Hetherington & Wheeler, 2007). In our work we plan to extend our experiences to the development of these virtual worlds with electronic health record simulators being available in these virtual organizations. These advancements in simulation are significant and will continue to influence software application prototyping, testing and evaluation. Such work is necessary as simulations can lead to cost savings. Cost savings associated with preventing health information system implementation, failure and the need for re-implementation as well as cost savings associated with health information system modification and reimplementation.

6. Conclusions

Use of simulations in health informatics is a rapidly expanding field of study. With the exponential rise in the development and implementation of health information systems globally by health care consumers and other health care organizations (e.g., clinics and hospitals), there has developed a growing need to evaluate these applications for their health care system effects. Current estimates suggest up to 65% of health information system applications fail to be adopted by health professionals (Rabinowitz et al., 1999). As well, many health information systems and devices fail to be used to their fullest extent by the individuals for whom they have been designed (such as patients, physicians, nurses and other health professionals). In addition to this, research has emerged suggesting that health information systems may negatively affect health professionals work processes through the introduction of cumbersome workflows (Kushniruk et al., 2006) and may inadvertently facilitate medical errors (i.e. technology-induced errors) (Koppel et al., 2005; Kushniruk et al., 2005).

Health informatics researchers have shown that clinical simulations, computer-based simulations and hybrid simulations can be used to test software applications for task-technology fit, their error facilitating features and functions, their effects on health care organizations and health care systems. Simulations can be used to evaluate software applications/devices. Clinical simulations can be used to evaluate the effects of differing constellations of software applications and devices upon aspects of health professional work (i.e., work processes and outcomes) with considerable ability to predict possible issues associated with software application and/or device usage (Borycki et al., 2009b). Such knowledge can provide organizations with information that can influence their decision-making during the organizational processes of procurement, selection and implementation of systems that can prevent downstream costs associated with application modification and switching to devices that better support health professional work. Future research will involve extending simulation from clinical and computer-based simulations to those involving computer controlled mannequins involving simulated electronic health records in virtual reality environments and virtual worlds.

7. References

Anderson, J.G. (2004). Information technology for detecting mediation errors and adverse drug events, *Expert Opinion on. Drug Safety.* 3(5), 449-455.

Anderson, J.G. (2003). A system's approach to preventing adverse drug events. In S. Krishna, Balas E.A., Boren S.A. (Eds.) *Information Technology Business Models for Quality Health Care: An EU/US Dialogue.* IOS Press, The Netherlands, pp. 95-102.

Anderson, J.G. (2002a). Evaluation in Health Informatics: Computer Simulation, *Computers in Biology and Medicine,* 32, pp. 151-164

Anderson, J.G. (2002b). A Focus on Simulation in Medical Informatics, *Journal of the American Medical Informatics Association*, 9(5), 554-556.

Anderson, J.G., Aydin, C.E. (2005). *Evaluating the organizational impact of healthcare information systems* (2nd ed.). New York: Springer Verlag.

Anderson, J.G, Ramanujam, R., Hensel, D., & Anderson, M. (2005). *Proceedings of Health Sciences Simulation 2005*, J.G. Anderson and M. Katzper (eds.), San Diego, CA, The Society for Modeling and Simulation International, pp. 9-14.

Armstrong, B., Kushniruk, A., Joe., R. Borycki, E. (2009). Technical and architectural issues in deploying electronic health records (EHRs) over the WWW. *Studies in Health Technology and Informatics, 143*, 93-8.

Ash, J.S., Sittig, D.F., Poon, E.G., Guappone, K., Campbell, E., Dykstra, RH. (2007). The extent and important of unintended consequences related to computerized provider order entry. *JAMIA, 14*(4), 415-423.

Banks, J. & Carson, J.S. (1984). *Discrete-Event System Simulation*, Prentice Hall, Englewood Cliffs, NJ.

Borycki, E.M., Kushniruk, A. W. (2005). Identifying and preventing technology-induced error using simulations: Application of usability engineering techniques. *Healthcare Quarterly, 8*, 99-105.

Borycki, E.M., Kushniruk, A.W. (2008). Where do technology induced errors come from? Towards a model for conceptualizing and diagnosing errors caused by technology (pp. 148-166). In A. W. Kushniruk and E. M. Borycki (Eds.) *Human, Social and Organizational Aspects of Health Information Systems*. Hershey, Pennsylvania: IGI Global.

Borycki, E.M. & Kushniruk, A.W. (in press). Use of Clinical Simulations to Evaluate the Impact of Health Information Systems and Ubiquitous Computing Devices Upon Health Professional Work. In S. Mohammed and Jinan Fiaidhi *Ubiquitous Health and Medical Informatics: The Ubiquity 2.0 Trend and Beyond*. Hershey: Pennsylvania: IGI Global.

Borycki, E.M., Lemieux-Charles, L, Nagle, L., Eysenbach, G. (2009a). Evaluating the impact of hybrid electronic-paper environments upon nurse information seeking. *Methods of Information in Medicine, 48*(2), 137-43.

Borycki, E.M., Kushniruk, A.W., Kuwata, S., Watanabe, H. (2009b). *Simulations to assess medication administration systems* (pp. 144-159). In B. Staudinger, V. Hob and H. Ostermann (Eds.). Nursing and Clinical Informatics: Socio-technical Approaches. Hershey, Pennsylvania: IGI Global.

Borycki, E.M., Kushniruk, A.W., Keay, E., Nicoll, J., Anderson, J., Anderson, M. (2009c). Toward an integrated simulation approach for predicting and preventing technology-induced errors in healthcare: Implications for healthcare decision makers. *Healthcare Quarterly*, in press

Byrick, R. J. & Wynands, J. E. (2009). Simulation-based education in Canada: Will anesthesia lead in the future? *Canadian Journal of Anesthesia, 56*: 273-278.

Campbell, E. M., Sittig, D.F., Ash, J.S. et al. (2006). Types of unintended consequences related to computerized provider order entry. *JAMIA., 13*: 547-56.

Denson, J. S. & Abrahamson, S. (1969). A computer-controlled patient simulator. *JAMA*, 208: 504-8.

Friedman C.P. & Wyatt J.C. (2005). *Evaluation methods in biomedical informatics.* New York: Springer Verlag.

Gaba, D. M. & DeAnda, A. (1988). A comprehensive anesthesia simulation environment: Recreating the operating room for research and training. *Anesthesiology, 69*: 387-94.

Granlien, M.F., Hertzum, M., Gudmundsen, J. (2008). The gap between actual and mandated use of an electronic medication record three years after deployment. *Studies in Health Technology and Informatics, 136*: 419-424.

Gordon, G. (1969). *System Simulation*, Prentice Hall, Englewood Cliffs, NJ.

Hannon, B.& M. Ruth, M. (1994). *Dynamic Modeling*, Springer-Verlag, NY.

Hargrove, J.L. (1998). *Dynamic Modeling in the Health Sciences*, Springer-Verlag, NY.

Katzper, M. (1995). Epistemological Bases of Postulational Modeling, In J.G. Anderson and M. Katzper (eds.), *Health Sciences, Physiological and Pharmacological Simulation Studies*, pp. 83-88. Society for Computer Simulation, San Diego, CA.

Koppel, R, Metlay P, Cohen A et al. Role of computerized physician order entry systems in facilitating medication errors. JAMA. 2005;293(10): 1197-1203.

Kushniruk, A., Triola, M., Stein, B., Borycki E., Kannry J. (2005). Technology induced error and usability: The relationship between usability problems and prescription errors when using a handheld application. *International Journal of Medical Informatics, 74*(7-8): 519-26.

Kushniruk, A.W., Borycki, E., Kuwata, S., Kannry, J. (2006). Predicting changes in workflow resulting from healthcare information systems: Ensuring the safety of healthcare. *Healthcare Quarterly, 9*: 114-8.

Kushniruk, A.W., Borycki, E.M., Myers, K., Kannry, J. (2009). Selecting electronic health record systems: Development of a framework for testing candidate systems. *Studies in Health Technology and Informatics, 143:* pp. 376-9.

Kushniruk, A.W., Borycki, E.M. (2005). Low-cost rapid usability engineering: Designing and customizing usable healthcare information systems. *Healthcare Quarterly, 9*(4): 98-100.

Law, A.M. & Kelton, W.D. (1991). *Simulation Modeling and Analysis*, 2nd ed. McGraw Hill, NY.

Maged, N., Boulos, K., Hetherington, L. & Wheeler, S. (2007). Second life: An overview of the potential of 3-D virtual worlds in medical and health education. *Health Information and Libraries Journal, 24*, 233-245.

National Library of Medicine. (February, 2009) The Visible Human Project. http://www.nlm.nih.gov/research/visible/visible_human.html

Oreskes, N., Schrader-Frechette, K. & Belitz, K. (1994). Verification, Validation and Confirmation of Numerical Models in the Earth Sciences, Science, *2163*: 641-646.

Patton, R. (2001). *Software testing.* Indianapolis, Indiana: SAMS.

Rabinowitz et al. (1999). Is there a doctor in the house? *Managing Care*, 8(9), 42-44.

Shulman, R., Singer, M., Goldstone, J., Bellingan, G. (2005). Medication errors: A prospective cohort study of hand-written and computerised physician order entry in the intensive care unit. *Critical Care, 9*(5): R516-21.

Swain, J.J. (1997). Simulation Goes Mainstream, 1997 Simulation Software Survey, *ORMS Today* 24(5): 35-46.

4

Modelling the Clinical Risk: RFID vs Barcode

[1]Vincenzo Di Lecce*, [1]Marco Calabrese, [2]Alessandro Quarto, [3]Rita Dario

[1]Politecnico di Bari – DIASS

[2]myHermes S.r.l

[3]Hospital Unit "San Paolo" ASL/Ba.

ITALY

1. Introduction

This chapter proposes an approach that can improve the identification of patients, products, equipment and so on in a hospital. The aim is to better the management of the clinical risk by automating the process through the use of Radio Frequency IDentification (RFID).

The clinical risk management refers to the procedures for avoiding risks associated with direct patient care. It is the analysis about the probability of a patient being victim of an adverse event or inconvenience resulted, although involuntary, from improper medical care provided during the hospitalization. Research defines that the common denominator of almost all adverse clinical events is the lack of the patient traceability. In the specific context of a hospital, "traceability of patients" means managing a whole set of input and output data related to those processes defined as critical for clinical facilities.

In this work we will discuss a model to archive and manipulate data concerning the proposed system. RFID is, in fact, identified as a method for storing and retrieving data remotely by using small and cheap devices called RFID tags or transponders. For applying this technology in hospital environment it is necessary to build a network of these objects, each one with a unique number. So, only if there is a valid model to manage the produced output, one can easily retrieve information and realize an interesting use case.

In the proposed model, the adoption of an active instrument for automatic patient identification and assistance can be considered as the central entity of the process: "medical treatment of a patient", this includes potentially every activity from initial consultation through discharge of a surgical patient. In particular, this approach allows for simplifying the reality in terms of observable entities and supporting a higher degree of interconnection among those sections that traditionally are called "functional areas" of the hospital organization. Indeed, a lot of different actors characterize a clinical environment and the use of RFID seems to be capable to track all of them and optimize their interaction (Liao et al., 2006). The proposed RFID applications are targeted to the:

- Verification of positive patient identification. This is realized by means of a smart wristband for each patient. The tag contains information about the patient name, date of

* corresponding author

birth, surgical information, allergic reactions, medication requirement, blood type, health condition;

- Monitoring of surgical equipment before and after the operations. This application is aimed to grant a more efficient knowledge of the hospital instrument thus avoiding the stealing and misuse of equipment;
- Asset identification, such as blood transfusion, pharmaceutical units, charts and specimen;
- Bed inventory;
- Tracking of hospital staff and patients. Scientific works demonstrate, in fact, that geographical location of transponders is realizable by using a network of RFID readers in an indoor area. The idea is to divide the area in a set of sub-regions and read the power level each tag produces in relation to a particular reading station (Sangwan et al., 2005).

This paper also deals with the impact that the application of the RFID model produces on the traditional organization of a hospital unit. To this end, it is worth noting that the staff work is partially influenced by the new process organization. Therefore, it is clear that for realizing a cost/benefit analysis it is necessary to consider the importance of training and transition.

The outline of the chapter is as it follows. Paragraph 2 introduces the definition of clinical risk management, sketches an abstract model of it and provides an overview of ICT impact on the healthcare process with particular reference to barcode and RFID technologies as they have been used and implemented in the healthcare according to recent literature. Paragraph 3 makes a comparison between barcode- and RFID-based data models in order to enlighten the different perspective and benefits introduced by RFID technology in the patient care. In particular, the shift from a model based upon the concept of medical record to a new representation where the patient is at the center of the healthcare process is thoroughly examined. This change allows for a step-by-step reengineering of the healthcare process *from within,* which is extremely difficult using the traditional approach. In addition to traceability requirements in fact, an RFID tag (positioned, for example, in the patient's wristband) provides a real-time event trigger mechanism, which is very useful when a complete overview on the instantaneous state of the healthcare process is needed. A real-world example of how RFID can be easily integrated in the existing hospital environment is then presented in Paragraph 4. Paragraph 5 draws conclusion.

2. The Clinical Risk Management

The public healthcare recently and before the private one has been giving particular attention to the question of the clinical risk management. With reference to the Italian situation, for example, the prescriptive requirement for this issue may be due to the need to confirm the healthcare process for delivering *quality* services and therefore the recognition of those health *protocols* being valid for the institutional accreditation of all hospitals. The same consideration may be extended to most of Western countries as well. At the core of the quality process within the healthcare system there is also the *traceability* of any healthcare action referred to patients/users; because just the lack of such requirement is one of the main causes of the "clinical error", hence it is often responsible of high clinical risk.

The "traceability" is defined by the norm UNI EN ISO 9000:2000 as the ability to trace the history, use or location of what is under consideration. In a hospital the maintenance of traceability is a critical concern involving transversely those processes controlled by the structure organization system, whether it is based on traditional paper records, both in the case of a fully computerized management system, as well as in all hybrid-type situations. In any case, the traceability maintenance is based on an appropriate set of information relating to input and output data of certain processes identified as critical.
Some of the most critical processes within a healthcare structure concern the management of a large amount of information about drugs to be administered to patients, the examinations to be performed, the results of the tests, the diagnosis and clinical picture of patients until their discharge from a hospital department. The criticality index of processes depends on the criticality of the patients and their ability to communicate in a non-linear but actually exponential way.
The most advanced technological method, which is currently in use and able to minimize the risk by an error in the traceability process, without necessarily revolutionizing the entire management system of the healthcare setting organization, is the one involving the use of bar-coding printed on labels (barcode), which in turn are applied on the patient's medical records or other (infusion bags, medication, wrist bracelet). The coding contains a minimum set of information that can be read by optical devices connected to an appropriate computer system.
A suitable alternative is provided by RFID technology, recently introduced in clinical engineering, which seems to offer considerable advantages in terms of reliability, efficiency, versatility and ability to provide information.
In comparison with the old barcodes through this technology a patient that wears a bracelet containing a RFID transponder, is physically and uniquely included in the management process of clinical data, while with traditional systems the patient can be recognized only by using personal data.

2.1. Modelling the Clinical Risk Management

The debate about the clinical risk began in the 70s in U.S. in order to prevent the increasing trend in compensation claims by patients who had suffered damage as a result of errors in delivering the treatment they were subjected to. The most significant system, which is mentioned as an example of the national healthcare monitoring is the Australian Incident Monitoring System (AIMS), with 50,000 reports in 2001, 26,000 of them were sent directly from health facilities, while the remaining part by the operators, often anonymously, to the departments in charge. In Italy, specifically in Emilia Romagna, a similar system, which involved 39 units from 5 local health authorities of the region, was tested in 2001.
The *risk management* is about the identification of risks associated with the organization activities and the use of appropriate and adequate practices to prevent these risks or minimize their effects. The fundamental elements of risk management are: risk identification, risk analysis, risk treatment and monitoring. In this context the main modalities of risk identification are: the use of administrative and information data, the *incident reporting* and structured review of health records.

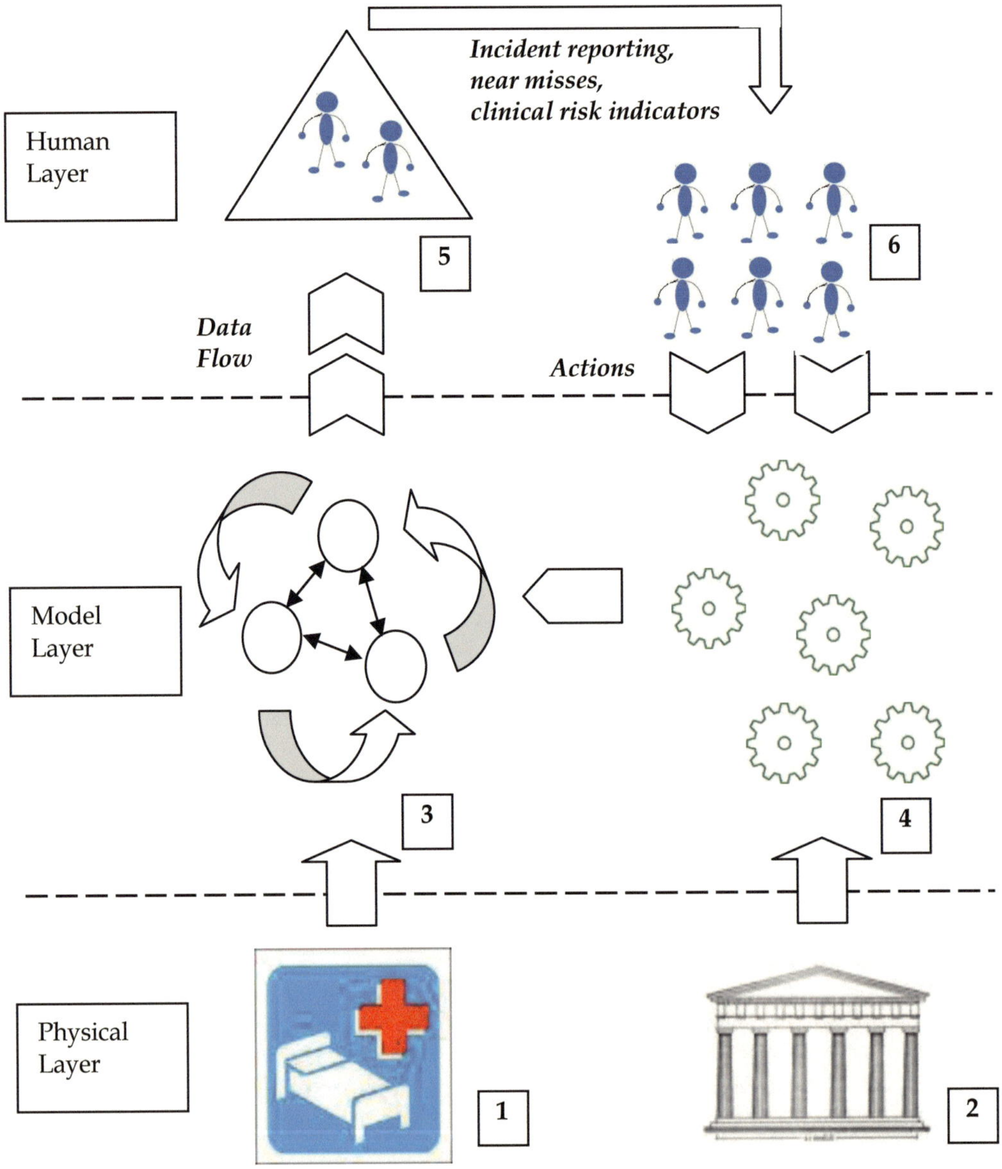

Legend

1. Healthcare Centres: hospitals, clinics
2. Normative Institutions: ministry of Health, Academies
3. Processes
4. Norms: protocols, guidelines
5. Supervisors
6. Stakeholders: medical staffs, patients

Fig. 1. Clinical Risk Management layered representation.

These data are useful to perform an assessment of adverse events that have already occurred (*misses*) or that are potentially verifiable (*near-miss*).
In order to produce a complete model of the risk management, a preliminary investigation on which variables are needed and what semantics they have is due. In-field data actually measured in real-world scenarios need in fact to be conceptualized within the ontological framework of the problem. As a rule of thumb, the more complex the underlying ontology in terms of numbers of independent concepts, the more the number of independent variables that should be considered. In computer science, ontology is defined as "a specification of a representational vocabulary for a shared domain of discourse - definitions of classes, relations, functions, and other objects" (Gruber, 1993). In other words, ontology can be considered as the formal specification of conceptualizations of certain domain knowledge. Ontology models the world of interest through assertions in a given language. Well formed assertions require a grammar, i.e. a way to assess the correct order of sequences of symbols used to describe the problem under consideration by means of formal rules. This would require an accurate ontological approach which goes beyond the scope of this work and will be investigated in future work on the subject.
For the scope of this chapter it is sufficient to describe the clinical risk management using a three-layer representation as depicted in Figure 1. The base layer accounts for places and institutions that are involved in the healthcare process. Hospitals and clinics are the physical places where processes come in action, while the Ministry of Health and other accredited institutions are responsible for providing formal informal guidelines and protocols that have to be implemented by medical operators. Processes and norms characterize the Model Layer: if correctly managed, they guarantee a suitable match between clinical theory and practice. At the upper layer two main groups can be found: stakeholders (such as medical staff and patients) and supervisors (that can be internal or external to the supervised structure depending on national healthcare systems). This last group supervises correct clinical risk management through in-field data collecting. In Italy, for example, this institution is called "Direzione Sanitaria" (Health Care Directorate) and works as a local control body in cooperation with the Ministry of Health. Supervising bodies are generally involved in the evaluation of the clinical risk through appropriate indexes which are produced through the accurate analysis and interpretation of recorded historical data. The acquisition of these data is generally achieved through incident reporting provided by medical staff.

2.2 Computerization of hospital healthcare data for clinical risk management

The automation of health records helps reduce the risk of error in healthcare, but contemporarily it involves new elements that must be analyzed; this implies necessarily and primarily a management of organizational flows referred to the clinical process. The automation procedure includes various components related to two areas and in each of them it is therefore possible to highlight the main sources of clinical errors:
A) Information Generation
  a. The information management operators
  b. The evidence of errors or omissions
B) Information Use
  a. The interpretation of the data
  b. The integration of information bases

c. The availability of the data
d. The redundancy of information
e. The storage of information

From this it appears that all the data being specific to an information system interact either directly or indirectly in the safety of clinical processes.

Information Generation. The first effect of computerization is the change in the way of recording information. In an ideal path it is necessary to provide for the complete elimination of paper-based materials and at the same time it is important that who performs the healthcare action, should be also in charge of registration, for example: the doctor who prescribes a treatment, will have also to carry out the same operation by means of an information system directly. Therefore, it is clear that it is not a true automation of the information flow where there is still a stage of the clinical process based on paper records, such as a prescription made first on paper and then subsequently computerized.
From the perspective of risk assessment, the computerization of data at a later phase leads to the introduction of such errors of interpretation or transcription, which remain hidden for the following user of the system, since these risks cannot be manageable and much less controllable.

Information Use. Automation facilitates the access to the data, which are presented in a modality that is more different than that of the paper: if ergonomic guidelines and architectural aspects for the user interface design are not taken into account, there will be the risk of an incorrect interpretation of the submitted data thus generating an error. The integrity of the data and its continuity (backup, redundancy and disaster recovery) will be protected by the adoption of universally recognized standards in the analysis process.
In 2005 the process of *incident reporting* was activated in all public health facilities referring to the Local Health Authority 4 in Chiavari (Genoa, Italy) introducing a risk warning report. 660 records between the years 2005-2007 have been analyzed, 10% of these are about errors or *near miss* related to the identification of patients. The highlighted issues were:

1. Non-application of the patient's identification bracelet for accessing to the operating room;
2. Misidentification of the patient for the therapy;
3. Misidentification of the documentation: reports, examinations, labels, etc..;
4. Misidentification of patient to perform non-invasive care practices

Furthermore, from this clinical experience, it has been shown that the critical processes are represented by the admission of patients in the structures of the Local Health Authority, the access of the patient in the operating room and the therapy administration.
In 2007, in Apulia Region, the Regional Health Agency has launched a survey about procedures and technologies for the patient identification in the main hospitals. In particular, the required data referred to identification procedures such as:

- identification of the patient;
- Identification of diagnostic reports;
- Identification of biological samples;
- Identification of drugs and therapies;
- Identification of operators.

From a technical point of view, the Apulia Region refers to three classes of encoding devices that should be present in the hospital:
1) Clear Information: The identification modality is based on the presence of some essential information (second name, first name, date of birth, tax code, etc..) readable in text mode directly by the operator and usually included in a wristband applied to the patient;
2) Barcode: identification system using a bar code system;
3) RFID: this latter alternative shows significant advantages in terms of reliability, efficiency, versatility and ability to hold information, as compared to the old bar code devices. In fact, with this technology, the patient wearing the wristband containing an RFID device is physically and unequivocally included in the computerization process of clinical data management.
The employment of such objective identification systems is of priority importance especially in those wards considered as the most critical ones for the clinical risk due to the sensitivity of patients as well as the delicacy of assistance procedures such as those of the intensive care, neonatal unit and transplant patients (Di Lecce et. al, 2008).
The results of this investigation are still in the experimental phase of acquisition and processing for the next operational provisions and the relevant evaluations will be acquired by the Working Group under the Regional Plan for the Electronic Healthcare activated in 2006 in the field of ICT (Dario et al., 2007.a).
Rothschild and colleagues (Rothschild et al, 2005) have studied in a medicine department of a hospital in Boston as the most sensitive patients hospitalized in intensive care units are more susceptible to the consequences derived from the effects of adverse events. In the same hospital, (Lehmann et al, 2005) have studied iatrogenic events, occurred during the administration of drug therapy, as the main source of clinical error.
An essential example of risk management analysis, from which the need of applying the RFID technology in a hospital arises, is represented by the database design for the hospital S. Giovanni Battista in Turin (Rapellino, 2005). This project has started since 2000 and contains data related to the identification of unfavourable events occurred within the hospital. From that work presented in 2006 it results that 47% of adverse events is due to technical-structural and organizational problems of the healthcare structure.
One of the most risky procedures for the possibility of falling into the therapeutic error refers to the administration of blood products. The barcode recognition on blood bags is one of the oldest and most useful traceability system that is worldwide recognized. Even Turner CL. et al. (Turner et al., 2003) had already shown in 2003 as the implementation for the identification of the patient, subject to blood transfusion, by using barcode system rather than the verbal or written modality has led to a significant increase in safety of blood transfusions.
In 2006 Wicks and colleagues (Wicks et al., 2006) described the potential benefits, application areas, the implementation changes of health care processes and the corresponding structural strategies in the use of RFID technology in a U.S. hospital department.
Some Dutch authors (Friesner et al., 2005) have recently presented again the need of a careful analysis of audit by users, before and after the introduction of each new technological application in hospital. In 2004, an American unit of intensive pneumology has conducted a survey of incident reporting; Osmon S. and collaborators (Osmon et al., 2004) have stressed that most of medical omission and commission of adverse events

occurred outside the department of intensive therapy, especially during the emergency transport of patients among the different floors of the Hospital.
An application model made with the international partnership between hospital units in Palermo-Sicily Region and the University of Pittsburgh Medical Centre, represents the experience described by the authors in 2007 (Brenni et al., 2007), i.e. an information system also extended to electronic medical records. The system presents the integration of RFID technology by means of disposable bracelets with single sign-on rewritable passive-type tags applied at the access time for the authentication of patients.

2.3. Related Works about use of RFID and Barcode in Clinical Risk Management

The hospital belongs, by its nature, to the framework of complex structures. The typical activities of this context regard concepts such as: traceability, reliability, security. Historically the use of protocols (therapeutic, surgical, pharmaceutical, logistics etc.) has characterized such activities. The matter regarding hospital logistics as operating framework, (i.e. knowledge acquisition of changing processes that take place within the hospital for the reorganization and reengineering of structures), or as quality improvement (i.e. safety and appropriateness of clinical care services) has been under consideration for many years. Basis of this operational framework is typically the traceability, which is classifiable in hospitals as:

- Traceability system of wards;
- Traceability system of emergency wards;
- Traceability system of pharmaceuticals (From the delivery of the drug produced by the manufacturer to the production of the single dose);
- Traceability system of medical devices;
- Traceability system of blood bags;
- Traceability system of implantable devices.

Numerous experiments carried out in the early nineties have validated this approach in view of technological supports in use. Current tendency is to focus, in particular, on the management of physical paths of patients (patient flow). A more rational management of the physical patient flow could solve the typical hospital problems such as: delays, long waiting times, queues, erased interventions, patients placed in inappropriate care setting, nursing staff under stress, waste and high costs etc. In this regard, a remarkable experience is that referring to the surgical patient in Boston Medical Center.
In Italy the USL 8 (Local Health Unit) of Asolo Hospital and Cardinal Massaia Hospital belonging to ASL 19 (Local Health Authority) in Asti, (both of them date back to 2006) may also be considered as qualifying experiences. Especially that of Cardinal Massaia Hospital (Asti - Piemonte Region, Italy), where the experimentation, started in 2006, has involved the wards of Pediatrics and Cardiology; here RFID wristbands, encoded during the First Aid in Emergency ward, are assigned only if the patient must be hospitalized in the two enabled wards. While in other wards barcode technology is still used. This experience also allowed for a comparative evaluation of the two technologies.
Bates et colleagues (Bates et al., 2001) analyze how the use of information technology can be a practical support for the reduction of accidents involving hospital patients. Among the criteria for the reduction of clinical risk, there is the need to develop efficient communication information systems able to involve hospital operators. The main difficulty is, in fact,

interpreting and rapidly exchanging data produced by each different health care settings, such as analytical laboratories or pharmacies. This separation of information is considered as the biggest barrier for achieving a real clinical risk reduction. It is therefore important to underline the concept of creating a channel for asynchronous data exchange, so that information flows, which are extremely important and characterized by a strong urgency,(i.e. critical results derived from a particular analysis cycle) can be exchanged with a minimized latency time. It is similarly important to underline the use of technology for identification of patients, drugs and hospital instruments, by means of barcode system applications, in order to significantly reduce accidents caused by poor communication.

The comparison between barcode and RFID technologies in patient identification is realized in (Aguilar et al., 2006). They underline the fundamental differences between them: barcode are scanned one at time and RFID can be scanned continuously by one reader; a barcode can be printed and cannot be modified whereas an RFID tag can be re-writable; barcode requires line-of-sight and RFID not, so RFID can be used in applications that aim to eliminate human intervention; RFID presents more complicated forms of data protections and encryption than barcode; barcode devices are typically cheaper than the RFID ones.

Young (Young, 2006) discusses the possibility of optimizing medical assistance activities by using RFID and barcode technology. In particular he has suggested a coordinated use of the two technologies in order to achieve an appropriate balance between the implementation costs and benefits derived from them. The use of RFID technology, in relation to a high unit cost and considering the classification of patients and irregular material is really advantageous thanks to their reusability and ease of reading data. The use of barcode system can be seen as the solution for producing regular material inventories, taking into account the low cost but, at the same time, the greater difficulty in querying these systems due to their passive nature.

Perrin and Simpson (Perrin & Simpson, 2004) highlighted how healthcare organization should make special efforts to adopt the so called Auto-ID/Bar-Code Enable Medication Administration system, either it employs active technologies or it employs the passive ones. The major difficulties concern the need of re-engineering organization procedures. On the other hand, by drastically reducing adverse events in the hospital there can be several benefits (also economic), the reduction of legal costs for services and the great satisfaction experienced by personnel in getting the reduction of accidents, as well as the ability to optimize the work organization of each functional sub-area thus increasing in efficiency.

Jiang and colleagues (Jiang et al., 2005) analyze the use of barcode and RFID technologies in management of blood. In particular, the research would propose an information management system to reduce the AIDS diffusion caused by the transfusion of infected blood. The authors start investigating the proprieties of a traditional information system based on barcode. The main disadvantage is that the barcode on the blood bag carries less information and cannot be reused, so it is not possible to store dynamic information about donors. The proposed solution to the problem is based on the use of RFID architecture. Jiang proposes the use of a donor's smart card to store all the details about the clinical life of donors. The research analyzes also the management of blood bag. The traditional barcode system is characterized by a static information management; so when a blood bag is sent to a hospital and the blood is used then its label is usually discarded. So the blood center cannot know what has happened to the blood. With the use of RFID, doctors can avoid some problems of quality about the blood during transfusion and all data can be written on the smart chip.

In (Fuhrer & Guinard , 2006), authors present how RFID technologies can contribute to build a smart hospital by optimizing business processes, reducing errors and improving patient safety. In particular, the paper underlines the importance to adopt an information system to manage usefully the data that the RFID technology can produce. In the proposed smart hospital many assets and actors would be tagged by RFID: the medical equipment and all the devices should contain an embedded tag; all the doctors, nurses, caregivers and other staff members should use a personal smart badge; each patient receives a wristband with an embedded RFID; all the paper medical files and other documents are tagged with self-adhesive RFID labels; the blister packs, other drugs' packages and bags of blood contain RFID labels. To produce dynamic information about the hospital activities RFID readers are placed at the entrances and exits of the smart hospital. Additional RFID readers are in each operating theater and in most important offices and strategic passages. At the same time a set of RFID palm readers is distributed to the staff members. Using this architecture, authors propose the possibility of producing XML real-time in correspondence to hospital events and store all the information in the information system.

Also Wu B. et colleagues in (Wu, 2005) analyze the application of RFID sensor networks in a smart hospital to improve efficiencies in operational aspects. The use of the RFID sensor nodes can generate large amounts of data. All the data are real and produced real-time, but they are not understandable without an appropriate middleware to manage them. The authors propose a middleware to connect the sensor networks to the real hospital applications.

In (Al Nahas & Deogun, 2007) a survey on the use of technologies for the patient identification is conducted. The main objective for the adoption of these technologies is the reduction of the clinical risk. Authors analyze barcode solutions, largely used prior of the RFID. It is estimated that the 70 percent of all medication containers had barcodes in 2006 and also staff and patients can be identified by barcodes. Limits of barcode refer to the fact that they are sensible to wrinkling, tearing and wetting and that cannot be used for real-time tracking. So the RFID looks like the solution for clinical tracking application. RFID, in fact, does not require line-of-sight for scanning and are resistant to tearing and moisture. Another advantage of RFID is that active tags can be used for tracking equipment, staff and patients in real-time.

The contemporary use of barcodes and RFIDs is proposed in (Sun et al., 2008). In this case, the problem under analysis concerns the reduction of medication error. The authors move from the consideration that the RFID is a good solution for patient identification in hospitals; however due to the high cost of tags and readers, most of healthcare industries hesitate to introduce them. So the proposed system requires that each unit-dose medication has a barcode and each patient needs to carry a wristband embedding a RFID tag. So the hospital information system works by managing the information produced by both the technologies and read by staff PC and PDA.

In (Clarke & Park, 2006) authors analyze the impact that the adoption of new technology has on the work of a hospital facility. The authors underline that the physician and staff satisfaction is heavily influenced by the degree to which the new work process disrupts existing practices. So the hospital management would prefer changes that can improve the workflow and information within existing practices. If it is necessary to adopt a disruptive change, also a cost planning and training must be considered. Typically the IT-based process changes involve the introduction of new technologies that can be difficult to integrate into the traditional workplace and workflow. In order to avoid these well known problems, the authors propose the use of a low invasive and semi-automatic technology such as the RFID. This solution can be used for passive tracking of people, objects and documents of a clinical environment.

Ni et colleagues produce a study and a survey about a number of wireless technologies that have been used for indoor location sensing. In particular they focus on the use of RFID technology and propose a prototype called LANDMARC to realize an accurate indoor location sensing system (Ni et al., 2004).

3. Healthcare – Data Model

Hereinafter ER models will be presented to describe the health procedures for patient identification and assistance during the hospital stay. In particular, two representative models have been identified: one for encoding barcode type and the other based on RFID systems.

The main difference between the two technologies refers to the operating principle; it will be passive in the case of optical systems and active for Radio Frequency Systems; this difference impacts also on the hospital organization in relation to the quality of health services for the patient.

The transit from the Barcode model to the RFID model proposes a strong analogy with the evolution of the World Wide Web. The biggest innovation is, in fact, that an active technology transforms the patient from a simple information consumer to a data producer.

3.1 The traditional Data Model

The Feature of barcode model is that it can identify a multiple number of organizational subsystems and each of them refers to a different functional area for the patient assistance.

In particular there are specific sub-areas describing:

- Medical services: the main entity is the "medical staff" actively involved in the production of tuples describing other entities: The performed "physical examinations", the issued "prognosis" and the associated "therapy". Of course, all information are stored in "medical record" in conformity with the time of production;
- Pharmacy services, laboratory analysis, diagnostic services: it is the sub-organization describing activity that the pharmacy staff performs in relation to the interpretation of medical record and medicine box packaging for the patient therapy. In this information system there is a second active entity, established by the "paramedical staff" responsible for the distribution of medicine boxes;
- Technical operating services: it is the model of functional reality associated with "hospital activities" conducted on the patient, such as: interventions, X-rays, ECG and other forms of health investigations. The active entity of this system is identified in the "operators" responsible for the different " hospital activities " associated with the production of specific outputs, that, as the diagrams show, are called: "report";
- Management control.

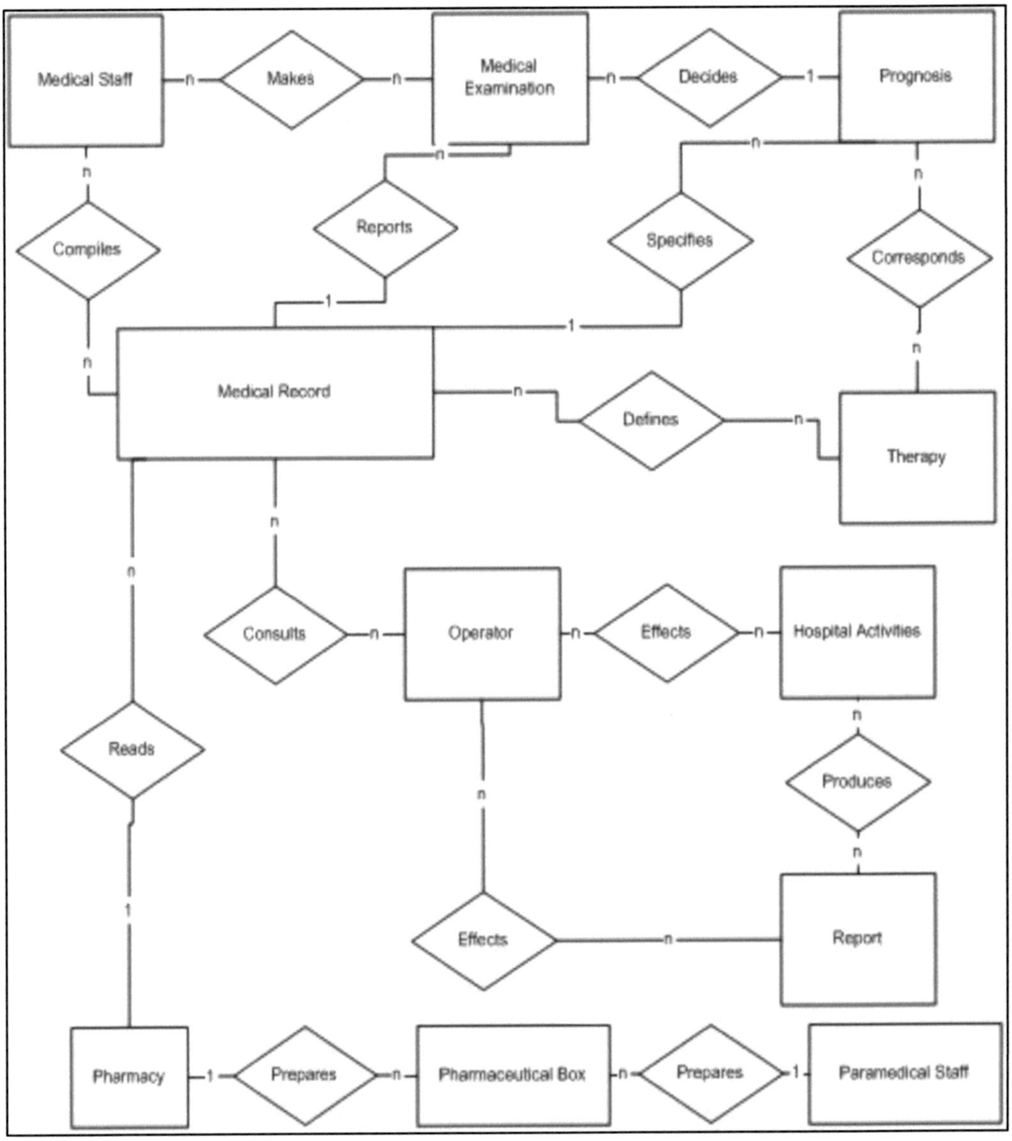

Fig. 2. - Medical system using Barcode autoidentification technologies.

The aggregation of summarized outputs from the produced information flows can be synthesized in the "medical record", i.e. a single centralizing entity allowing for the storage, in a strictly sequential mode, of data produced by each functional area in relation to the same patient (Figure 2). In other words, the traditional notion of "medical record" can be interpreted as the only entity in common among many information systems. Such a representation can be easily enhanced to support those passive technologies for the authentication of the patient, who is not characterized by any explicit diagrammatic presentation, but is an attribute of the before mentioned instrument for connection.

3.2 The "active patient" Data Model

The adoption of RFID as a tool for automatic patient identification can be considered as a central "active" entity of the whole model (Roark & Miguel, 2006). The alternative, presented in the associated diagram (Figure 3), is characterized by a simplification of reality in terms of observable entities; this means reducing the risk of information duplication that the traditional model shows (Brenni et al., 2007).

On the other hand, it is important to note a higher degree of interconnection among those that have been previously called "functional areas". In this model of reality, in fact, it is no longer possible to identify a clear separation among them, but their integration is recognizable and it is mainly identified in the "patient" and "health condition". The diagram is basically characterized by the disappearance of the "medical record" concept , seen as an instrument for getting information about activities produced by the system in relation to the patient, who it is associated to, and therefore the new entity "health condition" replaces the medical record and refers to the patient condition in a specific moment. Since the "health condition" is linked by a univocal relationship to the "patient" that it describes, it is clear that there is a direct relationship with the activities related to: "physical examinations" made by the medical staff; drug management (prescription, administration) made by the pharmaceutical staff and "performance" of other hospital operations for monitoring patient health condition (analysis and investigations) together with other correlated actions.

The comparison between the two proposed alternatives highlights the characteristics of simplification introduced by the RFID model, without having any increase in approximations made in view of the described reality. On the other hand, the presence of separate functional areas that are typical of barcode system draws attention to the problem of risks associated with information duplication. Indeed, the univocity of the chosen communication channel ("medical record") determines that the contact among different information flows can occur only after or before the processes have been developed by each functional unit (Dario et al., 2007.b).

So in relation to the clinical risk, asynchronism of communication can lead to lack of communication phenomena, which can be associated to the delta time characterizing the accesses for reading or writing the "medical record". However, the presence of a single communication node determines a possible break thus leading inevitably to the collapse of the whole macro system with all the relative risks connected to this (Brenni et al., 2007). In an interconnected model, similar to that using RFID technology, it is ensured that the temporary absence of information flow does not inhibit data exchange to all other entities of the system, which can continue to operate even under reduced conditions. The application of RFID model can be evaluated as optimizing also in terms of operation traceability. Certainly, a system producing a single intra-hospital communication output and characterized by sequential writing access, can easily suffer from the possibility of being improperly altered, differently from what actually occurs if the exchange of data and information among the operators takes place in real-time (Bates et al., 2001).

In conclusion, using such technology as RFID would mean several advantages to health care processes with only a slight reengineering of specific structures. A more rational use of hospital information systems could allow for a better organization of clinical data. Moreover it is noteworthy to remember the launch of RFID and Wi-Fi compliant transponders on the market. These would allow for unifying access points, thus simplifying them, (from a

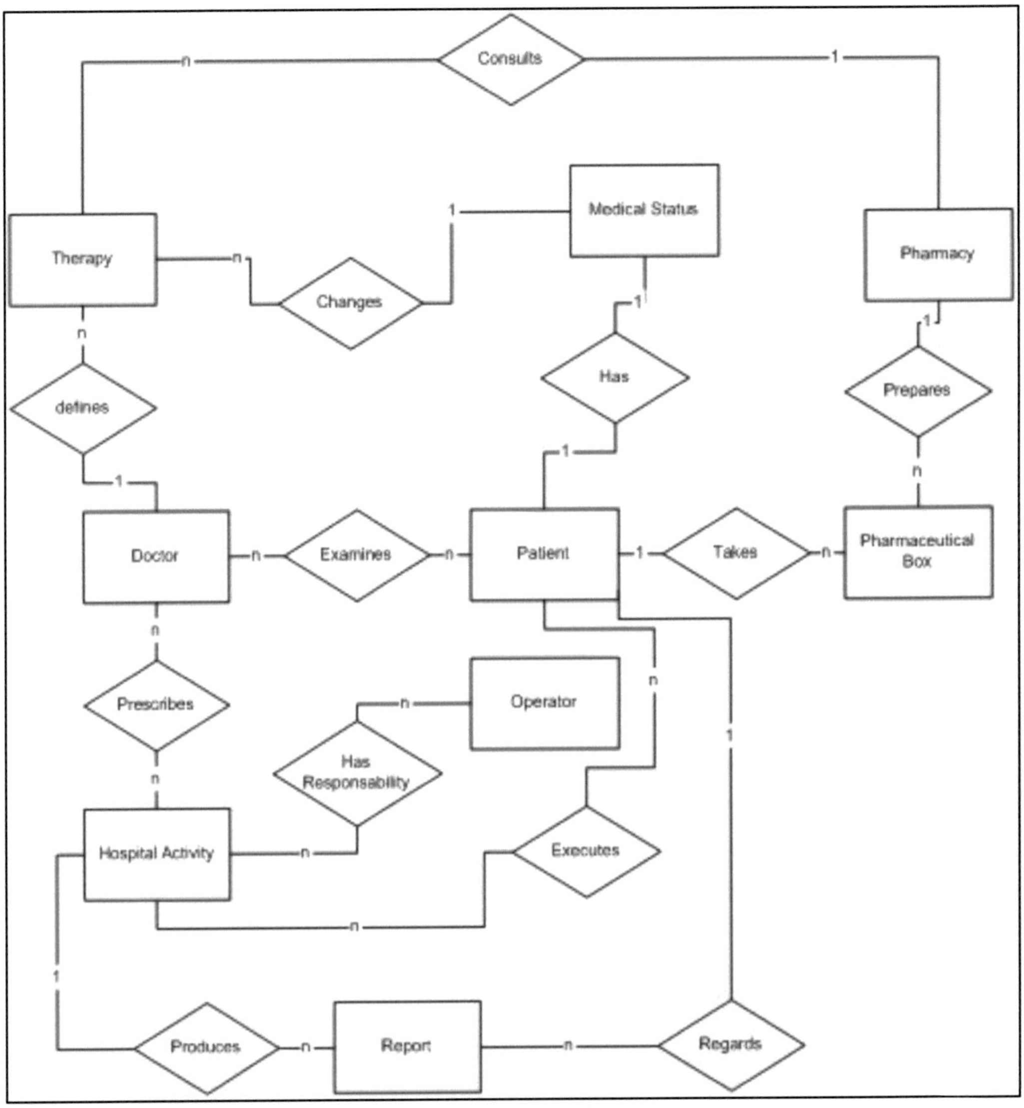

Fig. 3. - Medical system using RFID autoidentification technologies.

specialized portal to a pervasive wiring) and obtaining, through triangulation techniques and / or the power density calculation, the precise location of monitored entities. It is well known that the process for examining the clinical risk must start from identification of risks analytically, and therefore define the potential risks according to predetermined international grading scale in order to organize and implement the risk reduction project (Perilli, 2007). A possible solution for reducing the incidence of errors related to "mistaken identity" seems to be the use of identification wristbands with advanced RFID or barcode systems at the time of admission to hospital.

Of course this solution cannot be considered as the only or essential strategic element in the management clinical risk for the patient safety. To sum up, the use of an identification advanced system can not exclude the introduction of "best practices" relating to the implementation of the system for "incident reporting" and realization of campaigns focussing on specific issues, which are crucial to hospital security for both operators and citizens.

4. Advantages in using RFID-based healthcare systems: real-world example

The need to control and rationalize health expenditure for hospital services in Italy has led to the systematic recording of health data, through the introduction of the so-called S.D.O. "Scheda di Dismissione Ospedaliera" (Hospital Discharge Card), and the new reimbursement system by means of pre-determined charges as well as health services provided through D.R.G. (Diagnosis Related Group). The inclusion of the S.D.O. in the national health system, both public and private sectors, is regulated by the Ministerial Decree dated December, 28th 1991, and it has really replaced the previous system of data gathering, based on ISTAT (i.e. the Italian National Institute of Statistics) forms since 1995, also because of the dual role that currently this new document has: clinical summary and propaedeutic tool for billing the servicesperformed Although the D.R.G system classification can be traced back to 1983 in the U.S., its inclusion in Italy became effective only with the Ministerial Decree dated July 26th 1993 (the "Regulations of information flows about people discharged from public and private hospital institutions"). The introduction of S.D.O. and D.R.G. system brought about significant and radical changes in the organization of both public and private health facilities. The initial resistance to this change, due to the lack of competence in filling in these cards, with the different operating model, was overcome by launching a "navigation view" (as it happens for dialysis health services in Apulia Region), and this means that it is necessary to fix, update, manage more times the filling in procedure of the Hospital discharge card and the application of D.R.G. The completeness, accuracy, and timeliness of transmission from regions to the Ministry of Health in filling in the S.D.O. are obviously needed to monitor the regional and national progress of public and private health activity and therefore the following hospital expense.

4.1 Beyond "navigation view"

The technique of navigation view includes the non-systematic solution of medical errors (corrections, verification of the previous cases etc.) that are not always effective and, at the same time can be highly risky due to the "propagation of errors". The goal is the "automatic navigation" by using a series of information systems that can support the medical activity while filling in the S.D.O. and when assigning the D.R.G. This effort should be aimed at obtaining, real-time, the projection being as much accurate as possible in relation to the clinical diagnostic protocol that the patient follows during the period of hospitalization. The current legislation provides for the activation, through the health management administration, of systems for checking the completeness, timeliness and quality of the information contained in the S.D.O. The guidelines of the Health Ministry in June 1992 gave great opportunity for controlling the internal organization of the data flow system. However, up to the authors' knowledge, a comprehensive engineering approach to healthcare workflow management in Italy is quite far from being achieved. The proposed RFID-based approach moves towards reducing this gap.

S.D.O is uniquely attributed to the clinical history of one single patient's hospitalization. This means that its underpinning data model is in accordance with the ER diagram depicted in Figure 3 which adopts a patient-based view. A typical S.D.O. in Italy consists of two pages as shown in Figure 4 and 5. The first page is referred to patient's identification data and summary information about his/her hospitalization, while the second page reports on events related to diagnostic and therapeutic activities. In the medical practice, S.D.O. forms are often handwritten and many fields are generally left empty thus definitely providing only a small amount of all available information.

The process of compiling S.D.O. can be intensively automated by means of the proposed approach. In particular an RFID installed into the patient's wristband, when passing beside a receiver opportunely positioned in the proximity of a gate, can automatically inform the Hospital Information System about patient moving across hospital units. Three use cases have been here reported according to well-known Unified Modelling Language (UML) notation (Figure 6-11). They account for describing at an abstract level the automation of S.D.O. compiling activity. Use case diagrams are completed each one with a sequence diagram depicting the corresponding action flow.

- *Patient Identification*: this activity starts upon patient entrance in hospital for hospitalization. Medical staff (for example in first aid unit) identifies the patient and transmits patient data to the Hospital Information System. Consequently, patient id assigned by the system is copied onto an RFID tag hosted in a wristband which is then delivered to the patient to track all its hospital stay.
- *Patient Internal Transfer*: during hospitalization, the patient is bedded in one or more units depending on medical treatments (analysis, medical exams, surgery) he/she receives. Providing the gates of hospital units with an RFID reader, the entry/exit event of an RFID-equipped patient becomes straightforward. Each reading triggers an event that writes in the Hospital database updating the patient localization.
- *Patient receives treatment*: the medical doctor, after a medical visit or a surgical operation, writes the performed treatment on the patient's RFID by means of specific interfaces (for example a handheld device). This information is temporary stored into the RFID memory until a reading event, run by the passage through an RFID reader enhanced gate, causes data to be flushed towards the S.D.O. In this way, writing tasks are performed locally and remote database updating is managed asynchronously

5. Conclusion

In this chapter the improvement resulted by RFID-based modelling for the clinical risk management has been discussed. The comparison between barcode-based healthcare systems and RFID technologies has shown the possibilities for a significant process reengineering which would represent an essential key to efficacy and efficiency increase in personalized healthcare services. In this view, the new model is centred around the idea of patient as an active element in the clinical process, thus overcoming limits imposed by the concept of medical record. In addition to traceability requirements, an RFID tag (positioned, for example, in the patient's wristband) provides a real-time event trigger mechanism, which can be very useful when a complete overview on the instantaneous state of the healthcare processes is needed. A real-world example of how RFID technology may be integrated within the healthcare processes has been also presented and discussed.

In conclusion, throughout the text several benefits in using RFID technology in the hospital environment have been considered. They can be classified into two main categories: Benefits being tangible, measurable and attributable to a reduction in "cost" and Intangible benefits.
In the first group there are the benefits related to the efficiency and referable to the increasing of high quality processes and, consequently, a reduction of resources committed to solving the problems introduced by real or potential non-compliance concerns (corrective and preventive actions). Some classic examples of error, which should be corrected or prevented, refer, for instance, to the surgeon operating on the wrong side because of a transcription error or the doctor and the professional operator administering the incorrect therapy due to a homonymy of patients' names.
The intangible benefits can be subgrouped into further categories:
1. Benefits related to a strengthening of the information system;
2. Subjective benefits such as:
    a) Patient satisfaction in feeling more safe;
    b) Greater confidence in the structure by the patient;
    c) A better sense of belonging of staff due to the awareness that the system manages to avoid a large number of human errors; these factors are evaluated on the basis of the increase in the reference values of the quality indicators perceived by the users / patients and staff belonging to the structure (clinical audit).
3. Compliance with the requirements of Law for safe identification and treatment of data in accordance with the right to privacy of the patient;
4. Benefits attributable to the healthcare facility.
In light of what has been stated so far the authors have been considering the perspective that in the next future RFID-based models focused on a "patient-centric" view will be at the base of intensive healthcare process reengineering.

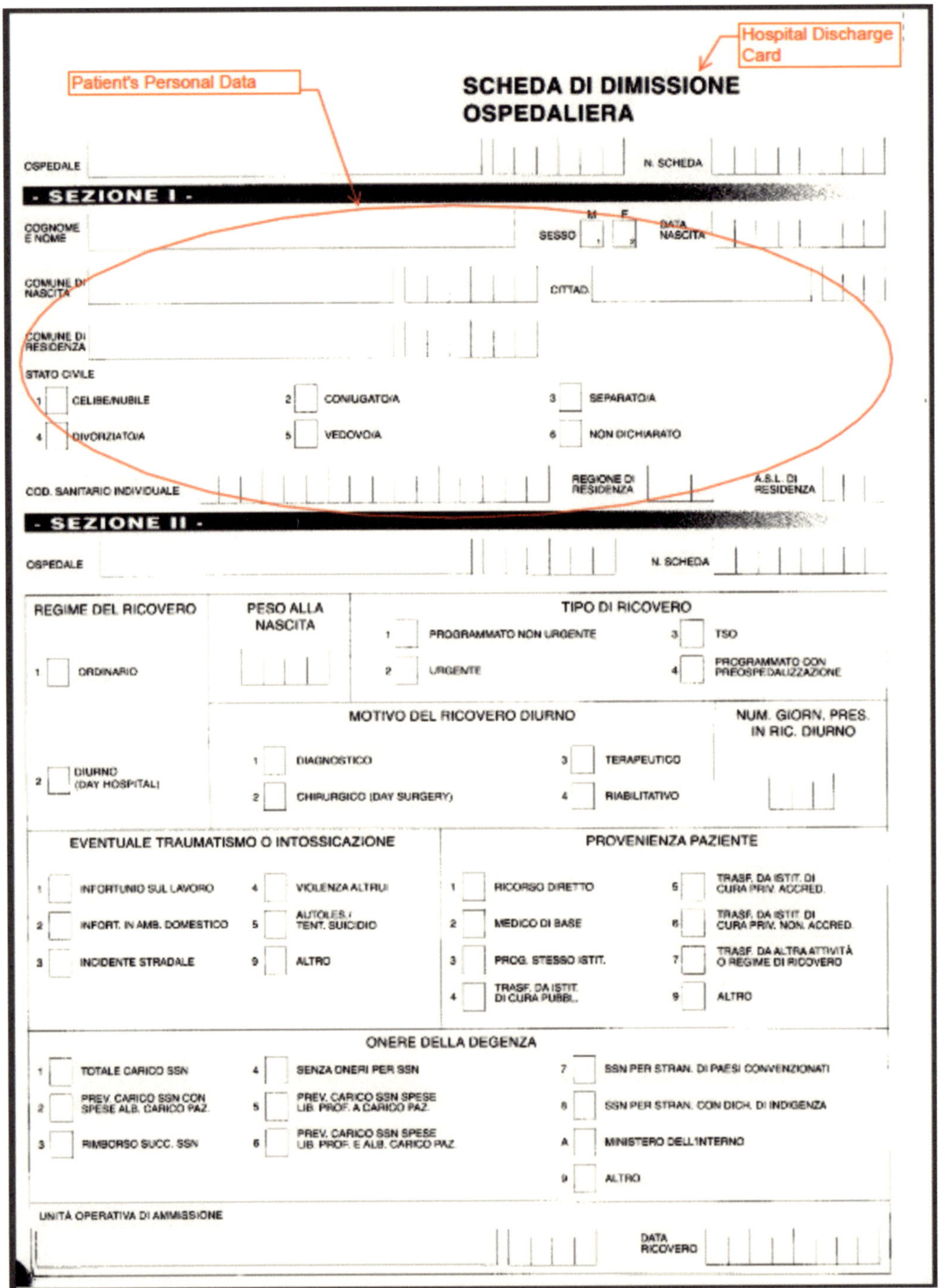

Fig. 4. – The patient's identification page of a S.D.O. document. This is the first page of a SDO and contains almost patient's personal data and summary information about hospitalization.

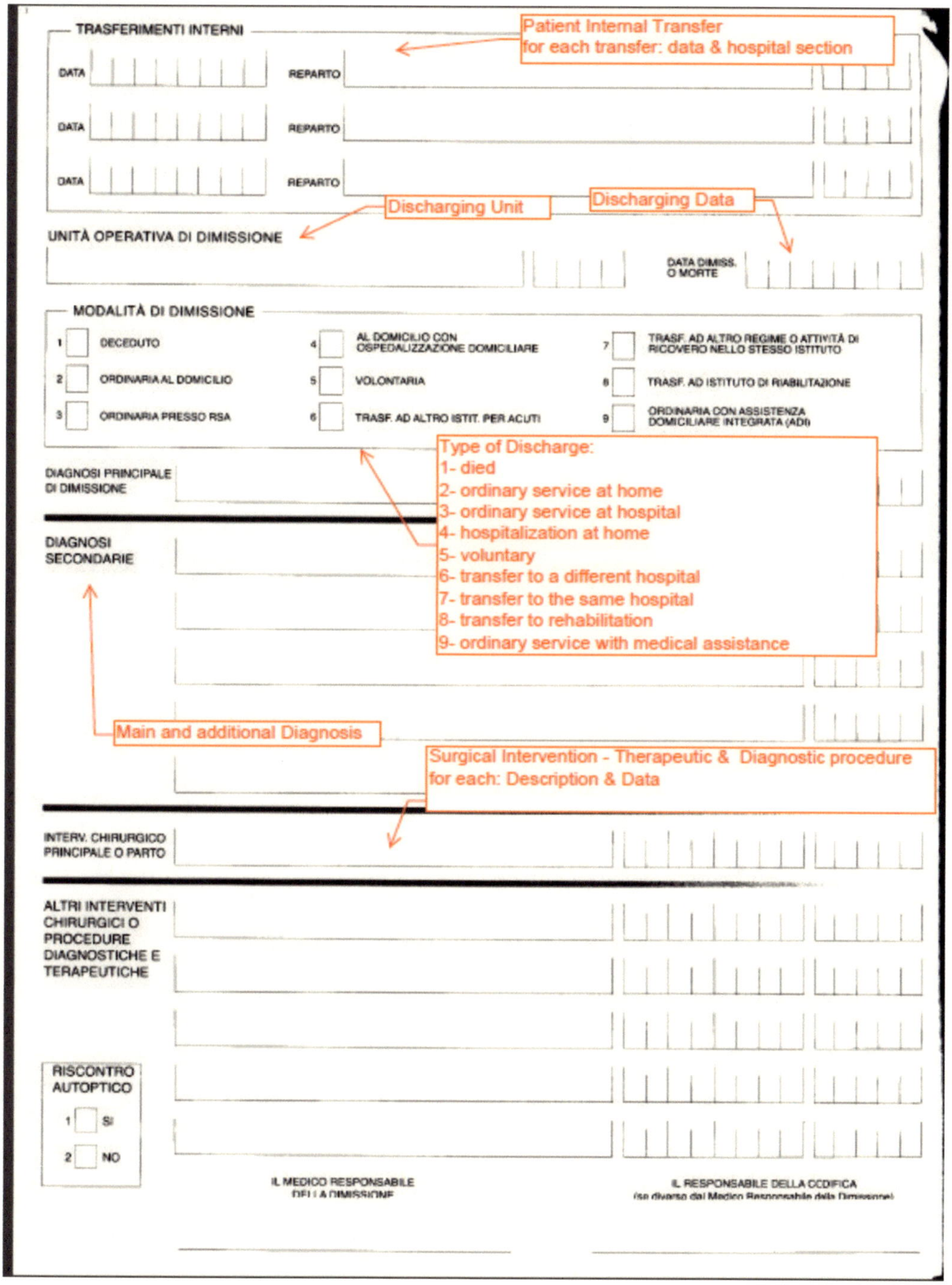

Fig. 5. - The patient's activity page of a S.D.O. This is the second page of a SDO and contains information about all the hospitalization, surgical, therapeutic and diagnostic procedure regarding a patient.

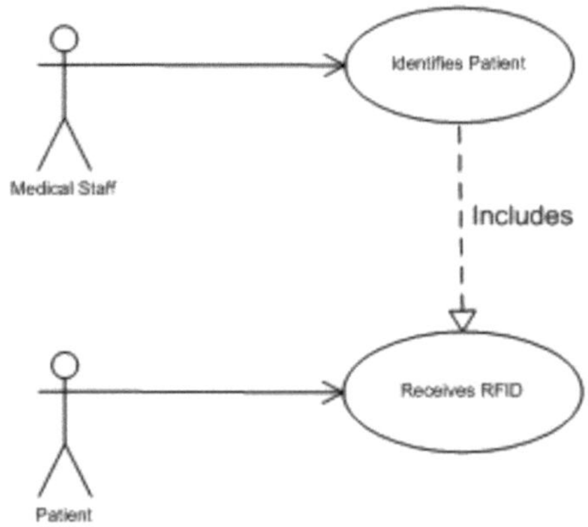

Fig. 6. - UML Use case of patient identification. This use case defines the filling process of the SDO for what concerns patient's identification (S.D.O. first page)

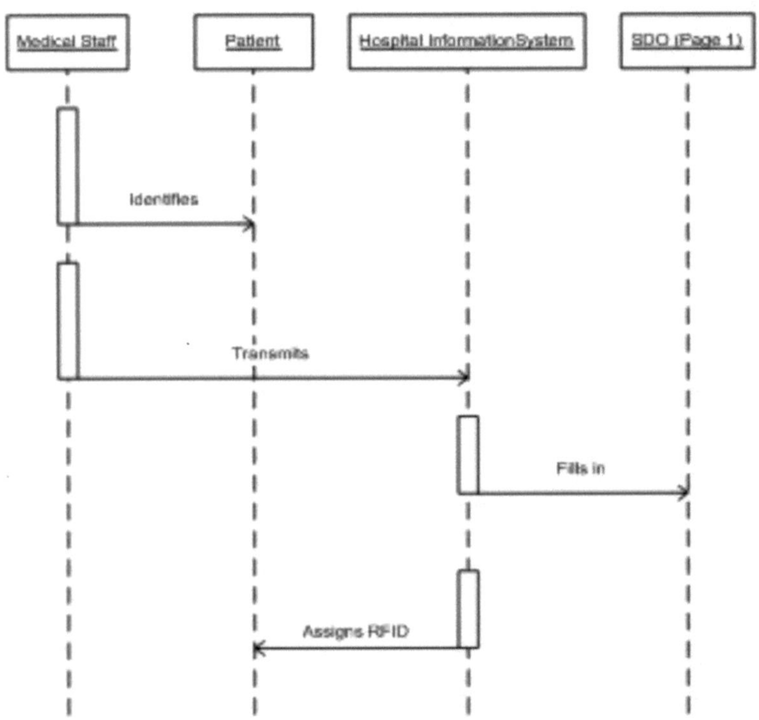

Fig. 7. - UML Sequence Diagram of patient identification. This UML diagram analyzes the sequences of patient identification, data acquisition and RFID assignation.

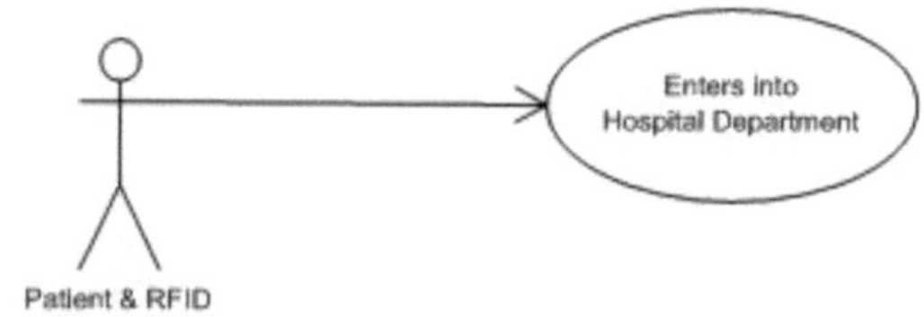

Fig. 8. - Use case of patient activity monitoring. This use case defines the filling process of the S.D.O. second page regarding the hospital departments in which the patient transits.

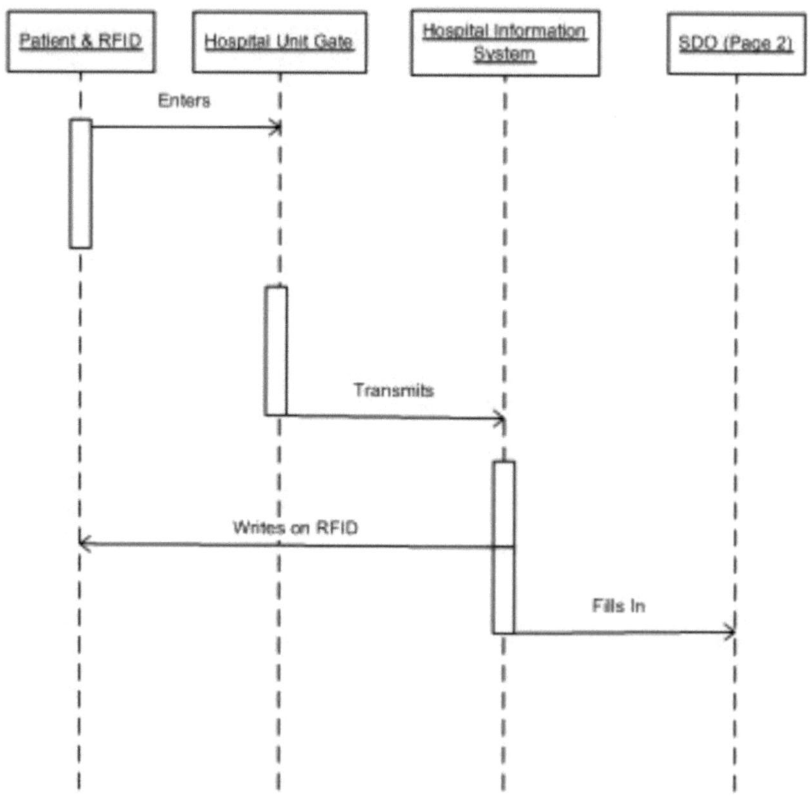

Fig. 9. - Sequence diagram of patient activity monitoring. This sequence diagram analyzes how information about the patient transit in hospital departments is managed by the proposed systems.

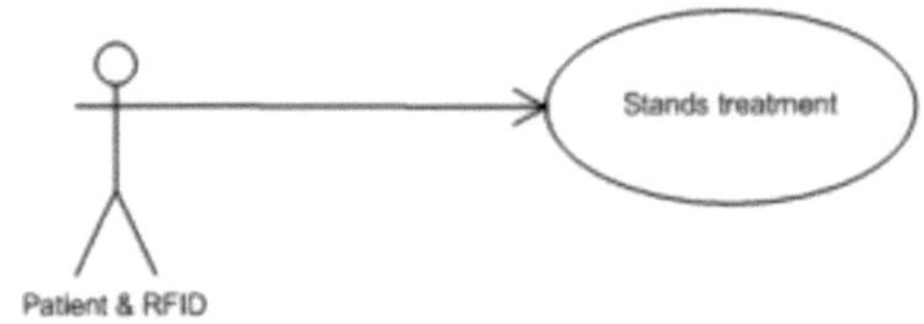

Fig. 10. - Use case of patient activity monitoring. This use case defines the filling process of the S.D.O. second page regarding the treatments (surgical, therapeutics and diagnostics) related to patient

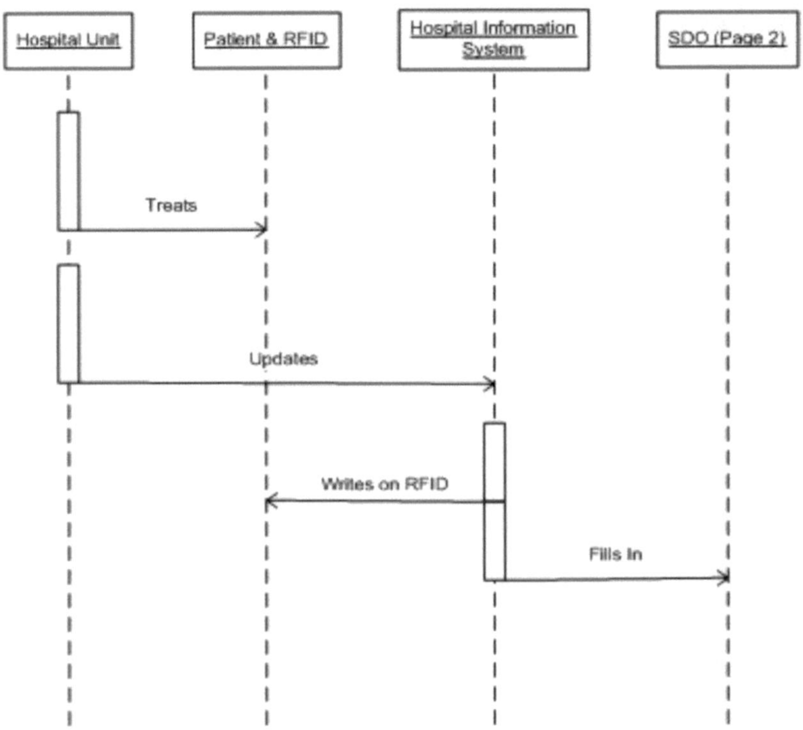

Fig. 11. - Sequence diagram of patient activity monitoring. This sequence diagram analyzes the sequence of operations in correspondence with the treatments of a patient (surgical, therapeutics and diagnostics).

7. References

Al Nahas, H. & Deogun, J.S. (2007). Radio Frequency Identification Applications in Smart Hospitals, *Proceedings of the 28th IEEE International Symposium on Computer-Based Medical Systems (CBMS07)*, pp. 337-342, ISBN 1063-7125, Maribor, Slovenia, June 2007, IEEE

Anguilar, A.; van der Putten, W. & Maguire, G. (2006). Positive Patient Identification using RFID and Wireless Networks, *Proceedings of the 11th Annual Conference and Scientific Symposium*, Health Informatics Society of Ireland, November 2006

Bates, D.; Cohen, M.; Leape, L.; Overhage, M.; Shabot, M. & Sheridan, T. (2001). Reducing the frequency of errors in medicine using information technology. *Journal of the American Medical Informatics Association*, Vol. 8, No. 4, July/August 2001, pp. 299-308, ISSN 1067-5027

Brenni, S.; Piazza, T. & Farinella E. (2007). La tracciabilità del paziente in strutture ospedaliere, *Notiziario dell'Istituto Superiore Sanità,* Vol. 20, No. 9, pp. 3-8, ISSN 0394-9303

Clarke, D. & Park, A. MD (2006). Active-RFID System Accuracy and ist Implications for Clinical Applications, *Proceedings of the 19th IEEE Symposium on Computer-Based Medical Systems (CBMS06)*, pp. 21-26, ISBN 0-7695-2517-1, Salt Lake City, UT, USA, June 2006, IEEE

Dario, R.; Quarto, A. & Di Lecce, V. (2007). Modello per la valutazione del rischio clinico: codice a barre vs RFID, *Proceedings of @ITIM 2007 8th National Congress*, pp. 31-36, ISBN 978-88-95614-02-1, Bari, Italy, December 2007, @ITIM

Dario, R.; Giove, A. & Calò, M. (2007). Intelligent Software Agency for Developing Multipurpose Health Care Information Systems, *Proceedings of @ITIM 2007 8th National Congress*, pp. 157-162, ISBN 978-88-95614-02-1, Bari, Italy, December 2007, @ITIM

Di Lecce, V.; Quarto, A.; Dario, R & Calabrese, M. (2008). Data Modelling for Complex Reality: an Application to the Clinical Risk Management, *The 17th IASTED International Conference on Applied Simulation and Modelling*, pp. 196-200, ISBN 978-0-88986-731-4, Corfu, Greece, June 2008, IASTED

Friesner, D.; Neufelder, D.; Raisor, J. & Khayum, M. (2005). Benchmarking patient improvement in physical therapy with data envelopment analysis, *International Journal of Health Care Quality Assurance*, Vol. 18, No. 6, pp. 441-457, ISSN 0952-6862

Fuhrer, P. & Guinard, D. (2006). Building a Smart Hospital using RFID technology, *Proceedings oft he 1st European Conference on eHealth (ECEH06)*, pp. 131-142, Fribourg, Germany, October 2006, GI-Edition - Lecture Notes in Informatics

Gruber, T.R. (1993). A Translation Approach to Portable Ontology Specifications, *Knowledge Acquisition*, Vol. 5, No. 2, pp. 199-220, ISSN 1042-8143

Jiang, M.; Fu, P.; Chen, H.; Chen, M.; Xing, B.; Sun, Z.; Deng, P.; Wang, G.; Xu, Y. & Wang, Y. (2005). A Dynamic Blood Information Management System Based on RFID, *Proceedings of the 2005 IEEE Engineering in Medicine and Biology 27th Annual Conference*, pp. 546-549, ISBN 0-7803-8741-4, Shanghai, China, September 2005, IEEE

Lehmann, L.S.; Puopolo, A.L.; Shaykevich, S & Brennan, T.A. (2005). Iatrogenic events resulting in intensive care admission: frequency, cause, and disclosure to patients and institutions, *American Journal of Medicine*, Vol. 118, No. 4, pp. 409-413, ISSN: 0002-9343

Liao, P.; Liu, L.; Kuo, F. & Jin, M. (2006) Developing a Patient Safety Based RFID Information System - An Empirical Study in Taiwan, *Proceedings of the IEEE International Conference on Management of Innovation and Technology*, pp. 585-589, ISBN: 1-4244-0147-X, Singapore, China, June 2006, IEEE

Ni, L.M.; Liu, Y.; Lau, Y.C. & Patil, A.P. (2004). LANDMARC: Indoor Location Sensing Using Active RFID, *Wireless Networks*, Vol. 10, No. 6, November 2004, pp. 701-710, ISSN 1022-0038

Osmon, S.; Harris, C.B.; Dunagan, W.C.; Prentice, D.; Fraser, V.J. & Kollef, M.H. (2004). Reporting of medical errors: an intensive care unit experience, *Critical Care Medicine*, Vol. 32, No. 3, pp. 727-733, ISSN 0090-3493

Perilli, G. (2007). *Le morti evitabili*, ASL/BA - Divisione Territoriale ex AUSL BA editore, Barletta (BA), Italy

Perrin, RA. & Simpson, N. (2004). RFID and Bar Codes - Critical Importance in Enhancing Safe Patient Care, *Journal of Healthcare Information Management*, Vol. 18, No. 4, November 2004, pp. 33-39, ISSN 1099-811X

Rapellino, M. (2005). Anatomia dell'errore: errore personale o errore di sistema?, *Atti del Simposio dalla Qualità percepita alla percezione dell'errore medico. Metodologia integrata per l'individuazione dell'errore medico*, Torino, Italy, Ottobre 2005, http://web.infinito.it/utenti/f/fappto/errore_medico_2005/rapellino_ab.html

Roark, DC & Miguel, K. (2006). RFID: bar coding's replacement?, *Nursing Management*, Vol. 37, No. 2, pp. 28-31, ISSN 0744-6314

Rothschild, J.M.; Landrigan, C.P.; Cronin, J.W.; Kaushal, R.; Lockley, S.W.; Burdick, E.; Stone, P.H.; Lilly, C.M.; Katz, J.T.; Czeisler, C.A. & Bates, D.W. (2005). The Critical Care Safety Study: The incidence and nature of adverse events and serious medical errors in intensive care, *Critical Care Medicine*, Vol. 33, No. 8, August 2005, pp. 1694-1700, ISSN 0090-3493

Sangwan, R.S.; Qiu, R.G. & Jessen, D. (2005). Using RFID Tags for Tracking Patients, Charts and Medical Equipment within an Integrated Health Delivery Network, *Proceedings of the 2005 IEEE Symposium on Networking, Sensing and Control*, pp. 1070-1074, ISBN 0-7803-8812-7, Malverna, PA, USA, March 2005

Sun, P.R.; Wang, B.H. & Wu, F. (2008). A New Method to Guard Inpatient Medication Safety by the Implementation of RFID, *Journal of Medical Systems*, Vol. 32, No. 4, August 2008, pp. 327-332, ISSN 0148-5598

Turner, C.L.; Casbard, A.C. & Murphy, M.F. (2003). Barcode technology: its role in increasing the safety of blood transfusion, *Transfusion*, Vol. 43, No. 9, pp. 1200-1209, ISSN 0041-1132

Wicks, A.M.; Visich, J.K. & Li, S. (2006). Radio frequency identification applications in healthcare, *International Journal of Healthcare Technology and Management*, Vol. 7, No. 6, pp. 522-540, ISSN 1368-2156

Wu, B.; Liu, Z.; George, R. & Shujace, K.A. (2005), eWellness: Building a Smart Hospital by Leveraging RFID Networks, *Proceedings of the 2005 Engineering in Medicine and Biology 27th Annual Conference*, pp. 3826-3829, ISBN 0-7803-8741-4, Shanghai, China, September 2005, IEEE

Young, D (2006). Pittsburgh Hospital combines RFID, bar codes to improve safety, *American Journal of Health-System Pharmacy*, Vol. 63, No. 24, December 2006, pp. 2431-2435, ISSN 1079-2082

Augmented Microscope System for Training and Intra-Operative purposes

Alessandro De Mauro[1], Jörg Raczkowsky[1], Reiner Wirtz[2], Mark Eric Halatsch[2], Heinz Wörn[1]
[1]*Institute for Process Control and Robotics, University of Karlsruhe (TH)*
[2]*University Hospital of Heidelberg*
Germany

1. Introduction

In recent years, neurosurgery has been deeply influenced by new technologies. Computer Aided Surgery (CAS) offers several benefits for patients' safety but fine techniques targeted to obtain minimally invasive and traumatic treatments are required, since intra-operative false movements can be devastating, leaving patients dead. The precision of the surgical gesture is related both to accuracy of the available technological instruments and surgeon's experience. In this frame, medical training is particularly important. From a technological point of view the use of the Virtual Reality (VR) for the surgeons training and Augmented Reality (AR) for the intra-operative aid for treatments offer the best results. This paper presents a prototype for a mixed reality system for neurosurgical interventions embedded on a real surgical microscope for pre- and intra- operative purposes. Its main purposes are:

- realistic simulation (visual and haptic) of the spatula palpation of Low-Grade Glioma (LGG);
- stereoscopic visualization in AR of relevant 3D data for safe surgical movements in the image guided therapy (IGT) interventions.

This is the first prototype of a training system using a real microscope for neurosurgery.

2. Motivation and Medical Background

In neurosurgical operating theatre (OR) almost all interventions are carried out using a microscope (Fig.1). All the best commercial systems provide the surgeon with only a real two-dimensional overlay of the region of interest (e.g. tumour) inside the oculars of the operating microscope related on the preoperative processed patient's image data. The 3D environment reconstruction from 2D is another difficult and critical mental work for the surgeon. A first motivation to this work is related to the last considerations and the target is the improvements of a prototype of an AR stereoscopic microscope for neurosurgical interventions developed in our institute (Aschke et al., 1999) optimizing and completing the information set visible for the surgeons needs. The goal is to enhance the surgeon's ability

for a better intra-operative orientation by giving him the three-dimensional view and other information he needs for a safe navigation inside the patients.
Another motivation is to enhance the current neurosurgical training in the specific frame of the realistic simulation (visual and haptic) of the spatula palpation of LGGs using a real surgical microscope. Traditional techniques for training in surgery include the use of animals, phantoms and cadavers. The main limitation of these approaches is that live tissue has different properties from dead tissue and also that animal anatomy is significantly different from the human. In other words, traditional surgical training is far from being realistic. Even if classical training is improved by the use of well illustrated books and excellent training movies recorded directly in the operating theatre, nowadays the main training for surgeons is still performed on the real patient. From several years simulation was validated by the scientific community and it was shown that VR simulators can speed-up the learning process and improve the proficiency of surgeons prior to performing surgery on a real patient (Tomulescu & Popescu, 1990). A comparison between computer-simulation-based training and traditional mechanical simulator for basic laparoscopic skills, found that trainees who trained on the computer-based simulator performed better on subsequent porcine surgery (Youngblood et al. 2005).
From the medical point of view LGGs are intrinsic brain tumours that typically occur in younger adults. The objective of related treatment is to remove as much of the tumour as possible while minimizing damage to the normal brain. Pathological tissue may closely resemble normal brain parenchyma when looked at through the neurosurgical microscope. As a result, efforts to remove all tumour cells inevitably remove some of the normal brain and can leave behind small sections of tumours cells. Neuronavigation can help only partially because the brain-shift phenomena affects the pre-operative patient data after craniotomy and tissue removal. The tactile appreciation of the different consistency of the tumour compared to normal brain requires considerable experience on the part of the neurosurgeon and is a vital point.
Hardware (microscope, tracking system, tools) and software (navigation system based on the patient dataset) are both involved in the training and intra-operative activities. This consideration justifies the idea of a mixed reality system that uses similar environments and architecture setups for pre- and intra-operative use, providing a natural continuum between training system (based on VR) and intra-operative system (based on AR).

3. Neurosurgical workflow

In order to facilitate the understanding of this research study it is crucial to give a brief introduction to the steps involved before and during the neurosurgical procedures (workflow) and the related technology.

3.1 Pre-operative phase

The geometric models of the organs or the region of interest (e.g. tumour) are reconstructed from data acquired by CT, MRI or other means by a radiologist. In the intra-operative phase a tracking system is used to track the relative positions of the patient, relevant tools, and microscope.

3.2 Intra-operative phase

In the OR, surgeon's eyes are typically on the microscope oculars but occasionally they need to see the screen in order to understand the correct position compared to the preoperative images (CT, MRI). All data are shown and navigated on the video using the normal three medical views (coronal, axial, sagittal) during the procedure. The position and orientation of an active tool tracked by the infrared tracking system and its relative position in the patient images are shown on the monitors. The two-dimensional contour of the region of interest is recognized as defined by the radiologist in the preoperative step. This two-dimensional shape is visible inside the commercial microscopes overlaid to the oculars views. The steps discussed here are shown in Fig.1

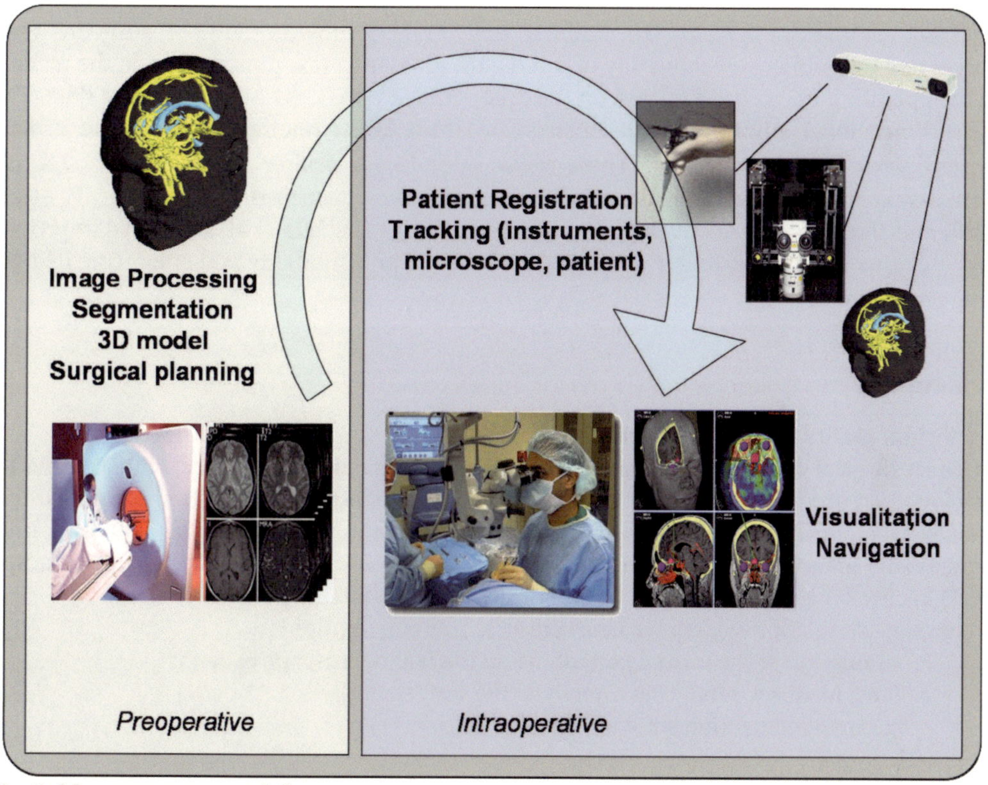

Fig. 1. Neurosurgery workflow

4. State of art

4.1 State of art in VR training for Surgery

The success of using haptic devices in medical training simulators has already been demonstrated by several commercial companies working in this field (i.e. Immersion Medical, Surgical Science, Mentice, and Reachin Technologies).

Other works show haptic simulation environment for laparoscopic cholecystectomy (Webster et al., 2003), for hysteroscopy (Montgomery et al., 2001) , interventional cardiology

procedures, incorporating blood flow models and models of cardiopulmonary physiology (Cotin et al., 2000), common bile duct exploration (Basdogan et al., 2001).
On the other hand, the state-of-the-art in neurosurgical simulation (Goh et al., 2005) shows only a few examples of VR based systems which use force feedback (Luciano et al., 2008, Sat o et al., 2006 and Wiet et al., 2000). Because a neurosurgical microscope is used in a large percentage of interventions, the realism of these simulators is limited by the architecture: they use either standard monitors or head mounted displays but not a real surgical microscope.

4.2 State of art in AR for Neurosurgery

The best commercial systems (i.e. Brainlab and Stryker) provide the neurosurgeons with only a real two-dimensional overlay of the region of interest (ex. tumour) inside the oculars of the operating microscope related on the preoperative processed patient's image data. The three-dimensional environment reconstruction from 2D is another difficult and critical mental work for the surgeon. There were only two working examples of AR 3D stereoscopic microscope for neurosurgery. The first was described in (Edwards, P. et al., 2000) and the second was developed in our laboratories (Aschke et al. 1999). We improved this previous work extending it with a higher level graphic modality and enhancing its real-time performances.

5. Methods

5.1 Virtual reality training system

In neurosurgical interventions monitors and operating microscopes are both commonly employed. In order to understand the correct tumour position compared to the preoperative images (CT, MRI) surgeon's eyes are normally on the microscope oculars and only occasionally glance at a larger screen. This second view is crucial in image guided therapy (IGT) to check the correct position of the surgical tools inside the patient brain.
A complete simulation system for neurosurgical training requires:

- simulation of the virtual patient inside the real microscope oculars;
- force feedback rendering directly at the user's hand;
- common navigation software used in OR.

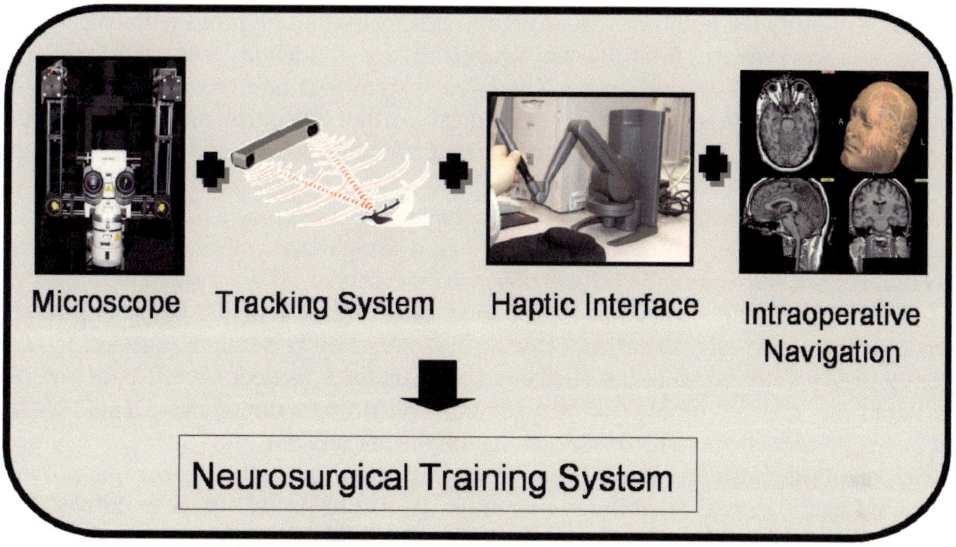

Fig. 2. Neurosurgical training system architecture

A virtual environment is geometrically built using real patients' data affected by a LGG from the standard medical imaging devices. During this process human organs are accurately reconstructed from real patient images using the open source software 3DSlicer.
Region growing algorithm has been used for segmentation, and next organ and region of interests are classified. The 3D triangularized surface model of the organ is obtained with a Marching cubes strategy and it's imported directly into our application, refined and converted from the VTK file format (3DSlicer output) to X3D. The 3D environment description language used is X3D because it is the natural successor of the well known VRML. It means that the complete scene in the application can be rendered in a web browser for future extension as web- collaborative and distributed training. Texturing is applied at this step in order to improve realism.
The registration step between these two virtual environments is carried out applying the right transformation matrices. To obtain the 3D models of the surgical tools we use a Laser ScanArm (FARO) as a rapid and accurate prototyping tool.
The visual output is provided by the rendering software developed in C++ and built on the open source GPU licensed and cross-platform H3D, a scene-graph API based on OpenGL for graphics rendering.
Collision detection module (requested to compute collision response) is based on based on model partition (Van den Bergen, C., 2004), the strategy of subdividing a set of objects into geometrically coherent subsets and computing a bounding volume for each subset of objects. It's connected to the physical model for the simulation of tool interactions and brain deformations and it's developed in OpenGL to obtain high level performance and realism.
The physical modelling method is based on Mass-Spring-Damper (MSD) and consists of a mesh of point masses connected by elastic links and mapped onto the geometric representation of the virtual object. This method is employed in our prototype to describe the mechanical properties of the virtual bodies computing the force feedback to the haptics and the organ deformations to be visualised. It is a discrete method characterized by low computable load, simplicity, low accuracy and low risk of instability because it uses Newton

dynamics to modify the point-masses positions and creates deformations with consideration to volume conservation. Brain tissue properties are modelled with MSD upon the OpenHaptics library (Sensable Tech.). The tissue parameters (stiffness, damping, friction, etc.) were evaluated together with our medical partner (Department of Neurosurgery, University Hospital of Heidelberg) using different training sections and processing empiric data.

Different haptic renderings were tested for a better optimization of the deformations. In order to have a complete training platform a video navigation system containing different 3D volume views is required. To achieve this, we have connected our system with the image guided therapy module of 3DSlicer. A haptic device (Phantom Desktop) provides the surgeon with an immersive experience during the interaction between the surgical tools and the brain or skull structures of the virtual patients. Its force feedback workspace and other important properties (nominal position resolution and stiffness range) make it suitable to be used in an ergonomic manner in conjunction with the microscope.

The 3D real-time position of the two viewpoints (one of each microscope ocular) is determined in the virtual environment through the use of passive markers affixed to the microscope and tracked by the infrared optical tracker (Polaris NDI). In order to speed up the simulation we modified the original library for tracking developed in our laboratories. In this way, data collected from Polaris is sent using the local area network to several given IP addresses and ports using the open-source OpenIGTLink of 3DSlicer modified for our needs. This allows a distributed architecture with the separation between rendering (graphical and haptic) and tracking PC with advantages in terms of computational load and realism (the average frame rate for graphical rendering is 31 fps and for the haptic 998 fps).

The collisions between organs and surgical tools produce forces which have to be replicated by the haptic interface and organ deformations, which have to be graphically rendered.

The main operating task simulated is the visual and tactile sensations of brain palpation (healthy or affected by LGG) pushing aside the human tissue using a neurosurgical spatula.

6. Augmented Reality extensions

The architecture described can be adapted for intra-operative purposes. In this instance, a surgeon needs the basic setup for the IGT interventions: microscope, monitors and surgical tools. The same virtual environment can be AR rendered onto the microscope optics with the difference that now the complete anatomy is considered rigid (deformable organs are not requested in this frame since only geometrical information are required) as well as the haptic interface replaced by new navigated infrared active tools.

The prototype is capable of tracking, in real time, the microscope, the patient's head and one or more surgical tool (pointer with active markers).

Fig. 3 shows the AR views inside the microscope oculars in which is possible identify the 3D region of interest (in this example the brain surface and craniotomy area is rendered). The microscope hardware related part was realized at our institute, as mentioned before and described in a previous work (Aschke et al. 1999). Registration with ICP (P.J. Besl & N.D. McKay, 1992) and camera calibration are carried out with similar procedure adopted in the previous prototype. Both are off-line steps and required for a perfect alignment between real and virtual world at the microscope view.

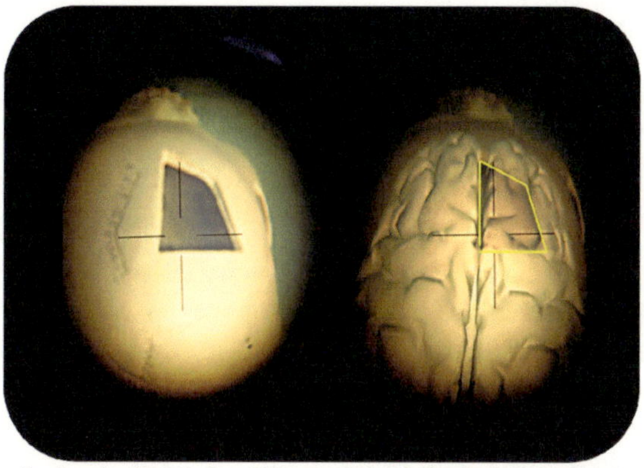

Fig. 3. AR microscope. Left: skull. Right: 3D model of the brain superimposed on the skull.

7. Conclusion

This paper presents the development of the first mixed reality system for training and intra-operative purposes in neurosurgery embedded on a real microscope. The main training task is the advanced simulation of brain tissue palpation enabling the surgeon to distinguish between normal and affected with a LGG brain tissue. Force feedback interaction with soft and hard tissues is made available to the surgeon in order to provide a complete immersive experience. The second feature allows the system to be employed as an AR microscope inside the OR. In this case a complex 3D environment is rendered by a stereoscopic image injection directly inside the microscope oculars for a better real time brain navigation and space cognition. 3DSlicer is, in both previous functional modalities, directly connected to the NDI tracking system in order to provide the navigation inside the real patient's images on the screen. The previously described software architecture guarantees performances and portability.

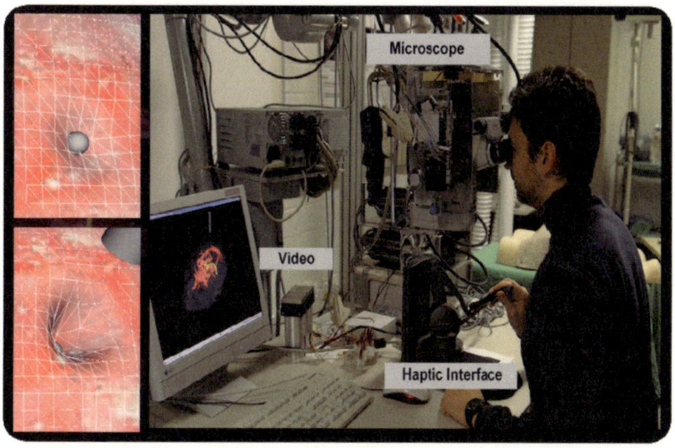

Fig. 4. Simulator. Left: brain tissue deformations. Right: complete prototype.

8. Acknowledgments

This research is a part of the European project "CompuSurge" funded by FP7 EST "Marie Curie" research network.

9. References

3DSlicer, URL: http://www.slicer.org/ [status January 2008]

Aschke, M. et al. (2003) Augmented reality in operating microscopes for neurosurgical interventions. Wolf and Strock editors, *Proceedings of 1st International IEEE EMBS Conference on Neural Engineering*, pp. 652--655

Besl, P.J. & McKay, N.D. (1992), A Method for Registration of 3-D Shapes, *IEEE Trans. Pattern Anal. Mach. Intell.*, vol. 14, 1992, pp. 239-256.

Basdogan, C., et al. (2001) Virtual Environments for Medical Training: Graphical and Haptic Simulation of Common Bile Duct Exploration. *IEEE-ASME Trans. Mechatronics*, vol. 6, no. 3, pp. 26—285.

Cotin S. et al. (2000) An Interventional Cardiology Training System. *Proceedings of Medicine Meets Virtual Reality*, pp. 59--65

Edwards, P. et al., (2000), Design and evaluation of a system for microscope-assisted guided interventions (MAGI), Medical Imaging, IEEE Transactions on, vol. 19, pp. 1082-1093.

Goh, K.Y.C. et al. (2005) Virtual reality application in neurosurgery. *Proceedings of the 2005 IEEE, Engineering in Medicine and Biology 27th Annual Conference*, Shanghai

H3D, URL: http://www.h3dapi.org/ [status January 2008]

Luciano, C. et al. (2008) : Second generation haptic ventriculostomy simulator using the immersivetouch™ system. Proceedings of Medicine Meets Virtual Reality 14, Long Beach, CA, USA.

Montgomery, K. et al.(2001), Surgical simulator for operative hysteroscopy, *IEEE Visualization 2001*, pp. 14—17.

OpenHaptics, URL: http://www.sensable.com/products-openhaptics-toolkit.htm [status March 2009].

Sato, D. et al. (2006), Soft tissue pushing operation using a haptic interface for simulation of brain tumor resection. *Journal of robotics and mechatronics*, vol. 18, pp. 634—642.

Tomulescu, V & Popescu, I. (1990) The use of LapSim virtual reality simulator in the evaluation of laparoscopic surgery skill. Preliminary result, *Chirurgia* (Bucharest, Romania), vol. 99, pagg. 523-7.

Van den Bergen, C. (2004), *Collision detection in interactive 3D environment*. Elsevier Morgan Kaufmann, S.Francisco, USA, 2004

Webster, R. et al. (2003) A haptic surgical simulator for laparoscopic cholecystectomy using real-time deformable organs. *Proceedings IASTED International Conference on Biomedical Engineering*, June 25–27, Salzburg, Austria.

Wiet, G. et al. (2000), Virtual temporal bone dissection simulation, *Proceedings of Medicine Meets Virtual Reality 2000*, pp. 378--384, J. D. Westwood, Ed., Amsterdam, The Netherlands.

Youngblood, P.L. et al. (2005) Comparison of training on two laparoscopic simulators and assessment of skills transfer to surgical performance, *Journal of the American College of Surgeons*, vol. 200, pp. 546-551.

6

A New Non-dominated Sorting Genetic Algorithm for Multi-Objective Optimization

Chih-Hao Lin and Pei-Ling Lin
Department of Information Management, Chung Yuan Christian University
Taiwan, R.O.C.

1. Introduction

Multi-objective optimization (MO) is a highly demanding research topic because many real-world optimization problems consist of contradictory criteria or objectives. Considering these competing objectives concurrently, a multi-objective optimization problem (MOP) can be formulated as finding the best possible solutions that satisfy these objectives under different tradeoff situations. A family of solutions in the feasible solution space forms a Pareto-optimal front, which describes the tradeoff among several contradictory objectives of an MOP. Generally, there are two goals in finding the Pareto-optimal front of a MOP: 1) to converge solutions as near as possible to the Pareto-optimal front; and 2) to distribute solutions as diverse as possible over the obtained non-dominated front. These two goals cause enormous search space in MOPs and let deterministic algorithms feel difficult to obtain the Pareto-optimal solutions. Therefore, satisfying these two goals simultaneously is a principal challenge for any algorithm to deal with MOPs (Dias & Vasconcelos, 2002).

In recent years, several evolutionary algorithms (EAs) have been proposed to solve MOPs. For example, the strength Pareto evolutionary algorithm (SPEA) (Zitzler et al., 2000) and the revised non-dominated sorting genetic algorithm (NSGA-II) (Deb et al., 2002) are two most famous algorithms. Several extensions of genetic algorithms (GAs) for dealing with MOPs are also proposed, such as the niche Pareto genetic algorithm (NPGA) (Horn et al., 1994), the chaos-genetic algorithm (CGA) (Qi et al., 2006), and the real jumping gene genetic algorithm (RJGGA) (Ripon et al., 2007).

However, most existing GAs only evaluate each chromosome by its fitness value regardless of the schema structure, which is a gene pattern defined by fixing the values of specific gene loci within a chromosome. The schemata theorem proved by Goldberg in 1989 is a central result of GA's theory in which a larger of effective genomes implies a more efficient of searching ability for a GA (Goldberg, 1989).

Inspired by the outstanding literature of Kalyanmoy Deb, this study proposes an evaluative crossover operator to incorporate with the original NSGA-II. The proposed evaluative version of NSGA-II, named E-NSGA-II, can further enhance the advantages of the fast non-dominated sorting and the diversity preservation of the NSGA-II for improving the quality of the Pareto-optimal solutions in MOPs. The proposed evaluative crossover imitates the gene-therapy process at the forefront of medicine and therefore integrates a new gene-evaluation method with a gene-therapy approach in the traditional uniform crossover scheme. The gene-evaluation method evaluates the merit of different genes between two mating parents by mutually exchanging these therapeutic genes one-by-one and observing the fitness variances. And then, the proposed evaluative crossover adopts a gene-therapy approach to cure the mating parents mutually with respect to their gene contribution to retain superior genomes in the evolutionary population.

The particular advantage of E-NSGA-II is that the gene-evaluation method can implicitly generate effective genome without explicitly analyzing the solution space by classical local search techniques. The performance of the proposed algorithm is experimented on nine unconstrained benchmark MOPs. The experiment results show that the E-NSGA-II not only can converge the nondominated solutions to the Pareto-optimal front but also can enhance the solution diversity to spread the achieved extent for all test MOPs.

The rest of this chapter is organized as follows. Section 2 introduces the genetic operators of the proposed E-NSGA-II. Section 3 describes numerical implementation and parameter setting. Section 4 reports the computational experiments on unconstrained MOPs and discusses the characteristics of E-NSGA-II. Finally, this chapter concludes with a summary in Section 5.

2. Algorithm Description

The NSGA proposed by Srinivas and Deb (1994) is one of the first EAs for MOPs (Srinivas & Deb, 1994). The main idea of the NSGA is the ranking process executed before the selection operation. In 2002, Deb et al. proposed a revised version, named NSGA-II, by introducing fast non-dominated sorting and diversity preservation policies (Deb et al., 2002). Three features of NSGA-II are summarized as follows:

1) **Computational complexity:** NSGA-II uses a fast non-dominated sorting approach to substitute for the original sorting algorithm of NSGA in order to reduce its computational complexity from $O(MP^3)$ to $O(MP^2)$, where M is the number of objectives and P is the population size. This feature makes NSGA-II more efficient than NSGA for large population cases.
2) **Elitism preservation:** Replacement-with-elitism methods can monotonously enhance the solution quality and speed up the performance of GAs significantly (Ghomsheh et al., 2007). NSGA-II adopts $(\mu+\lambda)$-evolution strategy to keep elitism solutions and prevent the loss of good solutions once they are found. Successive population is produced by selecting μ better solutions from μ parents and λ children.
3) **Parameter reduction:** Traditional sharing approach is a diversity ensuring mechanism that can get a wide variety of equivalent solutions in a population. However, a sharing parameter should be specified to set the sharing extent desired in a problem. Therefore, NSGA-II defines a density-estimation metric and applies the crowded-comparison operator with less required parameters to keep diversity between solutions.

In this study, the proposed E-NSGA-II stems from a concept different from traditional NSGA-II, particularly in terms of the gene-evaluation method. That is, the E-NSGA-II inherits the advantages of the NSGA-II and emphasizes the development of a new crossover operator and a modified replacement policy (Lin & Chuang, 2007).

2.1 Generation of Initial Population

A real coding representation is efficiently applied to solve numerical MOPs. Each test MOP is structured in the same manner and consists of M objective functions (Deb, 1999):

$$\text{Minimize } T(\vec{x}) = \left(f_1(\vec{x}), \cdots, f_M(\vec{x})\right) \quad (1)$$

$$\text{where } \quad \vec{x} = \left[x_1, x_2, \cdots, x_n\right]^T. \quad (2)$$

Each decision variable is treated as a gene and encoded by a floating-point number. Each chromosome representing a feasible solution is encoded as a vector $\vec{x} = [x_1 \ x_2 \cdots x_n]^T \in \Re^n$, where x_i denotes the value of the ith gene and n is the number of design variables in an MOP. Because the lower bound $\vec{l} = [l_1 \ l_2 \cdots l_n]^T$ and the upper bound $\vec{u} = [u_1 \ u_2 \cdots u_n]^T$ define the feasible solution space, the domain of each x_i is denoted as interval $[l_i, u_i]$.

The main components of the E-NSGA-II are chromosome encoding, fitness function, selection, recombination and replacement. An initial population with P chromosomes is randomly generated within the predefined feasible region. At each generation, E-NSGA-II applies the fast non-dominated sorting of NSGA-II to identify non-dominated solutions and construct the non-dominated front. And then, E-NSGA-II executes the rank comparison in selection operation to decide successive population by elitism strategy as the diversity preservation in NSGA-II (Deb et al., 2002). Therefore, the following sections only describe the details of the evaluative crossover operator and the diverse replacement.

2.2 Evaluative Crossover

For evaluation purpose, this study applies the crowding distance as an evaluation of chromosome's quality in the evaluative crossover. The crowding distance proposed in NSGA-II is used to estimate the density quantity of a particular solution in the population by calculating the average distance between other surrounding solutions with respect to each objective (Deb et al., 2002). After two parents have been selected from population, let the parent with larger crowding distance be named as the better parent ($\vec{x}_b$) and the other one is the worse parent ($\vec{x}_w$). Their crossover child is denoted as $\vec{y}$.

The proposed evaluative crossover imitates the gene-therapy process at the forefront of medicine, which inserts genes into an individual's cells to treat a disease by replacing a defective mutant allele by a functional one. Therefore, the evaluative crossover integrates a gene-evaluation method with a gene-therapy approach in the traditional uniform crossover scheme. By randomly generating a therapeutic mask with the same length as chromosomes, each parity bit in the therapeutic mask indicates whether the gene locus should be cured or not. For each gene locus, a random number in the interval [0, 1] is generated and compared to a pre-defined crossover rate p_c. If the random number is larger than the crossover rate, the parity bit in the therapeutic mask is assigned as 0 and no crossover occurs at this locus ($i \notin G_c$). Otherwise, the parity bit in the therapeutic mask is assigned as 1 and the child's gene is generated by the gene-therapy approach ($i \in G_c$).

Firstly, the gene-evaluation method mutually exchanges two parity genes between two mating parents and then compares their fitness variance as a measurement of these genes' merit. The exclusive features of the gene-evaluation method include that 1) the contribution of each gene is evaluated individually; and 2) the gene merit is estimated by the improvement of their density quantity during the gene-swap process (Lin & He, 2007).

Secondly, one temporary chromosome is generated for crossover locus i, denoted as $\vec{t}_i = [x_{b1},\cdots,x_{b(i-1)},\boldsymbol{x_{wi}},x_{b(i+1)},\cdots,x_{bn}]^T$. This temporary chromosome clones all alleles in the better parent and then replaces the selected gene of the better parent (x_{bi}) with the one of the worse parent (x_{wi}) in the same locus. The contribution of the gene x_{wi} is denoted as d_{wi} and approximated by the Euclidean distance between $\vec{t}_i$ and $\vec{x}_w$ by Equation (3). For comparison purpose, the Euclidean distance between $\vec{x}_b$ and $\vec{x}_w$ calculating by Equation (4) is the contribution of the gene x_{bi} and denoted as d_{bi}. Therefore, comparing d_{bi} with d_{wi} can reveal the contributions of x_{bi} and x_{wi} with respect to the genetic material of the better parent.

$$d_{wi} = dist(\vec{t}_i, \vec{x}_w) = \sqrt{\sum_{m=1}^{M} \left(f_m(\vec{t}_i) - f_m(\vec{x}_w)\right)^2} \tag{3}$$

$$d_{bi} = dist(\vec{x}_b, \vec{x}_w) = \sqrt{\sum_{m=1}^{M} \left(f_m(\vec{x}_b) - f_m(\vec{x}_w)\right)^2} \tag{4}$$

Finally, the gene-therapy approach can cure some defective genes in the better parent (i.e. x_{bi}) according to the genetic material of the other parent (i.e. x_{wi}) and then produce a child gene (i.e. y_i) for the evolutionary process. If the parity bit in the therapeutic mask is 0 (e.g. $i \notin G_c$), the offspring directly inherits the parity gene from the better parent, i.e. the gene in the better parent (x_{bj}) is equal to that in the child (i.e. $y_j = x_{bj}$) at the same locus. On the other hand, if the parity bit in the therapeutic mask is 1 (e.g. $i \in G_c$), the therapy gene of the child at the same locus (i.e. y_j) is arithmetically combined from the parity genes of the mated parents (i.e. x_{bj} and x_{wj}) according to their gene contributions. Each gene in the crossover child can be reproduced by Equation (5) in which *coef* is a random number in interval [0.5, 1.0].

$$y_i = \begin{cases} x_{bi}, & \text{if } (i \notin G_c) \\ x_{bi} \times coef + x_{wi} \times (1 - coef), & \text{if } (i \in G_c) \text{ and } (d_{bi} \geq d_{wi}) \\ x_{bi} \times (1 - coef) + x_{wi} \times coef, & \text{if } (i \in G_c) \text{ and } (d_{bi} < d_{wi}) \end{cases} \tag{5}$$

Example: In Fig. 1, the better parent with larger crowding distance (Cub_len = 0.8) is $P1$ and the worse parent (Cub_len = 0.6) is $P2$. The therapy gene is the 2nd gene in chromosomes. The temporary chromosome T clones all of genes in $P1$ except for the 2nd gene, which copies from x_{22} in $P2$. We assume that the Euclidean distance (d_{12}) between $P1$ and $P2$ is 0.5 and the distance (d_{22}) between $P1$ and T is 0.7, which are used to estimate the gene contribution of x_{12} and x_{22}, respectively. Because d_{22} is larger than d_{12}, the 2nd gene in $P2$ (x_{22}) is better than that in $P1$ (x_{12}). Therefore, the child's gene (x_{y2}) inherits more genetic material from x_{22} than x_{12}. The pseudo code of the evaluative crossover is described in Table 1.

2.3 Polynomial Mutation

Mutation operator is applied to enlarge the population diversity to escape from local optima and therefore enhance the exploration ability. E-NSGA-II inherits the polynomial mutation used by NSGA-II and operates as Equation (6) and (7) (Deb & Goyal, 1996).

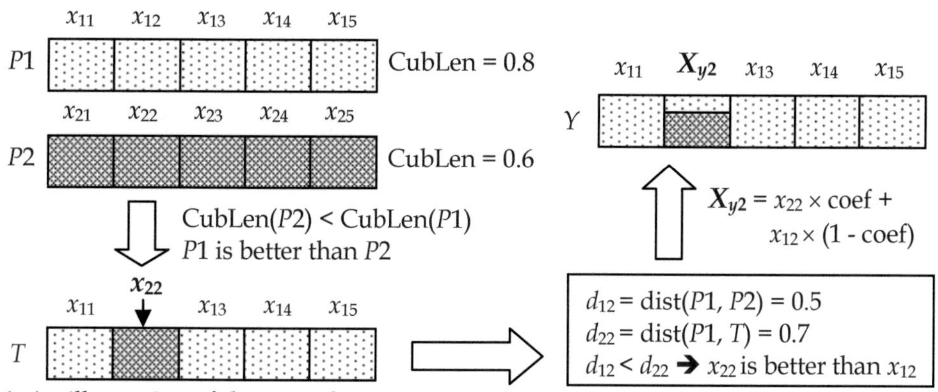

Fig. 1. An illustration of the gene-therapy approach

```
/* The Evaluative Crossover Operator */
Let  xoverPoint is a set of random selected gene loci;
   p1 and p2 denote parent chromosomes;
   child denote child chromosome;
   rand is a random value in [0~1];
   coef is a random value in [0.5~1.0];
   cubLength() is a density estimation function;
   dist() is an Euclidean distance calculator;
If cubLength(p1) is better than cubLength(p2)
   winner = p1;
   loser = p2;
Else
   winner = p2;
   loser = p1;
End If
copy chromosome(winner) to chromosome(child);
For i = 1 to chromosomeLength do
   generate a random number rand;
   If rand < crossover rate
      copy chromosome(winner) to chromosome(tempChromosome);
      tempChrimisime(i) = loser(i);
      If dist(tempChromosome, loser) >= dist(winner, loser)
         child(i) = winner(i) × coef + loser(i) × (1 - coef);
      Else
         child(i) = winner(i) × (1 - coef) + loser(i) × coef;
      End If
   End If
End For
```

Table 1. The pseudo code of the evaluative crossover operator

$$y_i^{(1,t+1)} = x_i^{(1,t+1)} + (x_i^{(u)} - x_i^{(L)})\overline{\delta_i} \tag{6}$$

$$\overline{\delta_i} = \begin{cases} (2r_i)^{1/(\eta_m+1)} - 1, & if \quad r_i < 0.5 \\ 1-[2(1-r_i)]^{1/(\eta_m+1)}, & if \quad r_i < 0.5 \end{cases} \tag{7}$$

In Equation (6), $x_i^{(u)}$ and $x_i^{(L)}$ are the upper and lower bounds of the mutation parameter. According to Deb's research, the shape of the probability distribution is directly controlled by an external parameter η_m and the distribution is not dynamically changed with generations (Deb, 2001). Therefore, parameter η_m is also fixed in this study.

2.4 Diverse Replacement

E-NSGA-II modifies the replacement strategy proposed by Ghomsheh et al. in 2007 to keep diversity and generate successive population (Ghomsheh et al., 2007). The replacement criteria relying on the fast non-dominated sorting and diversity metric can keep those better diversity individuals and provide larger search space for crossover and mutation operators.
In this study, a competitive population is generated by combining the parent population and the offspring population. In the competitive population, if the number of individuals with rank=1 is less than the population size, the successive population is firstly filled with the best non-dominated solutions and then selects the highest diversity solutions from the remaining individuals with rank>1 until the pre-specified population size is achieved. On the other hand, the successive population is sequentially filled with the best diversity solution from individuals with rank=1 until the size of the successive population is equal to the population size. According to these replacement criteria, the successive population can be generated. The pseudo code of replacement procedure is described in Table 2.

3. Numerical Implementation

For each test MOP, E-NSGA-II performs 10 runs with different seeds to observe the consistency of the outcome. The mean value of the measures reveals the average evolutionary performance of E-NSGA-II and represents the optimization results in comparison with other algorisms. The variance of the best solutions in 10 runs indicates the consistency of an algorithm. E-NSGA-II is implemented by MATLAB.

3.1 Performance Measures

Different performance measures for evaluating efficiency have been suggested in literature (Okabe et al., 2003). For comparison purpose, this study applies two metrics: 1) the convergence metric (Υ): approximating the average distance to the Pareto-optimal front; and 2) the diversity metric (Δ): measuring the extent of spread achieved among the obtained solutions (Deb, 2001).
For the convergence metric (Υ), a smaller metric value implies a better convergence toward the Pareto-optimal front. This study uses 500 uniformly spaced solutions to approximate the true Pareto-optimal. To measure the distance between the obtained non-dominated front (Q) and the set of Pareto-optimal solutions (P^*), this study computes the minimum Euclidean distance of each solution from 500 chosen points on the Pareto-optimal front by Equation (8). The average of these distances is used as the convergence metric as Equation (9).

$$d_i = \min_{k=1}^{|P^*|} \sqrt{\sum_{m=1}^{M} (f_m^i - f_m^{*(k)})^2} \tag{8}$$

$$\Upsilon = \left(\sum_{i=1}^{|Q|} d_i\right) / |Q| \tag{9}$$

```
/* The Diverse Replacement Operator */
Let R = 0.1;
    E = 0.01;
If members of rank1 < PopulationSize
  Put all individuals with rank=1 into Offspring;
  Put all individuals with rank>1 into unmarkedPool;
  Calculate all distance between individuals in unmarkedPool;
  Record the minimal distance as minDistance of each individual;
  While Offspring < PopulationSize do
    Select one individual in unmarkedPool;
    If minDistance > R
      Fill this individual into Offspring;
      Remove this individual from unmarkedPool;
    Else
      Move this individual into markedPool;
    End if
    If unmarkedPool is empty
      R = R - E;
      Move all individuals from markedPool to unmarkedPool;
    End if
  End while
Else
  Put all individuals with rank=1 into unmarkedPool;
  Calculate all distance between individuals in unmarkedPool;
  Record the minimal distance as minDistance of each individual;
  While Offspring < PopulationSize do
    Select one individual in unmarkedPool;
    If minDistance > R
      Fill this individual into Offspring;
      Remove this individual from unmarkedPool;
    Else
      Move this individual into markedPool;
    End if
    If unmarkedPool is empty
      R = R - E;
      Move all individuals from markedPool to unmarkedPool;
    End if
  End while
End if
```

Table 2. The pseudo code of the diverse replacement operator

In Equation (8), d_i is the Euclidean distance between the solution $i \in Q$ and the nearest member of P^*. Indicator k denotes the kth member in P^*. Notation M is the number of objectives and $f_m^{*(k)}$ is the mth objective function value of kth member in P^*. Indicator i in Equation (9) is the obtained non-dominated solution from E-NSGA-II.

For Diversity metric (Δ), the value of Δ would be close to zero if the non-dominated solutions of the obtained front widely and uniformly spread out. The diversity metric (Δ) measures the extent of spread achieved among the obtained non-dominated solutions and is calculated by Equation (10).

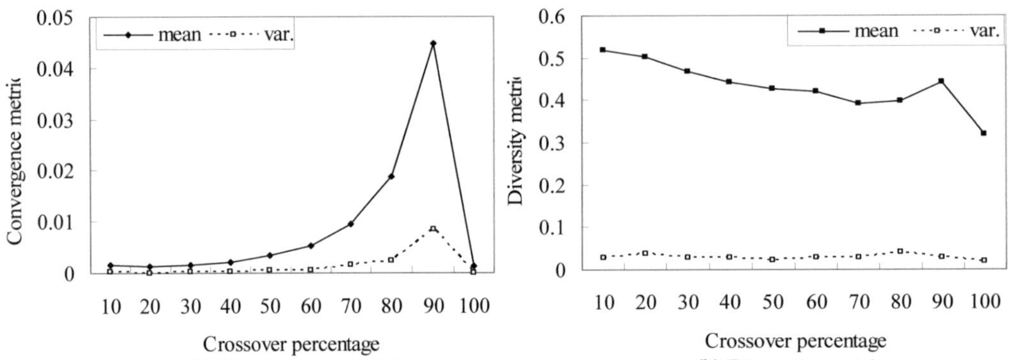

(a) Convergence metric (b) Diversity metric

Fig. 2. Effect comparison among ten crossover percentages on problem ZDT1

$$\Delta = \frac{d_f + d_l + \sum_{i=1}^{N-1} \left| d_i - \bar{d} \right|}{d_f + d_l + (N-1)\bar{d}} \tag{10}$$

The Euclidean distances between the extreme solutions of the Pareto front (P^*) is d_f. The distances between the boundary solutions of the obtained nondominated set (Q) is d_l, and the distances between the consecutive solutions in the obtained non-dominated set is d_i. Notation $\bar{d}$ is the average of d_i.

3.2 Parameter Setting

To discover the best configuration for E-NSGA-II, some comprehensive investigations for parameter setting are performed on a benchmark problem. Especially, the performance of the evaluative crossover is influenced by three parameters: 1) crossover percentage; 2) crossover rate; and 3) therapeutic coefficient. The experimental results are averaged in 10 runs and evaluated by the convergence metric and the diversity metric. Problem ZDT1 is selected to analyze the effect of different parameters with a reasonable set of values in these experiments. The test function ZDT1 proposed by Zitzler et al. has a convex Pareto-optimal front and two objective functions without any constraint. The number of decision variables is 30 and the feasible region of each variable is in interval [0, 1].

$$\text{Minimize} \quad T(\vec{x}) = \left(f_1(x_1), f_2(\vec{x})\right) \tag{ZDT1}$$

$$\text{where} \quad f_1(x_1) = x_1 \tag{11}$$

$$f_2(\vec{x}) = g(\vec{x})\left[1 - \sqrt{x_1 / g(\vec{x})}\right] \tag{12}$$

$$g(\vec{x}) = 1 + 9\left(\sum_{i=2}^{n} x_i\right)/(n-1) \cdot \tag{13}$$

1) Effect of Crossover Percentage

The crossover percentage decides how many successive individuals are produced by crossover operator. For example, 80% crossover percentage means that the crossover operator produces 80% offspring and the other 20% are produced by mutation operator. Especially, 100% crossover percentage means that all offspring are firstly recombined by crossover operator and then flipped one or more genes by mutation operator.

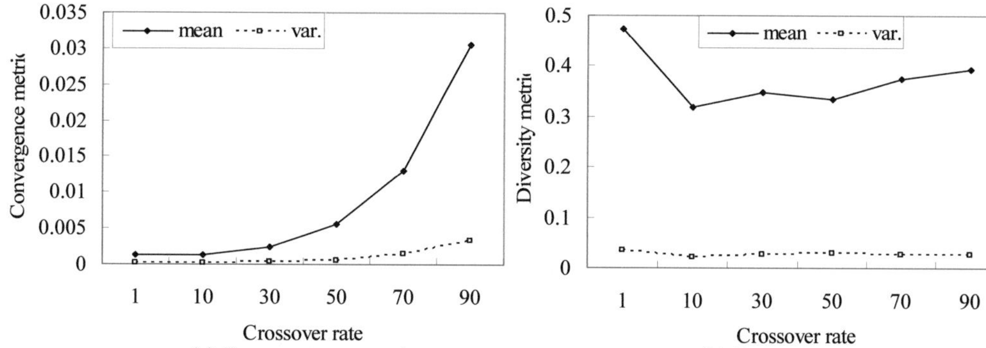

(a) Convergence metric (b) Diversity metric

Fig. 3. Effect comparison among ten crossover rates on problem ZDT1

To analyze the best percentage of crossover children in each generation, ten crossover percentages (from 10% to 100%) were tested on problem ZDT1. The mean and variance of the convergence and diversity metrics are depicted in Fig. 2(a) and Fig. 2(b), respectively.

In Fig. 2(a), a larger crossover percentage implies a worse convergence situation when the crossover percentage is assigned from 10% to 90%. However, the best convergence is obtained when the crossover percentage is 100%. For diversity metric, Fig. 2(b) shows that the diversity metric is slightly declined from 10% to 70% and then rises until 90%. In particular, the best diversity metric is also obtained when the crossover percentage is 100%. Therefore, all individuals in this study are firstly recombined by the evaluative crossover and then mutated by the polynomial mutation.

2) *Effect of Crossover Rate*

In the gene-evaluation method, a smaller crossover rate implies a lower computational effort because only the selected loci in the therapeutic mask need to be evaluated individually. To realize the effects of different crossover rates (p_c), six simulations with crossover rates from 1% to 90% are conducted on problem ZDT1 to discover the best crossover rate.

The convergence and diversity metrics of experimental results are depicted in Fig. 3(a) and 3(b), respectively. In Fig. 3(a), the convergence metric remains stable between p_c=1% and p_c=10%. Obviously, a larger crossover rate implies a worse convergence situation on problem ZDT1 while p_c is larger than 10%. The diversity metric in Fig. 3(b) is monotonically decreased from p_c=1% to p_c=10% and then slightly increased until p_c=90%. Considering the convergence and diversity metrics, the crossover rate applied in this study is 10%.

3) *Effect of Therapeutic Coefficient*

In the gene-therapy approach, each therapeutic gene of crossover child arithmetically combines two parity genes at the same locus of the mating parents. To test the effects of different therapeutic coefficient (*coef*), seven fixed coefficients and four variable ones for Equation (5) are tested on problem ZDT1. The mean and variance of the experimental results for seven fixed coefficients (from 0.01 to 1.0) are depicted in Fig. 4. The convergence metric depicted in Fig. 4(a) remains stable between 0.01 and 0.5. As the value of *coef* is larger than 0.5, the convergence situation is dramatically increased until *coef*=1. When the value of *coef* increases from 0.01, the diversity metric in Fig. 4(b) is decreased and levels off between *coef*=0.5 and *coef*=0.9. And then, the diversity metric increases at *coef*=1.0.

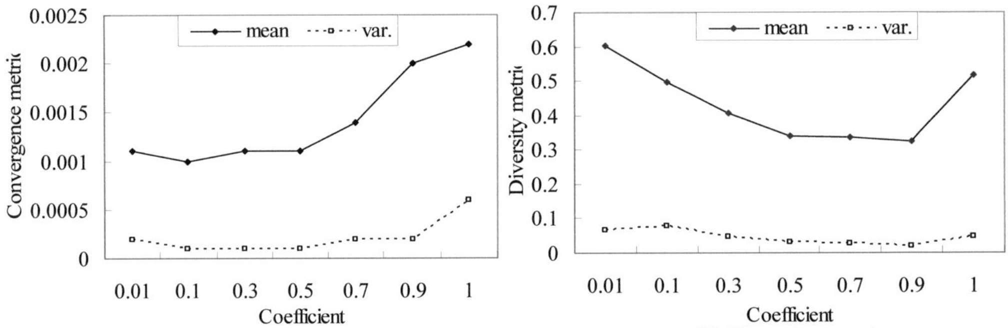

(a) Convergence metric (b) Diversity metric

Fig. 4. Effect comparison among fixed therapeutic coefficients on problem ZDT1

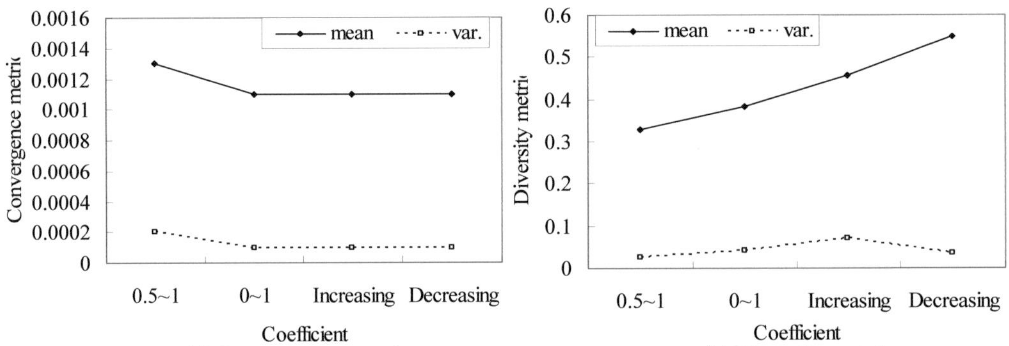

(a) Convergence metric (b) Diversity metric

Fig. 5. Effect comparison among variable therapeutic coefficients on problem ZDT1

E-NSGA-II Algorithm Setting	
Population size	100
Maximum generation	1000
Simulation times	10
Percentage of offspring reproduction from crossover operator	100%
Percentage of offspring reproduction from mutation operator	100%
E-NSGA-II Crossover Operator	
Crossover rate	0.1
Coefficient of arithmetical combination	Random [0.5,1]
E-NSGA-II Mutation Operator	
Mutation rate	1/ length of variable
Mutation scope	Rank *20

Table 3. Parameter setting of E-NSGA-II

Fig. 5 depicts the experimental results of four variable type of therapeutic coefficients, which consist of 1) random value in interval [0.5, 1]; 2) random value in interval [0, 1]; 3) monotonically increasing value (from 0 to 1); and 4) monotonically decreasing value (from 1 to 0). Obviously, the random coefficient in interval [0.5, 1] achieves the best diversity metric in Fig. 5(b) although its convergence result in Fig. 5(a) is slightly worse than others about 0.0002. Considering the tradeoff between the convergence and diversity metrics, this study suggests the random value in interval [0.5, 1] as the therapeutic coefficient in this study.

Prob.	n	Bounds	Objective Functions	Comments
SCH	1	$[-10^3, 10^3]$	$f_1 = x^2;\ f_2 = (x-2)^2$	convex
FON	2	$[-4,4]$	$f_1 = 1-\exp\left(-\sum_{i=1}^{3}(x_i - \frac{1}{\sqrt{3}})^2\right);\ f_1 = 1-\exp\left(-\sum_{i=1}^{3}(x_i + \frac{1}{\sqrt{3}})^2\right)$	nonconvex
POL	2	$[-\pi,\pi]$	$f_1 = [1+(A_1-B_1)^2+(A_2-B_2)^2];\ f_2 = [(x_1+3)^2+(x_2+1)^2]$ $A_1 = 0.5\sin 1 - 2\cos 1 + \sin 2 - 1.5\cos 2$ $A_2 = 1.5\sin 1 - \cos 1 + 2\sin 2 - 0.5\cos 2$ $B_1 = 0.5\sin x_1 - 2\cos x_1 + \sin x_2 - 1.5\cos x_2$ $B_2 = 1.5\sin x_1 - \cos x_1 + 2\sin x_2 - 0.5\cos x_2$	nonconvex, disconnected
KUR	3	$[-5,5]$	$f_1 = \sum_{i=1}^{n-1}(-10\exp(-0.2\sqrt{x_i^2+x_{i+1}^2}));\ f_2 = \sum_{i=1}^{n}(\lvert x_i\rvert^{0.8}+5\sin x_i^3))$	nonconvex
ZDT1	30	$[0,1]$	$f_1 = x_1;\ f_2 = g(x)\left[1-\sqrt{x_1/g(x)}\right];\ g(x) = 1+9(\sum_{i=2}^{n} x_i)/(n-1)$	convex
ZDT2	30	$[0,1]$	$f_1 = x_1;\ f_2 = g(x)\left[1-(x_1/g(x))^2\right];\ g(x) = 1+9(\sum_{i=2}^{n} x_i)/(n-1)$	nonconvex
ZDT3	30	$[0,1]$	$f_1 = x_1;\ f_2 = g(x)\left[1-\sqrt{x_1/g(x)}-(x_1/g(x))\sin(10\pi x_1)\right]$ $g(x) = 1+9(\sum_{i=2}^{n} x_i)/(n-1)$	convex, disconnected
ZDT4	10	$x_1 \in [0,1]$ $x_i \in [-5,5],$ $i = 2,\ldots,n$	$f_1 = x_1;\ f_2 = g(x)\left[1-\sqrt{x_1/g(x)}\right]$ $g(x) = 1+10(n-1)+\sum_{i=2}^{n}\left[x_i^2-10\cos(4\pi x_i)\right]$	nonconvex
ZDT6	10	$[0,1]$	$f_1 = 1-\exp(-4x_1)\sin^6(6\pi x_1);$ $f_2 = g(x)\left[1-(\frac{f_1(x)}{g(x)})^2\right];\ g(x) = 1+9\left[\frac{\sum_{i=2}^{n} x_i}{n-1}\right]^{0.25}$	nonconvex, nonuniformly spaced

Table 4. Unconstrained test MOPs (All objectives are minimization functions)

3.3 Configuration of the E-NSGA-II

After these comprehensive experiments, the configuration and parameter setting of the proposed evaluative crossover are determined. Other parameters used in this study are the same as those in the original NSGA-II (Deb et al., 2002). The configuration of E-NSGA-II is summarized in Table 3 and used in the following section for performance comparison.

4. Computational Experiments

4.1 Test Problems

Nine test problems for MOPs are used in these experiments to systematically evaluate the performance of E-NSGA-II. These unconstrained benchmark problems suggested by Zitzler et al. cover a broad range of functionality characteristics with two objective functions (Zitzler et al., 2000). In this study, the test MOPs are denoted as SCH, FON, POL, KUR, ZDT1, ZDT2, ZDT3, ZDT4 and ZDT6. Table 4 describes the problem identifier, the number of variables, the feasible regions of decision variables, the function formulations, and the nature of the Pareto-optimal front for each problem (Deb et al., 2002).

4.2 Existing Algorithms for Comparison

Several existing algorithms are applied for the entire test MOPs in literature. This study compares the results of five well-known algorithms with the proposed E-NSGA-II on nine test problems. These existing algorithms are:

1) NSGA-II (revised non-dominated sorting genetic algorithm) (Deb et al., 2002): By using the fast non-dominated sorting and diversity preservation, NSGA-II identifies non-dominated solutions in the population and then executing the rank comparison in selection operation to decide successor population by elitism strategy.
2) n-NSGA-II (niching-NSGA-II) (Ghomsheh et al., 2007): n-NSGA-II modifies the elitism strategy of the NSGA-II according to the diversity value of each candidate individual. The purpose of this algorithm is to guarantee a better spread among the solutions.
3) SPEA (strength Pareto evolutionary algorithm) (Zitzler & Thiele, 1999): By combining several features of previous multiobjective EAs in a unique manner, SPEA differs from several multi-criteria EAs in the kind of fitness assignment and the niching technique.
4) PAES (Pareto-archived evolution strategy) (Knowles & Corne, 1999): PAES is a (1 + 1) evolution strategy that comprises three parts: the candidate solution generator, the candidate solution acceptance function, and the Nondominated-Solutions archive. PAES represents the simplest approach to a multiobjective local search procedure.
5) MOTS (multi-objective Tabu search) (Jaeggi et al., 2004): Based on Tabu search, MOTS uses functional decomposition to perform parallel objective function evaluations at the H&J local search and the diversification search and becomes a parallel multi-objective continuous Tabu search algorithm.

4.3 Comparison Results among Algorithms

Simulation results of the proposed E-NSGA-II on nine test problems are compared with five multi-objective optimizers, which are NSGA-II, n-NSGA-II, SPEA, PAES and MOTS. Table 5 and Table 6 depict the convergence metric Y and the diversity metric Δ of the experimental results obtained using these six algorithms, respectively. The mean and variance of simulation results in 10 independent experiments are depicted in the first row and the second row of each algorithm in Table 5 and Table 6. The mean of the metrics reveals the average evolutionary performance and represents the optimization results in comparison with other algorisms. The variance of the metrics indicates the consistency of an algorithm.

Table 5 shows that using the proposed evaluative crossover can further improve the convergence quality of NSGA-II on almost all problems except on problem POL. E-NSGA-II performs as good as n-NSGA-II to converge in six MOPs and outperforms n-NSGA-II in FON, POL and ZDT6. Furthermore, E-NSGA-II significantly overcomes SPEA, PAES and MOTS in eight problems but slightly loses on problem POL. In all cases with E-NSGA-II, the variance of convergence metric in ten runs is also small except in POL. That is, E-NSGA-II is great and consistent as n-NSGA-II and outperforms NSGA-II, SPEA, PAES and MOTS on the convergence capability.

In Table 6, E-NSGA-II outperforms all other algorithms dramatically on the mean of the diversity metric in almost all test problems except in POL and KUR with NSGA-II. That is, E-NSGA-II is a brilliant algorithm for MOPs to ensure a better spread among solutions and provide a good diversity although it slightly loses on the mean of convergence metric in two problems with NSGA-II. That is, E-NSGA-II can find a better spread of solutions than other algorithms on almost all test problems.

Algorithm	ϒ	SCH	FON	POL	KUR	ZDT1	ZDT2	ZDT3	ZDT4	ZDT6
E-NSGA-II	Mean	0.0033	0.0011	0.1143	0.0165	0.0013	0.0010	0.0046	0.0011	0.0042
	Variance	0.0002	0.0001	0.1008	0.0031	0.0001	0.0001	0.0003	0.0001	0.0002
n-NSGA-II	Mean	0.0032	0.0023	0.2375	0.0161	0.0011	0.0008	0.0042	0.0011	0.0139
	Variance	0.0002	0.0002	0.0428	0.0034	0.0001	0.0001	0.0003	0.0002	0.0018
NSGA-II	Mean	0.0034	0.0019	0.0156	0.0290	0.0335	0.0724	0.1145	0.5131	0.2966
	Variance	0.0000	0.0000	0.0000	0.0000	0.0048	0.0317	0.0079	0.1185	0.0131
SPEA	Mean	0.0034	0.1257	0.0378	0.0456	0.0018	0.0013	0.0475	7.3403	0.2211
	Variance	0.0000	0.0000	0.0001	0.0001	0.0000	0.0000	0.0000	6.5725	0.0005
PAES	Mean	0.0013	0.1513	0.0309	0.0573	0.0821	0.1263	0.0239	0.8548	0.0855
	Variance	0.0000	0.0009	0.0004	0.0119	0.0087	0.0369	0.0000	0.5272	0.0067
MOTS	Mean	0.0032	0.0008	0.0158	0.0276	0.0414	0.0664	0.0154	22.689	0.3758
	Variance	0.0000	0.0000	0.0005	0.0047	0.0008	0.0016	0.0010	10.966	0.1745

Table 5. Mean (first rows) and variance (second rows) of the convergence metric ϒ

Algorithm	Δ	SCH	FON	POL	KUR	ZDT1	ZDT2	ZDT3	ZDT4	ZDT6
E-NSGA-II	Mean	0.2069	0.1629	0.9197	0.5771	0.1251	0.1311	0.5833	0.2001	0.1177
	Variance	0.0115	0.0125	0.0393	0.0377	0.0013	0.0093	0.0242	0.0201	0.0098
n-NSGA-II	Mean	0.3822	0.3590	0.9531	0.5004	0.4225	0.4238	0.6827	0.4623	0.4056
	Variance	0.0409	0.0270	0.0703	0.0404	0.0218	0.0368	0.0208	0.0371	0.0376
NSGA-II	Mean	0.4779	0.3781	0.4522	0.4115	0.3903	0.4308	0.7385	0.7026	0.6680
	Variance	0.0035	0.0006	0.0029	0.0010	0.0019	0.0047	0.0197	0.0646	0.0099
SPEA	Mean	1.0211	0.7924	0.9727	0.8530	0.7845	0.7551	0.6729	0.7985	0.8494
	Variance	0.0044	0.0055	0.0085	0.0026	0.0044	0.0045	0.0036	0.0146	0.0027
PAES	Mean	1.0633	1.1625	1.0200	1.0798	1.2298	1.1659	0.7899	0.8705	1.1531
	Variance	0.0029	0.0089	0.0000	0.0138	0.0048	0.0077	0.0017	0.1014	0.0039
MOTS	Mean	0.3789	1.1298	1.5933	1.1166	0.7714	0.8135	0.8234	1.0044	0.3722
	Variance	0.0251	0.0344	0.0120	0.1437	0.0789	0.0360	0.0225	0.0047	0.2648

Table 6. Mean (first rows) and variance (second rows) of the diversity metric Δ

4.4 Algorithm Analysis

According to the research by Huband et al. in 2006, each test problem can be characterized by four factors (Huband et al., 2006): 1) uni-modal/multi-modal, 2) convex/non-convex, 3) connected/disconnected, and 4) bias/non-bias. The modality of a test problem can determine the exploration ability of an algorithm for finding global optima. The geometric shape of the Pareto-optimal front can measure the selection and ranking ability of algorithms. The bias factor directly influences the convergence speed toward the Pareto-optimal front of algorithms. If the test problem has several disconnected Pareto-optimal sets, algorithms will feel difficult to find all regions of the Pareto optimal front. The characters of nine test problems are depicted in Table 7 and analyzed in the follows.

1) Multi-modal Problems

A multimodal function possesses numerous local optima that could trap an algorithm into its local optima and fail to find global optima. In general, solving multimodal problems is more difficult than unimodal ones. In this study, problem POL, KUR, ZDT3, ZDT4 and ZDT6 contain mutimodal objective functions.

Problem	Objective	Modality	Convexity	Bias	Connectivity
SCH	f1 f2	Uni-modal Uni-modal	Convex	Non-bias	Connected
FON	f1 f2	Uni-modal Uni-modal	Non-convex	Non-bias	Connected
POL	f1 f2	Multi-modal Uni-modal	Non-convex	Non-bias	Disconnected
KUR	f1 f2	Uni-modal Multi-modal	Non-convex	Non-bias	Disconnected
ZDT1	f1 f2	Uni-modal Uni-modal	Convex	Non-bias	Connected
ZDT2	f1 f2	Uni-modal Uni-modal	Non-convex	Non-bias	Connected
ZDT3	f1 f2	Uni-modal Multi-modal	Convex	Non-bias	Disconnected
ZDT4	f1 f2	Uni-modal Multi-modal	Non-convex	Non-bias	Connected
ZDT6	f1 f2	Multi-modal Multi-modal	Non-convex	Bias	Connected

Table 7. Characters of nine test problems

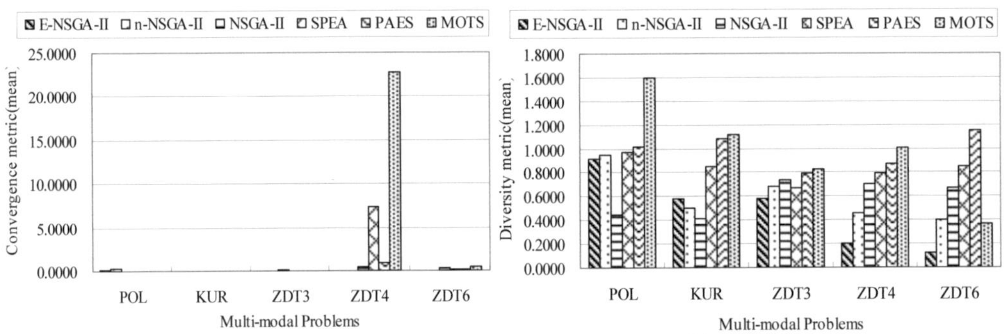

(a) Convergence metric (b) Diversity metric

Fig. 6. Comparison between E-NSGA-II and existing algorithms on multimodal problems

In Fig. 6(a), the proposed E-NSGA-II can converge in these five multimodal problems as better as n-NSGA-II. Nevertheless, E-NSGA-II overcomes considerably NSGA-II, SPEA, PAES and MOTS on KUR, ZDT3, ZDT4 and ZDT6. In Fig. 6(b), E-NSGA-II outperforms all other algorithms on the mean of the diversity metric in almost all test problems except in POL and KUR with NSGA-II.

2) *Convex Problems*

Convex Pareto optimal fronts can cause difficulty for algorithms to rank solutions by the number of their dominated solutions because solutions around the middle of the convex Pareto front have great chance to dominate more solutions (Deb, 1999). Problem SCH, ZDT1 and ZDT3 belong to convex problems. The convergence metric Y and the diversity metric Δ of the experimental results obtained using these six algorithms are depicted in Fig. 7(a) and Fig. 7(b), respectively.

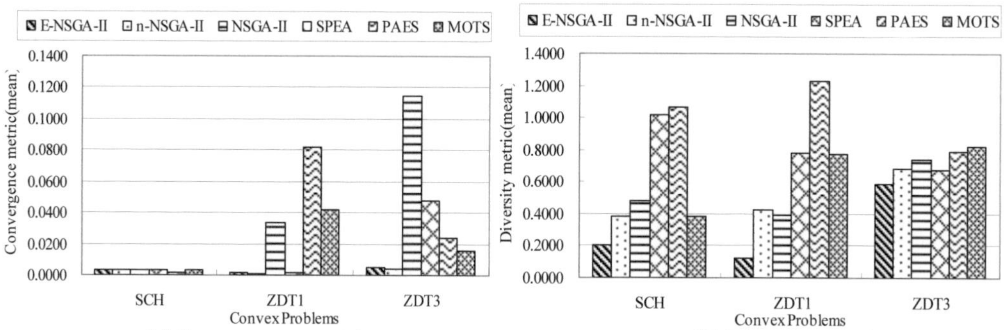

(a) Convergence metric (b) Diversity metric

Fig. 7. Comparison between E-NSGA-II and existing algorithms on convex problems

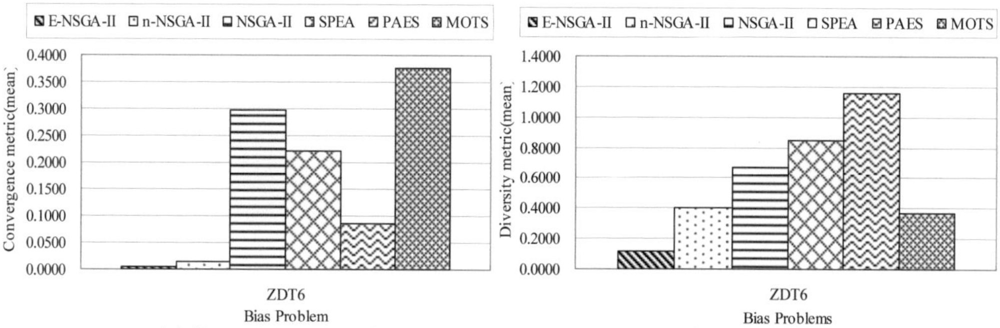

(a) Convergence metric (b) Diversity metric

Fig. 8. Comparison between E-NSGA-II and existing algorithms on bias problem

Although dealing with the convex problems is difficult, the proposed E-NSGA-II performs the best convergence metric in Fig. 7(a) and the best diversity metric in Fig. 7(b) on all convex problems than other five algorithms. That is, the evaluative crossover can further improve the ranking performance of NSGA-II for convex problems.

3) *Bias Problem*

A bias problem may directly influences the convergence speed toward the Pareto-optimal front of algorithms. A better exploitation ability of an algorithm is useful to be able to identify the presence of bias in a test problem. In this study, only problem ZDT6 belongs to the bias problem. In Fig. 8(a) and Fig. 8(b), the convergence metric (Y) and the diversity metric (Δ) show that E-NSGA-II with the proposed evaluative crossover is the best evolutionary algorithm among these six algorithms for handling the bias problem ZDT6.

4) *Disconnected Problems*

In this study, problem POL, KUR and ZDT3 have disconnected Pareto-optimal fronts, which will increase the likelihood that an algorithm will fail to find all regions of the Pareto optimal front. For KUR and ZDT3 in Fig. 9(a), the proposed E-NSGA-II can converge on the Pareto-optimal front and achieve a better convergence metric than other algorithms. Furthermore, E-NSGA-II also can spread solutions around and outperform other four algorithms (except for NSGA-II on POL and KUR) on the diversity metric in Fig. 9(b).

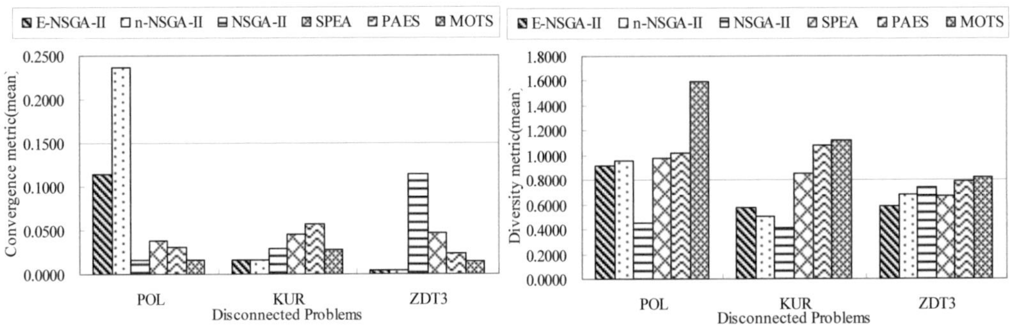

(a) Convergence metric (b) Diversity metric

Fig. 9. Comparison between E-NSGA-II and existing algorithms on disconnected problems

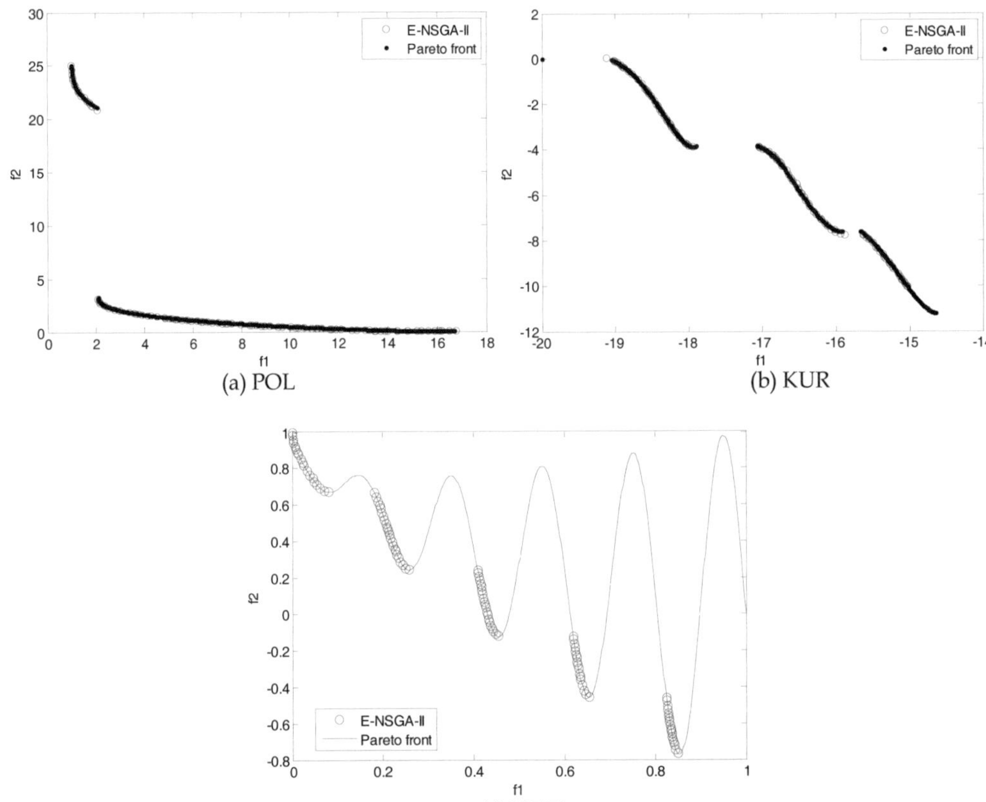

(a) POL (b) KUR

(c) ZDT3

Fig. 10. Nondominated solutions with E-NSGA-II on three disconnected test problems

For three disconnected problems, Fig. 10 shows all nondominated solutions obtained by using E-NSGA-II and the Pareto-optimal region. In their Pareto-optimal front, problem POL, KUR and ZDT3 have two, three and five regions of discontinuous curves, respectively. Fig. 10 demonstrates the ability of E-NSGA-II to converge the true Pareto-optimal front and spread diverse solutions in the front. Fig. 11 depict the Pareto-optimal front and non-dominated solutions obtained by E-NSGA-II for the other six test problems where solid line

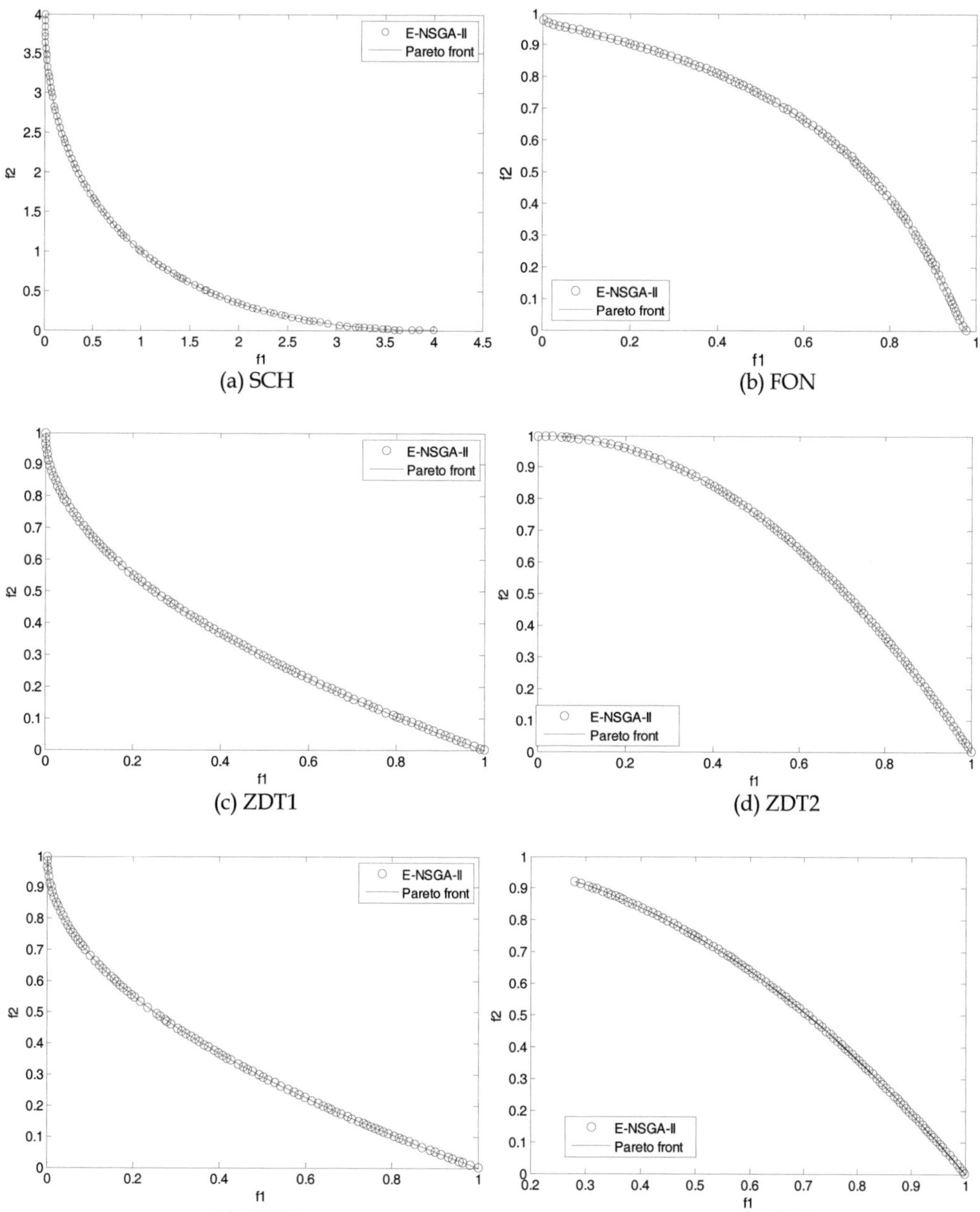

(a) SCH (b) FON
(c) ZDT1 (d) ZDT2
(e) ZDT4 (f) ZDT6

Fig. 11. Nondominated solutions with E-NSGA-II on six test problems

represents the Pareto-optimal front and the hollow circles represent the obtained non-dominated solutions with E-NSGA-II. Obviously, the solutions obtained by E-NSGA-II are very close to Pareto-optimal front and the spreading diversity is also excellent. Therefore, the E-NSGA-II is an effective GAs for solving MOPs and achieving excellent diversity metric.

5. Conclusion

This study imitates the gene-therapy process at the forefront of medicine and proposes an innovative evaluative crossover operator. The evaluative crossover integrates a gene-evaluation method with a gene-therapy approach in the traditional NSGA-II for finding uniformly distributed Pareto-optimal front of multi-objective optimization problems. To further enhance the advantages of fast non-dominate sorting and diversity preservation in NSGA-II, the proposed gene-evaluation method partially evaluates the merit of different crossover genes by substituting them in better parent and then calculating the fitness variances. The gene-therapy approach incorporates with the evaluative crossover to cure the mating parents mutually with respect to their gene contribution in order to retain superior genomes in the evolutionary population.

Some comprehensive investigations for parameter setting are performed on a benchmark problem. Especially, three parameters of the evaluative crossover with a reasonable set of values are analyzed to realize their evolutionary effect. The experimental results show that a 100% crossover percentage with 10% crossover rate and a random therapeutic coefficient can achieve the best performance for E-NSGA-II.

The proposed algorithm is tested on nine unconstrained multi-objective optimization problems. The experimental results are compared with five existing algorithms. The results show that the proposed E-NSGA-II is able to converge the Pareto-optimal front of all test problems, even though other algorithms experiences difficulties in approaching the global optima on some functions. E-NSGA-II can also achieve better diversity qualities than others. The results of algorithm analysis also reveal that the proposed evaluative crossover can intuitively evaluate gene contributions that can guide E-NSGA-II to perform an efficient search by dynamically shifting emphasis to significant genome in the feasible space without abdicating any portion of the candidate schemata. Although the convergence metric on the disconnected problem POL is slightly worse than four algorithms, E-NSGA-II outperforms almost all other algorithms on the mean of the convergence metric in other test problems. For the diversity metric, E-NSGA-II also performs better than all other algorithms dramatically in all test problems except for NSGA-II on POL and KUR.

In the future, the proposed E-NSGA-II should further develop the properties of a simple yet efficient evaluative crossover operator, a revised mutation operator and a parameter-less approach to deal with a wide spectrum of real world multi-objective problems.

6. Acknowledgement

The authors would like to thank Kalyanmoy Deb for his explicit writing and brilliant papers that inspire our mind. The research is supported by the National Science Council of Republic of China under grant NSC 96-2221-E-033-007.

7. References

Deb, K. (1999). Multi-objective genetic algorithms: Problem difficulties and construction of test problems. *Evolutionary Computation*, Vol. 7, No. 3, pp. 205-230.

Deb, K. (2001). *Multi-objective optimization using evolutionary algorithms*, New York: John Wiley and Sons.

Deb, K. & Goyal, M. (1996). A combined genetic adaptive search (GeneAS) for engineering design. *Computer Science and Informatics*, Vol. 26, No. 4, pp. 30-45.

Deb, K.; Pratap, A.; Agarwal, S. & Meyarivan, T. (2002). A fast and elitist multiobjective genetic algorithm: NSGA-II. *IEEE Transactions on Evolutionary Computation*, Vol. 6, No. 2, pp. 182-197.

Dias, A.H.F. & Vasconcelos, J.A. (2002). Multiobjective genetic algorithms applied to solve optimization problems. *IEEE Transactions on Magnetics*, Vol. 38, No. 2, pp. 1133-1136.

Ghomsheh, V.S.; Khanehsar, M.A. & Teshnehlab, M. (2007). Improving the non-dominate sorting genetic algorithm for multi-objective optimization, *Proceedings of Computational Intelligence and Security Workshops*, pp. 89-92.

Goldberg, D.E. (1989). *Genetic Algorithm in Search, Optimization, and Machine Leaning*, Addison Wesley.

Horn, J.; Nafpliotis, N. & Goldberg, D. (1994). A niched pareto genetic algorithm for multiobjective optimization, *Proceedings of the First IEEE Conf. on Computational Intelligence*, pp. 82-87.

Huband, S.; Hingston, P.; Barone, L. & While, L. (2006). A review of multiobjective test problems and a scalable test problem toolkit. *Evolutionary Computation*, Vol. 10, No. 5, pp. 477-506.

Jaeggi, D.; Asselin-Miller, C.; Parks, G.; Kipouros, T.; Bell, T. & Clarkson, J. (2004). Multi-objective Parallel Tabu Search. *Lecture Notes in Computer Science*, Vol. 3242, pp. 732-741.

Knowles, J. & Corne, D. (1999). The Pareto archived evolution strategy: A new baseline algorithm for multiobjective optimization, *Proceedings of the 1999 Congress on Evolutionary Computation*, pp. 98–105.

Lin, C.H. & Chuang, C.C. (2007). A rough set penalty function for marriage selection in multiple-evaluation genetic algorithms. *Lecture Notes in Computer Science*, Vol. 4481, pp. 500-507.

Lin, C.H. & He, J.D. (2007). Multiple-evaluation genetic algorithm for numerical optimization problems, *Proceedings of the Computability in Europe 2007: Computation and Logic in the Real World*, pp. 239-246.

Nebro, A.J.; Durillo, J.J.; Luna, F.; Dorronsoro, B. & Alba, E. (2007). A cellular genetic algorithm for multiojective optimization. *International Journal of Intelligent Systems*, pp. 1-12.

Nebro, A.J.; Luna, F. & Alba, E. (2005). New ideas in applying scatter search to multiobjective optimization, *Proceedings of IEEE Conference on Evolutionary Multi-Criterion Optimization Guanajuato*, Mexico, pp. 443-458.

Okabe, T.; Jin, Y. & Sendhoff, B. (2003). A critical survey of performance indices for multi-objective optimisation, *Proceedings of the Congress on Evolutionary Computation*, pp. 878-885.

Qi, R.; Qian, F.; Li, S. & Wang, Z. (2006). Chaos-genetic algorithm for multiobjective optimization, *Proceedings of the Sixth World Congress on Intelligent Control and Automation*, pp. 1563-1566.

Ripon, K.S.N.; Kwong, S. & Man, K.F. (2007). A real-coding jumping gene genetic algorithm (RJGGA) for multiobjective optimization. *Information Sciences*, Vol. 177, No. 2, pp. 632-654.

Srinivas, N. & Deb, K. (1994). Multiobjective optimization using nondominated sorting in genetic algorithms. *Evolutionary Computation*, Vol. 2, No. 3, pp. 221-248.

Zitzler, E. & Thiele, L. (1999) Multiobjective evolutionary algorithms: A comparative case studyand the strength pareto approach. *IEEE Transactions on Evolutionary Computation*, Vol. 3, No. 4, pp. 257-271.

Zitzler, E.; Deb, K. & Thiele, L. (2000). Comparison of multiobjective evolutionary algorithms: Empirical results. *Evolutionary Computation*, Vol. 8, No. 2, pp. 173-195.

7

Oscillators for Modelling Circadian Rhythms in Cyanobacteria Growth

Jaromír Fišer[a], Jan Červený[b] and Pavel Zítek[a]
[a] *Czech Technical University in Prague, Centre for Applied Cybernetics (cAk) Czech Republic*
[b] *Institute of Systems Biology and Ecology in Nové Hrady, Academy of Sciences CR Czech Republic*

1. Introduction

There is strong evidence that the behaviour of living systems is subject to biological clocks which can be considered as mutually coupled oscillators. These applications of oscillators were studied since very early (Minorsky, 1962; Pavlidis, 1973). In case of biological systems like algae populations or micro-organism cultures their varying growth rate and other living system activities are liable, first of all, to the diurnal cycles of light irradiation as the decisive model input. The living systems adopt these cyclic conditions as their inner circadian rhythms and exert a specific tendency to maintain their rhythm even if the cyclic external influences change their period or shape. In this way the model of system entrainment to circadian rhythms is based on the idea of nonlinear resonance phenomenon. The circadian rhythms, also referred to as internal biological rhythms, play a role as temporal regulatory pacemakers practically in any activity of living species, but their mechanism remains still largely unknown (Ditty et al., 2009). Experimental studies and mathematical modelling have demonstrated that circadian pacemakers working on periods close to 24 hours can be modelled as limit cycle oscillators (Pavlidis, 1973; Winfree, 1970; Wever, 1970). Typically a pacemaker model implementation involves a Van der Pol oscillator as a limit cycle generator influencing the model of population growth (Fišer et al., 2008). Then this circadian pacemaker structure can be identified with the experimentally obtained data. A part of the recent research in cyanobacteria growth modelling has been already described in the previous paper (Fišer et al., 2006), where an algae population growth is investigated.

In selecting a suitable oscillator for circadian pacemaker application the ability of the system to adapt its frequency and the shape of cycles according to the exogenous cyclic inputs, is to be kept in view in particular. Thus any oscillator considered as the pacemaker has to be endowed with the property that its limit cycle oscillations change gradually in frequency and shape according to the cyclic influences. These influences comprise light irradiance and other ambient inputs particularly temperature and nourishment supply (Johnson et al., 2004).

Beside the analytical nonlinear schemes mentioned above a chemical oscillator has already been developed as generator of circadian rhythms (Miyoshi et al., 2007), and its operation was tested on rhythms in cyanobacteria. The structure of this oscillator is relatively complex and the aim of this chapter is to find an approximation of the Miyoshi oscillator by a Van der Pol type oscillator for substituting its function by a simpler scheme in modelling the timing influence on the diurnal cycles in the cyanobacteria growth.

2. Experimental data acquisition

The authors' own data material used for working out the model presented below, originates from experiments with unicellular, diazotropic cyanobacterium *Cyanothece,* sp. ATCC 51142. The experiments were performed in a laboratory-scale bioreactor, developed by Photon Systems Instruments, Ltd. (Fig.1). Due to a programmable source of variable irradiance in this device and due to other adjustable experiment conditions artificially formed diurnal cycles can be provided and the consequent circadian rhythms in cyanobacteria culture can be observed and recorded. The used bioreactor provides capability to generate artificially defined cultivation conditions with controlled distribution of CO_2 nourishment, inevitable for obtaining consistent culture growth data. Furthermore, a controlled heating and/or cooling allows to maintaining a desired temperature for cultivation. Continuously recorded outputs include temperature, optical density and fluorescence emission representing the culture production performance. Among other artificial perturbations of the culture growth changes of the nourishing gas composition can be provided. Particularly the carbon dioxide concentration changes can be applied in the experiments. As the model output the optical density of cyanobacteria culture in 735 nm, as a parameter proportional to concentration of cyanobacteria culture, is used (Nedbal et al., 2008).

Fig. 1. Prototype of cultivation device

3. Population growth model

Among other approaches to modelling the population growth, the models based on Volterra population equation are applied. Their recent applications used to include the delay effects resulting from the age structure of the described population into the model (Cushing, 1993; Iannelli, 1994). The delayed Volterra model of population growth is usually referred to in a functional form which can be found in Kuang, (1993). To express the ageing influence on the inhibition of population growth an extension of the delayed Volterra model has been introduced by Fišer et al., (2007).

Consider the population growth model described by the delayed Volterra-type system (Červený et al., 2007)

$$\frac{dx(t)}{dt}=\left(\mu(x,y,I,\vartheta)-\int_0^T x(t-\tau)dA(\tau)-\int_0^T \frac{dx(t-\tau)}{dt}dB(\tau)\right)x(t) \tag{1}$$

where x is the cyanobacteria concentration in the culture, I is the incident light intensity, ϑ is the temperature of nourishing medium and $\mu(x,y,I,\vartheta)$ is the specific rate of cell growth. This growth rate is also affected by the timing activity of the biological clock of the culture represented by the cyclic variable y as the output of oscillator described below. The functions $A(\tau)>0$, $B(\tau)>0$ are delay distributions, $\tau\geq 0$, and T is the maximum delay length. As to the timing action its impact on the specific growth rate is considered in the following separated form

$$\mu(x,y,I,\vartheta)=\mu_p(x,I,\vartheta)+\mu_c(y) \tag{2}$$

where μ_p expresses the specific growth rate based on Monod kinetics and μ_c is a growth rate increment originating from the clock oscillator. The variable y is the output of a chemical cyclic action explained in Section 4 which controls the circadian rhythms. Due to the dimensional homogeneity its influence on the growth rate is supposed as proportional to one of the state variable derivatives of the oscillator in Section 4

$$\mu_c(t)=C\,y(t)=C\frac{d[CPKaiC_6]}{dt} \tag{3}$$

where C is a proportional gain coefficient.

The value of the main component μ_p of the growth rate results from both the Monod kinetics and Lambert-Beer law as follows

$$\mu(x,I,\vartheta)=\mu_{\max}\left(1-e^{-\frac{I_a(x,I)}{I_{sat}}}\right)p(\vartheta) \tag{4}$$

where I_a is the average light intensity inside the culture given by

$$I_a(x,I) = \frac{I\,k_w}{k_c x}\left[1 - e^{-k_c x}\right] \tag{5}$$

where I_{sat} is a saturation light intensity, and p is an auxiliary function expressing the dependance of the growth rate on the temperature. The parameters k_c , k_w determine the light absorption in cyanobacteria culture and glass wall, respectively (for more details see Li et al., 2003).

In the next the main attention is paid to circadian rhythm issue, i.e. the cyclic influence of $\mu_c(y)$ on the cyanobacteria growth rate.

4. Miyoshi chemical oscillator

The functional structure of circadian oscillator in cyanobacteria on molecular level was discovered by Ishiura et al. (1998). The experiment data were measured on *Cyanothece* sp. while one has to be concerned about already published models which are almost exclusively developed for another model cyanobacterium *Synechococcus elongatus* (e.g. Miyoshi et al., 2007; Mori et al., 2007; Rust et al., 2007; van Zon et al., 2007). For our modelling approach let be assumed that the features of interest in these two organisms are comparable. More details on molecular base of cyanobacteria circadian clock are well described recently by Ditty et al. (2009).

For purposes of diurnal cyanobacteria growth modelling we adopted the oscillator developed by Miyoshi et al. (2007) that allows entrainment by the light-dark forcing applied on the culture. Adopted mechanistic model of oscillator constitutes the set of 13 differential equations that describe changes in concentration of protein complexes involved in circadian clock system. The equations with state variable descriptions (Table 1) are as follows

$$\frac{d[KaiC_6]}{dt} = -[KaiC_6](k_1 + k_{21} + v_{cat1}[KaiC_6]^{-1}) + k_{22}[PPKaiC_6] + k_2[KaiC]^6 + v_{cat2} \tag{6}$$

$$\begin{aligned}\frac{d[PPKaiC_6]}{dt} = &-[PPKaiC_6](k_3 + k_{22} + k_{23}) + k_4[KaiC]^3[PKaiC]^3 + k_{21}[KaiC_6] + k_{24}[CPKaiC_6] \\ &+ v_{cat1} - v_{cat2} - v_{cat3} + v_{cat4}\end{aligned} \tag{7}$$

$$\frac{d[CPKaiC_6]}{dt} = y = -[CPKaiC_6](k_5 + k_{24}) + k_6[PKaiC]^6 + k_{23}[PPKaiC_6] + v_{cat3} - v_{cat4} \tag{8}$$

$$\begin{aligned}\frac{d[KaiC]}{dt} = &\,6(k_1[KaiC_6] - k_2[KaiC]^6) + 3(k_3[PPKaiC_6] - k_4[KaiC]^3[PKaiC]^3) \\ &+ (k_{tl2}[kaiBC\ mRNA] - k_{p\deg 3}[KaiC])L\end{aligned} \tag{9}$$

State variables	Description	Init. cond. [molecules/cell]
$[KaiC_6]$	non-phosphorylated KaiC hexameric complex	139.220
$[PPKaiC_6]$	partially phosphorylated KaiC hexameric complex	779.158
$[CPKaiC_6]$	completely phosphorylated KaiC hexameric complex	1229.563
$[KaiC]$	non-phosphorylated KaiC monomer	932.446
$[PKaiC]$	phosphorylated KaiC monomer	110.829
$[KaiB_4]$	KaiB-inactive tetramer complex	0.173
$[KaiB_{4i}]$	KaiB-active tetramer complex	3251.369
$[KaiB]$	KaiB monomer	1130
$[KaiA_2]$	KaiA dimer	166.559
$[KaiA]$	KaiA monomer	9.998
$[kaiA\ mRNA]$	kaiA mRNA	2.856
$[kaiBC\ mRNA]$	kaiBC mRNA	2.865
$[KaiA_2B_4]$	complex of a KaiA dimer and KaiB-active tetramer	51.022

Table 1. State variables description with initial conditions

$$\frac{d[PKaiC]}{dt} = -[PKaiC]^3 3\left(k_4[KaiC]^3 + 2k_6[PKaiC]^3\right) + 3k_3[PPKaiC_6] + 6k_5[CPKaiC_6] - k_{p\deg 4}[PKaiC]L \quad (10)$$

$$\frac{d[KaiB_4]}{dt} = -[KaiB_4](k_{10} + k_{11}[KaiA_2]) + k_9[KaiB]^4 + k_{12}[KaiA_2B_4] - v_{cat\_b1} + v_{cat\_b2} \quad (11)$$

$$\frac{d[KaiB_{4i}]}{dt} = v_{cat\_b1} - v_{cat\_b2} \quad (12)$$

$$\frac{d[KaiB]}{dt} = 4\left(k_{10}[KaiB_4] - k_9[KaiB]^4\right) + \left(k_{tl2}[kaiBC\ mRNA] - k_{p\deg 2}[KaiB]\right)L \quad (13)$$

$$\frac{d[KaiA_2]}{dt} = -[KaiA_2](k_7 + k_{11}[KaiB_4]) + k_8[KaiA]^2 + k_{12}[KaiA_2B_4] \quad (14)$$

$$\frac{d[KaiA]}{dt} = -[KaiA]\left(2k_8[KaiA] + k_{p\deg 1}L\right) + 2k_7[KaiA_2] + k_{tl1}[kaiA\ mRNA]L \quad (15)$$

$$\frac{d[kaiA\ mRNA]}{dt} = k_{a1}\frac{k_{bts1}[RNAP]}{1 + k_{bts1}[RNAP]}\frac{[CPKaiC_6]}{[PPKaiC_6]}L - k_{m\deg 1}[kaiA\ mRNA] \quad (16)$$

$$\frac{d[kaiBC\,mRNA]}{dt} = k_{a2}\frac{k_{bts2}[RNAP]}{1+k_{bts2}[RNAP]}\frac{[CPKaiC_6]}{[PPKaiC_6]}L - k_{m\deg 2}[kaiBC\,mRNA] \tag{17}$$

$$\frac{d[KaiA_2B_4]}{dt} = k_{11}[KaiA_2][KaiB_4] - k_{12}[KaiA_2B_4] \tag{18}$$

where rate variables formed from Michaelis-Menten equations are as follows

$$v_{cat1} = k_{cat1}\frac{[KaiA_2][KaiC_6]}{K_{m1}+[KaiC_6]} \tag{19}$$

$$v_{cat2} = k_{cat2}\frac{[KaiA_2B_4][PPKaiC_6]}{K_{m2}+[PPKaiC_6]} \tag{20}$$

$$v_{cat3} = k_{cat3}\frac{[KaiA_2][PPKaiC_6]}{K_{m3}+[PPKaiC_6]} \tag{21}$$

$$v_{cat4} = k_{cat4}\frac{[KaiA_2B_4][CPKaiC_6]}{K_{m4}+[CPKaiC_6]} \tag{22}$$

$$v_{cat\_b1} = k_{cat\_b1}\frac{[PPKaiC_6][KaiB_4]}{K_{m\_b1}+[KaiB_4]} \tag{23}$$

$$v_{cat\_b2} = k_{cat\_b2}\frac{[CPKaiC_6][KaiB_{4i}]}{K_{m\_b2}+[KaiB_{4i}]} \tag{24}$$

The parameter values and variable description, of all the rate constants starting in the notation with k and all the Michaelis constants starting in the notation with K are specified in the application example. Also the initial conditions of the set (6)-(18) are provided in the application example. Because some rate variables in (6)-(18) are activated by forcing light (for original reference see Miyoshi et al., 2007), while in dark these rate variables are relaxed, we apply to distinguish between the activation and relaxation of these rate variables a logical variable L already substituted into (6)-(18). This logical variable represents on/off irradiance state (for more details see Section 5).

For the simulation purposes (6)-(18) are viewed as the state equations in state variables specified by Table 1 and constituting the state vector as follows

$$\mathbf{w} = \begin{bmatrix} [KaiC_6],[PPKaiC_6],[CPKaiC_6],[KaiC],[PKaiC],[KaiB_4],[KaiB_{4i}],\ldots \\ \ldots[KaiB],[KaiA_2],[KaiA],[kaiA\,mRNA],[kaiBC\,mRNA],[KaiA_2B_4] \end{bmatrix}^T \tag{25}$$

Correcting several misprints in Miyoshi et al. (2007) the following changes were carried out in (11) and (13). Namely, the signs of rate variables $v_9 = k_9[KaiB]^4$, $v_{10} = k_{10}[KaiB_4]$ are exchanged, and at the same time the right-hand sides of expressions for v_9, v_{10} are mutually exchanged. Another correction was applied to parameters k_{cat4} and k_{pdeg4}. In addition, parameters K_{m1}, K_{m2} were increased 1000 times to achieve the circadian rhythms of 24 h period.

5. Approximation of biological clock by Van der Pol oscillator

An oscillator based on Van der Pol equation is proposed to approximate the chemical oscillator presented in previous section because of appreciable simplification concerning the number of both state variables and tuning parameters. Then, let the proposed Van der Pol oscillator be considered in the matrix form

$$\frac{d\mathbf{z}(t)}{dt} = \mathbf{A}\mathbf{z}(t) + \mathbf{F}(\mathbf{z})\mathbf{z}(t)z_1(t) + \mathbf{B}(\mathbf{z})\mathbf{u}(t,D) \tag{26}$$

where $\mathbf{z} = [z_1, z_2, z_3]^T$ is the state vector of the oscillator. Both the state and input matrices are

$$\mathbf{A} = \begin{bmatrix} 0 & 1 & 0 \\ 0 & a\varepsilon & 0 \\ 0 & 0 & -\dfrac{1}{T} \end{bmatrix}, \quad \mathbf{F}(\mathbf{z}) = \begin{bmatrix} 0 & 0 & 0 \\ -abz_2 & 0 & -1 \\ 0 & 0 & -\dfrac{1}{T} \end{bmatrix} \tag{27}$$

and

$$\mathbf{B}(\mathbf{z}) = \begin{bmatrix} 0 & \dfrac{q}{4\pi^2} z_3 & 0 \\ 0 & 0 & \dfrac{\Omega}{T} \end{bmatrix}^T \tag{28}$$

respectively. The constants a, ε ,b are the parameters of Van der Pol equation and the oscillator input vector is of the form $\mathbf{u}(t,D) = [I(t) \quad \Omega(t-D)]^T$, where $I(t)$ is the cyclic light intensity representing the diurnal cycles, and Ω is the frequency on which the oscillator is to be entrained. Gain q amplifies the light intensity and time constant T with pure delay D determines the dynamics of adaptation. The existence of limit cycle motion is conditioned by the inequality

$$\left(\varepsilon - bz_1^2\right) > 0 \tag{29}$$

where $\varepsilon > 0$, $b > 0$. The other parameters, a and q, are the weighting coefficients which influence the shape of limit cycle oscillations. The oscillator output is given by the equation

$$y(t) = C_d z_2(t) = C_d \frac{dz_1(t)}{dt} \tag{30}$$

where C_d is a normalization coefficient. Output y is then the input variable of specific growth rate (3) to modify the cyanobacteria growth by circadian rhythms as $\mu_c(t) = C\,y(t) = C\,C_d\,z_2(t)$.

6. Oscillator-based scheme for adapting to circadian rhythms

Basically equation (1) provides the model with the internal relationships which govern the growth of population but this model part does not express the circadian character and particularly the impact of diurnal cycles on the growth. The biological populations are specifically sensitive to changes in their environment and thus they are able to adapt themselves to these changes. All this suggests that a more complex mechanism than a pure sensory adaptation may be involved in the model. It is typical that the adaptation time constants tend to be rather longer than the ones typical for sensoric organ responses. This property of biological systems is provided by means of applying an oscillator (Pavlidis, 1973) influenced by a generator of diurnal cycles as in the block diagram in Fig. 2. Using the oscillator based on Van der Pol equation, the generator of diurnal cycles of light irradiation $I(t)$ may be applied to adapt the limit cycle frequency of the oscillator. Another oscillator, called chemical, is forced by sequence of 0 and 1, where 0 and 1 correspond to the dark phase and light phase, respectively. This is simply done using logical variable L, see Fig. 2, that either 0 or 1 are in the product with corresponding rate variables in right-hand sides of (8)-(20). We say that these rate variables are in on/off irradiance state.

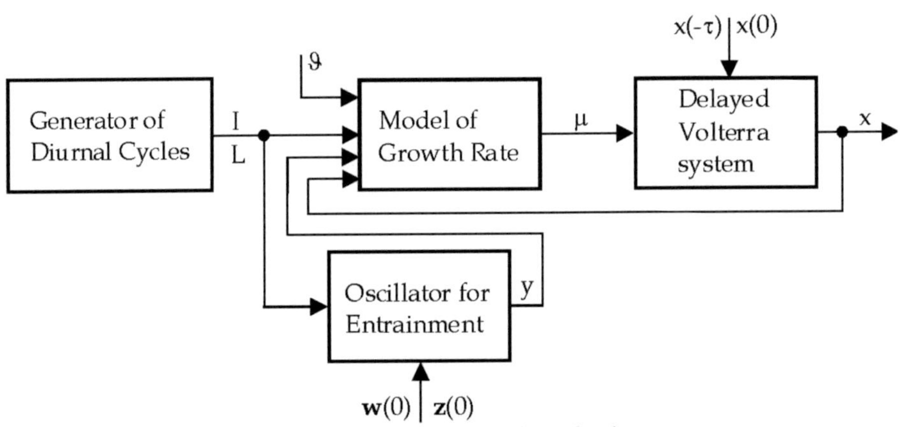

Fig. 2. Oscillator-based scheme for adapting to circadian rhythms

The modelling with the help of the scheme in Fig. 2 requires the setting of proper initial conditions comprised in vectors $\mathbf{w}(0)$, $\mathbf{z}(0)$ and initial cyanobacteria concentration (inoculum) $x(0)$ with relaxed $x(-\tau), 0 < \tau \le \tau_{\max}$.

7. Application example

In this section a growth model for cyanobacteria species *Cyanothece* is presented. For fitting the model the data from experiments reported in Section 2 were used. The samples of measured courses of cyanobacteria, like that in Fig. 5 were used to identify the model parameters. First, the parameters of specific growth rate μ were determined, for more details we refer to Červený et al., (2007), where the cultivated cyanobacteria species *Cyanothece* is investigated. In this paper the following parameters are considered: $\mu_{\max} = 0.028\,h^{-1}$, $I_{sat} = 126\,\mathrm{Wm}^{-2}$, auxiliary value $p(\vartheta = 30°\mathrm{C}) = 1$, coefficient $k_c = 3.4$, specific parameter $k_w = 31.6$. The remaining parameters of model (1) have been resulted in the distributions $A(\tau)$ and $B(\tau)$ as follows

$$A(\tau) = \begin{cases} 0, & \tau < 0 \\ 3.33 \cdot \dfrac{\tau}{24}, & \tau \in \langle 0,24 \rangle\ \mathrm{h} \\ 3.33, & \tau > 24 \end{cases}, \quad B(\tau) = 0 \qquad (31)$$

First, the parameters of chemical oscillator are determined in the table below (adopted from Supplementary Online Material in Červený & Nedbal (2009)).

Rate constants	*Description*
$k_1 = 1.615\,h^{-1}$	dissociation rate for $KaiC_6$
$k_2 = 2.039\times10^{-16}\,molecules^{-5}\,cell^5\,h^{-1}$	binding rate for KaiC
$k_3 = 1.615\times10^{-4}\,h^{-1}$	dissociation rate for $PPKaiC_6$
$k_4 = 1.019\times10^{-14}\,molecules^{-5}\,cell^5\,h^{-1}$	binding rate for KaiC and PKaiC
$k_5 = 0.162\,h^{-1}$	dissociation rate for $CPKaiC_6$
$k_6 = 1.019\times10^{-10}\,molecules^{-5}\,cell^5\,h^{-1}$	binding constant for PKaiC
$k_7 = 0.162\times10^{-1}\,h^{-1}$	dissociation rate for $KaiA_2$
$k_8 = 0.268\,molecules^{-1}\,cell^1\,h^{-1}$	binding rate for KaiA
$k_9 = 7.393\times10^{-17}\,molecules^{-3}\,cell^3\,h^{-1}$	binding rate for KaiB
$k_{10} = 1.615\times10^{-4}\,h^{-1}$	dissociation rate for $KaiB_4$
$k_{11} = 8.756\times10^{-4}\,molecules^{-1}\,cell^1\,h^{-1}$	binding rate for $KaiA_2$ and $KaiB_4$
$k_{12} = 8.788\times10^{-2}\,h^{-1}$	dissociation rate for $KaiA_2$
$k_{21} = 1.079\times10^{-8}\,h^{-1}$	autophosphorylation rate of $KaiA_2B_4$
$k_{22} = 1.079\times10^{-5}\,h^{-1}$	autodephosphorylation rate of $PPKaiC_6$
$k_{23} = 1.079\times10^{-6}\,h^{-1}$	autophosphorylation rate of $PPKaiC_6$
$k_{24} = 1.079\times10^{-8}\,h^{-1}$	autodephosphorylation rate of $CPKaiC_6$
$k_{a1} = 1.017\times10^{7}\,molecules\,cell^{-1}\,h^{-1}$	transcription rate of kaiA

$k_{a2} = 6.458 \times 10^{7}$ *molecules cell*$^{-1} h^{-1}$	transcription rate of kaiBC
$k_{cat1} = 0.539\ h^{-1}$	rate of $KaiC_6$ phosphorylation
$k_{cat2} = 0.539\ h^{-1}$	rate of $PPKaiC_6$ dephosphorylation
$k_{cat3} = 1.079\ h^{-1}$	rate of $PPKaiC_6$ phosphorylation
$k_{cat4} = 0.890\ h^{-1}$	rate of $CPKaiC_6$ dephosphorylation
$k_{cat\_b1} = 2.423\ h^{-1}$	rate of $KaiB_4$ inactivation
$k_{cat\_b2} = 0.346\ h^{-1}$	rate of $KaiB_{4i}$ activation
$k_{m\deg 1} = 0.133\ h^{-1}$	degradation rate of kaiA mRNA
$k_{m\deg 2} = 0.178\ h^{-1}$	degradation rate of kaiBC mRNA
$k_{p\deg 1} = 8.00 \times 10^{-3}\ h^{-1}$	degradation rate of KaiA
$k_{p\deg 2} = 0.490\ h^{-1}$	degradation rate of KaiB
$k_{p\deg 3} = 1.300\ h^{-1}$	degradation rate of KaiC
$k_{p\deg 4} = 0.200\ h^{-1}$	degradation rate of PKaiC
$k_{tl1} = 8.239 \times 10^{-3}\ h^{-1}$	translation rate of kaiA
$k_{tl2} = 1.701 \times 10^{2}\ h^{-1}$	translation rate of kaiBC
Michaelis and miscellaneous constants	*Description*
$k_{bts1} = 3.657 \times 10^{-12}$ *molecules*$^{-1}$ *cell*	binding constant for RNA polymerase in *kaiA*
$k_{bts1} = 1.000 \times 10^{-12}$ *molecules*$^{-1}$ *cell*	binding constant for RNA polymerase in *kaiBC*
$K_{m1} = 602$ *molecules cell*$^{-1}$	Michaelis constant for $KaiC_6$ phosphorylation
$K_{m2} = 602$ *molecules cell*$^{-1}$	Michaelis constant for $PPKaiC_6$ dephosphorylation
$K_{m3} = 0.602$ *molecules cell*$^{-1}$	Michaelis constant for $PPKaiC_6$ phosphorylation
$K_{m4} = 0.602$ *molecules cell*$^{-1}$	Michaelis constant for $CPKaiB_4$ dephosphorylation
$K_{m\_b1} = 0.602$ *molecules cell*$^{-1}$	Michaelis constant for $KaiB_4$ inactivation
$K_{m\_b2} = 6.675 \times 10^{1}$ *molecules cell*$^{-1}$	Michaelis constant for $KaiB_{4i}$ activation
$[RNAP] = 5000$ *molecules cell*$^{-1}$	RNA polymerase concentration

Table 2. Rate and other constants in equations (6) – (24)

Then the parameters of Van der Pol oscillator are found as follows: $\Omega = 0.26\ \text{rad} \cdot \text{h}^{-1}\ (2\pi/24)$, $\varepsilon = 1$, $b = 181$, $a = 0.03$, $q = 0.03$, $T = 1\,\text{h}$ and $D = 0$. Proportional gain C results in $5 \times 10^{-4}\ \text{molecules}^{-1} \cdot \text{cell}$ for the chemical oscillator and $2\ \text{molecules}^{-1} \cdot \text{cell}$ for the Van der Pol oscillator. In addition, normalization coefficient C_d in (30) is adjusted at the value $2\ \text{molecules} \cdot \text{cell}^{-1}$. For comparing both oscillators the initial conditions of the chemical oscillator are set in their "morning" values, introduced by Miyoshi et al. (2007), are listed in Table 1. Obviously, the third -order oscillator of Van der Pol type cannot satisfy these conditions but its limit cycle can be satisfactorily identified with that of the chemical oscillator. In order to set Van der Pol oscillator output close to limit cycle the following initial conditions are used

$$z_1(0) = -0.085, z_2(0) = 0, z_3(0) = \Omega^2 \tag{32}$$

where Ω is the frequency of desired circadian rhythm.

The initial conditions of the chemical oscillator are chosen to be synchronized with cyanobacteria circadian oscillator. In Fig. 3 the phase portraits of the chemical and Van der Pol oscillator are recorded.

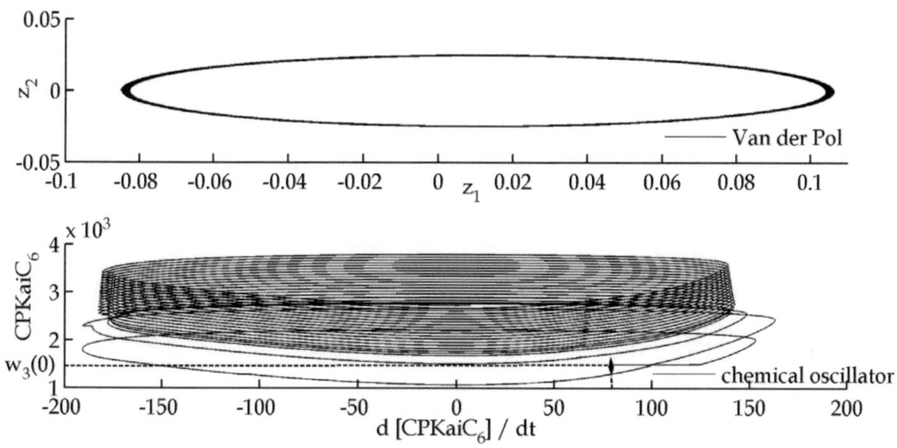

Fig. 3. Phase portraits of both oscillators with initial conditions in Table 1 and (32)

After comparing limit cycles of both oscillators the chemical oscillator tends to the limit cycle along a spiral while the Van der Pol oscillator immediately achieves the limit cycle. However, the subject of interest is to apply the variables on horizontal axes in Fig. 3 what are the derivatives changing the specific growth rate in (1).

The specific growth rate given by (2), composed from two components, is drawn in Fig. 4 under light conditions specified in Fig. 5.

In Fig. 5 the cyanobacteria growth is obtained in circadian LD 12:12 regime, where LD regime abbreviates light/dark regime in hours. Later on, the LD regime is switched to LL regime where LL denotes continuous light.

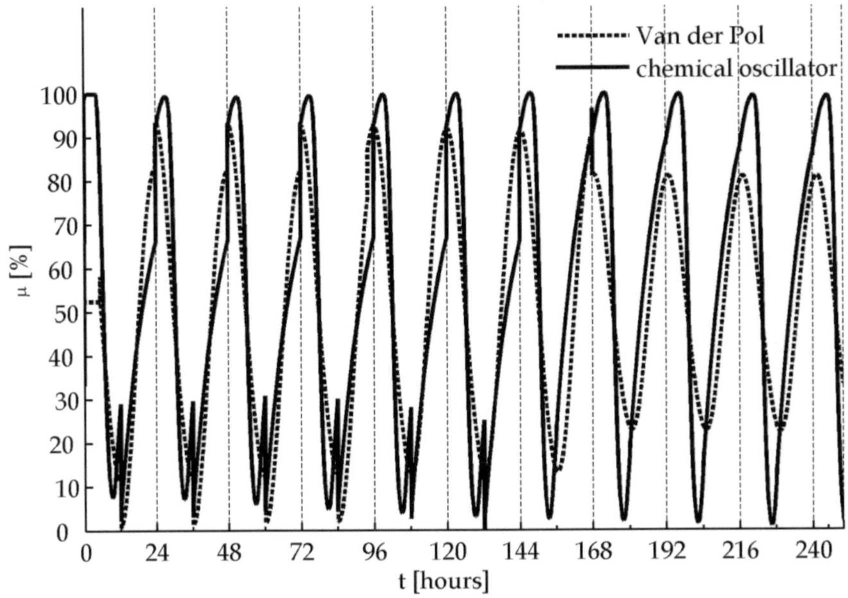

Fig. 4. Specific growth rate (2) in percents with respect to $\mu_{\max}$

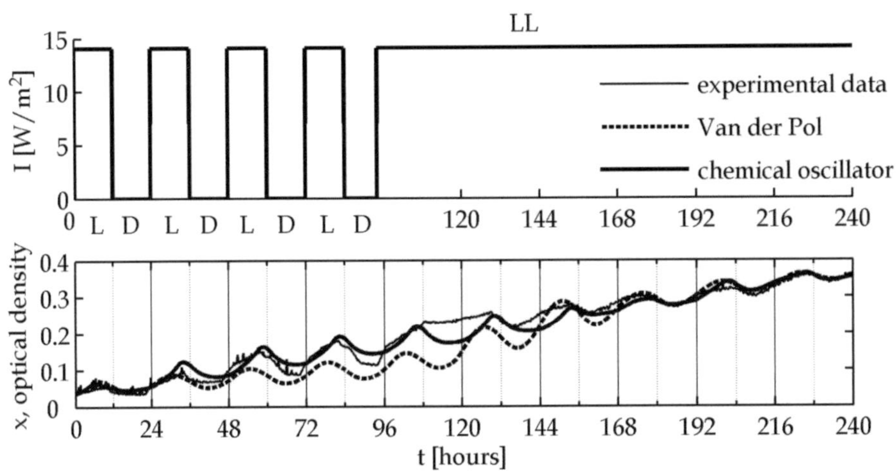

Fig. 5. Comparison of measured concentration x with the modelled one using the scheme in Fig. 2 with initial conditions $x(0)=0.045, x(-\tau)=0, \quad 0<\tau\leq 24\text{h}$

In Fig. 5 an experiment with cyanobacteria culture is recorded, where the cyclic lighting with 24 hours period is changed to a permanent light with constant intensity. The measured data of cyanobacteria growth are compared with the modelling results obtained from both the models with chemical and Van der Pol oscillators. Both the models fit well the undisturbed growth of the culture, however, the model version with the chemical oscillator is in a better agreement with the experiments, better than it is with the application of Van der Pol oscillator.

8. Conclusions

The issue of circadian rhythms is getting more importance with the emerging possibility of intensifying the biotechnological processes. The main aim of the paper is to show that the rather complex chemical oscillator can be substituted by a relatively simple Van der Pol oscillator in its timing function in modelling the circadian rhythms. While the chemical oscillator consists of thirteen state variables the simple Van der Pol is of the third order only. Apparently these oscillators cannot be fully equivalent in their state vectors, but both the oscillators can substitute each other in generating the clock limit cycle. The basic frequency is given by the 24 hour period and both these oscillators can be tuned to a different desired frequency. Nevertheless the adjustment of the period is not of the same dynamics in both the oscillators. Only in this respect the Van der Pol oscillator does not fit the growth oscillations in cyanobacteria as the chemical one, but this shortage is not substantial for the bioreactor application and is outweighed by the simplicity of the proposed approximation. As regards the presented results it is necessary to note that the experiment conditions were simplified as to the simplified nourishment technique, where only CO_2 was supplied while no fixable nitrogen was available. That is why in the presented experiments the cyanobacteria concentration drops during the dark phases, which is not typical in case of complete nourishment.

Acknowledgement

This work was supported by the Ministry of Education of the Czech Republic under Project 1M0567, and subsequently by grants AV0Z60870520 (Czech Academy of Sciences) and GACR 206/09/1284 (Czech Science Foundation) and through the FUNCDYN Programme of the European Science Foundation and European Commission, Contract no. ERAS-CT-2003-980409.

9. References

Cushing, J. M. (1993). An Introduction to Structured Population Dynamics, In: *Regional Conference Series in Applied Mathematics (No. 71),* Rozier, R., (Ed.), pp. 200, SIAM, ISBN 0-89871-417-6, Philadelphia

Červený, J.; Fišer, J. & Zítek P. (2007). A Model Solution to Adapting the Algae Population Growth to Diurnal Cycles, *Proceedings of 16th Int. Conf. Process Control (PC'07),* ISBN 978-80-227-2677-1, Štrbské Pleso, High Tatras, Slovakia, 11-14 June 2007, STU, Bratislava

Červený, J.; Nedbal, L. (2009). Metabolic rhythms of the cyanobacterium *Cyanothece* sp. ATCC 51142 correlate with modeled dynamics of circadian clock, *Journal of Biological Rhythms,* Vol. 24, No. 4, (Aug 2009), pp. 295-303, ISSN 0748-7304

Ditty, J. L.; Mackey, S. R. & Johnson, C. H. (2009). *Bacterial Circadian Programs,* Springer, ISBN 978-3-540-88430-9, Berlin

Fišer, J.; Červený, J. & Zítek P. (2006). Time Delay Model of Algal Population Growth in a Photobioreactor, *Proceedings of 5th MathMod,* Vol. 2, ISBN 3-901608-30-3, Vienna, Austria, 8-10 February 2006, Argesim, Wien

Fišer, J.; Červený, J. & Zítek P. (2007). Time Delay Model of Algal Population Growth in Tubular Photobioreactor, *SNE(Simulation News Europe)*, Vol. 17, No. 3-4, (Dec 2007), 14-18, ISSN 0929-2268

Fišer, J.; Zítek P. & Červený, J. (2008). Oscillators for Modeling Biomass Growth Adaptation to Circadian Rhythms, *Proceedings of UKSIM Tenth International Conference on Computer Modelling and Simulation*, pp. 175-179, ISBN 0-7695-3114-8, Cambridge, UK, 1-3 April 2008, IEEE Computer Society, Los Alamitos

Iannelli, M. (1994). Mathematical Theory of Age-structured Population Dynamics, In: *Applied Mathematics Monographs*, Vol. 7, Pasquali, A., (Ed.), pp. 174, Giardini Editori e Stampatori, ISBN 88-427-0250-1, Pisa

Ishiura, M.; Kutsuna, S.; Aoki, S.; Iwasaki, H.; Andersson, C. R.; Tanabe, A.; Golden, S. S.; Johnson, C. H. & Kondo, T. (1998). Expression of a gene cluster *kaiABC* as a circadian feedback process in cyanobacteria. *Science*, Vol. 281, No. 5382, (Sep 1998), 1519-1523, ISSN 0036-8075

Johnson, C. H.; Elliott, J.; Foster, R.; Honma, K-I. & Kronauer, R. (2004). Fundamental properties of circadian rhythms, In: *Chronobiology: Biological Timekeeping*, Dunlap, J. C.; Loros, J. J. & DeCoursey, P. J. (Ed.), pp. 66-105, Sinauer Associates, Inc. Publishers, ISBN 0-87893-149-X, Sunderland

Kuang, Y. (1993). Delay Differential Equations, with Applications in Population Dynamics. In: *Mathematics in Science and Eng.*, Vol. 191, Ames, W. F., (Ed.), pp. 400, Academic Press, ISBN 0-12-427610-5, San Diego

Li, J.; Xu, N. S. & Su, W. W. (2003). Online estimation of stirred-tank microalgal photobioreactor cultures based on dissolved oxygen measurement, *Biochemical Engineering Journal*, Vol. 14, No. 1, (April 2003), 51-65, ISSN 1369-703X

Minorsky, N. (1962). Nonlinear Oscillations, Van Nostrand Company, Inc., ISBN 0-442-05408-4, Princeton, New Jersey

Miyoshi, F.; Nakayama, Y.; Kaizu, K.; Iwasaki, H. & Tomita M. (2007). A Mathematical Model for the Kai-Protein-Based Chemical Oscillator and Clock Gene Expression Rhythms in Cyanobacteria, *Journal of Biological Rhythms*, Vol. 22, No. 1, (Feb 2007), 69-80, ISSN 0748-7304

Mori, T.; Williams, D. R.; Byrne, M. O.; Qin, X.; Egli, M.; McHaourab, H. S.; Stewart, P. L. & Johnson, C. H. (2007). Elucidating the ticking of an *in vitro* circadian clockwork. *PLoS Biology*, Vol. 5, No. 4, (March 2007), e93, ISSN 1544-9173, doi:10.1371/journal.pbio.0050093

Nedbal, L.; Trtílek, M.; Červený, J.; Komárek, O. & Pakrasi H. B. (2008). A Photobioreactor System for Precision Cultivation of Photoautotrophic Microorganisms and for High-Content Analysis of Suspension Dynamics, *Biotechnology and Bioengineering*, Vol. 100, No. 5, (Aug 2008), 902-910, ISSN 0006-3592

Pavlidis, T. (1973). *Biological Oscillators: Their Mathematical Analysis*, Academic Press, ISBN 0-12-547350-8, New York

Rust, M. J.; Markson, J. S.; Lane, W. S.; Fisher, D. S. & O'Shea, E. K. (2007). Ordered phosphorylation governs oscillation of a three-protein circadian clock. *Science*, Vol. 318, No. 5851, 809-812, ISSN 0036-8075

van Zon, J. S.; Lubensky, D. K.; Altena, P. R. H. & ten Wolde P. R (2007). An allosteric model of circadian KaiC phosphorylation. *Proceedings of the National Academy of Sciences of the United States of America*, Vol. 104, No. 18, (April 2007), 7420-7425, ISSN 0027-8424

Wever, R. (1987). Mathematical Models of Circadian One- and Multi-Oscillator Systems, In: *Some Mathematical Questions in Biology: Circadian Rhythms,* Carpenter, G. A., (Ed.), pp. 205-265, Lectures on Mathematics in the Life Sciences, Vol. 19, American Mathematical Society, ISBN 0-8218-1169-X, Providence

Winfree, A. T. (1970). Integrated View Resetting a Circadian Clock, *Journal of Theoretical Biology,* Vol. 28, No. 3, (Sept 1970), 327-335, ISSN 0022-5193

8

Study of factors affecting taper joint failures in modular hip implant using finite element modelling

Kassim Abdullah
Department of Mechanical Engineering, International Islamic University Malaysia
Malaysia

1. Introduction

The replacement of the natural hip with artificial components is a well established procedure in orthopaedic medicine to alleviate pain from the diseased joint. The total hip replacement (THR) consists of a femoral component or stem and an acetabular cup. These are made as either one piece or modular designs. Modular femoral components have become popular among surgeons because neck length and offset can be adjusted intra-operatively, providing increased versatility without any need for a large inventory. In addition, modular heads allow for mixed alloy systems such as the combination of a titanium alloy stem with a cobalt-chromium or ceramic head.

Apart from the neck/head connection, there are femoral stem designs with extra areas of modularity. Examples of these prostheses are the S-ROM (Joint Medical Products, Stanford, Connecticut), the Infinity (Dow Corning Wright, Memphis, Tennessee), the RHMS (Smith-Nephew Richards, Memphis, Tennessee), and PROFEMUR Hip System (Wright Cremascoli Ortho SA, France).

A major drawback for all modular orthopaedic devices is that each modular component interface becomes a potential site for corrosion, wear, fretting and fatigue of mating surfaces (Collier et al., 1992; Manley & Serekian 1994; Hallab & Jacobs, 2003; Goldberg & Gilbert, 2003; Hallab et al., 2004; Gilbert et al., 2009; Rodrigues et al., 2009). The products of these interface processes are believed to cause tissue reactions that lead to implant loosening and subsequent failure of the arthroplasty (Amstutz et al., 1992; Harris, 1994; Kraft et al., 2001; Goldberg et al., 2002).

Thus, to make implant designs successful in clinical applications, these concerns need to be adequately addressed during the design stage of the prosthesis in conjunction with the implant strength and integrity of the implant-host bone system.

Types of failures often encountered in modular hip implants are dissociation, corrosion, wear; fretting and fatigue of mating metal surfaces (Goldberg et al., 2002, Sporer et al., 2006; Rodrigues et al., 2009). There are varieties of design and material factors that may influence the failure of specific components. The most significant of these is fretting because is almost impossible to prevent and in many cases may lead to other form of failures.

Fretting is defined as a wear mechanism that occurs at low amplitude, oscillating, sliding movement between two mechanically joined parts under load. There are varying descriptions of the magnitude of the motion associated with fretting, but it is generally defined as ranging from few to 50 μm (Mutoh, 1995). Given the magnitude of loading, all modular junctions of total hip prostheses can be susceptible to fretting wear. Other failures associated with fretting are fretting corrosion and fretting fatigue.

Major concerns of fretting relate to the modular junctions with metal to metal contact surfaces. Even though fretting and associated problems of orthopaedic implants were recognized since late in 1960s and in 1970s (Cohen & Lunderbaum, 1968; Gruen & Amstutz, 1975), the concern is ever increasing because orthopaedic surgeons and implant companies are interested in implants with more areas of modularity and actually produce different designs such as those mentioned above. Because these implants pose more mechanical joints, the possibility of fretting damage increases markedly -- especially in titanium alloy materials. Notable examples of fretting damage are those described by Hallab & Jacobs (2003) and Bobyn et al. (1993).

Among the factors that promote fretting are the design characteristics of modular hip implants such as neck diameter, neck length and fabrication tolerances of the joined parts are particularly important. Looser manufacturing tolerances lead to smaller contact area, higher stress concentration, and higher interfacial motion. All are key factors in developing fretting wear. (Goldberg & Gilbert, 2003; Fessler & Fricker, 1989). Similar studies using FEA have been reported (Shareef & Levine, 1996; Kurtz et al., 2001).

In this study, a generic modular-neck femoral stem design was assessed for relative motion at the Morse taper junction. Non-linear finite element analysis (FEA) was used. The research was carried out with the objective to study the effect of different fits of the Morse cone and surface conditions on the extent of the relative micromotion at the mating taper interfaces.

2. Materials and Method

A three dimensional (3-D) model of a generic hip stem system was created and analysed using a commercially available finite element (FE) software package: ANSYS software. The model was developed to simulate a modular hip implant system which consisted of a neck, part of the stem, and the interface between the two. Node to node contact elements were used to model the interface between two parts. These are non-linear elements; therefore, the finite element problem required a non-linear analysis. The nonlinearity of the model was based on the contact aspect only. The model was made to represent a hip stem of simple shape that could be manufactured in a good quality machine shop.

2.1 Finite element model generation

The outline of the stem was developed using keypoints and lines based on the dimensions of the PCA No. 5 hip prosthesis, but was simplified by leaving out the rounded corners and slight curvatures. As these simplified surfaces were relatively far away form the modular interface, the simplification would not affect the results. This also facilitated model changes during the analysis.

The model was meshed using all hexahedral (brick) volume structural element (SOLID45). A fine mesh was used around the tapered hole at the proximal end of the stem and a coarser mesh was used for regions distant from the hole and for the distal section of the stem.

Constraint equations were used to tie together the finer proximal and coarser distal mesh regions of the stem as indicated in Figure 1 that shows the final FE mesh used in analyses. The techniques that were employed to determine the extent of mesh refinement in the present work was to perform initial analysis with an assumed "reasonable" mesh. Then, the problem was re-analysed using finer mesh in critical regions, and the two solutions were compared. This process was repeated until the optimum mesh was obtained. A very fine mesh would have improved the results further but could take longer to run than it was feasible. The choice of the optimum mesh was based on both accuracy and solution run time. Further validation of results of this model was performed using experimental stress analysis as indicated in Figure 2.

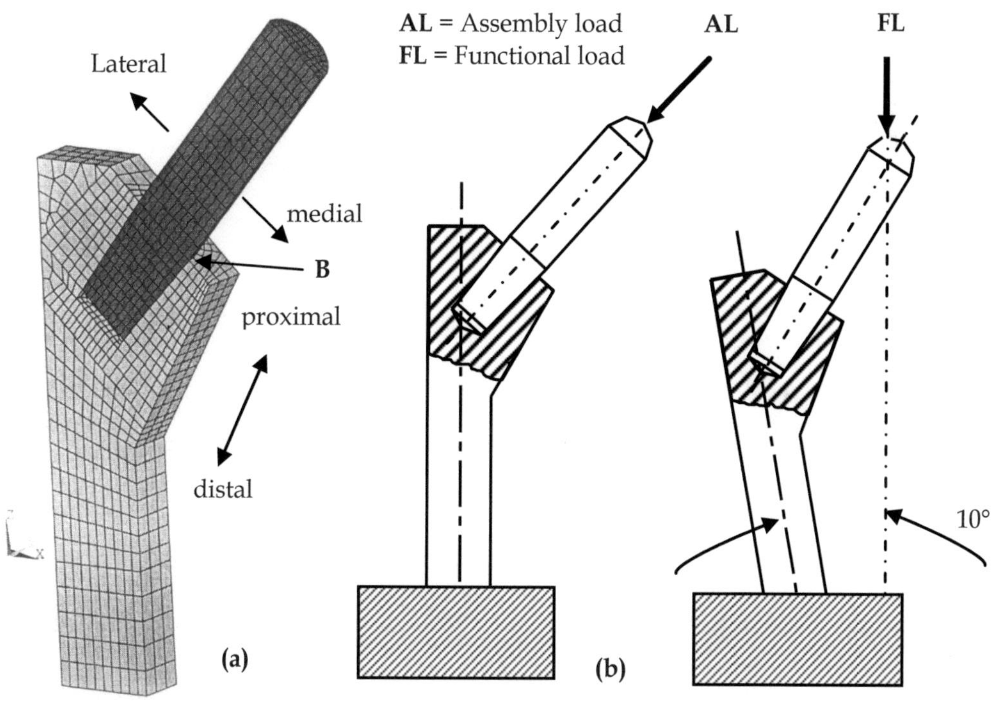

Fig. 1. **(a)** Meshed stem and neck. Only one half of the stem was modeled using symmetry constraints along the sagittal plane that divides the stem into two halves.
(b) Model alignment with respect to load. This arrangement was used for both FEA and experimental stress analysis.

2.2 Neck-stem contact definition

To simulate the neck-stem interface, the 3D node-to-node contact elements (CONTAC52) were used. These elements were used to represent two surfaces which could maintain or break physical contact and could slide relative to each other.

For successful contact problem, several contact element properties and options needed to be carefully selected. These properties include geometric input data, normal stiffness (KN), sticking stiffness (KS) and coefficient of friction. Geometric input is controlled by the mesh of contacting bodies. User defined options include specifying the type of friction model (elastic or rigid Coulomb fiction) and the contact time prediction control. In the determination of KN and KS, guidelines in the ANSYS reference manuals were followed so that the risk of numerical difficulties or slow convergence during the solution phase of the analysis could be minimized. Normal stiffness, KN, was determined based upon the stiffness of the surfaces in contact. KN had to be large enough that it could, reasonably, restrain the model from over-penetration, yet it had to be not so large that it could cause ill-conditioning of the stiffness matrix.

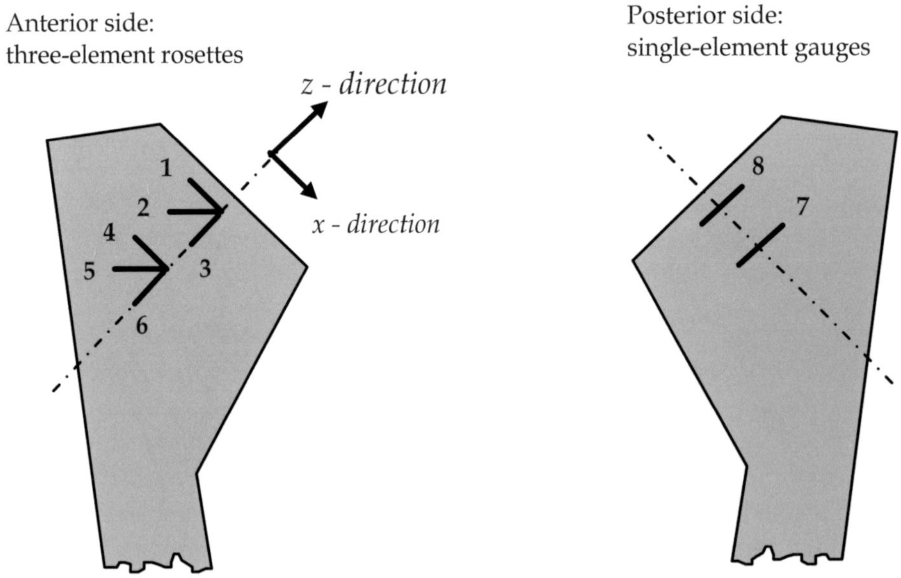

Fig. 2. Strain gauges installation. Two 3-element 45° staked rosettes and two single elements gauges were used. Numbers 1 to 8 represent gauge elements. Gauge elements 1, 4, 7, and 8 are aligned along the direction of principal stresses during the assemble loading.

Similarly, a suitable value for KS which would avoid numerical instability or excessive run times had to be determined. The default setting in ANSYS is KS = KN. Lower values reduce the run time. Value used were KN = 100*E and KS = 0.01*KN; after being tried and found to reduce the run time without affecting the stress and micromotion results. Elastic Coulomb friction was used because practical fretting couples exhibit dual micromotion regimes, normally referred to as elastic regime and gross slip regime (Zhou and Vicent, 1995; Mohrbacher et al., 1995). The values for the coefficient friction (μ) used in various analyses models were based on expermental measurements reported by Fessler and Fricker (1989) and the data from Budinski (1991).

2.3 Angular mismatch

Three model cases were developed to simulate three possible scenarios which could be realised when assembling stem and neck. The three cases defined in Figure 3 are:

i) No or zero angular mismatch
ii) Positive angular mismatch
iii) Negative angular mismatch

Tolerances of -2 to +2 minutes for the male taper were used, thus producing a maximum angular interference and clearance of 2 minutes. These tolerances are within the limits obtained by manufacturers. Design specifications for a particular manufacturer were 6° ±2 min. for female tapers and 5° 58' ±1 min. for male tapers. (Naesguthe, 1997).

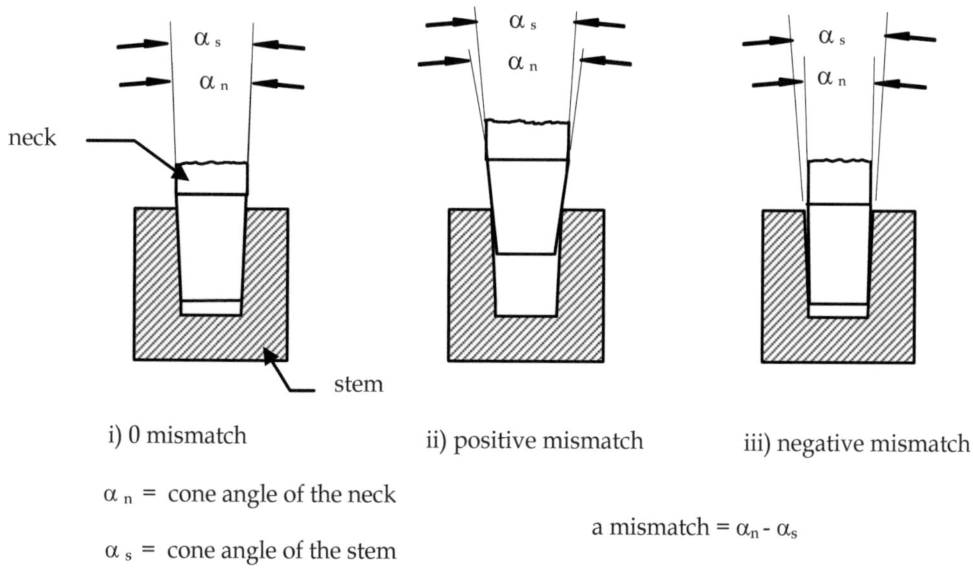

Fig. 3. Definition of mismatch cases used in FE analysis. Angular mismatch between the neck and the stem was achieved by changing cone angle of the neck by two minutes.

2.4 Boundary conditions and loading

Boundary conditions for finite element analysis and load application were set as in the experiment to determine the endurance properties of femoral stem of hip prostheses according to the ISO standard (ISO 7206-4: 1989 (E)). The angle between the load line and anatomical axis of the femur was set to be 10° when viewed perpendicular to the plane that includes the stem and the neck (Figure 1). Boundary conditions were established such that the finite element nodes at the bottom of the stem were constrained in all degrees of freedom (d.o.f). Only one half of the stem was modelled using symmetry constraints along the plane that divides the stem into two halves, (see Figure 1). The half-stem model ignored out-of-plane loads but was sufficient and was able to satisfy the purpose of the analysis.

Model loading was applied in six steps:
Step 1: A load was applied at the top and along the axis of the neck, as shown diagrammatically in Figure 1(b). This was termed an "assembly load"; it was applied to simulate the force a surgeon would use when inserting the neck into the stem hole during the operation.
Step 2: The assembly load was removed.
Step 3: A load was applied at the same point as in Step 1, but at an angle of 10° from longitudinal axis of the stem, as shown in Figure 1(b). This was termed a "functional load"; it was applied to simulate the force that would be applied to the implant during walking.
Step 4: The functional load was removed.
Step 5: The functional load was re-applied.
Step 6: The functional load was removed.

Five 'Load schemes' code-named 'First', 'Second', 'Third', 'Fourth' and 'Fifth' were used in various analyses. The magnitudes of the assembly and functional loads used in these 'Load schemes' are shown in Table I. The assembly loads were used in FE models to represent three possible cases of moderate, high and no tapping loads, respectively. The function loads were used to represent possible physiological loads as reported in the literature (Bergmann, et al. 1993; Viceconti et al., 1996)

Designation of the loading scheme	**Magnitude of the Assembly load (N)**	**Magnitude of the Functional load (N)**
First	3114	5500 (7.5 x BW*)
Second	5500	3114 (4 x BW)
Third	5500	2000 (3 x BW)
Fourth	3114	2000
Fifth	0	2000

*BW = Body weight of average person of 75 kg.

Table 1. Assembly and Functional loads used in FE analysis

3. Results and Discussion

3.1 Validation Results

Experimental stress analysis was performed for the purpose of validating FE results. It was sufficient to measure stresses only instead of both stress and micromotion because, theoretically, in finite element analysis, stresses are calculated from the primary displacement values. For instance, the press-fit stresses resulting from the application of assembly load were determined from the amount of interference at the neck-stem interface which in turn is determined from how much the neck moved relative to the stem. Therefore, if the stresses were proved valid, so would be the displacements from which the stresses were calculated. In this case, no relative micromotion was measured experimentally. Graphs that compare experimental with numerical results of the FE model show a good agreement on the two sets of results. These are shown in Figure 4 and 5 for stress prediction during assembly and functional loading, respectively. The differences between stress values obtained from strain gauges and stress values predicted by FE model were within 10% which is considered acceptable.

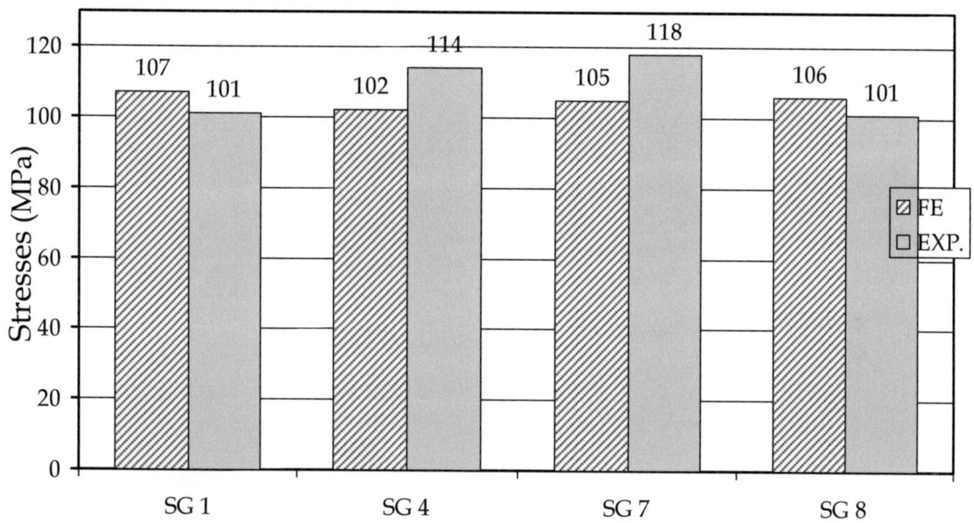

Fig. 4. Experimental and numerical stress values under assebly loading showing readings of gauges 1, 4, 7 and 8. The induced stresses at these gauge locations were mainly unidirectional (along x- direction).

3.2 Micromotion results in three angular mismatch cases

Figure 6 shows the relative micromotion of the First load scheme at a medio-proximal point (B) of the neck-stem interface for three mismatch cases. The selected point was characterised with the highest micromotion during the load cycle as shown in Figure 7. It was also a point of highest stress during the functional load. In this regard, the selected point was critical in terms of potential surface failure due to fretting and other surface degradation mechanisms.

At any particular instant during the loading of the implant system, the relative micromotion at the stem-neck interface was a result of a free body displacement of the neck or an elastic deformation of the neck and the stem, or the combination of the two. In all cases, application of the assembly load caused a non-recoverable relative micromotion between the neck and stem. This micromotion is termed non-recoverable because upon the removal of the assembly load, the neck did not move back to its initial position.

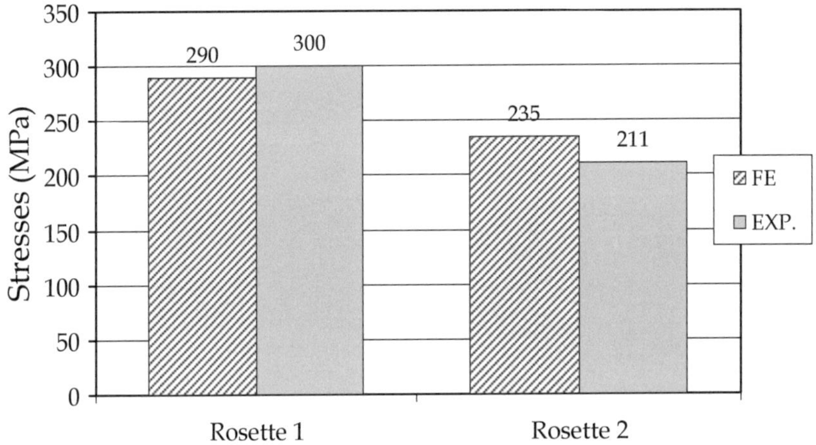

Fig. 5. Experimental and numerical stress values under functional loading. Since the stress state was multi-axial, the experimental results plotted are those from the rosettes only.

The interfacial micromotion observed during the application of the functional load was mainly due to elastic deformation of the parts. This observation can be justified from the fact that in models that had the assembly load of 5500 N, the micromotion was fully reversed upon the removal of the load (Figure 8).

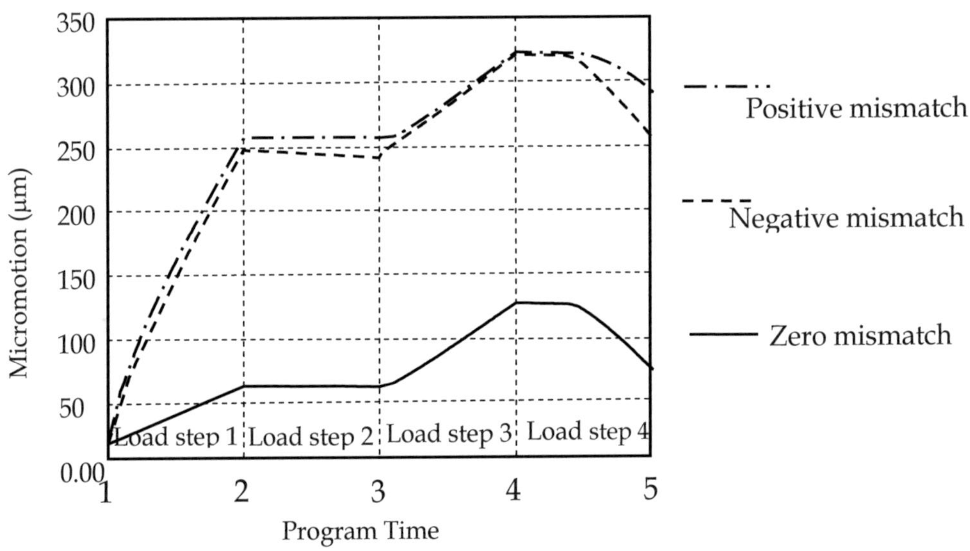

Fig. 6. Relative micromotion at the neck-stem interface for three mismatch cases at proximal medial point which experience highest relative motion.

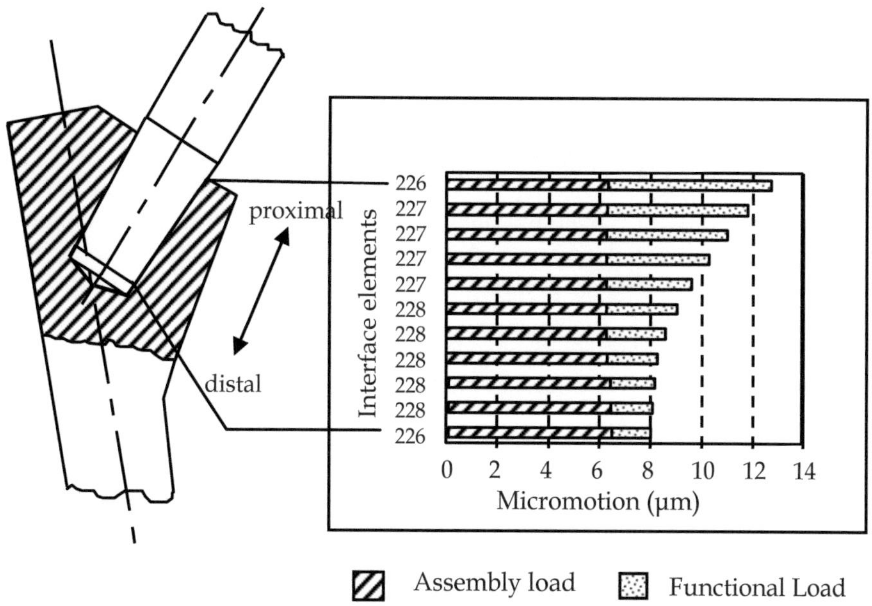

Fig. 7. Variation of micromotion along the contact area. Highest micromotion is observed at point B indicated in Figure 1 (a).

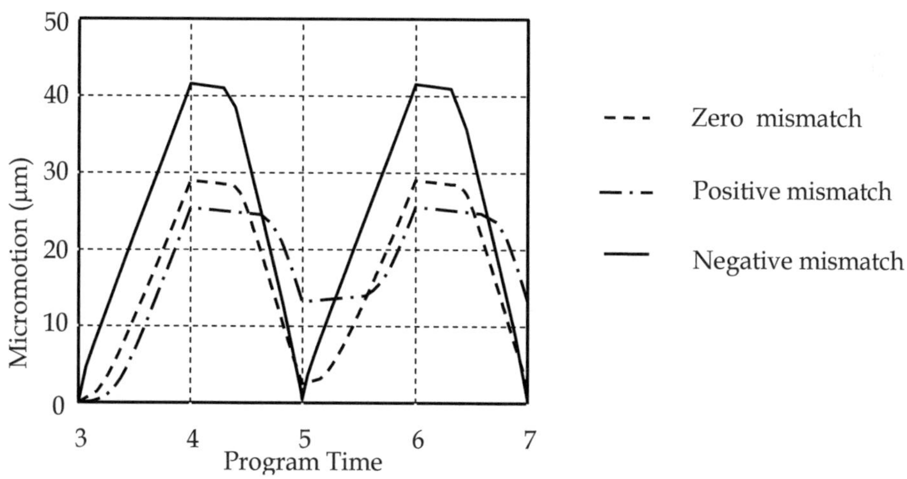

Fig. 8. Relative interface micromtion during two functional load cycles for three mismatch cases - Second load scheme (load steps 3 to 6).

For the First load scheme, the application of the functional load resulted in the magnitudes of relative micromotion of 65 µm, 70 µm and 80 µm in zero, positive and negative mismatch cases, respectively. When the functional load was removed, the micromotion in zero, positive and negative mismatch cases reversed to 52 µm, 32 µm and 65 µm. The subsequent cycles of functional loading and unloading resulted in repeated patterns of relative micromotion. This is clearly demonstrated in Figure 8 for micromotion variation curves for the Second loading scheme in two functional load cycles.

3.3 Results of other analysis models

Two models with zero angular mismatches were used to study the effect of the coefficient of friction and the magnitude of assembly load on variation of relative micromotion at the neck/stem mating surfaces. Figure 9 and 10, respectively, show the effects of coefficient of friction and assembly load on the neck-stem interface micromotion. The change of coefficient of friction had the greater effect on the reversible micromotion that occurred during the functional load cycle as shown in Figure 10. The increase in coefficient of friction from $\mu = 0.2$ to $\mu = 0.5$ had reduced the reversible micromotion from 50 μm to about 30 μm. Also, the magnitude of the assembly load affected the amount of micromotion caused by the subsequent functional load. Low assembly load resulted in highest micromotion as shown in Figure 10.

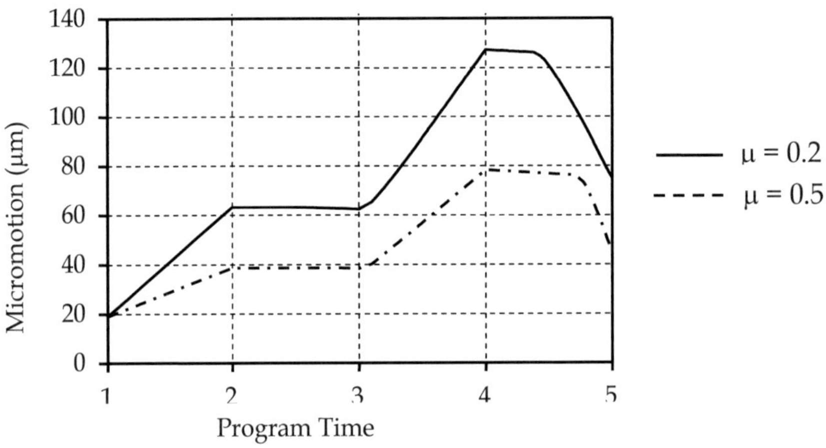

Fig. 9. Effect of coefficient of friction on the interface micromotion under assembly and functional load (load steps 1 to 4).

3.4 Model behaviour during the assembly load

The results of this study show that the magnitudes of the relative one time micromotion and reversible micromotion due to functional load depended on factors such as the magnitude of assembly force, coefficient of friction and the amount of angular mismatch between the male and female tapers.

The assembly load is used to achieve initial stability of the modular connection. A high assembly load is desirable in producing enough taper lock to prevent the neck from having further rigid body movement during the functional loading. This finding is consistent with the experimental study by Mroczkowski et al. (2006).

An extreme case of high interference is when the conical parts are pre-assembled as a shrink fit. This may result in considerable decrease in interfacial relative micromotion. Published experimental and retrieval data have indicated the absence of fretting damage in such press-fit situations (Brown et al., 1995; Mroczkowski et al., 2006).

Modular surfaces in real components are more complicated than they could practically be represented in FE models. Surface imperfections in real components will cause local yielding which will reduce the amount of mismatch when modular parts are assembled (Naesguthe, 1998). Material nonlinearity due to localized plastic deformation of surfaces was not included in the FE model. Therefore, the overall numerical micromotion predictions were likely to be higher than the values that would be obtained in real components.

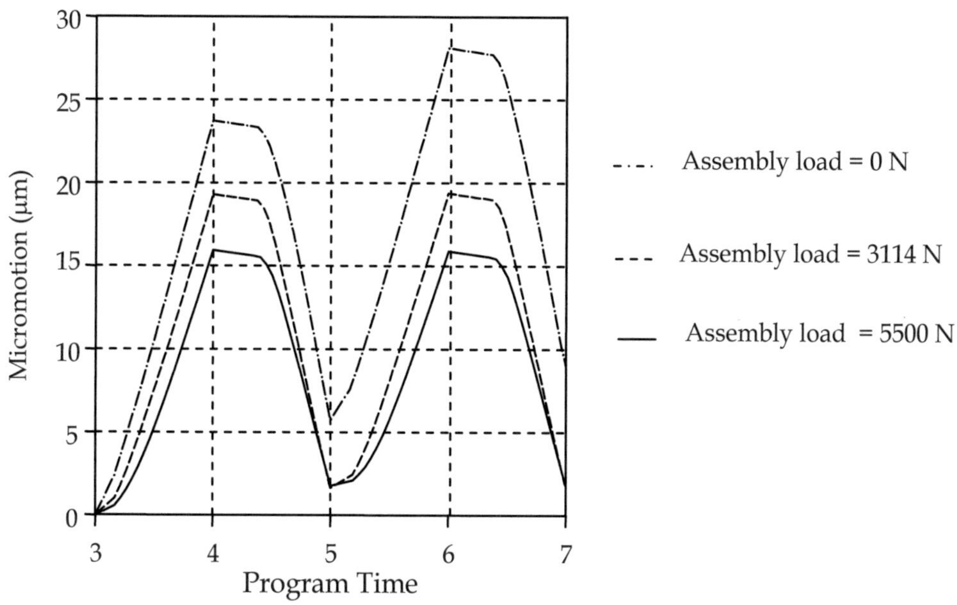

Fig. 10. Effect of assembly load on micromtion due to functional load. Third, Fourth and Fifth load schemes (load steps 3 to 6).

3.5 Effects of coefficient of friction

Maximizing the value of μ is beneficial in reducing conditions that promote fretting and fretting fatigue. The coefficient of friction has significant importance in actual performance of modular junction. Since, the interface micromotion is influenced by the load applied to the connected components of the modular hip stem; high friction surface is desirable to minimize interfacial relative motion.

3.6 Effects of angular mismatch

Zero angular mismatch is not the best and yields more micromotion. In determining the optimum angular tolerances, the individual case has to be judged based on its loading arrangement. For the modular neck hip prosthesis used in the present work, a positive mismatch is the optimum choice. The degree of mismatch should be limited to keep allowable stresses within the safe limits below the fatigue strength of the implant material.

Fatigue, fretting and corrosion: Model results have shown that application of a functional load results in relative interface micromotion which varies in magnitudes according to the nature of the modular connection, the surface properties, and the magnitude of both the assembly and functional load. The key parameter to fretting is slip amplitude which is defined as the peak-to-peak amplitude of the relative reversible micro-movement of the surfaces (Mohrbacher et al., 1995; Waterhouse, 1992).

In normal and fast walking, the load on the implant ranges from about 3 to 4 times body weight (Bergmann, et al., 1993). Even if the stress level on the component at these loads is lower than the failure values, the existence of relative micromotion at the modular interface may put the implant at a risk of fretting and fretting fatigue. Microscopic relative movement between mating surfaces of levels, as low as 0.125 μm or 3 μm, has been found sufficient to produce fretting debris (Mohrbacher et al., 1995; Waterhouse, 1992). The lowest slip range predicted in our models is higher than the above values. Fretting is therefore inevitable under predicted levels of reversible micromotion. Furthermore, in a surface micromotion characterised with sticking and sliding regimes, cyclic contact stresses can cause the formation of microcracks (Zhou & Vincent, 1997), which can lower the fatigue limit of the component by about 50% (Broszeit et al., 1985).

As shown in Figure 7 highest sliding micromotion occurs at medio-proximal location of the stem. This observation is consistent with findings reported by Viceconti et al. (1998). They observed repetitive parallel scars with an average length of 30-45 μm in specimens that were loaded at 300-3300 N. Our micromotion prediction at a functional load of 0-3114 N ranged between 13-41 μm.

Since the micromotion is inevitable, the only option available to minimize the fretting damage is to apply suitable fretting palliatives, as suggested by Beard (1988), that will reduce micromotion between mating surfaces. Even if the decrease of micromotion is apparently small, it can still have substantial effect in reducing fretting. Experimental data suggest that the specific wear rate (volume lost per unit load per unit sliding distance) varies as a function of the slip amplitude raised to the power of 2 to 4 (Beard, 1988).

4. Conclusion

A three dimensional, non-linear finite element model was used to analyse relative micromotion of the modular hip implant at the junction between the neck and the stem. Functional, design, surface and manufacturing features that can affect micromotion in the modular junction of hip implant were studied. From the results and discussions that followed, the conclusions are:

- A high assembly load reduces the magnitude of stress and micromotion fluctuations during ambulation, predicting lower fretting and fretting fatigue damage, hence, improved service life. Therefore, during operation, orthopaedic surgeons should aim at an assembly load of 6000 N or higher. The force to be used should be higher than the largest anticipated ambulatory load

- High friction at the modular interface with the coefficients of friction well above 0.5 up to complete binding between the surfaces is desirable in order to reduce the amount of relative micromotion at the modular mating surfcaes.
- In the modular neck stem, a positive mismatch is the best. This means a cone angle of the neck 2 minutes above the female taper on the stem. Our model showed low relative interfacial micromotion in the stem-neck connection with positive angular interference. It is therefore assumed that fretting damage of the modular interfaces can be minimized by a proper control of manufacturing angular tolerances of the mating parts.

5. References

Amstutz, HC.; Campbell, P.; Kossovsky, N. & Clarke, IC. (1992). Mechanism and clinical significance of wear debris induced osteolysis. *Clinical Orthopaedics and Related Research.* 276:7-18.

Beard, J. (1988). The avoidance of fretting, *Materials and Design*, 9 (4), 1988, 220-227.

Bergmann, G.; Graichen, F. & Rohlman, A. (1993) Hip joint loading during walking and running, measured in two patients. *Journal of Biomechanics*, 26, 969-990.

Bobyn, J., Dujovne; A. Krygier, J. & Young, D. (1993). Surface analysis of the taper junctions of retrieved and in vitro tested modular hip prostheses. In: *Biological Materials and Mechanical Considerations of Joint Replacement*, B.F. Morrey (ed.), 287-301, Raven Press ltd., New York.

Broszeit, E.; Kloos, K. & Shweighofer, B. (1985). The fretting fatigue behaviour of titanium alloy Ti 6Al 4V. In: *Titanium: Science and Technology*, 21-71, Deutsche Gesellschaft fur Metallkunde e.V, FRG.

Brown, S.; Flemming, C.; Kawalec, J.; Placko, H.; Vassaux, C.; Merritt, K., Payer; J. & Kraay, M. (1995). Fretting corrosion accelerated crevice corrosion of modular hip tapers, *Journal of Applied Biomaterials*, 6, 19-26.

Budinski, KC. (1991). Tribological properties of titanium alloys, *Wear*, 151, 203-217.

Cohen, J. & Lunderbaum, B. (1968). Fretting corrosion in orthopaedic implants, *Clinical Orthopaedics and Related Research*, 61, 167-175.

Collier, J.P.; Michael, D.E.; Mayor, B.; Jensen, R.E.; Surprenant, V.A., Surprenant, H.P., McNamara, J.L.; & Belec, L. (1992). Mechanism of failure of modular prosthesis. *Clinical Orthopaedics and Related Research*, 285, 129-139.

Fessler, H. & Fricker, D. (1989). A study of stresses in alumina universal heads of femoral prostheses, *Proceedings of the Institution for Mechanical Engineers. Part H: Journal of Engineering in Medicine*, 203, 15-34.

Gilbert, J; Mehta, M. & Pinder, B. (2009). Fretting crevice corrosion of stainless steel stem-CoCr femoral head connections: comparisons of materials, initial moisture, and offset length, *Journal Of Biomedical Materials Research. Part B, Applied Biomaterials*, Jan; Vol. 88 (1), 162-173.

Goldberg, J., Gilbert, J., Jacobs, J., Bauer, T., Paprosky, W. & Leurgans, S. (2002). A multicenter retrieval study of the taper interfaces of modular hip prostheses. *Clinical Orthopaedics and Related Research*, 401, 149–161

Goldberg, J. & Gilbert, J. (2003). In vitro corrosion testing of modular hip tapers. *Journal of Biomedical Materials Research: Part B, Appl Biomaterials*, 64B, 78–93.

Gruen, T & Amstutz, H. (1975). A failed vitallium/stainless steel total hip replacement: A case report with histological and metallurgical examination, *Journal of Biomedical Materials Research*, 9, 465-475.

Hallab, N. & Jacobs, J. (2003). Orthopedic implant fretting corrosion, *Corrosion Review*, 21(2-3), 183–213.

Hallab, N.; Messina, C.; Skipor, A. & Jacobs, J. (2004). Differences in the fretting corrosion of metal-metal and ceramic-metal modular junctions of total hip replacements, *Journal Of Orthopaedic Research*, Mar; Vol. 22 (2), 250-259.

Harris, WH. (1994). Osteolysis and particulate disease in hip replacement. *Acta Orthop Scand.* 65:113-123.

Kraft, C., Burian, B., Diedrich, O. & Wimmer, M. (2001). Implications of orthopedic fretting corrosion particles on skeletal muscle microcirculation, *Journal of Materials Science: Materials in Medicine*, 12, 1057–1062.

Kurtz, S. Srivastay, S., Dwyer, K., Ochoa, J. & Brown, S. (2001). Analysis of the stem-sleeve interface in a modular titanium alloy femoral component for total hip replacement, *Key Engineering Materials*, 198-199, 41-68.

Manley, MT. & Serekian, P. (1994). Wear debris; An environmental issue in total joint replacement. *Clinical Orthopaedics and Related Research*. 298:137-146.

Mohrbacher, H., Celis, J., & Roos, J. (1995). Laboratory testing of displacement and load induced fretting, *Tribology International*, 28 (5), 269-278.

Mroczkowski, M.; Hertzler, J.; Humphrey, M.; Johnson, T. & Blanchard, C. (2006). Effect of impact assembly on the fretting corrosion of modular hip tapers, *Journal Of Orthopaedic Research*, Feb; Vol. 24 (2), 271-279.

Mutoh, Y. (1995). Mechanisms of fretting fatigue, *JSME International Journal*, 38 (4), 405-415.

Naesguthe, E.A. (1998). Wear and corrosion analysis of modular hip implants: The ceramic head-metallic neck interface, *Ph.D thesis* , Queen's University, Canada

Rodrigues, C.; Urban, M.; Jacobs, J. & Gilbert, L. (2009). In vivo severe corrosion and hydrogen embrittlement of retrieved modular body titanium alloy hip-implants, *Journal Of Biomedical Materials Research. Part B, Applied Biomaterials*, Jan; Vol. 88 (1),, 206-219.

Shareef, N. & Levine, D. (1996). Effect of manufacturing tolerances on the micromotion at the Morse taper interface in modular hip implants using the finite element technique, *Biomaterials*, 17(6), 623-630.

Sporer, S.; DellaValle, C.; Jacobs, J. & Wimmer, M. (2006). A case of disassociation of a modular femoral neck trunion after total hip arthroplasty, *Journal Of Arthroplasty*, Sep; Vol. 21 (6), 918-921.

Viceconti, M.; Ruggeri, O.; Toni, A. & Giunti, A. (1996). Design related fretting wear in modular neck hip prosthesis, *Journal of Biomedical Materials Research*, 30, 181-186.

Viceconti, M.; Massimilia, B.; Stefano, S. & Toni, A. (1998). Fretting wear in a modular neck hip prosthesis, *Journal of Biomedical Materials Research*, 35, 207-216.

Waterhouse, R.B. (1992). Fretting fatigue, *International Materials Reviews*, 37, 77-97.

Zhou, Z. & Vincent, L. (1995). Mixed fretting regime, *Wear*, 181-183, 531-536.

Zhou, Z. & Vincent, L. (1997). Cracking induced by fretting of aluminium alloys, *Journal of Tribology*, 119, 36-42.

9

A MULTI AGENT SYSTEM MODELLING AN INTELLIGENT TRANSPORT SYSTEM

Vincenzo Di Lecce[1*], Alberto Amato[1], Domenico Soldo[2], Antonella Giove[1]
[1]Politecnico di Bari – DIASS
[2]myHermes S.r.l
Italy

1. Introduction

Nowadays, the globalization is one of the most significant phenomena of contemporary life. There are many debates about the real meaning of the globalization, its roots, effects and future. Among the most important aspects of the globalization is surely the global transportation system. In this framework it is clear how the availability of an advanced integrated transportation system, for moving goods and people as quickly as possible all around the world, is a crucial requirement that cannot be ignored in any case, but actually accomplished in the best way possible. In (Frank and Engelke, 2000) there is a remarkable work of review highlighting the steady interaction between transportation systems and human activities and how the former ones have a strong impact on the organization of the built environment. These ideas give explanation for the increasing interest that the scientific community has shown in the field of the transportation systems.

The recent improvements in ICT allow for the implementation of novel and pervasive systems. Indeed, in these days a wide spread of the Global Position System (GPS) and communication technologies (e.g. GSM, GPRS and UMTS network) has led to the implementation of interesting Intelligent Transportation System (ITS). These systems try to improve the optimization of many transportation system aspects such as vehicles, loads, routes and (overall) safety just by using these new technologies.

Route planning is an optimization problem that has been studied extensively in the past decades. Dijkstra's algorithm (Dijkstra, 1959) is the most well-known algorithm for determining the shortest path from one location to all other locations in a road network. Moreover it is noteworthy to mention other significant shortest path algorithms e, such as the Bellman-Ford algorithm (Bellman, 1958; Ford Jr. and Fulkerson, 1962), the D'Esopo-Pape algorithm (Pape, 1974), etc. An overview in this regard is given by (Bertsekas, 1998).

One of the biggest problems of these algorithms is the huge dimension of the solution space. This fact led the researchers to use parallel computing (Delle Donne et al., 1995) and/or to propose new heuristic methods often based on artificial intelligence techniques (Suzuki et al., 1995; Pellazar, 1998).

---

* corresponding author

An interesting technique of artificial intelligence that is having a large number of practical applications in the last years is the intelligent agent technology. In (Di Lecce et al., 2004) a multi-agent system was used in an environmental monitoring system, while in (Amato et al., 2007) and (Di Lecce et al., 2008.a) it was used in databases integration.

In literature there are also examples related to the application of this technology into complex decision support systems applied to traffic control (Danko and Jan, 2000; Fernandes and Oliveira, 1999). In (Danko and Jan, 2000) intelligent agents are used to build adaptive traffic control units that are seen as proactive upon changes (short- and long term) in traffic real-time. In (Fernandes and Oliveira, 1999) the characteristic of the agents' pro-activity is used to build a strategy for controlling traffic light systems.

Within the context of a research project financed by Apulia Region (Italy), the authors designed and developed a new ITS. This system, through advanced ICT technology aims at: planning transport services in order to calculate and avoid possible high risk situations; managing transportation in order to monitor and divert the movement of dangerous goods; supporting Emergency management by delivering all relevant information for the betterment in intervention of responsible forces. Route Planning is implemented to find the best route for each transport, by using specific algorithms that consider those areas to be protected, and nearby critical infrastructure and dangerous cargos.

The authors have modelled this ITS using the Multi Agent System (MAS) technology in order to reach all these objectives. According to the well known definition, a Multi Agent System (MAS) can be seen as an organization composed of autonomous agents and proactive agents that interact with each other to achieve common goals (Faulkner and Kolp, 2003). This technology has met with significant success in the Artificial Intelligent research community because the agent-based technology can be an interesting application for realizing new models able to support complex software systems. In a project based on distributed systems, software agents are typically designed to cooperate (with other agents or humans) in an intelligent way. That is why, in this work particular attention will be given to the communication languages used by the different intelligent agents of the structure.

Information referred to vehicle locations may be seen as the experience acquired from the system that, improving day by day, ensures the reduction of false alarm dispatches, control of transporters habits and traffic conditions on their usual routes.

For the automatic recognition of anomalous situations through intelligent analysis algorithms, the data about the movement of vehicles carrying materials, subject to specific rules, prove to be useful (Bond and Gasser, 1988). These algorithms allow for the implementation of an intelligent control system, capable of interpreting the information obtained in real time by vehicles carrying dangerous materials, and therefore correlating these data with the information within the intelligence base of the system (which evolves dynamically and autonomously) and recognizing then the alarm situations.

The aim of this chapter is to describe the proposed ITS highlighting some communication aspects of the decision support system used to define vehicle routes.

This chapter will start with a brief introduction about the ITS systems followed by an overview of the latest improvements in ITC allowing for their implementation. Then, the proposed system architecture will be described from a functional point of view. At this point the proposed agent based on decision support system to route planning is introduced. The communication acts among agents are analyzed from the language theory point of view. Then some experimental results will be described for highlighting some interesting aspects of the proposed system. Finally, the conclusions will close the chapter.

2. Technologic Improvements

The key technological elements of an ITS are: positioning system, communication channels and computing elements. In the latest years, various technologies implementing very reliable wireless communication channels also with high throughput were developed. Examples of such channels are GPRS, UMTS and EDGE technology.
As it is well known, the computing power grows according to the Moore's law. So today there are ever smaller and faster computation units.
In the latest years also the positioning systems have had interesting developments as the progresses, achieved by the Global Positioning System (GPS), shows. It consists of a constellation of continuously orbiting satellites run by the United States Department of Defence (DOD). Two levels of positioning accuracy are available: Standard Positioning Service (SPS) using the Coarse/Acquisition (C/A) code signals and Precise Positioning Service (PPS). PPS is encoded and not accessible to civilian users. SPS was intentionally degraded to obtain an accuracy of 100m (95% probability). This error source was eliminated after May 1, 2000 (Mosavi et al., 2004).
A GPS receiver antenna is used to detect signals from several of the DOD's NAVSTAR satellites at the same time. The receiver utilizes precise time and satellite position data, as well as other information in the transmitted signals, to calculate position coordinates. The time that the signal uses to travel from the satellite to the receiver is one of the essential values that the receiver must process. The variable atmospheric conditions, affecting how fast the signals travel, can generate small errors in the calculated coordinates. Under some conditions the receiver can get unclear signals from one or more satellites due to reflections of the same signals from water surfaces or buildings that are nearby (multipath). The most relevant elements influencing the GPS position accuracy are:

1. Satellite clock and position errors
2. Atmospheric delay of the transmitted satellite signals
3. Receiver noise and receiver clock errors
4. Multipath
5. Sky Satellite position relative to receiver

This latter element, satellite positions related to the receiver, refers to the satellites that a receiver is using to compute its position coordinates. Once or twice each day there is a short period of an hour or two when the only satellites, whose signals the receiver, can detect are in positions that do not allow for accurate coordinate determinations. The effect of this improper satellite positioning is to multiply the effects of the actual sources of error.
Several methods are known to improve the GPS position accuracy. Some methods use only a GPS receiver, while others use two or more receivers. An example of method based on a single GPS receiver is the averaging method. This method works averaging the latitudes and longitudes of computed GPS positions. This operation can reduce error and get better position accuracy. To reduce error by any great measure, positions must be computed at frequent intervals over a period of several hours and then averaged. It is difficult to predict exactly the amount of error reduction to be expected from averaging a certain number of positions over a given time period. This method is widely used when an accurate localization of a given fixed point is required, while it is not usable in dynamic conditions.

Various methods based on two or more GPS receivers are exploited in the differential correction in order to improve the position accuracy. Differential correction can remove most of the effects of Selective Availability (S/A) and other ordinary sources of error in GPS computed positions. In this method a reference station broadcasts corrections on common view satellites on a regular basis to the remote GPS receiver, which provides a corrected position output. A typical application of this method is the navigation guidance. On the other hand, any interruption of DGPS (Differential GPS) service will lead to the loss of navigation guidance, which can get into a vehicle accident, especially in the phase of precision approach and landing (Mosavi, 2005).
In agreement with a large number of experimental observations and the work in (He et al., 2005), and in (Di Lecce et al. 2008.b) the authors propose a method to improve the GPS position accuracy using a single receiver.

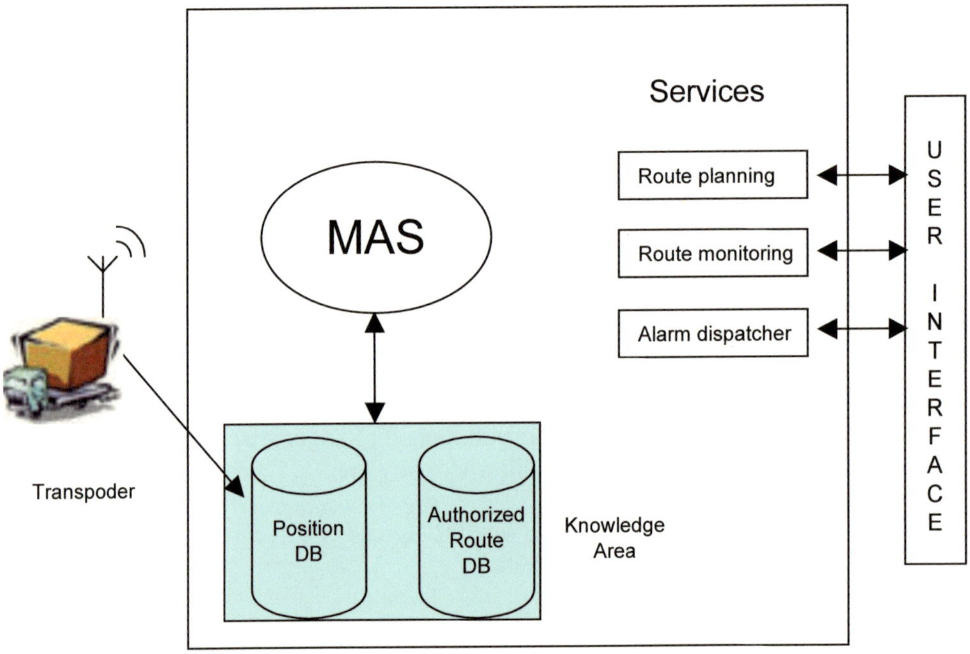

Fig. 1. A schematic overview of the proposed system

3. Proposed system

This paragraph deals with a comprehensive description of the whole proposed system for the management of hazardous material transport. Figure 1 shows a schematic overview of the described system. The goal of this system is: planning transport services in order to predict and prevent possible high risk situations; managing transportation in order to monitor and divert the movement of dangerous goods; supporting emergency management by providing all relevant information for the improvement in intervention of responsible forces, etc.
The implemented user interface is web based. It consists of two main sections:

1. transport manager: this section allows a transport manager to query the system in order to obtain an authorized route compliant with all the constraints imposed by the system (minimization of transport risk according to the law of this field).
2. monitoring interface: this section allows for monitoring the actual state of each vehicle involved into transportation.

All the vehicles involved in the transport are equipped with a transponder able to communicate its position and other data to a central system (DB positions in figure 1). The transponder uses the GPS technology for its localization and the GPRS as communication channel with the central server. The information sent by each transponder is acquired and catalogued by a computer system. These data become the knowledge base of the system that can be used to evaluate a large number of parameters (traffic conditions, mean time required for a route, etc.). These data are used to identify preferential routes and possible infringements of existing rules concerning this type of transport.

A fundamental component of the project regards an intelligent system for detecting infringements and distinguishing the alarm level of danger in order to simplify the development of institutional control tasks (often slowed down by false alarm dispatches).

The bodies in charge for the control of this transport modality are so informed in real time of any infringement occurring, thus obtaining more efficient operations.

Along the route, the system automatically provides the central server with data about the vehicle position and other parameters described further in the next sections. This information is used to:

- Check the actual vehicle route and travel condition, for security and statistical purposes and control operations performed by relevant authorities.
- Assess any possible suspicious behaviour such as: route changes, prolonged stops, unsafe load conditions or driving style, etc.
- Update a database about travelling times in the covered areas.
- Monitor the driver behaviour and the vehicle state.

4. Proposed route planning system and agents communication

In this section, the decision support system handling the route planning service implemented in the proposed system is described. Aim of this system is to find the route for a given transport that satisfies a big number of constraints such as: minimizing the hydro-geologic risk, minimizing the impact of the transport on the anthropic activities (i.e.: school, places with high density of human presence, etc.), minimizing the transport execution time, etc. The main characteristics of the proposed system are its scalability and its flexibility. The number of constraints satisfied by the proposed system as the number of handled transports are virtually unlimited. This result is due to the use of the multi agent system approach and the implemented negotiation algorithm.

Traditional systems, based on multi-objective functions optimization, have serious limits regarding the scalability both of the considered parameters and the number of vehicles involved into transport. The current technological advances in computing offer potential for deployment of agent-based negotiation systems. Negotiation can be seen as a search process where the participants are jointly searching for, in a multi-dimensional space, a single point at which they reach mutual agreement and meet their objectives. As shown in (Dospisil and

Kendall, 2000), the main approaches to design of negotiation strategies are: analytical (based on game theory), evolutionary (genetic algorithm) and intelligent agents' negotiation.
In this work the authors used the agent negotiation method due to its flexibility and scalability. One of the most relevant aspects of agents' negotiation is the inter-agent communication process. Agent communication acts are processes of paramount importance in designing MAS because the building block for intelligent interaction is knowledge sharing that includes both mutual understanding of knowledge and the communication of that knowledge. Agents communication has been widely investigated in literature and some standard agent communication languages (ACL) were proposed. Two interesting examples of such languages are:

1. KQML (Knowledge Query Manipulation Language) is a common framework via which agents could exchange knowledge. This language can be seen as composed of two modules:
    a. an "outer" module that defines the intended meaning of a message by using simple LISP-like format.
    b. A separate Knowledge Interchange Format (KIF) defining the content of messages using a first-order predicate logic. KIF is not considered part of the KQML standard.
2. the Agent Communication Language (ACL) defined by the Foundation for Intelligent Physical Agents (FIPA). Similarly to KQML, it defines an "outer" module for messages but it does not mandate any specific language for message content. The FIPA ACL defines a formal semantics in terms of a Semantic Language (SL) that is a quantified multi-modal logic.

An interesting contribute in the clear identification of the conditions bounding agent communication languages is to be found in (Wooldridge, 1998). Indeed, in that work the author investigates the possibility of defining an abstract formal framework to verify the semantics of agents communication languages. A framework of this type is useful because its implementation could address the problem of inter-operability of independent agents. The main problems that the author outlines in building such a framework are:

- the semantics of SL are expressed in the normal modal logic of Kripke semantics that are not connected with computational systems. In other words, given a generic program (written in any programming language) there is not a known way to characterize its states in terms of a SL formula (in this situation the SL are defined ungrounded).
- Computational complexity: the problem of verifying if an agent communication act is compliant with a given semantics can be reduced to a logical proof problem. This fact makes the complexity of this problem well-known. If a SL has an expressive power equal to a propositional logic, the problem is computable. This fact is not valid for first order logic and multi-modal logic.

Starting from these considerations, the authors proposed in this work an ontological based approach. In computer science, ontology is defined as "a specification of a representational vocabulary for a shared domain of discourse - definitions of classes, relations, functions, and other objects" (Gruber, 1993). In other words, ontology can be considered as the formal specification of conceptualizations of certain domain knowledge. Ontology models the world of interest through assertions in a given language.

The key objects of our model are: routes, nodes and risk index. A node is a generic point (typically a crossroad) described by means of geographic coordinate (latitude and longitude). A route is a set of sequential nodes joining the starting and the ending points. The risk index refers to a weight associated to each route and it is in inverse proportion to the satisfaction level of a given constraint. Each constraint is modelled as a risk map that is a map associating the level of risk, concerning that constraint, with each point (with a resolution of 200 meters per pixel).

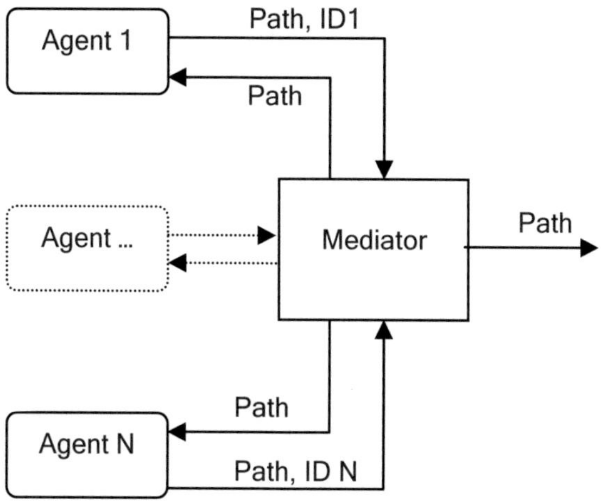

Fig. 2. A block diagram of the proposed negotiation process

The levels of risk are quantized in six values (the numbers between 1 and 6) where 1 indicates low risk and 6 indicates very high risk. These maps are geo-coded in order to associate the corresponding geographic coordinate (the latitude and longitude couple) with each pixel in the map. Using each one of these maps it is feasible to correlate a risk value, concerning the parameter modelled by the given map, with each route.

The system includes various "path agents" and a mediator agent. Each "path agents" has the ability to compute a route and associate a risk value, using a single risk map, to it. In other words, each agent is able to compute a route analysing only one constraint. In the agency there are as many path agents as many constraints are required. This fact introduces a strong level of system scalability indeed adding a new constraint to the system does not require a re-engineering of the whole system but it requires the simple creation of a new path agent. Each intelligent agent has the ability to interact with the mediator agent.

From a linguistic perspective, the agents communicate by means of performative messages (Wooldridge, 1998).

Figure 2 illustrates a schematic overview of the negotiation process. When the route planning process starts up, each agent computes N routes and the corresponding risk levels. After this stage, each path agent proposes the route with the lowest risk level to the mediator. The main task of the mediator is to assist the path agents in finding a shared solution that minimizes the overall risk associated to the chosen route. This solution is reached through a phase of cooperative negotiation, namely an interleaved succession of proposals and counter-proposals that goes on until the proposals of the agents converge to a stable agreement or a timeout expires (agency optimization).

The following pseudo-code shows the main aspects of the negotiation phase:

```
10) Each path agent:
    computes a route and its associated risk level and sends them to the mediator
20) The mediator chooses the route with the lowest risk level and asks each agent to evaluate
    this new proposal
30) Each agent computes the risk level associated to this proposed route according to its risk
    map (namely the constraint that it is handling) and sends the computed risk level to the
    mediator
40) The mediator computes the overall risk level (riskID) associated to this path and
    IF riskID is less than a given threshold T
        choose this path
        goto (50)
    ELSE goto (10)
50) END
```

The following characteristics of the proposed algorithm should be highlighted:

- Each path agent memorizes its last analysed route and it generates the various proposals introducing variations in this route.
- Each agent proposes different paths in the step (10) but they converge to a single path in step (30).
- Each path agent is characterized by a parameter regulating its bent for the change. This optional parameter is useful to introduce a mechanism of flexible priority among the various considered constraints.

5. Experiments and results

With the intent of testing the effectiveness of the proposed negotiation method, a heavy stage of simulation was carried out. After this first stage, the system was applied to the real case. Both stages are described in this section.

5.1 Simulation stage

This simulation begins by considering a hypothetic travel between two points: A and D. These points are components of a network composed of N full connected points as shown in figure 3. In the real world, this structure represents a generic travel between a source point and a destination with N possible intermediate legs. Each couple of legs is connected by a route.

Figure 3 is a schematic representation of this model. In this figure only four points are represented for its readability. Figure 3.a shows the topologic model of the possible routes while figure 3.b represents a model of the risk map owned by each agent (see section 4). In this model, the punctual and distributed information in the risk map has been concentrated in a single cell of the matrix (called risk matrix) in figure 3.b that represents the whole risk level associated to that route. In the proposed example (figure 3), the risk level associated to the travel between the points A and C is 4 while that between the points B and D is 2. In other words, 4 is the mean risk level associated to the path between A and C. This value is the mean of all the values related to the points in the risk map falling on the (real world) road joining the point A and C.

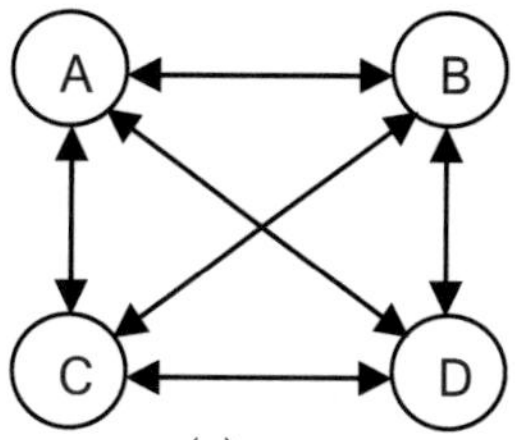

(a)

	A	B	C	D
A	0	1	4	6
B	1	0	3	2
C	4	3	0	5
D	6	2	5	0

(b)

Fig. 3. Schematic representation of the proposed model

As result of this model, the risk matrix is symmetric. In each simulation the first column of the matrix represents the starting point, while the last one is the destination point of the route (so figure 3 represents all the possible routes between A and D).
This matrix is realized in a semi-random way, namely, its elements are generated randomically, but the direct route between source and destination point (A-D in the above example) is penalized imposing the max level risk.
The experiments were conducted by using the Matlab® environment.
Aim of the simulation was to understand the performance of the proposed system in terms of its ability to find a solution. The problem could be briefly formulated in the following way:
Given a network composed of N full-connected legs, find a route between 2 points (let say A-D) satisfying M different constraints within a threshold value T.

Number of experiments (asked routes)	100
Number of constraints	5+1
Mean number of iteration	16.27
Number of routes without solution	5
Maximum number of steps	100
T	2.5
N	5

Table 1. Results achieved through the proposed experiments

After looking into this problem it is clear that there are cases where there is no solution, while in other cases it is possible to find it. In order to handle the cases in which the solution could not exist, a limit in the number of negotiation steps has been introduced. Table 1 provides a schematic view outlining the obtained results. In these experiments, the system was queried 100 times (Number of experiments (asked routes)) with a route between two given points. The number of possibly legs was N=5. There were five specific constraints each one handled by an intelligent agent plus the constraint regarding the general low level risk that should be less than T (2.5 in these experiments). The results show that the negotiation phase requires a mean number of 16.27 steps to reach a good solution in the cases in which it exists. When the solution does not exist (or it is not found in the prefixed 100 steps), the mediator chooses among the various proposed solutions the one with the risk level closer to T.

5.2 Real case application

The proposed system was put in practice for specific reasons in the context of concrete cases under analysis, namely it was the kernel of the prototypal decision support system developed by the authors and tested for handling the transport of hazardous material in the Apulia Region (Italy).

This system implies the use of 4 agents facing the following constraints: hydro-geologic risk, road traffic, archaeological zones and sensible targets (schools, fabrics, etc.). As explained above, each constraint was modelled as a risk map. The possible risk values vary between 1 (very low risk) and 6 (very high risk). It should be noticed that the road traffic map may present variations during the different hours of the day. In this work, the day was divided into six time bands each one of four hours. The agent handling this constraint uses a risk map according to the time of the transport.

As stated before, the proposed system relies on a web based interface (figure 4) and it uses as routing engine the Google-map API and the AJAX technology to obtain the various routes. When the system is queried with a route request between a source and a destination location each agent works with the routing engine to get various routes and with the mediator to find the best route satisfying all the imposed constraints as explained above.

Fig. 4. A screen shot of the proposed system interface

6. Conclusions

In this work the authors have presented a new ITS, developed in the framework of a research project funded by Apulia Region (Italy), focusing the attention on some aspects related to the route planning module.
The proposed route planning module is based on a multi-agent cooperative negotiation paradigm. For this reason, particular attention was paid to the linguistic aspects of the problem and an ontological approach was used to define the communication acts among agents.
The achieved results reveal how a multi-agent cooperative negotiation paradigm can be useful in solving the problem of multi-objective route optimization. The proposed approach considers individual agent optimization (the process that each agent uses to choose a new route) and agency optimization, performed according to our negotiation protocol, by which the agents achieve a global agreement.
The implementation of a multi-agent paradigm gives great flexibility and scalability to the system. As the proposed real case application shows, this system is able to handle time variant constraint. The presence of the mediator introduces a significant level of scalability into the system. Indeed, if there is the need to tackle a new constraint, it will be sufficient to create a new agent dealing with it. The proposed results demonstrate the suitability of the proposed system as support decision system in route planning problems.

7. References

Amato, A.; Di Lecce, V.; Piuri, V., (2007), Distributed Database for Environmental Data Integration in proceedings of IEEE Symposium on Virtual Environments, Human-Computer Interfaces and Measurement Systems, 2007. VECIMS 2007. 25-27 June 2007 Page(s): 47 - 51 Digital Object Identifier 10.1109/VECIMS.2007.4373926

Bellman R., (1958) On a routing problem, Quarterly of Applied Mathematics 16, 87–90.

Bertsekas D. P., (1998) Network Optimization: Continuous and Discrete Models, Athena Scientific, Nashua, New Hampshire, United States.

Bond, A. H., Gasser, L. (Eds.) (1988). Readings in Distributed Artificial Intelligence. Morgan Kaufmann.

Danko A. R., Jan L.H. R., (2000), Agent controlled traffic lights ESIT 2000, 14-15 September 2000, Aachen, Germany.

Delle Donne, V.; Reiher, E.; Wolfe, R.; Vezina, G.; Van Dongen, V., (1995) Passport: parallel land route planning software, in proceedings of Canadian Conference on Electrical and Computer Engineering. Volume 2, 5-8 Sept. 1995 Page(s):933 - 936 vol.2 Digital Object Identifier 10.1109/CCECE.1995.526581

Di Lecce V., Pasquale C. and Piuri V., (2004), A Basic Ontology for Multi Agent System Communication in an Environmental Monitoring System, in proceedings of CIMSA 2004 - International Conference on Computational Intelligence for Measurement Systems and Applications Boston, MA, USA, 14-16 JULY 2004, pp. 45-50, ISBN: 0-7803-8342-7.

Di Lecce, V.; Amato, A.; Calabrese, M., (2008.a). Data integration in distributed medical information systems in proceedings of Canadian Conference on Electrical and Computer Engineering, 2008. CCECE 2008.

Di Lecce V., Amato A., Piuri V., (2008.b), Neural Technologies For Increasing The GPS Position Accuracy, CIMSA 2008 - IEEE International Conference on Computational Intelligence for Measurement Systems And Applications Istanbul - Turkey , 14-16 July 2008, DOI: 10.1109/CIMSA.2008.4595822, ISBN: 978-1-4244-2305-7

Dijkstra, E.W., (1959), A note on two problems in connexion with graphs, Numerische Mathematik 1, 269–271.

Dospisil, J. and Kendall, E., (2000) Designing Agents with Negotiation Capabilities. In internet Commerce and Software Agents: Cases, Technologies and Opportunities (ed. Syed Rahman and R. Bignal), Idea Group Publishing, 2000.

Faulkner S., Kolp M., (2003). "Ontological Basis for Agent ADL", The 15th Conference on Advanced Information Systems Engineering, CAISE, Velden, Austria, 16 - 20 June.

Fernandes, J. M. and Oliveira E., (1999), "TraMas: Traffic Control through Behaviour-based Multi-Agent System", Proceedings of the Fourth International Conference on The Practical Application of Intelligent Agents and Multi-Agent Technology (PAAM99), pp 457- 458, London, April 1999

Ford Jr., L.R., and d.r. Fulkerson, (1962) Flows in Networks, Princeton University Press, Princeton, New Jersey, United States.

Frank L. D. PhD and Mr. Engelke P. (2000) How Land Use and Transportation Systems Impact Public Health: A Literature Review of the Relationship Between Physical Activity and Built Form, City and Regional Planning Program College of Architecture, Georgia Institute of Technology

Gruber, T. R., (1993) A Translation Approach to Portable Ontology Specifications, Knowledge Acquisition, vol. 5, Issue 2, pp. 199 - 220, June

He Yong, Yu Haihong, Hui Fang, (2005) "Study on Improving GPS Measurement Accuracy", IMTC 2005 - Instrumentation and Measurement Technology Conference Ottawa, Canada, 17-19 May 2005, pp. 1476-1479

Mosavi M. R., Mohammadi K., and Refan M. H., (2004). "A New Approach for Improving of GPS Positioning Accuracy by using an Adaptive Neurofuzzy System, before and after S/A Is Turned off", International Journal of Engineering Science, Iran University of Science and Technology, vol. 15, pp. 101-114

Mosavi M. R. (2005). "Comparing DGPS Corrections Prediction using Neural Network, Fuzzy Neural Network, and Kalman Filter", Journal of GPS Solution, pp. 1-11.

Pape, U., (1974) Implementation and efficiency of Moore-algorithms for the shortest route problem, Mathematical Programming 7, 212–222

Pellazar, M.S., (1998) Vehicle Route Planning With Constraints Using Genetic Algorithms, in Aerospace and Electronics Conference, 1998. NAECON 1998. Proceedings of the IEEE 1998 National 13-17 July 1998 Page(s):392 - 399

Suzuki, N.; Araki, D.; Higashide, A.; Suzuki, T., (1995) Geographical route planning based on uncertain knowledge, in Tools with Artificial Intelligence, 1995. Proceedings., Seventh International Conference on 5-8 Nov. 1995 Page(s):434–441 Digital Object Identifier 10.1109/TAI.1995.479838

Wooldridge M., (1998) Verifiable Semantics for Agent Communication Languages, in *Proceedings of the 3rd International Conference on Multi Agent Systems*, Page: 349, 1998 ISBN:0-8186-8500-X

10

A Graphical Development Method for Multiagent Simulators

Keinosuke Matsumoto, Tomoaki Maruo, Masatoshi Murakami, Naoki Mori
Osaka Prefecture University
Japan

1. Introduction

A multiagent system (Weiss, 2000); (Russell & Norving, 1995) is proposed as an approach to social phenomena and complex systems in recent years. Agents are connected with networks, and they cooperate and negotiate with each other to solve problems by exchanging information. In addition, many multiagent simulators (MAS) are proposed, and some frameworks for developing MAS are also developed. These frameworks make the amount of work reduce. But it is necessary to build models that are required to develop simulators from scratch. It becomes a burden to developers. The models correspond to a model of MVC (Model-View-Controller) pattern. These models would be specialized in the framework and lack in reusability. Problems of these simulator frameworks are shown in the following:

- Implementing models takes time and cost.
- Managing models is very difficult.
- The reusability of models is low.

To solve these problems, this paper proposes a graphical model editor that can build models diagrammatically and a simulator development method using the editor. The method is compared with a conventional method from the viewpoint of usability and workload. The proposed method is applied to some examples and the results show that our method is effective in construction of multiagent simulators.

2. Multiagent Simulators

A multiagent system consists of the following components:

- Agent

An agent is an actual piece of operating software. It senses an environment and acquires information. It acts according to the information.

- Environment

An environment is a field where agents act. It also includes objects.

- Object

An object is a non-autonomous entity arranged in an environment. It does not influence the environment and agents.

In addition to them, a multiagent simulator has schedules for simulations:
• Schedule
A schedule prescribes behaviour of agents, state transitions of an environment, etc. It is invisible for simulations.

In a multiagent simulator, an agent works with other agents or an environment, and gives some influences. The MAS may show an unexpected aspect as a result. Such emergent phenomena are useful for analyzing complex systems.

3. Frameworks for Multiagent Simulators

A multiagent simulator is software for actually simulating behavior of agents on a computer. It is also called an agent base simulator. There are mainly two kinds of methods in building a multiagent simulator. One, you could develop it using existing programming languages from scratch. The other, you could also develop it implementing only required components (multiagent models) by the aid of simulator frameworks. The former, while flexibility is very high, the quality of the software depends on a developer's skill. Because all parts are implemented from scratch, the burden of development is very heavy. The latter, components common to simulations are already implemented, and the burden of development is cut down greatly. In addition to this, the latest simulator frameworks have various functions, and they become very convenient to analyze. This paper focuses on a development method that uses simulator frameworks. Typical existing simulator frameworks are listed in the following:

• Swarm
• Mason
• KK-MAS
• TeamBots
• Repast
• StarLogo
• Ascape
• Breve

Among these frameworks, Repast (North et al., 2005) and Mason (Luke et al., 2003) are made to be target frameworks in the following. These two frameworks take many concepts from Swarm (Swarm Development Group, 2004), and their flexibility and functionality are very high.

4. Graphical Model Editor

In order to describe multiagent models by diagrams, a dedicated editor is needed for drawing the diagrams. This section proposes a graphical model editor.

4.1 Definition of Drawing

Data of agents, environments, objects, and schedules are required to define multiagent models. It is also necessary to determine which diagrams should be used to express these data. These data can be divided into static and dynamic ones. We use class diagrams for static data, and flowcharts for dynamic data respectively. Some examples of model diagrams are shown in Fig. 1.

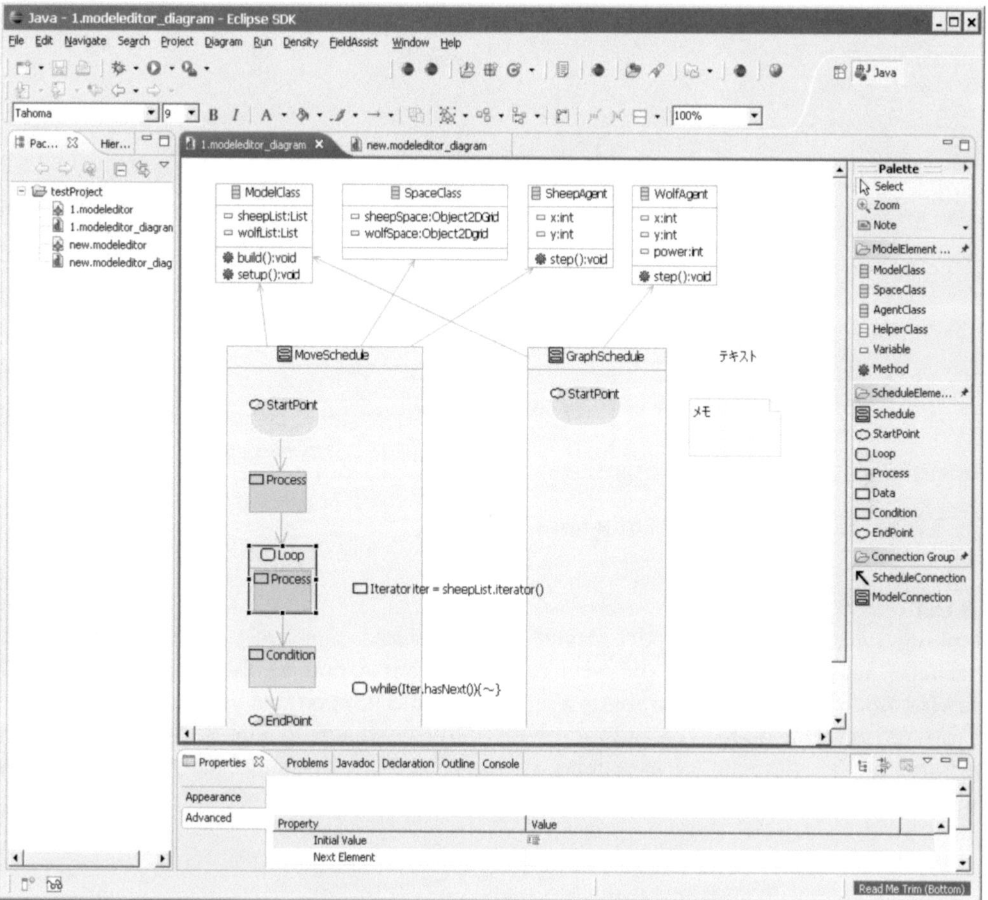

Fig. 1. Examples of model diagrams.

4.2 Definition of Model Structure

In defining model structure, we use a meta-model. A meta-model is a meta-level model for defining specific models. It gives definitions using the data about agents, environments, objects, and schedules. Adding the definitions of model structure as constraints of the model editor, an editing that is contrary to the constraints is prohibited.

The outline of the meta-model is shown in Fig. 2. In this figure, classes under the class object correspond to class diagrams, and classes under the schedule area to flowcharts. Some kinds of class objects and schedule objects are prepared, and these are used as nodes on the editor. The following two things are realized by using this meta-model in Eclipse: If you try to draw an entity that does not meet drawing constraints of the meta-model, the model editor would not allow us to do. When the model is stored, model structure is preserved in the same structure of the meta-model. The meta-model restricts users to use the editor semantically wrong. In addition, the editor use a format called XMI (XML Metadata Interchange) (OMG, 2008) when the model is stored. There is an advantage that this model can be used with other tools in future. This format can raise the reusability of the model.

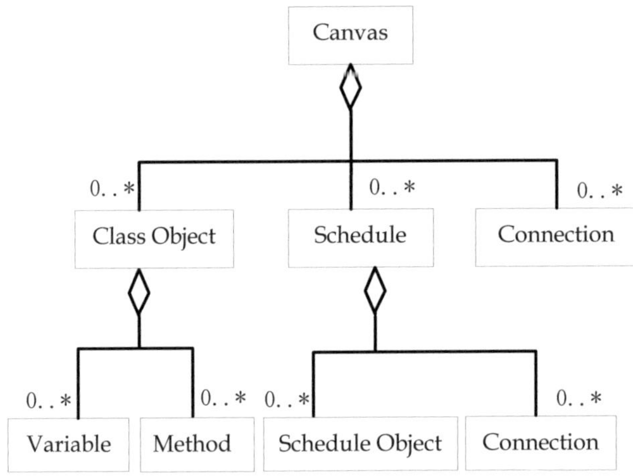

Fig. 2. A definition of the model by a meta-model.

4.3 Definition of Mapping

Drawing information and model structure are defined separately. These data must be connected to each other. We define a mapping from a part of the meta-model to each drawing node. Without this mapping, a situation could happen that you cannot save it even if you can draw a node. The outline of mapping is shown in Fig. 3. Mapping from an attribute of the meta-model to a label of drawing objects enables us to deliver model information.

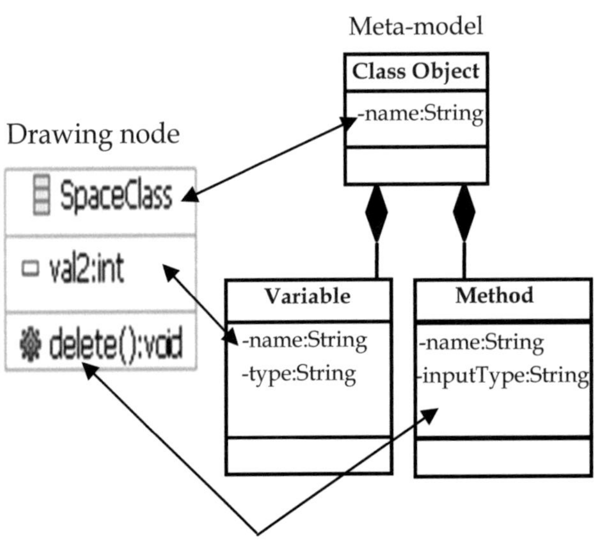

Fig. 3. Mapping of a drawing node and a model structure definition.

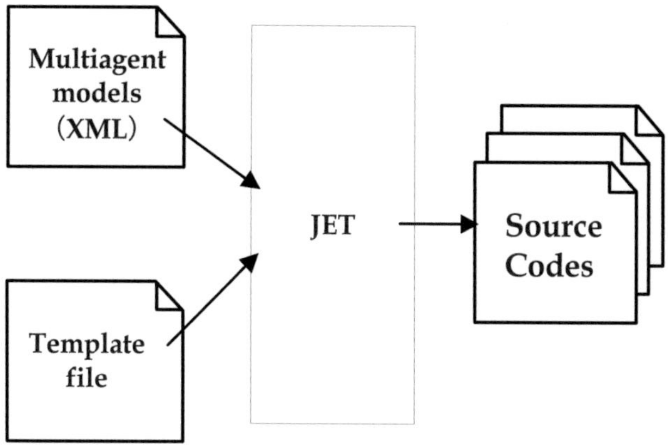

Fig. 4. Technologies for transforming models into codes.

It is necessary to modify the mapping if a definition of drawing, such as a form or colour of an object, is modified. But there is no necessity of changing the meta-model, and vice versa. Since the mapping is only tying up two items, so modification is very easy. Thereby, we can flexibly modify definitions of drawing and the meta-model.

5. Development Method by Model-Code Transformation

This section describes a simulator development method using the proposed graphical model editor. A transformation process of the method is shown in Fig. 4.

5.1 Transforming Multiagent Models into Source Codes

JET (Java Emitter Templates) (Marz & Aniszczyk, 2006) is used for transforming multiagent models into source codes. JET is one of Eclipse project results and it is a code generation technique for improvement in productivity. A code-generator is an important component of Model Driven Development (MDD). The goal of MDD is to develop a software system using abstract models (such as UML models or EMF/ECORE models), and then refine and transform these models into source codes. Although it is possible to create abstract models, and manually transform them into codes, the real power of MDD comes from automating these processes. Such transformations accelerate the MDD processes, and result in better code quality. In JET, codes are outputted using templates. Models can be applicable to various frameworks by changing templates. JET is useful to raise the reusability of models. It needs an XML file storing the model information and a template file for transforming the model into codes. The template file is described for every target language using XPath (XML Path Language).

The model describes XML forms as a tree structure. A template corresponds to a medium which creates source codes by reading information of the model. The tags in the template are simplified tags of XPath, and it is possible to take out the information of input models by designating these tags directly. Source codes corresponding to each platform are generated on the basis of this information.

5.2 Templates

A template is created for Java language because one of the target simulator frameworks, Repast, corresponds to Java. The flexibility of the template depends on the contents in the template. Existing many sample programs are referred to make template's schema as general as possible.

A part of the created template is shown in the following:

```
<?xml version="1.0" encoding="utf-8"?>
public class <c:get select="$element/@elementName" /> {
<c:iterate select="$element/variables" var="vari">
   private <c:get select="$vari/@type" />
    <c:get select="$vari/@elementName" />;
  public void set<c:get select="$vari/@elementName" /> (
     <c:get select="$vari/@type" /> <c:get
     select="$vari/@elementName" />) {
        this.<c:get select="$vari/@elementName" /> = <c:get
        select="$vari/@elementName" />;}
   public <c:get select="$vari/@type" /> get<c:get
     select="$vari/@elementName" />() {
     return <c:get select="$vari/@ elementName" />;}
</c:iterate>
<c:iterate select="$element/methods" var="meth">
   public <c:get select="$meth/@outputType" /> <c:get
     select="$meth/@elementName" />(<c:get
     select="$meth/@inputType" />){}
</c:iterate>
}
```

6. Experimental Results and Evaluations

To evaluate the proposed method, the method is applied to some multiagent simulators, and it is compared with a conventional method from the viewpoint of usability and workload.

6.1 Model Editor

The model editor enables us to edit models graphically and to add information in detail using a property sheet. Code based model generation could be replaced with diagram based model generation by the editor. The model editor is built using the framework of Eclipse, it can be customized, and easily changed. It also increases the reusability of the models created by the model editor.

On the flowchart expression, there is a problem that it can not deal with multiplex loops. As a result, coding by hands still remains. Expressions used in the editor are similar to programming languages such as class diagrams and flowcharts, so that some knowledge is needed for understanding them. To solve these problems, it is necessary to improve the contents of drawing and to consider more intelligible expressions.

6.2 Automatic Code Generation

Some sample simulators were developed using the model editor. The developed sample simulators are taken from sample programs of Repast (http://repast.sourceforge.net/repast_3/examples/index.html) and reference (Yamakage & Hattori, 2002). We examined how much codes were generated automatically by this proposed method. To be more precise, we compared the amount of codes automatically generated by the model editor and model-code transformation with the amount of codes that are manually added. These situations are shown in Fig. 5. The developed sample simulators are shown in Table 1.

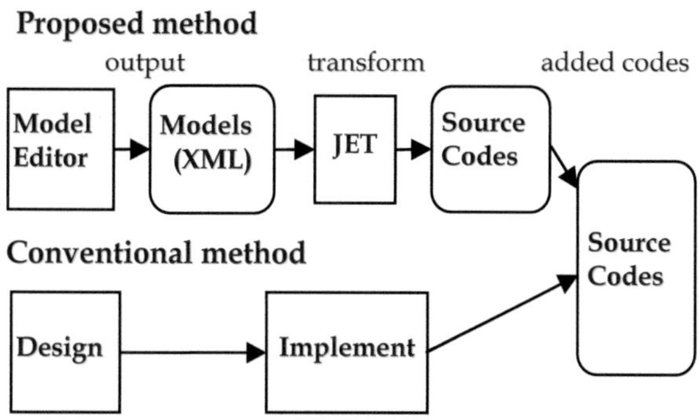

Fig. 5. Comparison of the proposed method and the conventional method.

	Sample name	Total codes (lines) (A)	Automatically generated codes (lines) (B)	Automatic code generation rate (C)=(B)*100/(A)
1	Heat Bug	585	261	44.62%
2	Sugar Scape	490	233	47.55%
3	Regression Office	580	239	41.21%
4	Rabbit Population	364	192	52.75%
5	Open map	296	164	55.41%
6	Neural from file	186	74	39.78%
7	Neural Office	647	199	30.76%
8	Mousetrap	282	128	45.39%
9	Game of life	555	196	35.32%
10	JinGirNew	359	176	49.03%
11	Jiggle Toy	310	116	37.42%
12	Jain	332	142	42.77%
13	Hypercycles	712	201	28.23%
14	Hexa Bug	426	193	45.31%
15	Gis Bug	184	85	46.20%
16	Genetic Office	519	203	39.11%
17	Enn	566	224	39.58%
18	Asynchagents	435	178	40.92%
19	Lotka-Volterra	478	247	51.67%
20	Carry Drop	418	186	44.50%
average		436.2	181.9	42.88%

Table 1. Automatic code generation rate using the model editor.

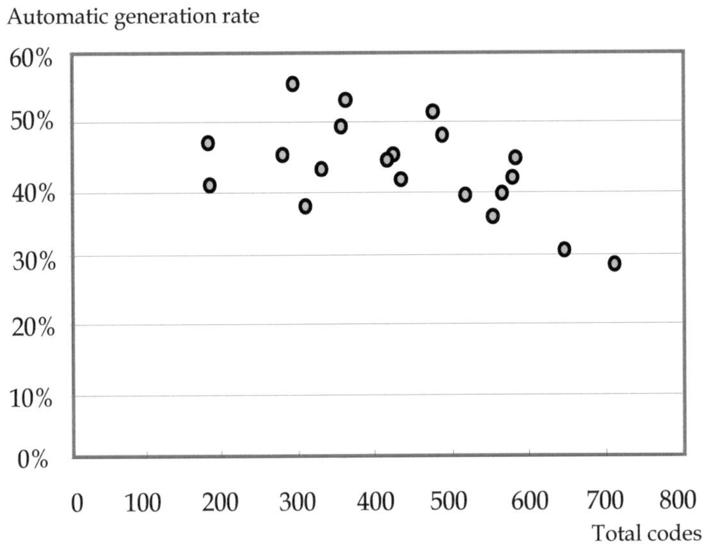

Fig. 6. Automatic code generation rate.

This table shows automatic code generation rates by using the model editor. Fig. 6 depicts the results graphically. It turns out that every sample automatically generates about 40% - 50% of the total codes. The average rate of the automatic code generation attains about 43%. The automatic code generation rates tend to decrease with the increase of total codes. This tendency is caused by the model editor's ability that cannot deal with complex logics. The larger the total codes are, the more codes you need to add by hand. It is necessary to improve the model editor as a future subject.

6.3 Workloads

This section investigates how much the proposed method reduces workload. Unless the workload of drawing models by the editor is less than that of developing models from scratch, it does not make the burden of development reduce. These two workloads were measured. We compare the automatic generated codes to the number of nodes placed on the model editor. The amount of lines per one node is computed in Table 2. The numeric value (E) of Table 2 expresses how many lines are generated from one node on average. The average value of (E) is 2.46.

The workload of arranging one node (two clicks and some little things) seems to be less than that of writing by hand the codes of 2.46 lines (about 62 characters, (G) = (E)*(F)). It is difficult to compare these correctly, and we assume that the workload of arranging one node and that of writing one line are equivalent for the simplicity. Under this assumption, Fig. 7 depicts how much workloads are reduced. First, in the area of automatic code generation,

$$\text{Nodes} : \text{Codes} = 1 : 2.46 \tag{1}$$

because the workload of arranging one node and that of writing one line are assumed to be equivalent, the proposed method can be suppressed in 41% (1*100/2.46) of the amount of workload of the conventional method. There is no difference in the area of the manual generation, since these parts are generated by hand for both the proposed method and the conventional one. The average automatic code generation rate (C) in the Table 1 is about 43%. The workload of the nodes part corresponds to 18% (=43%*41%) as a whole. As a result, 25% of the total workload is reduced as shown in the Fig. 7. The validity of the proposed method is also shown from the viewpoint of workloads.

	Sample name	Total noses (D)	Lines per node (E) =(B)/ (D)	Average characters per line (F)	Characters per node (G)=(E) * (F)
1	Heat Bug	99	2.64	24.1	63.62
2	Sugar Scape	72	3.24	23.7	76.58
3	Regression Office	88	2.72	25.9	70.42
4	Rabbit Population	67	2.87	26.8	76.81
5	Open map	61	2.69	23.2	62.46
6	Neural from file	22	3.36	31.4	105.47
7	Neural Office	110	1.81	24.5	44.32
8	Mousetrap	63	2.03	22.7	46.19
9	Game of life	92	2.13	22.6	48.12
10	JinGirNew	64	2.75	25.8	70.83
11	Jiggle Toy	68	1.71	24.6	41.93
12	Jain	57	2.49	25.2	62.76
13	Hypercycles	110	1.83	24.0	43.77
14	Hexa Bug	76	2.54	23.6	60.00
15	Gis Bug	33	2.58	25.7	66.09
16	Genetic Office	78	2.60	29.1	75.82
17	Enn	100	2.24	23.6	52.85
18	Asynchagents	71	2.51	28.3	70.83
19	Lotka-Volterra	103	2.40	22.8	54.74
20	Carry Drop	90	2.07	23.9	49.43
	average	76.2	2.46	25.1	62.15

Table 2. The amount of codes per one node.

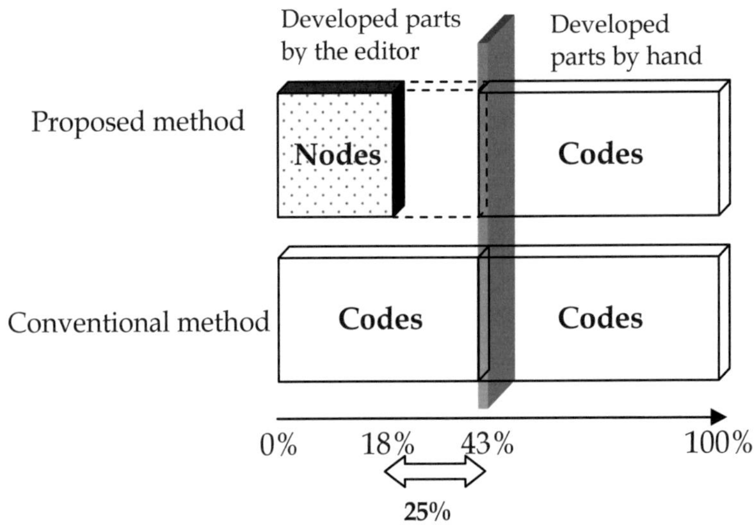

Fig. 7. Difference of the two methods.

7. Conclusion

This paper proposed a model editor that can create graphically multiagent models, and a simulator development method using the editor to build multiagent simulators. Development and management of the models became very easy. In addition, reusability of the models also became very high, and simulator platforms could be changed flexibly. The proposed method was applied to some multiagent simulators and the results show that our method is effective in developing multiagent models and simulators.

As future problems, we must improve the model diagrams to increase automatic code generation rates, and prepare other templates for various frameworks.

8. Acknowledgment

This work was partially supported by JSPS KAKENHI 21560430.

9. References

Luke, S.; Balan, G. C.; Panait, L.; Cioffi-Revilla, C. & Paus, S. (2003). MASON: A Java Multi-Agent Simulation Library, *Proceedings of Agent 2003 Conference on Challenges in Social Simulation*, pp. 49-64, Chicago, USA, October 2003.

Marz, N. & Aniszczyk, C. (2006). Create more -- better -- code in Eclipse with JET, *IBM Developer Works Article*.

North, M.J.; Howe, T.R.; Collier, N.T. & Vos, J.R. (2005). The Repast Symphony Runtime System, *Proceedings of Agent 2005 Conference on Generative Social Processes, Models, and Mechanisms,* ANL/DIS-06-1, ISBN 0-9679168-6-0, pp. 159-166, Chicago, USA, October 2005.

OMG (2008). XMI, See http://www.omg.org/technology/documents/formal/xmi.htm.

Russell, S.J. & Norving, P. (1995). *Artificial intelligence: A Modern Approach,* Prentice-Hall, ISBN 0-13-103805-2, Englewood Cliffs.

Swarm Development Group (2004). Swarm 2.2, See http://wiki.swarm.org.

Weiss, G. (2000). *Multiagent Systems: A Modern Approach to Distributed Artificial Intelligence,* The MIT Press, ISBN 9780262731317, Cambridge.

Yamakage, S. & Hattori, S. (2002). *Artificial society in computers – multiagent simulation model and complex systems* – (in Japanese), Kyoritsu Shuppan, ISBN4-320-09735-1, Tokyo.

11

Multi-Agent Geosimulation in Support to Qualitative Spatio-Temporal Reasoning: COAs' "What if" Analysis as an Example

Hedi Haddad and Bernard Moulin
Laval University
Canada

1. Introduction

Multi-Agent Geosimulation (MAGS) is a relatively novel approach to model-building and application in the geographic sciences and geocomputing (Torrens, 2008). It is mainly characterized by the use of Agent-Based Models - particularly Multi-Agent Systems (MAS) - and Geographic Information Systems (GIS) in order to model, simulate and study complex phenomena taking place in geographical environments (Benenson and Torrens, 2004; Moulin et al., 2003). Recent research works in MAGS focused on two main trends. The first trend consists in improving different conceptual and computational aspects of MAGS models such as development methodologies (Ali, 2008), 2D and 3D virtual geographic environments models (Silva et al., 2008; Paris et al., 2009), agents perception and navigation models (Silva et al., 2008), generic MAGS platforms (Blecic et al., 2008) and models calibration and validation (Hagen-Zanker and Martens, 2008). The second trend consists in applying MAGS techniques to solve new problems such as parking policies evaluation (Benenson et al., 2007), prediction of house prices evolution (Bossomaier et al., 2007) and public health risk management (Bouden et al., 2008), to mention a few. Although these works allow modeling and simulating several geospatial phenomena, they do not guarantee that the simulation results will be well understood by a human user. In fact, results of geosimulations are usually presented using statistical, mathematical and / or graphical techniques (Ali et al., 2007). The complexity of the simulated phenomena and the huge volume of generated data make these techniques difficult to be interpreted by users. Indeed, human reasoning is mainly qualitative and not quantitative. Therefore, we believe in the importance of linking MAGS models with qualitative reasoning techniques, and we think that this link will allow the development of new systems which support qualitative reasoning in spatial contexts. While some recent works have been interested in this issue (Furtao and Vasconcelos, 2007), to our knowledge there is a lack of works that address its theoretical and computational aspects. Our contribution in this chapter aims at proposing an approach that uses MAGS techniques to support qualitative spatio-temporal reasoning. Particularly, we are interested in supporting a specific kind of qualitative reasoning called "What-if" reasoning and its particular application to the planning of courses of actions

(COAs). In this chapter we present a general overview of the proposed approach from its theoretical foundations to its computational implementation. More specifically, we highlight how this approach requires integrating several disciplines in addition to MAGS techniques. The structure of the chapter is as following. In Section 2 we present the "What-if" thinking process and its application to the COAs' analysis problem. In Section 3 we present our MAGS-based approach. We explain its principle and present its main steps. We also list the main requirements that must be dealt with in order to implement it. These requirements are respectively presented in sections 4, 5, and 6. In Section 7 we present MAGS-COA, a tool that we developed as a proof of concept of the proposed approach. We also present how we used MAGS-COA to implement and evaluate scenarios in the search and rescue domain. Finally, in Section 8 we discuss the limits of the proposed approach and we conclude with future work.

2. "What-if" Thinking Process and the COAs' Analysis Problem

We aim to propose a MAGS-based approach to support a kind of qualitative spatio-temporal reasoning called *COAs' "What-if" analysis*. *"What-if" reasoning* is a kind of counterfactual thinking used by humans to deal with uncertainty when it is either impossible or impractical to conduct physical experiments (Lebow, 2007). Practically, "What-if" reasoning allows a human being to explore the consequences of different alternatives by asking questions of the form "WHAT will the situation be IF ...". From a cognitive perspective, "What-if" reasoning is a qualitative mental simulation-based process consisting of three steps: 1) elaborating an analogical mental model of a situation (mental visualization); 2) mentally carrying out one or several operations on it; and 3) seeing what occurs. During the third phase qualitative *causal reasoning* is used to interpret the results of the manipulation(s) carried out during the second phase (Trickett and Trafton, 2007).
In practice, "What-if" counterfactual thinking is usually applied to explore the consequences of several alternatives in order to either plan future activities or explain historical events (Ferrario, 2001; Gaglio, 2004). As an example, we are interested in the application of "What-if" reasoning to the problem of courses of action (COAs) planning. A *COA* is an outline of a plan specifying the tasks to be performed by a set of resources (i.e. people, planes, teams) as well as the spatio-temporal and coordination constraints that must be satisfied in order to achieve a desired objective. Consequently, the success of the COA widely depends upon the performance of the resources when carrying out their tasks. Considering the context of planning COAs in a geographical environment, this performance is constrained by several factors, two among them being characterized by an inherent uncertainty: 1) On the one hand, there are several unpredictable natural phenomena that may occur in the geographic environment; 2) On the other hand, there are other entities acting in the environment and reacting to the COA resources' activities. In order to deal with such an uncertainty, human planners usually apply "What-if" reasoning in order to think about the implications of different assumptions by playing out different alternatives, and then by evaluating the plausibility of their consequences. However, human beings have some limits when reasoning in the context of changing geographic spaces. In fact, it has been proved that trying to mentally encompass changes (mental simulation) is a difficult task for humans (Forbus, 1981; Kahneman and Tversky, 1982). It is even more difficult in a large scale space because of the complexity and the diversity of phenomena which take place in it. In

addition, the human mental representation of space presents some limits, such as difficulties to judge distances and to estimate the three-dimensional aspects of the geographic space (Rothkegel et al., 1998; Tversky, 2005). Moreover, human planning is often carried out under stressful conditions such as time pressure and tiredness which affect human attention and memory, hence influencing the quality of decisions. For these reasons, the use of decision support systems that somewhat alleviate the mental charge of human decision makers is considered to be helpful during the COAs' "What-if" analysis process.

3. A MAGS-Based Approach to Support COAs' "What-if" Analysis

Multi-Agent Geosimulation (MAGS) inherits from two research fields: multi-agent systems (MAS) and geographic information systems (GIS) (Fournier, 2005). On the one hand, some AI research works have been interested in agent and multi-agent simulations in a spatial context, and the concept of spatial multi-agent systems has emerged (Rodrigues and Raper 1999; Batty and Jiang 2000; Frank et al., 2001). More recently, GIS have attracted a growing interest within the MAS research community as an explicit representation of spatial environments in multi-agent simulations (Gimblett, 2002; Brown and Xie, 2006; Phan and Amblard, 2007). On the other hand, geographers have been interested in MAS in order to introduce a temporal (dynamic) dimension in GIS which are typically static. By combining advanced characteristics of artificial agents and explicit and faithful representations of the geographic space, MAGS has been recognized as an effective technique for simulating complex systems composed of interacting agents in a simulated geographic environment. It has been recognized that such an approach is of great potential for verifying and evaluating hypotheses about how real spatial complex systems operate (Albrecht, 2005).
Therefore, we think that a MAGS-based approach is suitable for the COAs' "What-if" analysis problem. In the remainder of this section we present a general view of our approach; we discuss its principle, we present its main steps and finally we identify the main requirements that must be satisfied in order to implement it.

3.1 Principle

In Section 2 we presented the COAs' "What-if" thinking process as a kind of qualitative spatio-temporal reasoning based on a mental simulation. The key idea we are defending here is that combining MAGS techniques with qualitative modelling and reasoning techniques is suitable to support such a reasoning process. Consequently, we propose an approach that enriches MAGS techniques with spatio-temporal qualitative reasoning techniques (Figure 1). The approach mainly consists in: 1) using MAGS techniques to simulate the execution of COAs in a *Virtual Geographic Environment* (*VGE*) which can change during the simulation; 2) then allowing the user to explore various assumptions through different simulations and to analyze their outcomes. Results of the simulation are then transformed into a qualitative representation and therefore can be analyzed using qualitative reasoning techniques.

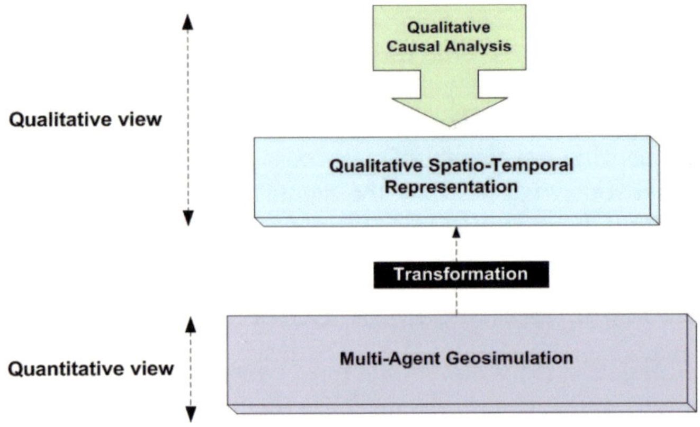

Fig. 1. Linking MAGS models with qualitative spatio-temporal reasoning

Our approach can be thought of as a new form of knowledge representation and reasoning about dynamic geographical phenomena which relies on integrating both quantitative and qualitative representation approaches. Indeed, multi-agent geosimulations - taking advantage of technological advances in autonomous agents, GIS data and natural phenomena modeling - provide a somewhat faithful analog representation of the geographic reality and of its dynamism. It can be a good support to the "what-if" mental simulation and a good way to represent the dynamism corresponding to the behaviours of the resources involved in the COA and their interactions. However, spatial reasoning, in our every day interaction with the physical world, is often driven by qualitative abstractions rather than complete quantitative knowledge (Cohn and Hazarika, 2001), and, as we mentioned in Section 2, human beings have cognitive difficulties when reasoning about various quantitative aspects of the geographic space. Therefore, it becomes interesting to exploit the geosimulation results in a qualitative manner by transforming them into models of dynamic situations which can be used to carry out different kinds of qualitative reasoning.
We think that such a combination of quantitative and qualitative representations allows us to take advantage of both of them. On the one hand, geosimulation is a good way to support a human being during her mental simulation and guaranties that our qualitative models are based on more realistic sources. On the other hand, qualitative representations take the user away from non-relevant details, by capturing only relevant information. The integration of quantitative and qualitative approaches is not a new idea: it has been widely supported by the GIS community (Winchester, 2000). However, to our knowledge it is still not fully implemented in current spatial decision support systems.

3.2 Steps

Considering the characteristics of the COAs' "What-if" analysis process presented in Section 2, we propose an approach composed of three steps: scenarios specification, MAGS and data causal analysis (Figure 2).
During the first step, the user specifies the *scenario* to be analyzed. We call a scenario the description of both a COA and the set of related assumptions specified by the user. The description of a COA indicates the initial positions of the involved resources in the *VGE* and

shows *how* (which tasks or goals need to be carried out), *when* (temporal constraints) and *where* (spatial positions) they must achieve a given mission. Assumptions mainly correspond to the different "happenings" or events that may occur in the *VGE* and that are not caused by the resources' intentional actions, as for example rain falls and movements of fog patches[1].

The second step consists in using a multi-agent-based geosimulation system to simulate the specified scenario in a *VGE*. The resources of the COA are represented by software agents that are inserted in the *VGE* and that autonomously carry out their activities. They react to the actions of other agents, they are constrained by the characteristics of the *VGE* and they are influenced by the effects of the different "happenings" that occur in it.

The third step consists in analyzing the results generated by the simulation. Since we aim to support a "what-if" analysis, we are particularly interested in causal reasoning and in identifying the causal relationships between the user's assumptions and the geosimulation results.

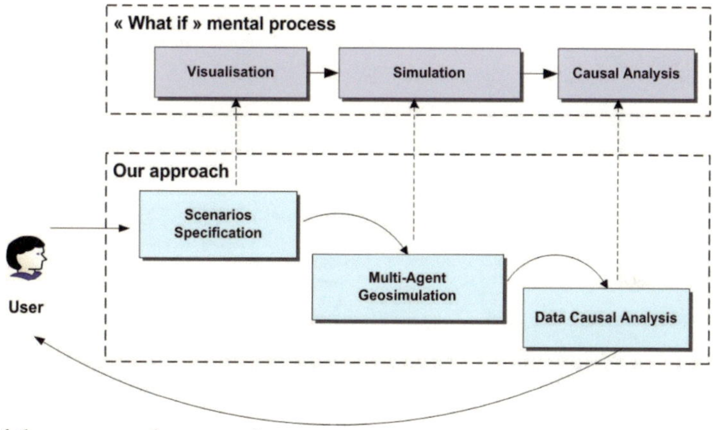

Fig. 2. Steps of the proposed approach

3.3 Requirements for MAGS Applied to "What-if" Analysis

Once the steps of the proposed approach are identified, the important question that must be dealt with is the following: what does the implementation of such an approach means in terms of conceptual and computational requirements? To answer this question, let us start from the end. Indeed, the goal is to establish cause / effect relationships between certain "elements". Let us call the "concepts of interest" these elements. However, we must first be able to express the results of geosimulations in terms of these concepts of interest, and therefore we have a new requirement of data transformation. Of course, we must have a MAGS platform allowing the simulation of the considered scenarios. Since we already have such a platform (which will be presented in Section 7) we do not consider it as a requirement in this chapter. Finally, we have a requirement of defining and modeling the concepts of interest that will be used to express the results of the MAGS and to apply causal reasoning on them.

---

[1] In historical "What-if" reasoning, assumptions can be related to the decisions or actions that may have been taken by a resource of the COA. An example will be presented in Section 7.2.

The fundamental question is thus the following: what are these concepts of interest? In the literature, situations describing changes in a spatial context are usually called *spatio-temporal phenomena* (or dynamic geographical phenomena). Therefore, the scenarios which we are interested in (simulation of COAs and happenings) are considered as spatio-temporal phenomena. Consequently, our first requirement consists in proposing a conceptual model of such spatio-temporal phenomena, i.e. COAs and happenings occurring in a virtual geographic environment. Our second and third requirements respectively consist in expressing the results of our geosimulations using the concepts of the proposed model, and in applying causal reasoning techniques on these concepts (Figure 3). In the following sections we detail the solution that we propose to deal with the three above-mentioned requirements. Section 4 introduces the concept of *spatio-temporal situations* that we use to model dynamic geographical phenomena. Section 5 presents data transformations required to express the results of the simulated scenarios in terms of spatio-temporal situations. Section 6 presents our model of causal reasoning about spatio-temporal situations and how it is used to analyze the results of the MAGS.

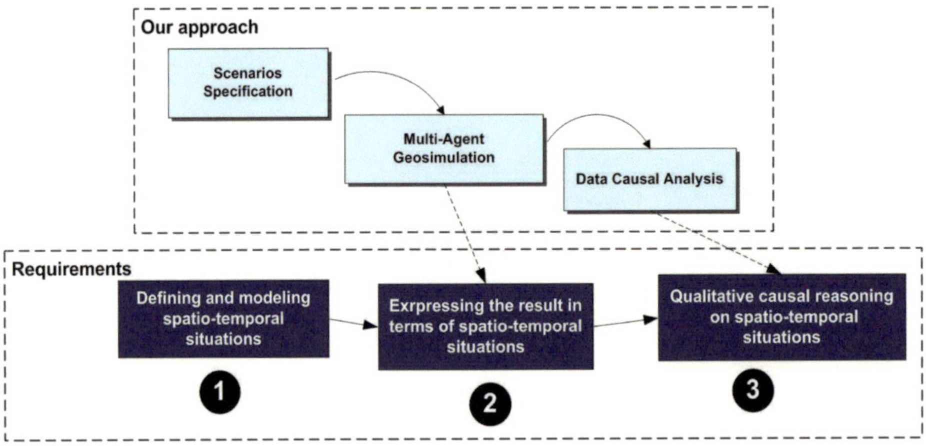

Fig. 3. Requirements to implement the proposed approach

4. A Model of Spatio-Temporal Situations

We aim to model dynamic phenomena in a geographic environment in which there are different kinds of complex spatial entities (such as rivers and buildings). There are also different kinds of objects (such as people and cars) which may move in this geographic environment and modify its state (for example, "block a road"). In addition, different "happenings" may occur in the environment (for example, explosions or floods) and may influence it (for example, "destroying a bridge may block a road and disrupt a river").

The study of dynamic phenomena consists of studying properties of the world that change over *time*. Spatial dynamic phenomena describe changes over both *time* and *space*, and are therefore called *spatio-temporal* phenomena. Several models have been proposed in the literature in order to model spatio-temporal phenomena. A review of these models and their limits with respect to the COAs' "What-if" problem is beyond the scope of this chapter and will be presented in a subsequent paper (see (Haddad, 2009) for further details). However, our model differs from existing models with respect to two main aspects: its theoretical foundations and its knowledge representation formalism.

In contrast to the majority of existing approaches, the theoretical roots of our spatio-temporal model derive from natural language research community. This community assumes that we use language to describe *situations* of the world (Helbig, 2006): "states of affairs and courses of events in which objects have properties and stand in relations to each other at various space-time locations" (Lindström, 1991). A situation is a finite configuration of some aspect of the world in a limited region of space and time and is characterized by various properties or relations that hold among the various objects in that situation (Sowa, 1984). As the world evolves through time, it changes from one state to another. Such changes of state are brought about by the occurrences of events (Georgeff et al., 1993). Consequently, a situation "may be a static configuration that remains unchanged for a period of time, or it may include processes and events that are causing changes" and "it may include people and things with their actions and attributes" (Sowa, 1984). Several conceptual models of static and dynamic situations expressed by natural language have been proposed by linguists. In our project, we push further works of the French linguist Desclés (Desclés, 1990; 2005) in order to define the concept of *spatio-temporal situations* which we use to model our spatio-temporal phenomena (Section 4.2).

With respect to knowledge representation language, we formalize our spatio-temporal situations using the conceptual graphs (CGs) formalism. Sowa (Sowa, 1984) introduced CGs as a system of logic based on Peirce's existential graphs and semantic networks proposed in artificial intelligence. We decided to use CGs because they are known to express meaning in a form that is logically precise and computationally tractable. In fact, there is a well-defined mapping between conceptual graphs and corresponding first-order logical formulae, although CGs also allow for representing temporal and non-monotonic logics, thus exceeding the expressive power of first-order logic (Hensman and Dunnion, 2004). In addition, they provide extensible means to capture and represent real-world knowledge and have been used in a variety of projects for information retrieval, database design, expert systems, qualitative simulations and natural language processing. However, their application to model dynamic phenomena in geographic spaces and to reason about them is an innovative issue (Haddad and Moulin, 2007). More details about CGs and their theoretical foundations can be found in (Sowa, 1984), among others.

Figure 4 illustrates the concepts of our model for spatio-temporal phenomena in a geographic space. Besides the work of the linguist Desclés which we used to define the concept of *spatio-temporal situations* and to capture a qualitative view of dynamic phenomena, we take advantage of ontological works on geographic space and geographic objects to define the structure of space in our model. Indeed, according to Grenon and Smith (Grenon and Smith, 2004) we may distinguish two *modes of existence* for entities populating the world. The first mode corresponds to an *'endurant' view* according to which there are entities "that have continuous existence and a capacity to endure through time even while undergoing different sorts of changes". The second mode corresponds to an *occurrent view* that describes 'occurrent entities' that "occur in time and unfold themselves through a period of time" (Grenon and Smith, 2004). Similarly to this classification, we define two views in our model: the *endurant* view and the *dynamic* view (Figure 4). Our *endurant view* is composed of the geographic space and the objects located in it. A geographic space is composed of geographic objects (*Geo-Object*) such as rivers, mountains and cities. For spatial referencing purposes, each geo-object is projected onto a spatial zone. Other endurant entities of the world (such as people, cars and animals) are represented using the *Actor* concept. Actors are located in the geo-objects composing the geographic environment and may navigate between them. Different relationships (as for example spatial relationships) may hold between geo-objects. Our *dynamic view* is composed of spatio-temporal situations. A spatio-temporal situation may be static (a state) or dynamic (an event or a process). A situation may involve[2] actors and geo-objects, and is characterized by various properties or relations that hold between them. Dynamic situations introduce changes in static situations. We say that they modify states. In addition, a process is characterized by an event that marks its beginning and an event corresponding to its end. These concepts are detailed in the following sub-sections.

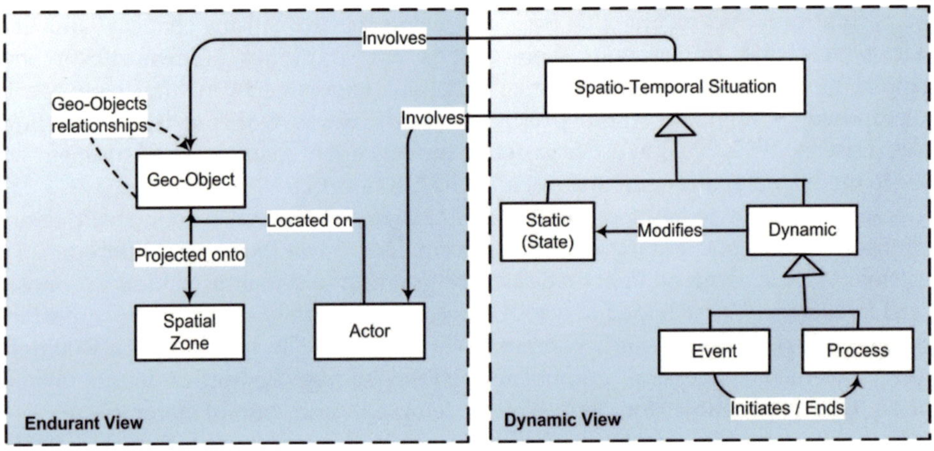

Fig. 4. Our model for spatio-temporal situations

4.1 Endurant View

This view describes the structure of the geographic space and the actors that may be located in it. We define and use the following concepts:

- ***Space* and *Spatial zone***: We adopt the definition of *Space* and *spatial zone* proposed in (Grenon and Smith, 2004). *Space* is the entire spatial universe (the maximal spatial region) and all spatial zones are parts of it. However, we use a different partition of *Space*. At a first elementary level, the *Space* is partitioned into a set of regular cells called pixels. Then, *spatial zones* are incrementally constructed in *Space*. A spatial zone is thus associated with a set of pixels. At a second level, *Space* is completely partitioned by a set of adjacent *spatial zones* in a manner that *Space* is totally covered. Let n be the number of spatial zones of *Space*, we have: *Space* = m Mereological[3] sum (z_i), $i = 1 .. n$. Spatial zones are used as a reference framework to localize geographic objects in *Space*.

---

[2] The term involvement is used by (Grenon and Smith, 2004) to refer to the relations that objects may have with events and processes (objects participate in situations and situations involve objects).

[3] Mereology (also called Part/Whole) formalizes the relation between a complex object and its parts. More details can be found, among others, in (Casati et al., 1998).

- **Geographic object**: According to (Mark et al., 1999), the domain of geographic objects "comprehends regions, parcels of land and water-bodies, topographic features such as bays, promontories, mountains and canyons, hills and valleys, roads, buildings, bridges, as well as the parts and aggregates of all of these". "Geographic objects are thus in every case spatial objects on or near the surface of the earth. They are objects of a certain minimal scale; they are typically complex, and they have parts". A geographic object has borders that distinguish it from other geographic objects in the environment. These borders can be concrete (*bona fide*) such as mountains and rivers or abstract (*fiat*) such as cities and municipalities (borders which exist only in virtue of the different sorts of demarcations effected cognitively by human beings) (Smith, 1994). We use the concept of *Geo-Object* to designate a geographic object (Fonseca et al., 2002). A geo-object has several descriptive attributes, a geometrical representation and is associated - by projection - to a spatial zone which represents its position in *Space*. The form and the size of the spatial zone are thus identical to the form and the size of its equivalent geo-object.

- **Geo-Objects relationships**: These are spatial relationships which describe the relative spatial positions of geo-objects. In the spatial literature we may distinguish the following conceptual categories of spatial relationships:

- *Topological relationships*: In the area of qualitative spatial reasoning, topology "is intended to describe properties of and relationships between spatial entities such as regions of points of a certain space, for instance, of two- or three-dimensional Euclidean space" (Renz, 2002). Several topological relations are proposed in the literature depending on the structure of the spatial objects (for example, simple or composite objects) and on computational models used to implement them (for example, *raster* or *vector* GIS data models).
- *Superposition relationship*: Superposition is an important relationship when reasoning about geographic space. Providing a formal definition of the superposition relationship is not an easy task (Desclés, 1990). A simple solution proposed by (Grenon and Smith, 2004) consists of adding another dimension in the projection function to specify that a geo-portion is located *over*, *under* or *on* a spatial zone.
- *Proximity relationships*: There are several models proposed in the literature to determine proximity relationships between spatial objects. An example of a generic model is proposed by (Kettani and Moulin, 1999) based on objects' *influence areas* to define a set of proximity relationships between spatial objects. This model can be used to compute proximity relationships such as *Close to* (*near*) and *Distant* (*far from*).

- **Actor:** Actors are used to specify endurant entities other than geo-objects. In the context of our project, actors represent the resources participating in the COA. Therefore, and depending on the application domain, actors may correspond to several entities such as people and cars. An actor has several descriptive attributes and can be stationary or mobile. In our model, at a given instant of time, an Actor is located in one and only one geo-object.

4.2 Dynamic View

We adopt Desclés' definitions of static and dynamic situations (Desclés, 1990). According to Desclés, a static situation represents the absence of change, while a dynamic situation introduces change and is abstracted as a transition of the world from an initial situation Sit_1 to another posterior situation Sit_2. The transition comprises three temporal zones: *before transition* (Sit_1), *during transition* from Sit_1 to Sit_2, and *after transition* (Sit_2). In addition to the model of Desclés, we extend the model of *temporal situations* proposed by Moulin (Moulin, 1997). A temporal situation is associated with a time interval which characterizes its temporal location on a time axis. An elementary time interval is specified by a list of parameters, essentially the begin-time *BT*, the end-time *ET*, the time scale *TS* and the time interval duration *DU*. We extend the concept of temporal situation to define the concept of *spatio-temporal situation*. A spatio-temporal situation is a temporal situation associated with a set of *spatio-temporal positions*.

Formally, a spatio-temporal situation is a quadruple <*SD, SPC, STI, SSTP*> where:

-The situation description *SD* is a pair [situation-type, situation-descriptor] used to identify the spatio-temporal situation. The situation type is used to semantically distinguish different kinds of spatio-temporal situations: states, events and processes. The situation descriptor identifies an instance of a situation and is used for referential purposes.

-The situation propositional content *SPC* is a non-temporal knowledge structure described by a conceptual graph. It makes a situation's semantic characteristics explicit.

-The situation time interval *STI* is a structure which aggregates the temporal information associated with the spatio-temporal situation.

-The situation's spatio-temporal position *SSTP* is a knowledge structure which describes positions of a spatio-temporal situation in space and time. The *SSTP* is formalized as a set of triples <$time_1$, $time_2$, *geo-obj*> indicating that during the interval time [$time_1$, $time_2$], the spatio-temporal situation is localized in a certain geo-object *geo-obj*.

Spatio-temporal situations are related by *temporal relations*. Based on Allen's temporal relations (Allen, 1983) we consider three basic relations called "*BEFORE*", "*DURING*" and "*AFTER*". Given two time intervals X and Y, the relation *BEFORE*(*X, Y, Lap*) holds if we have the following constraints between the begin- and end-times of X and Y compared on a time scale with the operators {>, <, =}: $BT(X) < ET(X); BT(Y) < ET(Y); BT(X) < BT(Y); ET(X) < ET(Y); BT(Y) - ET(X) = Lap, Lap => 0$. The *Lap* parameter is a real number that measures the distance between the beginning of interval *Y* and the end of interval *X* on their time scale. *DURING* and *AFTER* relations are defined in the same way (Moulin, 1997).

Graphically, we represent a spatio-temporal situation by a rectangle composed of three parts, top, middle and bottom respectively representing knowledge associated with the SD & STI, the SPC and the SSTP (examples are presented later).
Using this notation we formalize three kinds of spatio-temporal situations: state, event, and process.

- State: A state corresponds to a static situation (i.e. a finite configuration of some aspect of the world in a limited region of space that remains unchanged for a period of time). We have already mentioned that a situation is characterized by various properties or relations that hold among the various objects in that situation (Sowa, 1984). Desclés (1990) distinguished between localization states (spatial and temporal) and attribution states (assign a property to an object). Figure 5 illustrates a simple example of an attribution state identified by *st1*. Note that in conceptual graphs formalizm, each conceptual graph is associated with a propositional content, which is set to *true* by default. If the negation symbol "¬" is associated with a conceptual graph, the propositional content is set to *false*. In

Figure 5, the SPC of *st1* specifies that the person Dany is sick[4]. The STI specifies that Dany was sick during the time interval [September 23 2004, January 20 2005]. The SSTP specifies that during his state of illness, Dany was in Québec till December 11 2004 then in Paris from December 12 2004. Note that STI and SSTP's information is optional because, depending on the context, it can be unavailable or partially available. In this case, the temporal and spatio-temporal parameters are not specified.

Attribution_State: st1 BT: September 23 2004; ET: January 20 2005; TS: Date
[PERSON: Dany]->(ATT)->[Sick]
{<23-09-2004, 11-12-2004, Québec>, <12-12-2004, 20-01-2005, Paris>}

Fig. 5. An example of state

- Event: We adopt Desclés' definition (Desclés, 1990). An event expresses a temporal occurrence that appears in a static background, which may or may not change the world. It marks a break between the "before-event" and the "after-event". However, in our model we consider that events are punctual, i.e. their duration corresponds to a single time unit. Using the temporal relations *BEFORE* and *AFTER*, we define two relationships *BEFORE-SITUATION* and *AFTER-SITUATION* respectively corresponding to the initial situation (before the event) and the final situation (at the end of the event). Figure 6 illustrates an example of a simple event of type *Spatial_Zone_Entry_Event* identified by *ev1*. Its propositional content makes explicit the agent and the destination of the movement. Its time interval parameters are: BT: 10:00:00; ET: 10:00:00; TS: Time; DU: 1 (Duration = ET - BT + 1) and DS. In addition, its SSTP specifies that the event occurred at Laval University's campus at time 10:00:00. The event triggers a change from a "before event situation" to an "after event situation". The first situation is a localization state identified by *st1*. It has only two time parameters: ET: 09:59:59 and TS: time. Its propositional content describes the fact that the person Hedi is located outside Laval University's campus. This state is related to the event *ev1* by the *Before-Situation* relationship. The second situation is a localization state identified by *st2*. It also has only two time parameters: BT: 10:00:00 and TS: time. Its propositional content describes the fact that Hedi is located inside Laval University's campus. This state is related to the event *ev1* by the After-Situation relationship.

---

4 Syntactically, a conceptual graph is a network of concept nodes linked by relation nodes. Concept nodes are represented by the notation [Concept Type: Concept instance] and relation nodes by (Relationship-Name). The concept instance can either be a value, a set of values or a CG. The formalism can be represented in either graphical or character-based notations. In the graphical notation, concepts are represented by rectangles, relations by circles and the links between concept and relation nodes by arrows. The character-based notation (or linear form) is more compact than the graphical one and uses square brackets instead of boxes and parentheses instead of circles.

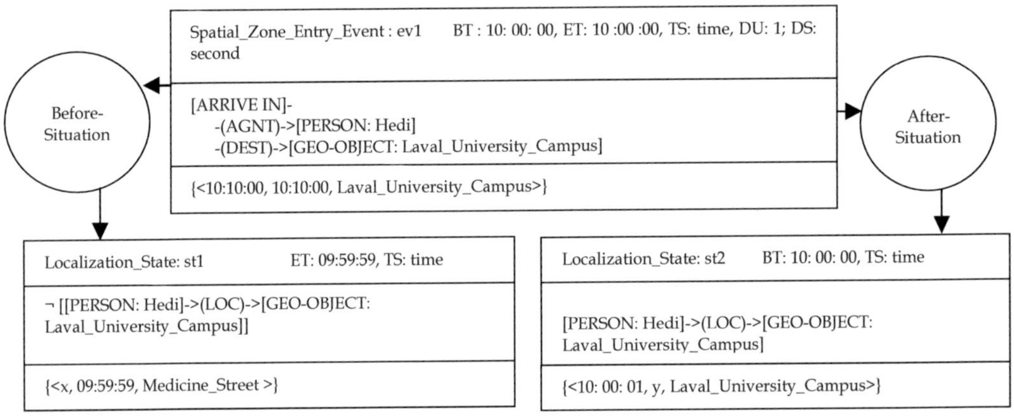

Fig. 6. An example of event

-Process: We adopt Desclés' definition of a process (Desclés, 1990). A process expresses a change initiated by an event that marks the beginning of the process, and may have an end-event and a resulting state. A process makes the universe transit from an initial situation corresponding to the "before-process" to a final situation describing the "after-process". In contrast to an event, a process has a significant duration, and we can talk about "a situation holding during the process". Using the temporal relation *DURING*, we define the relationship *DURING-SITUATION* corresponding to the intermediate situation which holds during the process. Figure 7 illustrates a process corresponding to the fact that "Hedi takes 10 minutes to go from home to Laval University Campus using his bicycle". The situation is a movement process, identified by *cp1*. It has an initial and a final situation specified similarly to those that we presented for the event. In addition, a process may be associated with a situation describing the state that holds during its progress. In the case of *cp1*, the 'during situation' is a localization state identified by *st3*. It has the same temporal parameters as the process *cp1*. Its propositional content describes the fact that the person Hedi is located neither at home nor in Laval University Campus (we don't know where exactly, that is why the SSTP of *st3* and *cp1* are empty). It is related to the process *cp1* by the During-Situation relationship.

Different relationships can be defined between states, events and processes. In Figure 4 we presented only some of these relationships (an event initiates or ends a process, and a process modifies a state). Other relationships can be defined, such as facilitation and blocking (Worboys and Hornsby, 2004).

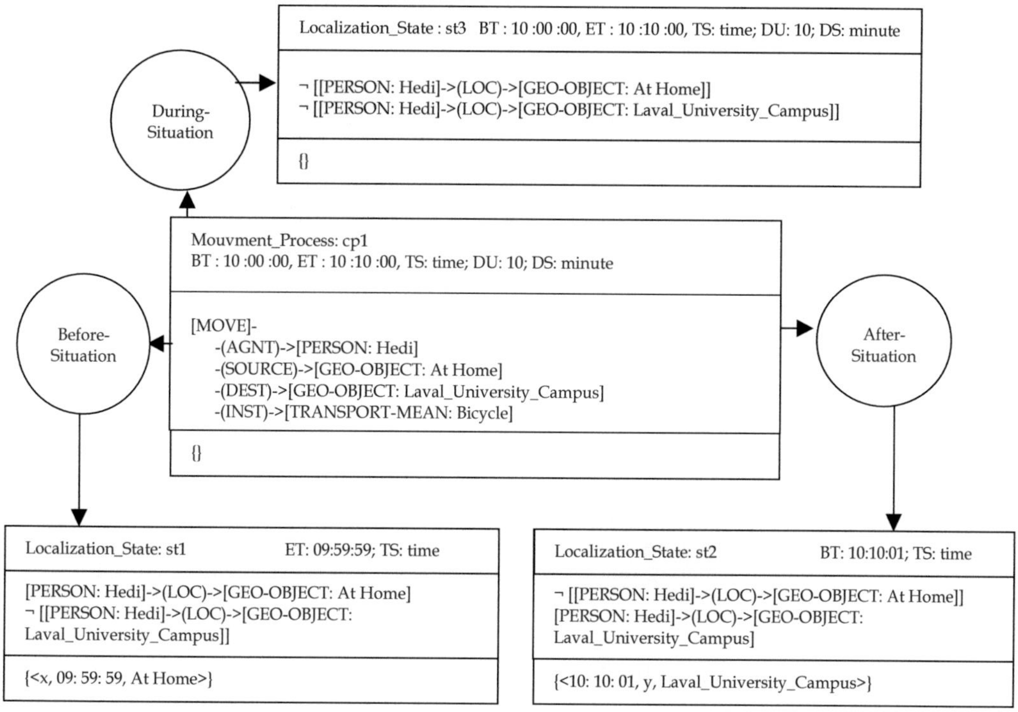

Fig. 7. The representation of a process

In this section we presented our conceptual model for representing dynamic geographic phenomena using the concept of *spatio-temporal situations*. This model represents our solution for the first requirement of our MAGS-based approach. In the following section we present our solution for the second requirement, which consists of expressing the results of the geosimulations in terms of spatio-temporal situations.

5. From Quantitative Geosimulations to Qualitative Spatio-Temporal Situations

The second requirement of our MAGS-based approach is to be able to express the results of geosimulations using the concepts of spatio-temporal situations (states, events and processes). In order to meet this requirement, we developed a data collection and transformation approach which is explained using the example of Figure 8.

Let us consider a COA composed of only one resource: agent *A*. Suppose that the agent is initially located in the geo-object *zone06*. Suppose also that we assign to this agent the task to go to *zone12* following a predefined path <*zone06, zone08, zone12*>. Finally, let us suppose that the agent is characterized by two attributes, "Location" (position) and "Tiredness-level" which are respectively initialized to "zone06" and "normal".

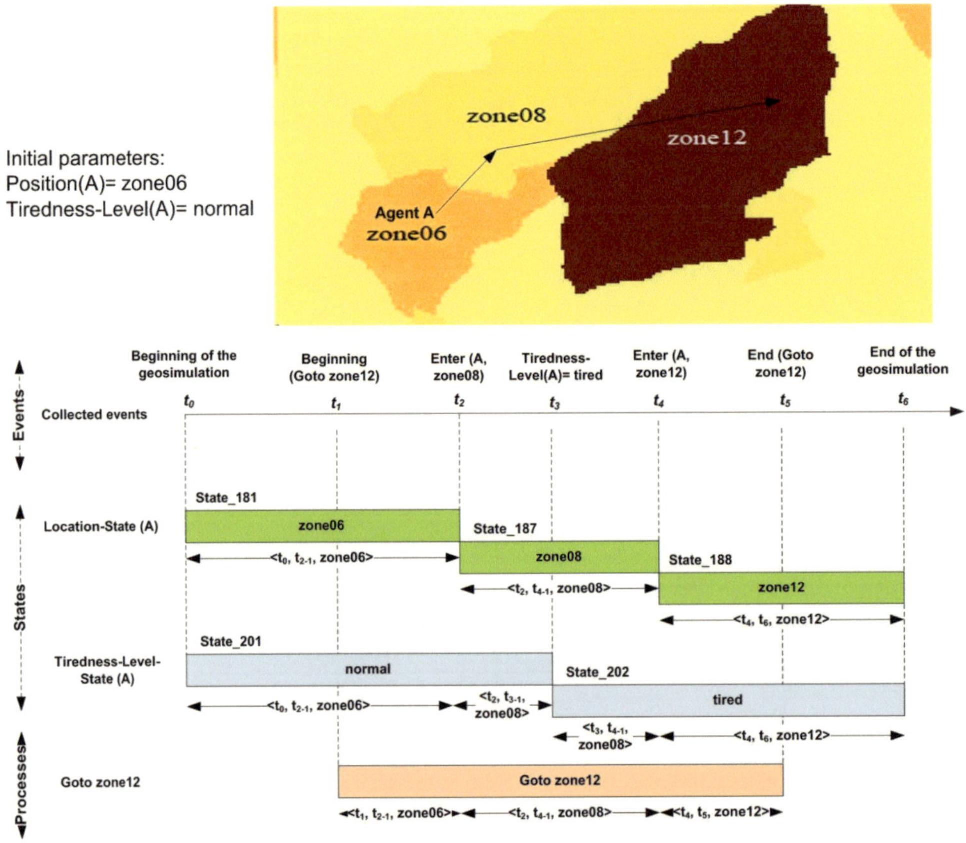

Fig. 8. An example illustrating data transformation

The key idea is that the system should collect, during the geosimulation, data describing changes of attributes of entities manipulated in the geosimulation. Therefore, the results that are initially collected during the simulation only correspond to punctual events. Based on these events, the system should deduce states and processes and identify their spatio-temporal positions. In the example illustrated in Figure 8, the initial results of the geosimulation correspond to situations describing punctual events, such as the beginning of the execution of the task *Goto zone12*, the change of the location of the agent from *zone06* to *zone08* (the event *Enter(A, zone08)*) and the change of the attribute "Tiredness-Level" of the agent *A* (the agent is tired at t_3). These events are formalized in CGs according to the model presented in Section 4. At the end of the geosimulation, algorithms are applied to identify, from these events, an explicit representation of states and processes. For example, from the punctual event describing the fact that agent *A* entered the geo-entity *zone08* at time t_2 we can identify the state *State_181* of type *Location-State* and describing the fact that agent *A* is located in *zone06* during the time interval $[t_0, t_{2-1}]$ (Figure 8). Similarly, from the punctual event describing the fact that agent *A* is tired at t_3 we can explicitly identify the state *State_201* of type *Tiredness-level-State*: this state describes the fact that agent *A*'s tiredness level is normal during the temporal interval $[t_0, t_{3-1}]$, and that the spatio-temporal position of this state is {<t_0, t_{2-1}, *zone06*>, <t_2, t_{3-1}, *zone08*>}. Of course, we raised the assumption that the

spatio-temporal position of a state corresponds to the spatio-temporal position of the entity described by this state during its temporal interval. Therefore, the spatio-temporal position of *State_201* corresponds to the spatio-temporal position of agent *A* during the interval [t_0, t_{3-1}], which is {<t_0, t_{2-1}, *zone06*>, <t_2, t_{3-1}, *zone08*>} (Figure 8). Processes are identified using the same principle. For example, considering the two punctual events that respectively describe the beginning and the end of execution of task *Goto zone12*, we identify an explicit representation of the process *Goto zone12* which takes place during the time interval [t_1, t_5]. Using a similar assumption that the spatio-temporal position of a process corresponds to the spatio-temporal position of the entity executing this process, we can identify that the spatio-temporal position of the process *Goto zone12* is {<t_0, t_{2-1}, *zone06*>, <t_2, t_{4-1}, *zone08*>, <t_4, t_5, *zone12*>}.
Presenting the detailed algorithms used for data transformation is beyond the scope of this chapter, for more details the interested reader can refer to (Haddad, 2009).

6. Causal Reasoning about Spatio-Temporal Situations

After applying the data transformation presented in Section 5, the results of the geosimulation are expressed in terms of spatio-temporal situations, i.e. states, events and processes with their temporal and spatio-temporal positions. Causal analysis can now be carried out. Our aim is to identify causation relationships between spatio-temporal situations. Causation is a semantic relationship that holds between two individual situation instances. One situation instance plays the role of cause while the other plays the role of effect. In the literature, a distinction is made between causation and causality (Lehmann and Gangemi, 2007). While causation refers to a causal relationship between two individual situation instances, causality refers to a causal relationship between two situation types. Therefore, reasoning about causation relies on knowledge about causality. In the literature, a causality relationship in a spatial context is based on temporal and spatial constraints. These constraints are derived from the fact that human recognition of causal relations is based upon recognition of precedence and contiguity between the cause and the effect (Kitamura et al., 1997). In this view, cause occurs before effect and both are spatially contiguous. We use the temporal causal ontology proposed by (Terenziani and Torasso, 1995) to model temporal constraints. The ontology distinguished different semantic causal relationships between temporal situations (states, events and processes) depending on their temporal intervals (i.e., the cause occurs before or at the same time as the effect and the cause ends before, after or at the same time as the effect). For example, there is a difference between causal relations in which "the presence of the cause is only momentarily required to allow the effect to begin", and causal relations in which "the continued presence of the cause is required in order to sustain the effect" (Terenziani and Torasso, 1995). In order to model the spatial constraints, we use the model proposed by (El-Geresy et al., 2002). In this regard, cause must be spatially connected to its effect in either one of two ways: indirect (distant) or direct connection. In the case of distant connection, a path must exist between the spatial positions of the cause and of the effect which allows the propagation of a certain *causing property*, such as, for example, a lake does not allow the spread of fire (El-Geresy et al., 2002). In addition, when cause and effect are not spatially co-located, cause takes a delay to reach its effect (*diffusion delays*).

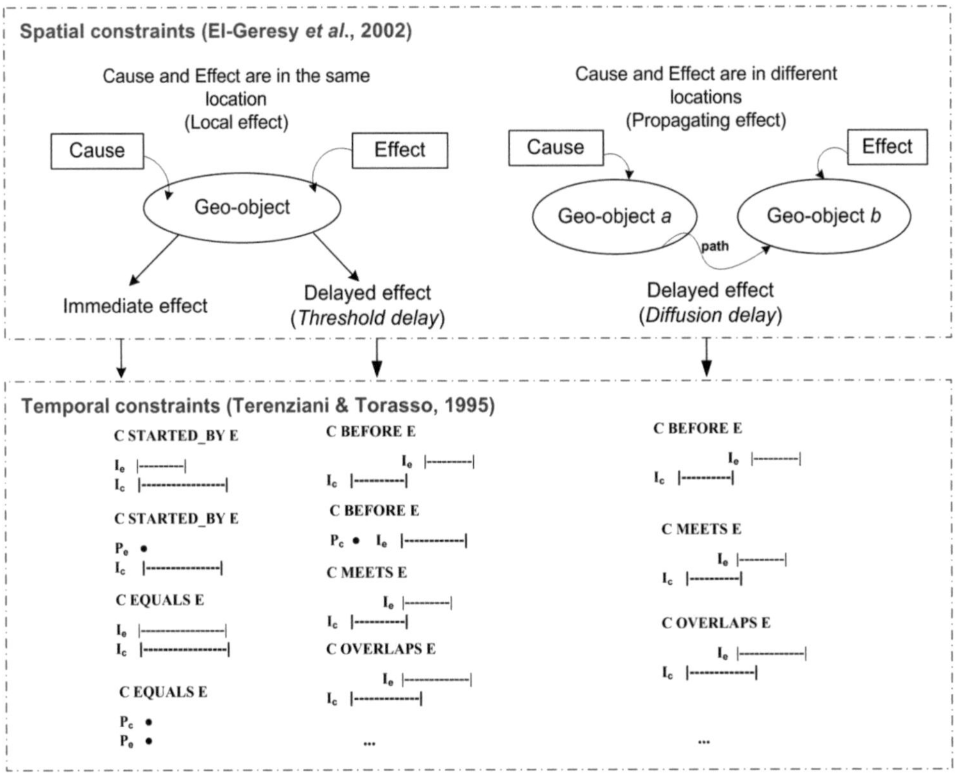

Fig. 9. Spatio-temporal causal constraints

By combining the aforementioned temporal and spatial models, it is possible to represent the spatio-temporal causal constraints illustrated in Figure 9. With respect to the spatial causal constraint, a cause may have a local or a propagating effect. On the one hand, a local effect takes place at the same spatial position as the cause situation. From a temporal perspective, a local effect can be immediate or delayed. Immediate effect starts at the same time as its cause. Delayed effect corresponds to the fact that the cause "may not be able to deliver its effect before reaching a certain level over a certain period of time, e.g. flooding will not occur before the water in the river increases beyond a certain level" (El-Geresey et al., 2002). Spatio-temporal immediate effects and threshold-delayed effects are formalized using Allen's temporal relationships (Allen, 1983). For example, an immediate effect can be formalized by the respective following spatial and temporal constraints: Location(cause) = Location(effect) and {*Started_By* (Cause, Effect) or *Equals* (Cause, Effect)}. On the other hand, a propagating effect takes place at a different spatial position than the cause situation. Thus, we always talk about a delay corresponding to the time taken by the cause to reach its effect. Similarly, spatio-temporal diffusion delayed effects are formalized using Allen's temporal relationships. The spatio-temporal positions (SSTP) of our spatio-temporal situations are used to verify the different spatio-temporal causal constraints between a cause and an effect.

Using these causal spatio-temporal constraints, we specify knowledge about causality thanks to the concept of *causality relation* (Figure 10). A *Causality Relation* defines a causal link between a typical cause situation (the *HasCauseSituation* relationship) and a typical effect situation (the *HasEffectSituation* relationship) and specifies the spatio-temporal constraints that characterize this link (the *Temporal Constraints* and *Spatial Constraint* concepts). Cause and effect situations are actually configurations of spatio-temporal situations (the *Situations Configuration* concept). Consisting of one or more spatio-temporal situations, a configuration describes how a set of typical spatio-temporal situations is organized in order to play the role of a typical cause or effect in a causality relation.

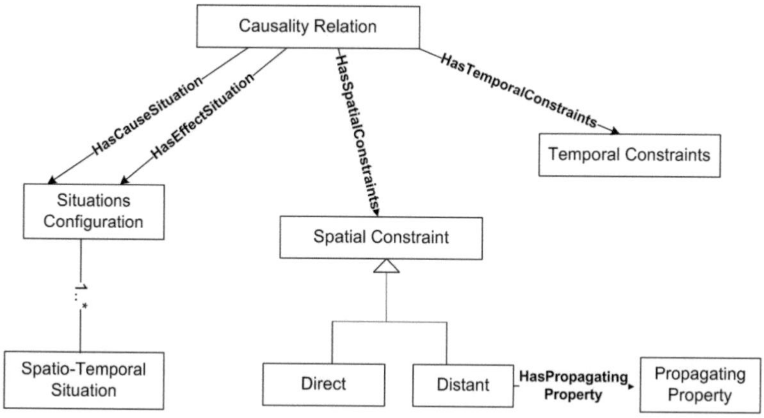

Fig. 10. Semantic of a causality relation

Causality relations are used to specify knowledge about causality and to infer causation relationships between instances of spatio-temporal situations obtained as a result of a geosimulation. Simply, we say that an individual spatio-temporal situation sts_a of type *A* is a cause of another individual spatio-temporal situation sts_b of type *B* if there is a causality relation specifying that typical situations of type *A* cause typical situations of type *B*.

In this section we covered all the requirements identified in Section 3.3 in order to implement our MAGS-based COAs' "What-if" analysis approach. In the following section we present how our approach was implemented in the center of the MAGS-COA Project.

7. The MAGS-COA Project

Our team developed the MAGS-COA System, a proof of concept of the proposed approach. The objectives of the MAGS-COA Project are 1) to illustrate the technical feasibility of the proposed approach and 2) to evaluate the relevance of the approach to support the resolution of real problems. We present the technical architecture of the system in Section 7.1. In Section 7.2 we give a general idea about how we used the system to implement scenarios in the search and rescue (SAR) domain and to qualitatively evaluate the relevance of the approach with SAR domain experts.

7.1 Architecture

The MAGS-COA system is designed to support the steps of the approach which were presented in Section 3.2. Figure 11 illustrates the system's architecture which is composed of three main modules: the experiment specification module, the geosimulation module and the evaluation module. In the followingparagraphs we give a general presentation of these modules.

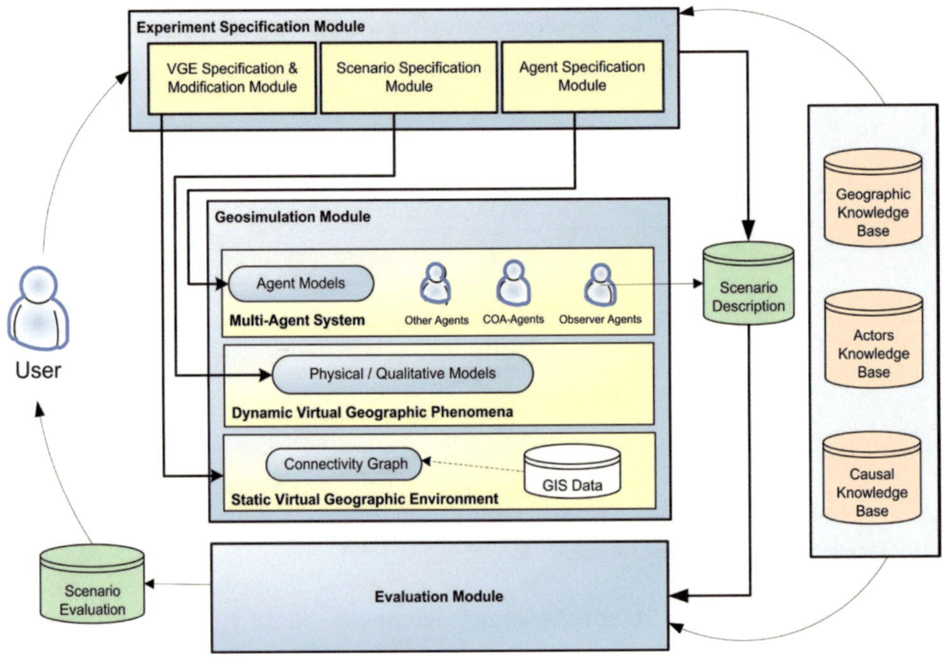

Fig. 11. The architecture of MAGS-COA

COA "What-if" Experiment specification

The first step consists in initializing the COA's "What-if" experiment. To do so, the user first selects the *VGE* (Virtual Geographic Environment) where the scenario will be executed, using the *VGE Specification and Modification Module*. This allows loading and initializing the geographic environment into the geosimulation module (Figure 11). The geographic environment is a GIS-based data model augmented with the elements presented in Section 4.1. There are different systematic ways of coupling GIS and multi-agent simulation environments (Schüle et al., 2004). In our project, we use a loose coupling, i.e. data is generated using a GIS tool and then imported into the virtual geographic environment where it can be manipulated by the agents during the simulation run. Geo-Objects (mountains, lakes, etc.) and their topological relationships are directly generated by the GIS tool. This knowledge is stored in a data structure manipulated by the simulation environment (as a connectivity graph). In addition, semantic knowledge about geographic objects is specified in a geographic knowledge base containing types of entities of the geographic environment (i.e. Geo-Objects, such as mountains and lakes, and natural processes, such as rain and snow) and their attributes.

The user then uses the *Agent Specification Module* to select the actors participating in the experiment (from a list of actors specified in the Actors knowledge base) and to locate them in the VGE. The Actors knowledge base is an application ontology containing information about types of actors, their attributes and the tasks that they are able to carry out. Tasks correspond to the activities that an actor can perform, from simple movements to complex and sophisticated activities (such as "lead an attack operation" in the military domain). Knowledge about tasks is defined using the concept of spatio-temporal situation presented in Section 4.1.

Then, the user specifies the scenario describing the COA and the assumptions (using the *Scenario Specification Module*). The COA specifies the sequence of tasks and the constraints imposed on the actors (the agents of the geosimulation) in order to achieve their mission. The assumptions are formalized as different "happenings" located in space and time (as for example, the explosion of a bridge or the beginning of wind blowing at a specific time, in a given location and in a given direction). The different types of happenings and their attributes correspond to the physical spatio-temporal processes and events specified in the geographic base knowledge. The *Agent Specification Module* and the *Scenario Specification Module* respectively allow initializing the attributes and the behaviours of the corresponding agents' models in the geosimulation module (Figure 11).

MAGS

Then, the user launches the geosimulation in the *VGE*. The actors of the COA are represented by autonomous software agents simulating the behaviours of the real actors. We use an enhanced version of the MAGS platform (Moulin et al., 2003) as a multi-agent geosimulation environment. In this platform, agents are characterized by internal states corresponding to their attributes and are equipped with perception, navigation and behavioural capabilities according to a *perception-decision-action* loop (Figure 12, left side). With respect to the perception capabilities, an agent has a perception field which enables it to perceive 1) terrain features such as elevation and slopes, 2) the geographic objects and the other agents located in the agent's range of perception, and 3) dynamic areas or volumes whose shapes change during the simulation (such us smoky or foggy areas). Regarding the navigation capabilities, MAGS agents may use two navigation modes: *Following-a-path-mode* in which agents follow specific paths such as roads or *Obstacle-avoidance-mode* in which the agents move through open spaces avoiding obstacles. Finally, in the MAGS platform, an agent is associated with a set of objectives that it tries to reach. The objectives are organized in hierarchies composed of nodes representing composite objectives and leaves representing elementary objectives associated with actions that the agent can perform (Figure 12, right side). An agent makes decision about its objectives based on several parameters, such as its internal states and the perceived features of the *VGE*. Further details about agents' capabilities in the MAGS platform can be found in (Moulin et al., 2003).

The tasks of the scenario are transformed into agents' objectives. Depending on the natural phenomena to be simulated and the available data models, happenings and their effects can be simulated either using mathematical models (such as models of flood (Herath, 2001), fire propagation (Farsite, 2008) and soil erosion (Shen et al., 2006)), qualitative simulation models or agent-based models. In the current version of MAGS-COA, these phenomena are simulated using agent-based models. However, the behaviour of an agent simulating a natural phenomenon can be defined using either qualitative models (such as the wind triangle (NASA, 2006) to calculate the effect of wind on flying objects) or mathematical physical models (such as the above mentioned fire propagation model). Details about this aspect are beyond the scope of this chapter.

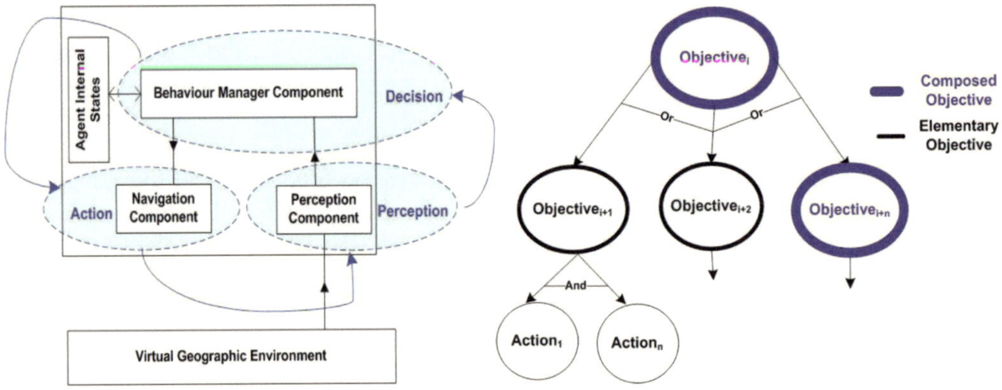

Fig. 12. Architecture of an agent (left) and agents' objectives hierarchy (right) in the MAGS platform

In Section 5 we presented a summary of our strategy to collect and transform the results of the geosimulation. Practically, we use a specific kind of agents, called *observer agents*, to collect and record information about relevant events occurring in the geosimulation virtual environment (Moulin et al., 2003). As it was explained in Section 5, observer agents collect information describing changes of values of geosimulation entities' attributes: attributes of continuant entities such as actors and geo-objects and attributes of occurrent entities such as actors' objectives and actions and computational processes simulating the physical phenomena. These collected events are formalized in our CG formalism and inserted in a log file which must be analyzed by the evaluation module.

Evaluation module

As we explained in Section 5, the evaluation module first applies the required transformations in order to create an explicit representation of the results of the geosimulation as a set of spatio-temporal situations instances. The evaluation then consists in applying causal reasoning in order to infer causation relationships among these situations instances. The evaluation process consists of: 1) establishing a temporal ordering of the initial set of spatio-temporal situations instances and 2) for every pair of these instances, verifying if they verify the constraints of a certain causality relation in the causal knowledge base (Figure 11). If these constraints hold, a new CG is created, making explicit the causal link between the individual cause and effect spatio-temporal situations.

We used the *Amine* platform (Kabbaj et al., 2006) to support reasoning about the geosimulation outputs. *Amine* is a Java Open Source platform that provides an integrated architecture to build intelligent systems. More specifically, we used the ontology and the *Prolog+CG* modules of this platform. Amine's ontology module allows building, editing and using ontologies and knowledge bases expressed in CGs. We used this module to define the knowledge bases of our project. *Prolog+CG* is an object-based and CG-based extension of the Prolog language including an interface with Java. We used *Prolog+CG* to develop the algorithms of the evaluation module.

7.2 Illustrative Scenario and Approach's Evaluation

As we mentioned in the beginning of Section 7, the second objective of the MAGS-COA Project was to evaluate the suitability of our approach as a support to real problems solving. As an example, we chose the aerial search and rescue (SAR) application domain in which "What-if" reasoning is frequently used to analyze historical events. More specifically, "What-if" analysis is used in this domain to determine why a specific COA has failed. For example, let us consider that a lost plane was performing a COA (flying plan) and that its desired objective (the mission) was to reach a specific destination at a specific time. Nevertheless, in a search and rescue context the plane was lost (it did not reach its destination) and consequently the COA failed. The main reasoning in a SAR scenario consists in raising hypotheses to infer the potential reasons that may have caused this failure. In a SAR Center, the human controller usually uses a map to study the characteristics of the terrain and to manually delimit the extent of the search area according to predefined rules (doctrine). In the case of a lost aircraft, the controller crafts certain hypotheses and attempts to validate them by confronting them to information received from various sources (information given by the pilot's relatives, weather agencies, on-site observers, etc.) and spatial constraints that he observes on the map.

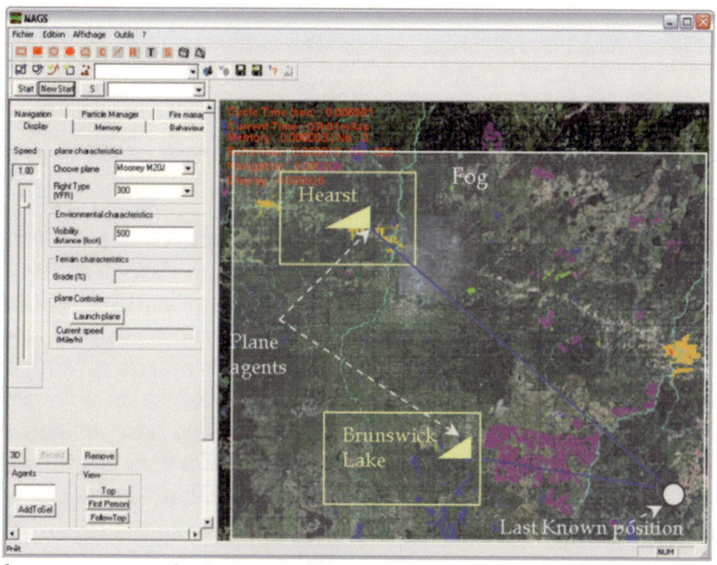

Fig. 13. Two plane agents exploring scenarios

Working with a historical real case study (the JOANIS case, occurred in Ontario, Canada), we implemented a scenario allowing a controller to make assumptions about different alternatives and to evaluate their credibility. Figure 13 illustrates the graphical interface of the implemented scenario. The system allows the controller to make assumptions about weather conditions (movement of fog patches in this case) and the decision that may have been made by the pilot (such as for example choosing an alternative landing site). In Figure 13, the controller evaluates the credibility of two alternative scenarios: because of the reduced visibility caused by fog the pilot has either: 1) selected Hearst as an alternative destination or 2) decided to look for a landing site near Brunswick Lake. For every scenario, we simulated the movement of fog and the behaviour of the plane in a *VGE* built from real GIS data.

Figure 14 illustrates an example of scenarios evaluation returned by the system. The evaluation shows that the process *Fog_01* caused the agent *mooney_01* to execute an objective of Visual Flight Rule (*process_53*). After that, the fact that the *fuel level* reached a critical level (the punctual event *event_52*) immediately caused the plane to execute an objective of finding the nearest landing place (*process_89*). The fact that the plane found a suitable landing place (*event_67*) immediately caused it to execute an objective of emergency landing (*process_67*). The system evaluates this alternative scenario as possible because the plane successfully completed its emergency landing objective. Note that *ThresdelayedCause* and *ImmCause* are two typical causality relations defined in the causal knowledge base with their temporal and spatial constraints.

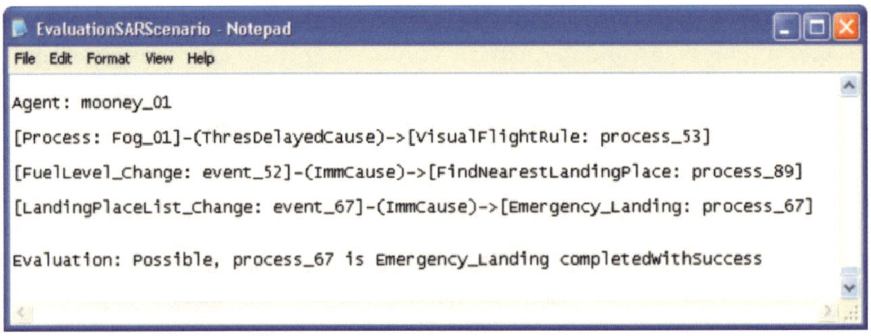

Fig. 14. An example of "What-if" scenario evaluation

We used the implemented scenario to evaluate the relevance of the approach by three SAR domain experts. The evaluation was *subjective* and *qualitative*. After a demo of the scenario, experts expressed their opinions using questionnaires and/or by direct discussions. Experts expressed positive feedback about the approach in general. Especially, they judged the approach relevant as a tool for training novice staffs and as a decision support about some precise aspects that must be considered when solving real cases. For example, experts appreciated the help given by the system to identify suitable landing sites that may have been chosen by a pilot, especially in a large scale geographic environment.

From an experimental point of view, our subjective and qualitative evaluation is not enough in order to conclude about the suitability of our approach as a support to real problem solving. Further experimentations are needed and planned to be carried out on different application domains in the future.

8. Conclusion and Future Work

In this chapter we proposed an approach that associates MAGS models with qualitative spatio-temporal reasoning techniques to support qualitative analysis in the context of dynamic geographic spaces. We studied the COAs' "What-if" analysis problem as a practical example. This multidisciplinary approach led to other interesting contributions such as the model of *spatio-temporal situations* and its application to the problem of causal reasoning in a dynamic spatial context. Besides, the MAGS-COA system shows the potential of the proposed approach as a support to real problem solving.

However, additional work is required to fully exploit the advantages of the proposed approach and to address its limits. From a computational perspective, we plan, in the near future, to evaluate the performance of the MAGS-COA system on scenarios involving a large number of agents and more complex spatio-temporal situations. From a theoretical perspective, we plan in a first step to apply our approach to support "What-if" reasoning in other domains such as fire forests and crowd control. In a second step we plan to extend our approach to other kinds of qualitative spatio-temporal reasoning and to explore how to take advantage of the concept of *qualitative spatio-temporal patterns* to analyze MAGS results. Indeed, causality relations are an example of qualitative spatio-temporal patterns, and generalizing the approach to support other kinds of qualitative spatio-temporal patterns is an interesting theoretical and practical area to be explored.

9. Acknowledgments

This research is supported by GEOIDE, the Canadian Network of Centers of Excellence in Geomatics (MUSCAMAGS Project), by Valcartier Defence R&D Canada (DRDC), Quebec, Canada (MAGS-COA Project) and by the Natural Science and Engineering Research Council of Canada (Discovery Grant Program).

10. References

Albrecht, J. (2005). A new age for geosimulation. *Transactions in GIS*, Vol. 9, No. 4, pp. 451–454

Ali, W. (2008). *2D/3D MultiAgent GeoSimulation: A Generic Method and its Application*, VDM Verlag Dr. Mueller e.K., ISBN-10: 3836472295

Ali, W.; Moulin, B.; Bédard, Y.; Proulx, M.J. & Rivest, S. (2007). Coupling Multiagent Geosimulation and Spatial OLAP for Better Geosimulation Data Analysis. *URISA Journal*, Vol. 19, No. 2, pp. 5-14

Allen, J. F. (1983). Maintaining Knowledge about temporal intervals. *Communications of the ACM*, Vol. 26, pp. 832-843

Batty, M. & Jiang B. (2000). Multi-agent Simulation: Computational Dynamics within GIS, In: *Innovation in GIS VII: Geocomputation*, Martin D. and Atkinson P. (Eds.), pp. 55–71, Taylor & Francis

Benenson, I. & Torrens, P.M. (2004). *Geosimulation: Automata-based modeling of urban phenomena*, WILEY edition, ISBN 0-470-84349-7, England

Benenson, I.; Martens, K. & Birfir, S. (2007). Agent-Based Model of Driver Parking Behavior As a Tool for Urban Parking Policy Evaluation, *Proceedings of the 10th AGILE International Conference on GISience 2007*, Aalborg University, Denmark

Blecic, I.; Cecchini, A. & Trunfio, G.A. (2008). A Software Infrastructure for Multi-agent Geosimulation Applications, In: *ICCSA 2008, Part I, LNCS 5072*, O. Gervasi et al. (Eds.), pp. 375–388, Springer-Verlag, ISBN:978-3-540-69838-8, Berlin, Heidelberg

Bossomaier, T.; Amri, S. & Thompson, J. (2007). Agent-Based Modelling of House Price Evolution, *Proceedings of the 2007 IEEE Symposium on Artificial Life (CI-ALife 2007)*, pp. 463-467, Honolulu, HI

Bouden, M.; Moulin, B. & Gosselin, P. (2008). The geosimulation of West Nile virus propagation: a multi-agent and climate sensitive tool for risk management in public health. *International Journal of Health Geographics*, Vol. 7, No. 35

Brown, D. & Xie, Y. (2006). Spatial agent-based modeling. *International Journal of Geographical Information Science*, Vol. 20, No. 9, pp. 941–943

Casati, R., Smith, B. and Varzi, A.C. (1998). Ontological Tools for Geographic Representation, In: *Formal Ontology in Information Systems*, N. Guarino (Ed.), pp. 77 - 85, IOS Press, Amsterdam

Cohn, A. & Hazarika, S. (2001) Qualitative Spatial Representation and Reasoning: An Overview. *Fundamental Informaticae*, Vol. 46, No. 1-2, pp. 1-29

Desclés, J.-P. (1990). *Langages applicatifs, langues naturelles et cognition*, Hermès, ISBN: 2-86601-227-5, Paris

Desclés, J.-P. (2005). Reasoning and Aspectual-Temporal Calculus, In: *Logic, Thought & Action*, Vanderveken, D. (Ed.), pp. 217–244, Kluwer Academic Publishers, Springer

El-Geresy, B.; Abdelmoty, A. & Jones, C. (2002). Spatio-Temproal Geographic Infromation Systems: A causal Perspective, In: *ADBIS 2002, LNCA 2435*, Manolopoulos, Y. and Navrat, P. (Eds.), pp. 191–203, Springer, ISBN: 978-3-540-44138-0, Berlin

FARSITE simulator (2008). http://www.firemodels.org/content/view/112/143/, last update: Sunday, 17 February 2008, Last access: Wednesday, 27 February 2008.

Ferrario, R. (2001). Counterfactual Reasoning, In: *Modeling and Using Context, Proceedings of the Third International and Interdisciplinary Conference, CONTEXT 2001, LNAI 2116*, Akman et al. (Eds.), pp. 170-183, Springer, Berlin Heidelberg

Fonseca, F.; Egenhofer, M.; Agouris, P. & Câmara, G. (2002). Using Ontologies for Integrated Geographic Information Systems. *Transactions in GIS*, Vol. 6, No. 3, pp. 231-257

Forbus, K.D. (1981). A Study of Qualitative and Geometric Knowledge in Reasoning about Motion. Massachusetts Institute of Technology, Arctificial Intelligence Laboratory, AI-TR-615, 1981

Fournier, S. (2005). Intégration de la dimension spatiale au sein d'un modèle multi-agents à base de rôles pour la simulation: Application à la navigation maritime. PhD thesis, Université de Rennes 1, France

Frank, A.U.; Bittner, S. & Raubal, M. (2001). Spatial and Cognitive Simulation with Multi-agent Systems, In: *Spatial information Theory: Foundations for Geographic Information Science, LNCS 2205*, D. Montello (Ed.), p. 124-139, Springer

Furtado, E.; Furtado, V. & Vasconcelos, E. (2007). A Conceptual Framework for the Design and Evaluation of Affective Usability in Educational Geosimulation Systems, In: *INTERACT 2007, LNCS 4662, Part I*, Baranauskas et al. (Eds.), pp. 497–510, Springer

Gaglio, C.M. (2004). The Role of Mental Simulations and Counterfactual Thinking in the Opportunity Identification Process. *Entrepreneurship Theory and Practice*, Vol. 28, No. 6, pp. 533-552

Georgeff, M.; David, M. & Anand, R. (1993). Events and processes in situation semantics, In *Situation Theory and Its Applications*, P. Aczel; D. Israel; Y. Katagiri & S. Peters (Eds.), CA: Stanford University Press, Stanford

Gimblett, R. (2002). *Integrating geographic information systems and agent-based modeling techniques for simulating social and ecological processes*, Oxford University Press, New York

Grenon, P. & Smith, B. (2004). SNAP and SPAN: Towards dynamic spatial ontology. *Spatial Cognition and Computation*, Vol. 4, No. 1, pp. 69-103

Haddad, H. (2009). Une approche pour supporter l'analyse qualitative des suites d'actions dans un environnement géographique virtuel et dynamique, l'analyse « What-if » comme exemple. PhD Thesis, Laval University, Canada, 2009

Haddad, H. and Moulin, B. (2007). Using Cognitive Archetypes and Conceptual Graphs to Model Dynamic Phenomena in Spatial Environments, In: *ICCS 2007, LNAI 4604*, U. Priss; S. Polovina & R. Hill (Eds.), pp. 69–82, Springer-Verlag, Berlin Heidelberg

Hagen-Zanker, A. & Martens, P. (2008). Map Comparison Methods for Comprehensive Assessment of Geosimulation Models, In: *LNCS 5072*, pp. 194-209, Springer, ISBN 978-3-540-69838-8

Helbig, H. (2006). Semantic Characterization of Situations, In: *Knowledge Representation and the Semantics of Natural Language (Cognitive technologies)*, pp. 85–111, Springer-Verlag, ISBN: 978-3-540-24461-5

Hensman, S. & Dunnion, J. (2004). Using Linguistic Resources to Construct Conceptual Graph Representation of Texts. *Speech and Dialogue* , vol. 3206, pp. 81-88

Herath, S. (2001). Geographical Information Systems in Disaster Reduction. *Information Technology For Disaster Management*, No.1, pp. 25-31

Kabbaj, A. (2006). Development of Intelligent Systems and Multi-Agents Systems with Amine Platform, In: *ICCS'06, LNAI 4068*, Springer, pp. 286-299, ISBN: 3-540-35893-5, Berlin

Kahneman, D. & Tversky, A. (1982). The simulation heuristic, In: *Judgement under uncertainty: Heuristics and biases*, D. Kahneman, P. Slovic and Tversky (Eds.). Cmabridge university Press, New York

Kettani, D. & Moulin, B. (1999). A Spatial Model Based on the Notions of Spatial Conceptual Map and of Object's Influence Areas, In: *Spatial Information Theory, Cognitive and Computational Foundations of GIS, LNCS 1661*, C. Freska, D. M. Mark (Eds.), pp. 401-415, Springer Verlag

Kitamura, Y.; Ikeda, M. & Mizoguchi, R. (1997). A Causal Time Ontology for Qualitative Reasoning, *Proceedings of the Fifteenth International Joint Conference on Artificial Intelligence IJCAI-97*, pp. 501-506, Maurgan Kaufmann Publishers

Lebow, R.N. (2007). Counterfactual Thought Experiments: A Necessary Teaching Tool. *History Teacher*, Vol. 40, No. 2, pp. 153-176

Lehmann, J., Gangemi, A. (2007). An ontology of physical causation as a basis for assessing causation in fact and attributing legal responsibility. *Artificial Intelligence and Law*, Vol. 15, No. 3, pp. 301–321

Lindström, S. (1991). Critical Study: Jon Barwise and John Perry, Situations and Attitudes. *NoFBs*, Vol. XXV, No. 5, pp. 743-770

Mark, D.; Smith, B. & Tversky, B. (1999). Ontology and geographic objects: An empirical study of cognitive categorization, In: *Spatial Information Theory: Cognitive and Computational Foundations of Geographic Information Science, LNCS 1661*, Freksa, C. & Mark, D. (Eds.), pp. 283-298, Springer

Moulin, B. (1997). Temporal contexts for discourse representation: An extension of the conceptual graph approach. *Applied Intelligence*, Vol. 7, pp. 227-225

Moulin, B.; Chaker, W.; Perron, J.; Pelletier, P.; Hogan, J. & Gbei, E. (2003). MAGS Project: Multi-Agent Geosimulation and Crowd Simulation, In: *Spatial Information Theory, LNCS 2825*, Springer, pp. 151-168, ISBN: 978-3-540-20148-9, Berlin

NASA (2006). Guided Tours to the Beginner's Guide to Aeronautics. http://www.grc.nasa.gov/WWW/K-12/airplane/move.html, Last update: Mar 14 2006, Last access: Wednesday, 27 February 2008

Paris, S.; Mekni, M. & Moulin, B. (2009). Informed virtual geographic environments: an accurate topological approach, *Proceedings of the International Conference on Advanced GIS & Web Services (GEOWS)*, IEEE Computer Society Press

Phan, D. & Amblard, F. (2007). *Agent-based modelling and simulation in the social and human sciences*, Oxford: The Bardwell Press, ISBN-10: 1905622015

Renz, J. (2002). *Qualitative Spatial Reasoning with Topological Information*, Springer, LNCS 2293, ISBN: 978-3-540-43346-0

Rodrigues, A. & Raper, J. (1999). Defining Spatial Agents, In: *Spatial Multimedia and Virtual Reality, Research Monographs Series*, J. Raper & A. Câmara (Eds.), pp. 111-129, Taylor & Francis, London, UK

Rothkegel, R.; Wender, K. & Schumacher, S. (1998). Judging spatial relations from memory, In: *Spatial Cognition – An interdisciplinary approach to representation and processing of spatial knowledge*, C. Freksa, C. Habel & K. F. Wender (Eds.), pp. 79-105, Springer

Schüle, M.; Herrler, R. & Klugl, F. (2004). Coupling GIS and Multi-agent Simulation – Towards Infrastructure for Realistic Simulation, In: *MATES 2004, LNAI 3187*, G. Lindemann et al. (Eds.), pp. 228–242, Springer

Shen, D.Y.; Takara, K.; Tachikawa, Y. & Liu, Y.L. (2006). 3D simulation of soft geo-objects. *International Journal of Geographical Information Science*, Vol. 20, No. 3, pp. 261-271

Silva, V.; Plazanet, C.; Carneiro, C. & Golay, F. (2008). 3D LIDAR Data Application for Urban Morphogenesis Multi-agent Vector Based Geosimulation, In: *ICCSA 2008, Part I, LNCS 5072*, O. Gervasi et al. (Eds.), pp. 179–193, Springer

Smith, B. (1994). Fiat Objects. In: *Parts and Wholes: conceptual Part-Whole Relations and Formal Mereology*, N. Guarino, L. Vieu & S. Pribbenow (Eds.), pp. 15–23, European Coordinating Committee for Artificial Intelligence, Amsterdam

Sowa, J.F. (1984). *Conceptual Structures: Information Processing in Mind and Machine*, Adison-Wesley, ISBN: 0201144727 Massachusetts

Terenziani, P. & Torasso, P. (1995). Time, Action-types, and Causation: An Integrated Analysis. *Computational Intelligence*, Vol. 11, No 3, pp. 529–552

Torrens, P.M. (2008). Geosimulation will infiltrate mainstream modeling and geoprocessing on the Web, In: *Signtific: The Future of Science and Technology*, Pang, Alex Soojung-Kim (Ed.), Palo Alto: Institute for the Future

Trickett, S. & Trafton, J. G. (2007). "What if": The Use of Conceptual Simulations in Scientific Reasoning. *Cognitive Science*, Vol. 31, pp. 843- 875

Tversky, B. (2005). Visuospatial reasoning, In: *The Cambridge Handbook of Thinking and Reasoning*, K. Holyoak & R. Morrison (Eds.), Cambridge University Press

Winchester, H. (2000). Qualitative research and its place in human geography, In: Qualitative Research Methods in Human Geography, Hay, I. (Ed.), pp. 1-21, Oxford University Press, Victoria, Austria

Worboys, M.F. & Hornsby, K. (2004). From objects to events: GEM, the geospatial event model, In: *the 3d International Conference on GIScience, LNCS 3234*, pp. 327–344, Springer

12

Computational Spectrum of Agent Model Simulation

Kalyan S. Perumalla
Oak Ridge National Laboratory
USA

1. Introduction

1.1 Overview

The study of human social behavioral systems is finding renewed interest in military, homeland security and other applications. Simulation is the most generally applied approach to studying complex scenarios in such systems. Here, we outline some of the important considerations that underlie the computational aspects of simulation-based study of human social systems. The fundamental imprecision underlying questions and answers in social science makes it necessary to carefully distinguish among different simulation problem classes and to identify the most pertinent set of computational dimensions associated with those classes. We identify a few such classes and present their computational implications. The focus is then shifted to the most challenging combinations in the computational spectrum, namely, large-scale entity counts at moderate to high levels of fidelity. Recent developments in furthering the state-of-the-art in these challenging cases are outlined. A case study of large-scale agent simulation is provided in simulating large numbers (millions) of social entities at real-time speeds on inexpensive hardware. Recent computational results are identified that highlight the potential of modern high-end computing platforms to push the envelope with respect to speed, scale and fidelity of social system simulations. Finally, the problem of shielding the modeler or domain expert from the complex computational aspects is discussed and a few potential solution approaches are identified.

1.2 New Computational Challenges

Computational social science has been an area of research for several decades now. Generally speaking, experiments in computational social science so far have been on the side of small scale (perhaps, at the limit, a few thousands of interacting entities). Lately, a general surge is apparent in an interest to represent and capture detailed effects at much larger scale. Scales of interest include population counts of cities, states, nations or even the world (10^4-10^9). Computational aspects that were not prominent at the smaller scale are now becoming pronounced at larger scale. Important orthogonal dimensions are emerging, making it necessary to revisit the computational problem with a fresh look. Dimensions such as simulation speed, model scale, simulation system usability, and multi-system interoperability, which were all once implicitly combined together and insignificant in and by themselves for small scale models, are now separating themselves out as independent dimensions at larger scale. This separation is requiring the exploration and investigation of optimal locations in the dimension space for specific problems (or problem classes) of interest.

A meta-level question of course remains, namely, whether, and to what degree, simulation-based study is useful for the purposes of studying large-scale social systems. Perhaps new modeling and analysis methods are to be invented and applied to better deal with accuracy, precision, sensitivity and other concerns. In the absence of a generally applicable, comprehensive alternative modeling paradigm, simulation-based analysis remains the best promise towards studying these large-scale social systems. Simulation, in combination with additional theoretical methods such as design of experiments, seems to be the method of vogue and acceptance in the community. It is in this context that we focus on the new computational ramifications of large-scale social science simulations.

An important insight we put forward here is that simulation-based studies fall into distinct classes, each class being characterized by its specific combination of scale and accuracy. The purpose (also known as "use-case") behind using a particular class of simulation models becomes important to articulate and define, since the purpose defines both the way in which results from the simulation are to be interpreted, as well as the computational effects that one has to expect from using that class of models. For example, when a simulation is intended to generate an overall qualitative result (such as stumbling upon or uncovering surprising behavior), the simulation runs must be fast enough to qualitatively explore a large search space, yet the exact quantitative outcomes must not be interpreted literally. Similarly, population models intended to serve as reasonable situational surrogates for the masses (e.g, in order to test a detailed model of an antagonist group leader) must be capable of sustaining a large number of individuals, yet be computationally fast to allow for multi-scenario experimentation; consequently, a high degree of fidelity may not be an appropriate expectation for the masses in such a usage.

The challenge, then, is to either automatically find the right level of fidelity for a specific usage, or be able to sustain as high a fidelity level as possible at any scale that may be presented by the modeler to the simulation system. This is a grand challenge, which perhaps will remain unsolved in the near future. An intermediate step is to become aware of the issues and realize the distinctions so that expectations and choices are made appropriately.

The rest of document is organized as follows. The main computational dimensions underlying the simulations are presented in Section 2, along with placement of popular modeling systems in the space of speed, scalability and fidelity dimensions. The notion of simulation usage scenarios and some of the common usage classes are described in Section 3. A quantitative estimate of computational time requirements is presented in Section 4, for different ranges of factors constituting simulation execution. Two case studies are presented on state-of-the-art large-scale simulation systems to highlight the potential of next generation social behavioral simulation systems. The first is a graphics processor-based solution called GARFIELD, presented in Section 5, and the second is a cluster computing-based solution called μsik, benchmarks of which have been scaled to supercomputing platforms, presented in Section 6. The observations of the article are summarized in Section 7.

2. Orthogonal Computational Dimensions

As mentioned before, the computational side of social behavioral simulation can be split into multiple dimensions in light of the new generation of large-scale simulation scenarios that are being contemplated. We identify five important dimensions, which are mutually orthogonal. The orthogonality is defined in the sense that any given combination of values along the five dimensions can correspond to a desired combination for some social science simulation scenario of interest.

2.1 Dimensions

The five dimensions are: scale, speed, fidelity, usability and interoperability. Each of these dimensions is discussed next.

Scale

Scale can be defined as the largest number of encapsulated units logically or actually instantiated in the model during simulation. The encapsulated units correspond to concepts widely referred to as entities, agents, actors, players, components and so on. In agent-based simulations, for example, the number of agents is a natural measure of scale; each agent is an encapsulated unit in the model and the agents are actually instantiated in the model during simulation. In aggregate methods, the determination of scale is less obvious, since the units being modeled might be logically represented, rather than actually instantiated. Nevertheless, logically aggregate representation can be used to define the scale. For example, in epidemic models that are based on differential equations (e.g., the SIR model (Daley and Gani 2001; Staniford, Paxson et al. 2002; Zou, Gao et al. 2003)), the number of units is represented by a single variable N. Each of the units (from the uninfected, susceptible or infected populations) constitutes a logically encapsulated modeling unit, although they are lumped together in one model variable. For our purposes, the scale is therefore N.

In general, scale is harder to identify in aggregate models, while it is easier in more detailed models that have an approximately one-to-one mapping from system-level units to modeled units. However, when logical representation is included in the account, along with instantiated representation, this definition of scale makes the computational dimension of scale orthogonal to other dimensions, especially to fidelity (discussed later in this section).

Speed

Speed is the inverse of wall clock time elapsed from configuration/initialization to the end of simulation. This is a dimension that is easily measured for an execution in a given simulation system. Speed does depend on some of the other dimensions in a fundamental sense. However, for a given system, different implementation approaches can exist, each giving a different level of speed. The computing hardware platform can also have a significant bearing on the speed. There is, however, an upper bound on speed for any given combination of model and platform. Often, of interest is either the raw speed (e.g., to help estimate the time for parameter sweeps in a multi-simulation design of experiments), or the real-time scale factor (a fraction less than unity being slower than real-time, unity being exactly real-time, larger than unity being that many fold faster than real-time). Clearly, speed is affected by many variables, including the complexity of underlying algorithms, synchronization efficiency, hardware/software implementation platform and so on.

Fidelity

Fidelity of a model is a concept that is harder to define absolutely yet possible to discuss about in a comparative fashion. Fidelity in general is the extent of detail of the system captured by the model. Note that this is distinct from scale in the sense that scale measures the count of encapsulated units, where as fidelity measures the amount of behavioral detail captured per encapsulated unit. In general, the detail could be not only intra-unit, but also inter-unit (e.g., additional global phenomena, such as ambient economic conditions, that span multiple units). Operationally, fidelity is a qualitative combination of the size of state and the number of activity "threads" representing the behavior in each encapsulated entity. Fidelity clearly has implications on computational efficiency; this is discussed later in Section 0.

For some objectives, adding more detail to the simulation may not bring a proportional amount of precision to the results. Nevertheless, the issue of value of fidelity is a separate concern; the dimension of fidelity can be discussed without necessarily linking it to overall value.

Note that coarseness of model is different from level of fidelity. Coarseness of modeling unit is typically reflected in the number of entities modeled as one modeling unit. For example, either an entire town could be modeled as one unit (giving several thousand modeled units per entity), or each individual is explicitly represented as a modeled unit. Fidelity on the other hand can be viewed as the amount of detail assigned to the behavior of each modeled unit. Of course, in this view, there is an implicit assumption on the separation of constituent entities from their behavioral dimensions.

Usability

An important concern that has practically dominated computational social science so far is that of usability. Usability is simply the inverse of the total amount of effort expended by the modeler to define, develop, debug, test, execute, animate, visualize, interpret and analyze simulations. Since social system modelers are not necessarily computational experts, there is emphasis on reducing the amount of effort needed to pose questions, explore, and get answers (often visually), in a point-and-click fashion.

Many of the popular social simulation systems today are driven primarily by this dimension. Once this usability is achieved to some good degree, other dimensions are explored as additional "wishes", such as scale and speed, in a secondary fashion. Usability simply reigns as supreme among the dimensions in social science simulation systems today.

In light of next generation modeling and simulation of social systems, unfortunately, the usability concern is no longer an easy one to address without having to consider its interaction with the other dimensions. While it is relatively straightforward to attain high levels of usability (ease of overall use) at low levels of scale, speed and/or fidelity, it is an entirely different matter to do so at large scale, high fidelity and/or high speed.

With current usability techniques, unfortunately, scale and/or fidelity cannot be increased without significantly affecting speed. Performance penalties, hidden heretofore under small scale/fidelity, rise to significant levels, with slowdowns exceeding 1000×. The sources of the penalties are varied, from the slow speed nature of interpreted languages, to overheads of heavy graphics, to instrumentation overhead for runtime flexibility of configuration and monitoring.

Interoperability

Interoperability is the ability to interface and integrate disparate, complementary subsystems into an integrated system. In social science simulations, interoperability can be used to reuse previously developed models in a new scenario or to interoperate models at different resolutions. For example, a model of a popular leader may be interfaced with a model of the general masses, in order to exercise the leader model dynamically or to uncover overall system behaviors under various scenarios.

Interoperability is a hard problem. In general, it remains hard even in the simplest setting, namely, of two models developed in the same programming language, same modeling framework and simulation system. There is quite a bit of literature on interoperable systems, many of the systems falling under the category of syntactic interoperability. Semantic interoperability, on the other hand, is the more difficult component.

Interoperability is a dimension orthogonal to the rest in the sense that one could achieve any combination of the rest four dimensions without making any headway in the interoperability aspect. Alternatively, one could strive for interoperability but that needs to be done with awareness of the regimes of the other dimensions at which the system being interoperated spans. For example, interoperability of graphics processor-based automata models with supercomputing-based agent models can only be undertaken at the levels of fidelity and scale that the automata and agent models on those platforms afford.

2.2 Modeling Approaches Spanning Scalability and Fidelity

There are several modeling frameworks that are available to use in modeling social systems. Each framework is implemented in some software system; a (non-exhaustive) list of implemented systems includes JSAF(Davis, Lucas et al. 2005), SEAS(Chaturvedi, Foong et al. 2005), PMFServ(Silverman 2008), CultureSim(Silverman 2008), NetLogo(Wilensky 1999), Mason(Luke, Cioffi-Revilla et al. 2004), Repast J/.Net(North, Collier et al. 2006), Symphony, Swarm(Walter, Sannier et al. 2005), TeD(Perumalla, Fujimoto et al. 1998), Maisie(Bagrodia and Liao 1994), SSF(Cowie, Liu et al. 1999), Arena and NetLogic, to pick a few representative ones from each type of framework.

Each modeling framework possesses its ranges of scalability, fidelity and speed. The typical ranges of some of the prominent frameworks are shown in Fig. 1. The region below the real-time diagonal indicates the combination of fidelity and scalability levels that can be executed fast enough to meet or beat real-time. The region above the diagonal line indicates the specific combinations of fidelity and scalability that take more than one second of wall clock time for each second simulated in the model.

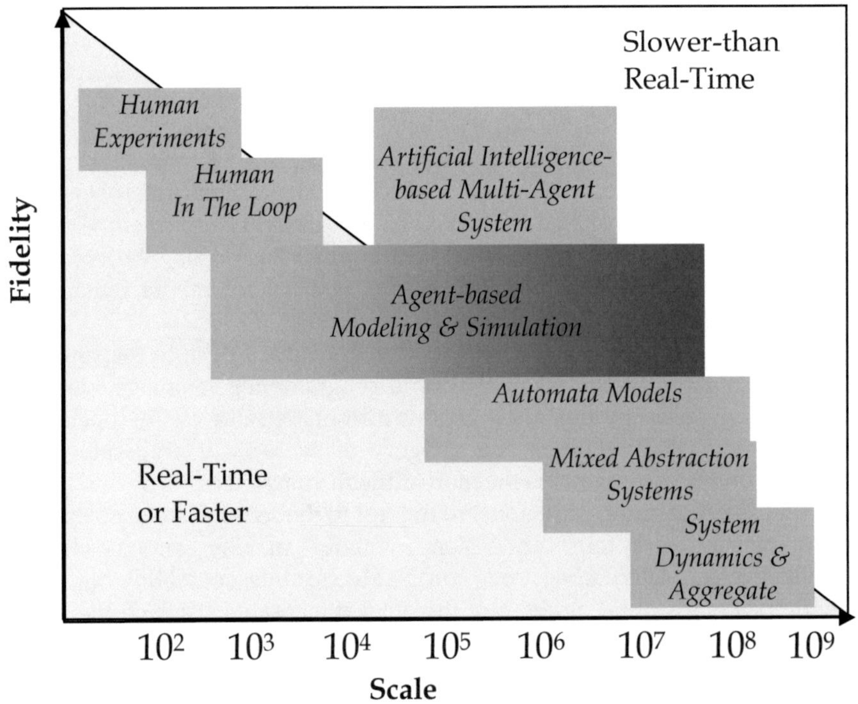

Fig. 1. Spectrum of behavioral modeling alternatives, and the scalability and fidelity ranges they afford.

Experiments involving real humans affords the maximum fidelity, but can only be practically performed with at most 10^2-10^3 individuals. Human-in-the-loop systems, such as semi-automated forces, can conceivably be performed with 10^2-10^3 human participants coupled to the system containing other artificially generated behaviors. The fidelity afforded is high on the human participation side of the system, but is reduced due to bi-directional interaction with artificial behaviors. Agent-based Modeling and Simulation(North and Macal 2007) affords the maximum range of scalability at moderate levels of fidelity. It is shown with extended (darkened) range to the right, denoting the recent increase in the number of agents that could be simulated using novel computing solutions such as data-parallel execution on graphical processors(D'Souza, Lysenko et al. 2007; Perumalla and Aaby 2008) and reverse computation-based control-parallel execution on supercomputers. Automata-based models are computationally simple enough to be executed in large entity counts, but at the cost of strictly lower fidelity. Mixed abstraction systems are those that combine more than one modeling paradigm, for ease of modeling or increase in speed. A classic example is the use of a small number of agent models placed in the context of a large population of automata models, delivering the higher fidelity of the agent models for important components while delivering the high speed of automata models for the less detailed population behaviors. *System Dynamics* and aggregate models are based on coupled differential equations. They afford the maximum level of scalability, since increasing the unit count could be as simple as increasing the value of a variable in the equations. However, they are also the lowest in fidelity.

2.3 Computational Aspects of Fidelity

A note can be made about the interaction of fidelity with computational burden. The issue at heart of tradeoffs between scale, speed and fidelity is the nature of computational artifacts that underlie the modeling primitives. An activity, such as random walk on a plane, can be realized as a computational thread instantiated in the context of an entity. Each activity thus consumes computational resources (computer memory and wall clock time), and also typically comes with additional state size represented in the entity (e.g., current location, movement pattern specification, etc.). Each entity can in general have several such activities coordinating with each other to realize the overall entity behavior. The number of activities translates to a corresponding number of computational threads that are instantiated during simulation execution. At runtime, these activities need to be allocated, scheduled, de-scheduled, synchronized and so on, all of which consume wall clock time as well as computer memory. Fidelity of the model translates to greater number of activities, more complex computation within each activity, and/or greater frequency of invocations to activity functionality. An automata-based model is a special case in which each entity contains a singleton activity which manipulates a (simple) state according to a state transition table. Thus, automata models typically are computationally lighter in weight, enabling larger scale at the same simulation speed level as agent-based models.

3. Simulation Usage Scenarios

In order to understand the computational challenges underlying computational social sciences, it is important to distinguish among various typical usage scenarios of social behavioral simulations. The usage scenarios are sufficiently disparate from each other, both qualitatively and quantitatively, whose distinction becomes prominent only at higher levels of scale and fidelity. At low scale (10^1-10^3 entities), the implications of the type of usage are not as pronounced as when the scale is increased beyond (10^4-10^9 entities). At low scale, one can resort to the modeling system that affords the highest fidelity, and be able to simulate without runtime effects becoming noticeable or problematic. At a larger scale, however, it becomes important to select the simulation system with the right tradeoff between scale and fidelity to stay within the simulation speed requirements. Using a low-fidelity simulation framework (e.g., automata-based system) can help scale to millions of entities, but the same system might be inappropriate when greater behavioral detail is attempted to be incorporated into the entities. Similarly, a high level of detail for entities in an application might not scale if most of the entities are merely used as background activity in a simulation.

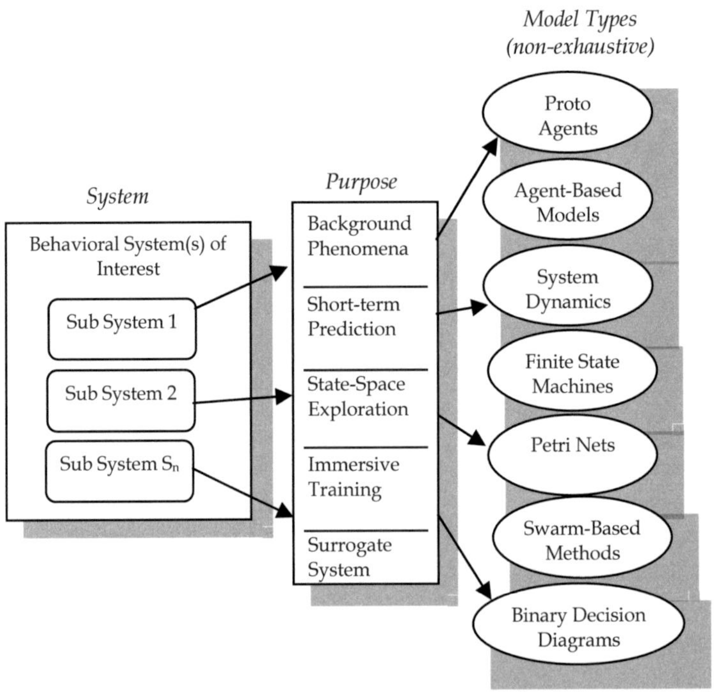

Fig. 2. Relation among Modeled System, Modeling Purpose, and Modeling Alternatives

To make an analogy, in financial market applications, simulation is used in different ways with different end goals and computational demands. Off-line simulations such as financial analytics and portfolio risk analysis are performed at relatively higher computational cost but with emphasis on longer-term prediction. Online simulations such as real-time trading solutions are a relatively recent trend in which the focus is on short-term prediction; but with as a high a fidelity as can be accommodated under real-time constraints. The important distinction is that the expectations of result quality and execution speed are set based on the intended usage of the particular type of simulation.
Here, we identify a few important classes of simulation usage in social behavioral simulations.

Situational Background Phenomena

In this class of simulations, the objective is to achieve reasonably rich, heterogeneous behavior among a large population of entities, but the emphasis is relatively less on sophistication in any one entity. Examples of this type of simulation usage are:

1. Evaluation of key social players; their behavior and influence are evaluated in the context of large low-fidelity populace (e.g., LeaderSim(Silverman 2008))
2. Animation of background crowds; need low fidelity but good heterogeneity of background entities; the main (foreground) entities, such as police force, are of much higher-fidelity (e.g., crowd simulation(Reynolds 2006))
3. In an unrelated field (Internet simulations), evaluation of distributed computing/communication applications; the network application can be evaluated

under the effects of background traffic and general network operation (e.g., fluid and packet-level simulation (Nicol, Liljenstam et al. 2003))

Short-Term Prediction

Prediction of immediate trajectory constitutes another class of simulations, in which heavy initialization is performed based on data and calibration, followed by short extrapolation via simulation. The assumption is that prediction will be more accurate due to closeness of initial state to reality and shortness of future period, together minimizing chance of deviation. Typically, this type of simulation is performed in a series of what-if case analysis to choose the best recourse from among a set of possible actions. Simulation needs are characterized by the need for extensive assimilation of configuration data and for high simulation speed for each scenario. Accuracy expectations tend to be relatively high.

Emergent Phenomena

This class of efforts is characterized by its emphasis on exploration of interesting aggregate behaviors evolved from disaggregated behaviors of an ensemble of entities. The emphasis on exploration brings the needs of long simulation times and large number of simulation runs. However, generally speaking, the level of fidelity is relatively low, since the focus is on observing the nature of overall patterns from relatively simple individual behaviors. Examples of this type of simulations include Ising Spin (Tomov, McGuigan et al. 2005), Segregation (Schelling 1978), and SugarScape models.

Training and Entertainment – Surrogate or Immersive

A class of behavioral simulations deals with training and/or entertainment objectives. For example, to train government agencies in emergency management, population reactions and responses are modeled and simulated in a synthetic environment; the environment serves as surrogate of the real world for training purposes (Chaturvedi, Foong et al. 2005). Similarly, for law enforcement and military purposes, immersive environments are used that include intelligent agents serving the role of antagonists (and sometimes allies as well) (Mastaglio and Callahan 1995; Devine and Gross 1998; Verdesca, Munro et al. 2005). The level of fidelity expected is extremely high for high quality training. Semi-automated forces fall in this category(Davis, Lucas et al. 2005). In civilian use, corporations can use such surrogate or immersive environments for management training in negotiation, team building, and so on. Again, the fidelity level expected of the automated behavior is very high, with consequent indulgence in higher-end computing platforms. Analogous needs are arising in entertainment industry, in which intelligent actors in a highly realistic synthetic environment are employed (e.g., SimCity). However, there is typically a tradeoff between fidelity and speed for real-time performance on commodity (low-end) computing platforms.

4. Computational Time Requirements

A truly enabling generation of simulation tools for computational social science would, ideally, bring progress along all five dimensions simultaneously. While progress along any single dimension is not difficult, achieving any two together is difficult, achieving three is daunting, four is heroic and all five is a grand challenge.

Among the five, of immediate interest for moving to next generation is simultaneous progress along scale and speed. In this combination, the components at play can be itemized in order to get an estimate of the computational requirements at hand. For an estimate, we will focus on agent-based view of the model, although equivalent measures can also be defined for other modeling frameworks.

The overall organization of agent-based simulation is that a series of experiments is run (e.g., with different leadership theories in an anti-establishment simulation), each experiment being executed using multiple scenarios (e.g., with different levels of displeasure among populations). Each scenario is executed multiple times, to arrive at good confidence intervals (e.g., with different random number seeds). Each simulation is typically organized as a series of time steps, each time step advancing the state of the entire model to that time step. At each time step, the rule sets of each agent are executed. A table itemizing these components of computational runtime that affect the speed of simulation is shown in Table 1.

Factor	Notes	Factor-Specific		Cumulative	
		Low	High	Low	High
Agent Rule Execution Time	From μs (for simple algebra) to ms (for complex optimization)	10^{-6} seconds	10^{-3} seconds	10^{-6} seconds	10^{-3} seconds
Number of Agents	From handful of team agents up to global world populations	10^{1} agents	10^{9} agents	10^{-5} seconds	10^{6} seconds
Number of Time Steps	Simple evolution to complex dynamics	10^{1}	10^{9}	10^{-4} seconds	10^{7} seconds
Number of Simulation Runs	Single sample run to multiple trials	10^{0}	10^{2}	10^{-4} seconds	10^{9} seconds
Number of Scenarios	From a few to full parameter sweeps or with Monte Carlo	10^{1}	10^{6}	10^{-3} seconds	10^{15} seconds
Number of Experiments	From focused contexts to cross-domain/cross-context	10^{0}	10^{2}	10^{-3} seconds	10^{17} seconds

Table 1. Range of Computational Time (on One Processor) Depending on Different Factors

4.1 Symbolic Simplicity vs. Computational Complexity

When dealing with computational complexity, it is worth noting that apparent simplicity or complexity of symbolic representation of rule sets does not necessarily have a direct correlation with computation time. A common misconception is that "simple" rules translate to "simple" computation. In particular, there is a prevalent notion that simulations aimed at discovering emergent behavior are characterized by simple computation. The fallacy in logic is the translation from simplicity of symbolic expression of rules to simplicity of computation. Here, we present two counterexamples to illustrate.

Richness of Temporal Behavior despite Symbolic Simplicity

An example of a "simple" rule set that requires long simulation times is the Manneville-Pomeau Map:

$$x_{n+1} = x_n + x_n^z (mod 1)$$

This map is useful to model turbulent, sporadic or intermittent behavior: The state variable x_n corresponding to time step n could represent a behavioral component, such as the mood of a person, or level of resentment towards oppression. Although this rule is relatively "simple" with respect to its symbolic expression, it is well-known that this map exhibits interesting behavior only when evaluated along the span of prolonged iteration. For $z \geq 3$ and $x_0 = 10^{-3}$, the onset of interesting behavior does not arrive until about 10^9 iterations. This type of model is an example of scenarios in which, although the dynamics are relatively "simple" to express symbolically, very long simulation times are needed to adequately exercise and capture the relevant dynamics.

Algorithmic Complexity despite Small Formulation Size

Yet another instance of simplicity of symbolic expression not equating to simplicity of computation is optimization-based rule sets. For example, Mixed Integer Programming-based model formulations are widely used in social behavioral models to capture individual optimization capabilities of interacting entities. For example, a behavioral model of people acting for/against an order from a leader is formulated as an integer programming problem in Ref(Whitmeyer 2007). These types of formulations are prone to heavy computational demands, despite simplicity of formulation. Consider the following "simple" model based on a Mixed Integer Programming formulation:

$$\begin{aligned}
&\max x_1 + x_2 \\
&5x_1 - 5x_2 \leq 6 \\
&5x_1 + 5x_2 \leq 9 \\
&x_1 \geq 0, x_2 \leq 5 \\
&x_1, x_2 \text{ int}
\end{aligned}$$

Solving this problem via branch-and-bound involves solving 29 instances of its linear-programming relaxations, each relaxation being solved by Simplex method. The cost thus adds up even for a simple problem, at the level of each agent. Note that the cost of this integer solving operation is incurred at every time step of every agent. At large scale, the computational cost can become prohibitive for reasonable use in a design of experiments.

4.2 Continuous vs. Discrete Event Execution – Semantics and Implementation

Another important class of computational considerations involves resolving notions of continuous and discrete time advancement mechanisms among model entities.

Most social science simulations are commonly defined in terms of time-stepped execution, in which time is advanced globally in fixed increments, and all agents are updated at each time step. However, some models are either inherently asynchronous in their formulation, or amenable to an alternative, asynchronous execution style for faster evolution. In such asynchronous execution models, updates to agents are processed via staggered timestamps across agents. An example of such asynchrony of agent activity in the model definition itself is a civil violence model(Epstein 2002). In general, asynchronous (discrete event) execution can deliver much faster advances in simulation time than naïve time-stepped approaches. Computational consideration arises in this regard for speeding up simulations via asynchronous model execution(Perumalla 2007), both in sequential and parallel execution contexts.

In the sequential execution context (executing on one processor), a computational consideration is in automatically converting a time-stepped execution to an asynchronous (discrete event) execution, with consequential improvement in speed of simulation. Techniques for executing continuous models in a discrete event fashion are known(Nutaro 2003) and additional ones are being developed(Perumalla 2007), which could be applied to social system execution.

In the parallel execution context, additional complexity arises. While it is relatively straightforward to map synchronous (time-stepped) execution to parallel computing platforms, the mapping of asynchronous execution is not so obvious. Efficient execution of asynchronous activity requires much more complex handling. The fundamental issue at hand is the preservation of correct causal dependencies among agents across time instants(Fujimoto 2000). Correctness requires that agents be updated in time-stamp order.

A naïve method would be to compute the minimum time of update required among all model units (e.g., agents), and perform a parallel update of all units' states up to only that minimum update time. Clearly, only one unit (or only a very few number of units, if more than one unit has the same minimum time of update) can be processed at each iteration. The cost of computing the global minimum time can constitute a large overhead; additionally, parallel execution of all units when only one (or very few) units are eligible for update can add significant overhead. Specialized time synchronization algorithms are needed to resolve these challenges (e.g., see (Perumalla and Fujimoto 2001)).

5. Case Study: GARFIELD

Lately, the state-of-the-art is advancing the computational capabilities of social behavioral simulations. The focus has increased on improving scale, speed or both. One of the recent directions is exploiting graphics processors' data parallel execution capabilities for fast agent-based simulations. Here we present some performance results from a system called GARFIELD (Graphical Agents Reacting in a Field) for simulating agent-based models on graphics processors. Additional implementation details can be found in Ref. (Perumalla and Aaby 2008).

One of the strengths of systems like GARFIELD is the combination of large scale and high speed achievable on some low- to medium fidelity models. Fig. 3 shows graphical snapshots of a few example simulations executed under GARFIELD. Fig. 4 shows the speed differential that can be obtained by optimizing fine-grained models to GPUs, as compared to the speed of interpreter-based frameworks such as Repast and NetLogo.

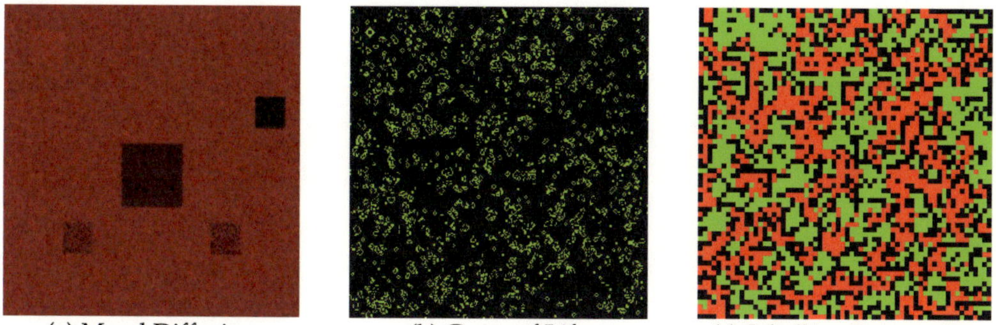

(a) Mood Diffusion (b) Game of Life (c) Schelling Segregation

Fig. 3. Graphical Snapshots from Large-scale Execution of Different Behavioral Simulation Models using GARFIELD

Benefits of large-scale simulation: The Game of Life invented by John H. Conway, published in (Gardner 1970), is a simulation when executed on large grid sizes exhibits some interesting benefits of large-scale execution. In Game of Life, it is well-known that several interesting patterns emerge both spatially and temporally. With a small-scale execution (e.g., with 100×100 grids), several experiments have to be initiated in order to explore and cover many possible patterns and to exercise their dynamic behaviors. However, in an execution with a 2048×2048 grid randomly initialized with live and dead cells, a large number of patterns emerge naturally, reducing the need for instantiating a simulation run for exercising/exploring each pattern separately. It is edifying to see the patterns emerge out of evolution from a randomized initial condition. The laborious and painstaking process of cogitating about potentially interesting behaviors can be substituted by exploration via the brute force of scale.

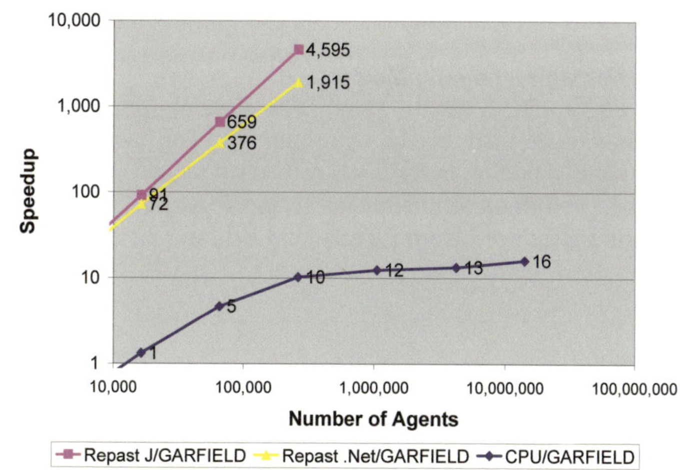

Fig. 4. Speedup of GARFIELD compared to Repast for the Game of Life Model. GARFIELD simulations are over 4000-fold faster than with traditional tool kits, and also scale to over 100-fold larger scenarios. However, usability is not as high as with other traditional toolkits.

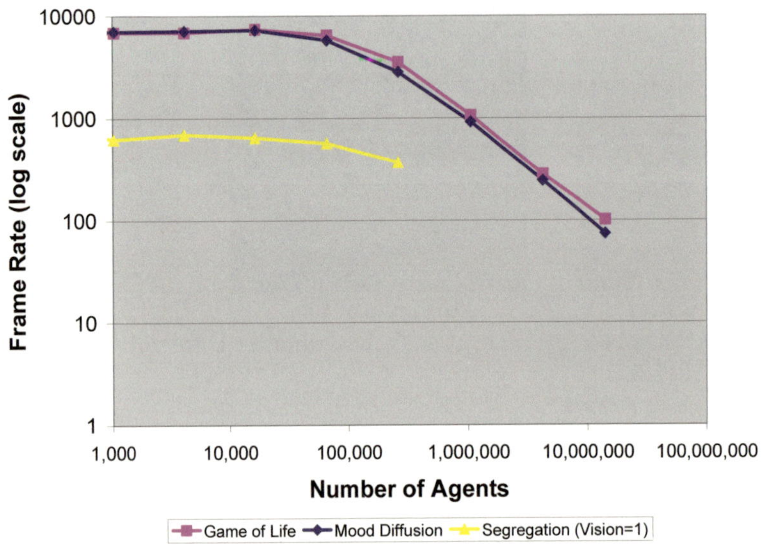

Fig. 5. Number of iterations per wall-clock second (absolute frame rate) achieved with the models on GPU

With regard to real-time aspect of speed, Fig. 5 shows the frame rate achieved for increasing number of agents in three applications. Real time execution is seen to be achievable in GARFIELD, with over 100 frames (time steps) per second clocked even in the largest grid sizes, of over 16 million agents. In smaller configurations, the frame rate is orders of magnitude higher.

5.1 Emergent Behavior with a Loyalty Model

In a more sophisticated application, it is possible to simulate populations of over several million agents with fine-grained model computation. For example, a scenario of a "leadership model" with 16 million individuals can be simulated, each individual obeying a loyalty-based leadership model that maximizes an individual's "utility" at each time step. The example model is reproduced from (Brecke and Whitmeyer 2007; Whitmeyer 2007) as follows:

$$
\begin{aligned}
&\text{Order} &&= O \in \{-1,0,1\} \\
&\text{Behavior} &&= B \in \{-1,0,1\} \\
&\text{Position} &&= P \in \{-1,0,1\} \\
&\text{Loyalty} &&= L = \lambda \frac{|O-B|}{2} \\
&\text{Lambda} &&= \lambda = \lambda_{previous}(1-\delta) + M_l \delta \\
&M_l &&= \text{Mean (previous) Loyalty of Neighbors} \\
&\text{Coercion} &&= C = R\frac{|O-B|}{2} \\
&\text{Idealogy} &&= I = \frac{|P-B|}{2} \\
&\text{Utility} &&= U = 1 - w_l L^2 - w_c C^2 - w_i I^2
\end{aligned}
$$

Given an order O, of interest is the variation of behavior B that is chosen by each individual to maximize the individual's utility U. Lambda's time dependence induces variation of B over time.

When M_l is defined as the mean loyalty of neighbors, the variation of B is less interesting, as lambda follows some sort of a diffusion process which can be expected to converge to an overall average across all individuals. To accommodate some dynamics, we make one change, namely, M_l is defined as the *maximum* loyalty, instead of *mean* loyalty, among neighbors. The rationale behind this variation is that the neighbor with the largest loyalty, even if there is only one, potentially has an overbearing influence on all its neighbors.

Fig. 6(a)-(f) shows snapshots of simulation for a population of over 2 million individuals, each executing the preceding loyalty model, with O=1, R=0.25, W_l=0.33, W_c=0.33, W_i=0.34, and δ=0.01. P is uniformly randomized across the population.

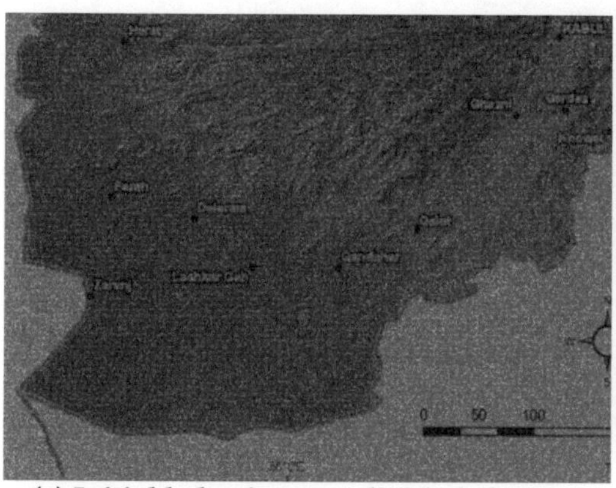

(a) Initial behavior map divided along a country border; loyal behaviors are below the diagonal (blue), and opposite are above

(b) Behavior smoothens after a few time steps, but neutral behaviors emerge along diagonal [geographical map is omitted]

(c) Fluctuations and growth of neutral behavior from the diagonal is observed

(d) Growth smears over time into the interiors, away from the diagonal

(e) Spread of neutral behavior is sustained even after thousands of time steps

(f) Neutrality waves are regenerated despite intermediate ebbs in prior time steps

Fig. 6. Interesting spatial and temporal variation in the behavior of population under a "loyalty-based" model (Brecke and Whitmeyer 2007; Whitmeyer 2007). Blue denotes behavior loyal to leadership, green denotes neutrality and red represents anti-order stance. Sustained waves of switching from/to neutral position indicates prolonged "unrest" due to divisions in initial conditions

The high simulation speed of GARFIELD was helpful in uncovering this emergent phenomenon, which was discovered when key parameters were varied in a large number of combinations.

6. Case Study: µsik

While systems like GARFIELD are designed with scale and speed in mind for low- to medium fidelity applications, new scalable systems are needed for the general class of social behavioral simulations that can include high fidelity models, possibly enhanced by usability features. For such applications, a system that scales from traditional multi-core desktop machines to supercomputing platforms is very useful.

The parallel discrete event simulation engines, such as μsik (Perumalla 2004; Perumalla 2005; Perumalla 2007), and ROSS (Holder and Carothers 2008), execute time-stepped and discrete event simulations at very high speed on a single desktop machine for users with limited compute power. The same engines are also capable of scaling to much larger problem sizes on cluster machines, multi-core workstations, or even supercomputers. In particular, the performance of the engine on supercomputing platforms is of particular relevance, as it shows the potential of realizing extremely large-scale social behavioral model simulations at very high speeds by leveraging tens of thousands of processor cores. Recent demonstration of the possible performance shows the capability to simulate up to half a billion events per wall clock second on 16,384 processors of a Blue Gene supercomputer.

6.1 Agent Interaction Model

The performance benchmark used to demonstrate this capability is the PHOLD application, which was designed as a generalized core of most simulations that include multiple interacting entities that interact via time stamped events/messages. The PHOLD benchmark (Perumalla 2007) is an abstraction of the interaction among multiple encapsulated units, to capture the simulation dynamics of computational performance. Most interacting-entity simulations map well to this model. In a way, good performance of this model is a necessary condition for good performance of other detailed behavioral models.

In this benchmark, each unit selects a target unit at random for interaction in the future. The selection of the destination unit is made at random, with some bias towards those units that are instantiated on the same processor (more than one unit/agent is mapped to the same processor). The interaction is scheduled with a period drawn from an exponential distribution with mean 1.0, plus a minimum increment of 1.0 (i.e., a "lookahead" of 1.0).

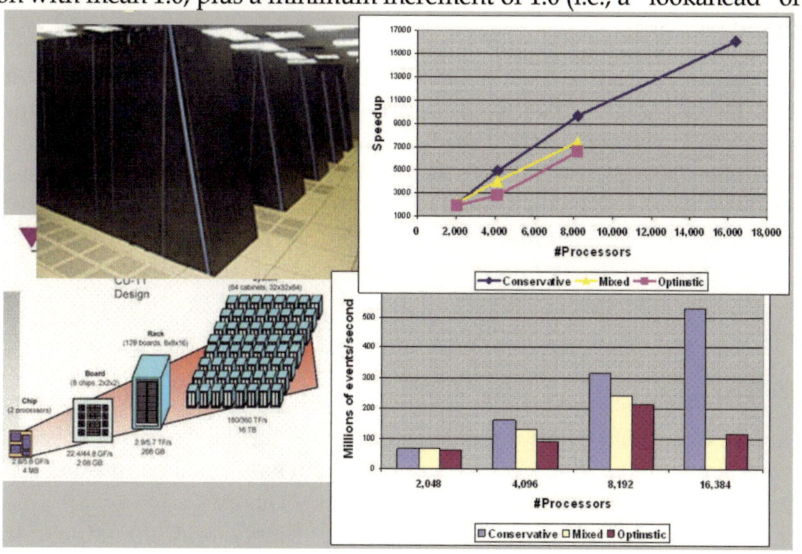

Fig. 7. Runtime Performance of μsik on the PHOLD Benchmark on up to 16,000 Cores of a Blue Gene Supercomputer.

The performance results are shown in Fig. 7, for the PHOLD scenario containing 1 million interacting entities. These results are reproduced from Ref. (Perumalla 2007). The most important metric to note is the number of events simulated per second, which translates to a per-event overhead that is on the order of 20 to 30 microseconds per event. Such a low event overhead makes it possible to contemplate executing even the finest grained agent simulations at high efficiency. In other words, the engine is capable of sustaining synchronized agent state evolution across processors with excellent parallel speedup.

7. Summary

The time seems to be ripe with respect to motivation as well as promise for next generation modeling and simulation tools in support of computational social science. Dimensions such as scale, speed, fidelity, usability and interoperability, which were once implicitly merged together at small-scale, are now getting separated as a result of focus on next levels along combinations of those dimensions. It is now possible to consider organizing the various modeling frameworks along their respective features, and select the best combination based on their fit with the specific purpose behind the simulation. The purposes behind simulations are equally important to distinguish among themselves, in order to be able to place the right levels of expectations on scale, fidelity and speed. Interoperability remains a difficult challenge, as is the problem of shielding the modeler from complexities of computational aspects driving the next generation systems. Automated compiler-based parallel execution on shared memory, LAN, GPU and/or supercomputers is potentially achievable, as is the possibility of integrating models at varying resolutions. The future looks bright for lifting computational social science to a new "enabling" plane.

8. Acknowledgements

This article has been authored by UT-Battelle, LLC, under contract DE-AC05-00OR22725 with the U.S. Department of Energy. Accordingly, the United States Government retains and the publisher, by accepting the article for publication, acknowledges that the United States Government retains a non-exclusive, paid-up, irrevocable, world-wide license to publish or reproduce the published form of this manuscript, or allow others to do so, for United States Government purposes. This effort has been partly supported by the RealSim project at Oak Ridge National Laboratory sponsored by the Department of Homeland Security.

9. References

Bagrodia, R. and W.-T. Liao (1994). "Maisie: A Language for the Design of Efficient Discrete-Event Simulations." IEEE Transactions on Software Engineering **20**(4): 225-238.

Brecke, P. and J. Whitmeyer (2007). Data for Leadership Theory Test.

Chaturvedi, A., C. M. Foong, et al. (2005). Bridging Kinetic and Non-kinetic Interactions over Time and Space Continua. Interservice/Industry Training, Simulation and Education Conference, Orlando, FL, USA.

Cowie, J., H. Liu, et al. (1999). Towards Realistic Million-Node Internet Simulations. International Conference on Parallel and Distributed Processing Techniques and Applications.

D'Souza, R., M. Lysenko, et al. (2007). SugarScape on Steroids: Simulating Over a Million Agents at Interactive Rates. AGENT 2007 Conference on Complex Interaction and Social Emergence. Evanston, IL.

Daley, D. J. and J. Gani (2001). Epidemic Modelling: An Introduction. Cambridge, UK, Cambridge University Press.

Davis, D. M., R. F. Lucas, et al. (2005). "Joint Experimentation on Scalable Parallel Processors." Journal of the International Test and Evaluation Association.

Devine, P. and G. Gross (1998). Lessons Learned from Human-in-the-Loop Trainer HLA Implementation. Proceedings of the 1998 Interservice/Industry Training, Simulation and Education Conference. Orlando, FL.

Epstein, J. (2002). "Modeling Civil Violence: An Agent-based Computational Approach." PNAS **99**(3): 7243-7250.

Fujimoto, R. M. (2000). Parallel and Distributed Simulation Systems, Wiley Interscience.

Gardner, M. (1970). Mathematical Games: The fantastic combinations of John Conway's new solitaire game "Life". Scientific American. **223:** 120-123.

Holder, A. O. and C. D. Carothers (2008). Analysis of Time Warp on a 32,768 Processor IBM Blue Gene/L Supercomputer. European Modeling and Simulation Symposium. Italy, Liophant.

Luke, S., C. Cioffi-Revilla, et al. (2004). MASON: A New Multi-Agent Simulation Toolkit. SwarmFest Workshop.

Mastaglio, T. W. and R. Callahan (1995). "A Large-Scale Complex Environment for Team Training." IEEE Computer **28**(7): 49-56.

Nicol, D., M. Liljenstam, et al. (2003). Multiscale Modeling and Simulation of Worm Effects on the Internet Routing Infrastructure. International Conference on Modeling Techniques and Tools for Computer Performance Evaluation (Performance TOOLS), Urbana, IL.

North, M. J., N. T. Collier, et al. (2006). "Experiences Creating Three Implementations of the Repast Agent Modeling Toolkit." ACM Transactioins on Modeling and Computer Simulation **16**(1): 1-25.

North, M. J. and C. M. Macal (2007). Managing Business Complexity: Discovering Strategic Solutions with Agent-Based Modeling and Simulation, Oxford University Press.

Nutaro, J. (2003). Parallel Discrete Event Simulation with Application to Continuous Systems. Department of Electrical and Computer Engineering. Tucson, AZ, University of Arizona. **Ph.D.:** 182.

Perumalla, K., R. Fujimoto, et al. (1998). "TeD - A Language for Modeling Telecommunications Networks." Performance Evaluation Review **25**(4).

Perumalla, K. S. (2004). "μsik - Software Package Homepage." Retrieved 2004/04/01, 2004, from www.cc.gatech.edu/computing/pads/kalyan/musik.htm.

Perumalla, K. S. (2005). μsik - A Micro-Kernel for Parallel/Distributed Simulation Systems. Workshop on Principles of Advanced and Distributed Simulation, Monterey, CA, USA.

Perumalla, K. S. (2007). Model Execution. Handbook of Dynamic System Modeling, CRC Press.

Perumalla, K. S. (2007). Scaling Time Warp-based Discrete Event Execution to 10^4 Processors on the Blue Gene Supercomputer. International Conference on Computing Frontiers, Ischia, Italy.

Perumalla, K. S., Ed. (2007). Symposium on Asynchronous Methods in Scientific and Mathematical Computing (ASYM). International Workshop on Principles of Advanced and Distributed Simulation. San Diego, CA, USA, IEEE.

Perumalla, K. S. and B. Aaby (2008). Data Parallel Execution Challenges and Runtime Performance of Agent Simulations on GPUs. Agent-Directed Simulation Symposium.

Perumalla, K. S. and R. M. Fujimoto (2001). Virtual Time Synchronization over Unreliable Network Transport. Workshop on Parallel and Distributed Simulation.

Reynolds, C. (2006). "Big Fast Crowds on PS3." Retrieved 2006/09/12, 2006, from www.research.scea.com/pscrowd.

Schelling, T. (1978). Micromotives and Macrobehavior, W. W. Norton.

Silverman, B. G. (2008). "Human Behavior Model Research." Retrieved 2008/01/15, from www.seas.upenn.edu/~barryg/HBMR.html.

Staniford, S., V. Paxson, et al. (2002). How to Own the Internet in Your Spare Time. USENIX Security Symposium, San Francisco, CA.

Tomov, S., M. McGuigan, et al. (2005). "Benchmarking and Implementation of Probability-based Simulations on Programmable Graphics Cards." Computers and Graphics **29**(1).

Verdesca, M., J. Munro, et al. (2005). Using Graphics Processor Units to Accelerate OneSAF: A Case Study in Technology Transition. Interservice/Industry Training, Simulation and Education Conference (IITSEC).

Walter, B., A. Sannier, et al. (2005). UAV Swarm Control: Calculating Digital Phermone Fields with the GPU. Interservice/Industry Training, Simulation and Education Conference (IITSEC), Orlando, FL.

Whitmeyer, J. (2007). Learning Theories for Loyalty-based Leadership Model.

Wilensky, U. (1999). NetLogo. Evanston, IL, Center for Connected Learning and Computer-Based Modeling, Northwestern University.

Zou, C. C., L. Gao, et al. (2003). Monitoring and Early Warning for Internet Worms. ACM Conference on Computer and Communication Security (CCS), Washington, DC.

HLA-Transparent Distributed Simulation of Agent-based Systems

Daniele Gianni[1],
Andrea D'Ambrogio[2], Giuseppe Iazeolla[2] and Alessandra Pieroni [2]
[1]*Computing Laboratory, University of Oxford,*
United Kingdom
[2]*Dept. of Computer Science, University of Rome TorVergata*
Italy

Abstract
The adoption of the agent-based approach to the modelling and simulation of physical systems has proved to considerably increase the simulation realism and accuracy. Simulation systems of such a kind, however, require computational resources that might become unfeasible when the number of simulated agents scales up. A *Distributed Simulation (DS)* approach might improve the execution of such systems, particularly in the case of scenarios populated by a large number of agents. Building an agent-based DS system, however, requires both specific expertise and knowledge of distributed simulation standards and a non-negligible amount of effort with respect to conventional local simulation systems. In this book chapter, we introduce a simulation framework named *Transparent_DS* (TDS), which enables the use of distributed environments while making affordable the development of agent-based simulators. TDS raises developers from the specific issues of the distributed environment. By use of TDS, the simulation agents can be locally developed and tested, and then transparently deployed in a DS environment, bringing significant savings in terms of effort and development time. In addition, TDS provides a uniform interface to the JADE framework, which further facilitates the work of developers of JADE-based *Multi-Agent Systems* (MAS) in the production of agent-based DS systems. By the TDS approach, any HLA- and agent-based distributed simulation system can practically be developed as conventional local MAS, with no extra effort and no extra knowledge. An example development of a simulation system is presented which is a common abstraction in several domains that involve the motion of individuals in a multi-storey building to simulate operations in normal or emergency situations.

1. Introduction

Distributed Simulation (DS) gives three main advantages with respect to *Local Simulation* (LS), namely [Fujimoto]: 1) scalability of needed computational resources, 2) reusability of existing simulation systems, 3) composability of available simulation subsystems. These features can be particularly exploited by agent-based simulation systems for at least three reasons:

1) the modelling of the agents (i.e.: the incorporation of intelligence, adaptation, and learning abilities into agents [Jennings]) requires computational capabilities that might become inadequate in a LS approach. Such capabilities can be scaled up in the DS approach by connecting various execution platforms;
2) a wide variety of agent-based software components is available and could be incorporated into an agent-based simulation system. Such components are however in many cases heterogeneous for implementation languages or platforms, and therefore their incorporation into an LS system might be problematic. This problem can be overcome by use of existing DS standards (e.g. *IEEE High Level Architecture (HLA)* [IEEE-HLA]) that give ways to interconnect heterogeneous systems;
3) by use of the same standards, various and heterogeneous LS subsystems can be aggregated into a unique DS system.

The use of DS environments, however, requires both specific expertise and knowledge of the DS standard and a non-negligible amount of effort to develop ad-hoc components, or to reuse existing ones, or else aggregating them. In this chapter, we address the problem of making the development of distributed agent-based simulators HLA-transparent. To this purpose, in this chapter we introduce the *Transparent_DS* (TDS) framework that easies the development of DS agent-based systems by raising the system developer from all the concerns of the HLA standard. Moreover, TDS is built on top of the popular *Multi-Agent System (MAS)* platform JADE [JADE] and provides a uniform interface with it, both in LS and DS environments.

The chapter is organized as follows. Section 2 presents the related work and outlines the TDS contribution with respect to state-of-the-art works. Section 3 is the background section that recalls concepts and terminology of HLA and of JADE. Section 4 introduces the TDS framework, and Section 5 gives an example case study which is a common abstraction in several domains that involve the motion of individuals in a multi-storey building to simulate operations in normal or emergency situations.

2. Related work

The TDS framework aims to make the development of distributed agent-based simulation systems HLA-transparent. The framework also introduces two main innovations:

(i). the incorporation of DS facilities into existing agent-based frameworks;
(ii). the effortless development of DS systems by transparent extension of conventional LS systems.

Current state-of-the-art systems that relate to TDS can be identified in: the *Agent-based DEVS/HLA* system [Sarjoughian], the *JAMES* system [Uhrmacher], the *HLA_AGENT* system [Lees], and the *JADE-HLA* system [Wang].
The *Agent-based DEVS/HLA* shares TDS's objectives and peculiarities, but differs considerably in the adopted solutions. *Agent-based DEVS/HLA* aims to introduce a layered

architecture that can indifferently execute simulated agents either in local or distributed environment. This system is based on seven layers and includes the agent reasoning layers besides the simulation layers. TDS, on the other hand, aims to 1) make the development of DS agent-based systems effortless by transparently extending conventional LS systems; and to 2) make transparent the development of the simulation system once the agent system is available. Although objectives 1 and 2 are also achieved by *Agent-based DEVS/HLA*, the way these objectives are achieved is considerably different from the TDS one. TDS integrates with widely adopted and standard MAS frameworks, rather than introducing new ones. By this approach, TDS gains several advantages, such as the availability for immediate reuse of agent adds-on, such as agent reasoning and planning [Pokahr], agent inference [Jess], or agent ontologies [Ontology-Bean] - all of which can be transparently and effortlessly incorporated into the DS agent-based.

The *JAMES* system provides a similar framework using the DEVS formalism in a Java-based environment. This system differs from the TDS for similar reasons to the ones already mentioned for *Agent-based DEVS/HLA*. In particular, *JAMES* uses platforms and formalisms that are not commonly adopted by agent-based systems. Differently, TDS uses JADE, a widely adopted MAS framework, and inherits all the add-ons already available for popular agent-based systems.

The *HLA_AGENT* system also provides a framework to develop agent-based simulation systems, and mainly gives a distributed extension of the *SIM_AGENT* framework [Sloman]. This system differs from TDS in two ways: 1) the use of the HLA standard is not made transparent; and 2) the reasoning, the planning, and the other agent peculiarities are directly incorporated into the simulation framework.

The system that, similarly to TDS, provides distributed simulation facilities and integrates with JADE is *JADE-HLA*. Despite of these similarities, TDS presents the following differences:

- TDS uses SimArch [Gianni08a] and makes the use of HLA completely transparent;
- TDS adopts a general *Discrete Event Simulation* (DES) modelling approach, and thus is not tied to any specific distributed simulation standard;
- TDS implements an agent-based conceptualisation of DES systems [Gianni08b];
- TDS is compliant with the JADE design outline, and therefore enables JADE developers to easily carry out agent-based modeling and simulation activities.

3. Background

3.1 High Level Architecture

The *High Level Architecture* (HLA) is an IEEE standard [IEEE-1516] that provides a general framework within which software developers can structure and describe simulation applications. The standard promotes interoperability and reusability of simulation components in different contexts, and is based on the following concepts [Kuhl]:

- *Federate*, which is a simulation program and represents the unit of reuse in HLA;
- *Federation*, which is a distributed simulation execution composed of a set of federates;
- *Run Time Infrastructure (RTI)*, which is the simulation oriented middleware that provides the services to build federates. The middleware consists in *RTI*

Locals, which reside on each federate site, and a *RTI Executive,* which is deployed on a central server.

The standard is defined by four documents:

- *1516 HLA Rules,* which govern the behaviour of both the federation and the federates [IEEE-HLAA];
- *1516.1 Interface Specification,* which defines both the RTI - federate (*RTIAmbassador*) and the federate - RTI (*FederateAmbassador*) interfaces [IEEE-HLA1];
- *1516.2 Object Model Template,* which defines the formats for documenting HLA simulations [IEEE-HLA2];
- *1516.3 Federate Execution and DEvelopment Process,* which provides a reference process for the development of HLA simulations [IEEE-HLA3].

The major improvement that HLA brings in with respect to its predecessors is an API-oriented development of distributed simulation systems. Compared to Protocol-oriented techniques, this approach raises developers from all the concerns related to the communication and synchronization of the distributed simulation systems. Despite of this improvement, the HLA approach still suffers from a considerable drawback. This derives from the set of service which is rather complex. These services consist of a wide set of generic simulation services, beyond the scope of *Discrete Event Simulation (DES),* that ranges from the management of the simulation life cycle to advanced updating techniques. Furthermore, the services concern only with the distributed environment and a considerable effort is always needed to develop the synchronization and communication logic between the local and the distributed environment. As a consequence, a considerable extra effort is necessary when using HLA to develop a DS system (compared to an equivalent LS one).

3.2 JADE

JADE [Bellifemmine] is a popular Java-based framework for the implementation of *Multi-Agent Systems* (MAS). JADE's base element is the agent, which maintains an internal state and whose dynamics is described through a set of pluggable behaviours. The behaviour is a sequence of internal operations and communication acts with other agents, and it is possibly composed of sub-behaviours according to several composition structures (e.g. parallel or serial).

The most fundamental JADE aspect is the communication, which is carried out according to the FIPA specifications [FIPA] through an asynchronous mail-box based mechanism. As FIPA defines, JADE messages are composed of the following attributes: sender, list of recipients, performative action, content, content language reference, content ontology reference, and a set of minor fields to control concurrent conversations. Besides attributes of immediate understanding, the message contains a performative action attribute, and two references to the content coding language and to the shared ontology, which needs to be further detailed.

The *performative action* attribute specifies the type of communication, which has been classified by FIPA into twenty-five different communication acts. For example, this attribute can be of value REQUEST when the sender agent asks for a service request to the recipient agents, or can be of value INFORM in the case of "notification" of state change.

Concerning the reference attributes to the *content language* and to the *content ontology*, these provide the recipient agents with the information needed to decode and interpret the semantics of the content field, respectively. JADE ontologies are in turn built on top of the basic ontology, which provides basic concepts for primitive data types, and can define three types of elements: predicates, concepts, and actions. *Predicates* represent facts in the modelled world, and can be true or false. *Concepts* represent complex data structures, which are composed of standard simple types like String and Integer. Finally, *actions* define special concepts that are internally associated to the actions an agent can perform.

4. The TDS Framework

The *Transparent_DS (TDS)* framework consists of a set of software libraries that can be configured and used to transparently implement HLA- and agent-based DS systems. The framework achieves this by integrating the *SimArch* layered approach [Gianni08, Gianni07, D'Ambrogio08] with the JADE framework. *SimArch* is a software architecture that structures simulation systems in four layers, which separate the program (coded in a high level simulation language) from the HLA-based distributed simulation infrastructure (denoted as layer 0, and not belonging to the architecture). The layers numbering proceeds bottom-up, from layer 1 to layer 4 as follows [Gianni08a]:

Layer 4: the simulation model program
Layer 3: the simulation language implementation
Layer 2: the execution container (i.e., the simulation engines)
Layer 1: the Distributed Discrete Event Simulation (DDES) abstraction
Layer 0: the distributed simulation infrastructure (HLA in this work)

In conventional development scenarios, the primitives of the distributed simulation standard (e.g. HLA) are used to code the simulation model. By use of SimArch, differently, a DS system can be developed as a conventional LS system, because developers are not to be concerned with the knowledge, the details and the practice of the specific distributed simulation infrastructure. Moreover, the developers are saved from the non-negligible efforts needed to implement the synchronization logic between the local and the distributed environment, which every distributed simulation infrastructure currently needs.
As a result, effort savings can be obtained of about 60% for beginners and of about 30% for experienced developers with respect to the development effort usually required by a DS system. Besides that, an additional saving can be recognized in an estimated 1.25 man_months per federate according to the SED effort model [Grable] when applied to the saving of about 3.5 Klines of code per federate [D'Ambrogio06a].
The TDS approach has the potential of obtaining similar results [Gianni09] and its architecture is illustrated in Fig.1, as resulting from the integration of the 4 layers structure of *SimArch* and of the JADE framework, as better described in next section.

4.1 Description of the TDS Layers

Each TDS layer has a well defined scope and its interfaces are for communication with the adjacent layers only. The interfaces and the communication protocols are defined independently from the layers internal implementation so that they are completely decoupled and can be replaced by custom layer implementations without any extra rework.

This is essential in many scenarios, for example when porting a simulation system onto a different distributed simulation infrastructure, when running the same simulation model in a different distributed environment, or when needed to meet specified performance requirements.

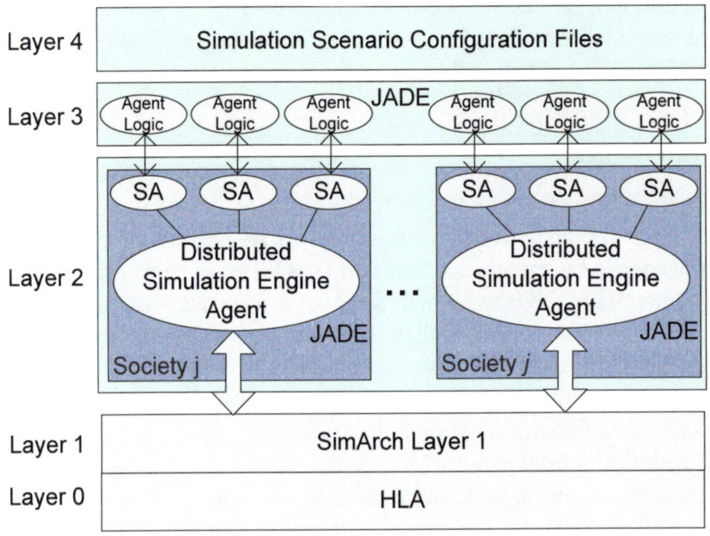

Fig. 1. The TDS architecture

The bottom layer, *Layer 1*, provides general synchronization and communication services in the distributed environment. These include *sendEvent*, *waitNextDistributedEvent* and *waitNextDistributedEventBeforeTime*, on top of the distributed simulation infrastructure conventionally identified by *Layer 0*, which is HLA in the current implementation, with the corresponding *RTIAmbassador* and *FederateAmbassador* communication interfaces, for communication from Layer 1 to 0 and from Layer 0 to 1, respectively. The current implementation of Layer 1 is coded on top of HLA, and thus benefits of the above mentioned reduced effort when developing HLA-based simulation systems because of the higher abstraction level, the higher components reusability, and the reduced necessary know-how that is obtained by this approach. Layer 1 also incorporates the *Federation Manager* [Kuhl], which manages the federation life cycle. The manager first creates the federation, then waits for all the federates to join and finally starts the simulation. When the run ends, the manager also coordinates the resigning of the federates. The role of the Federation Manager is to guarantee the DES-based execution throughout all the federation life cycle. The reader may refer to [Gianni07, D'Ambrogio06a] for further details on this layer implementation.

Layer 2 is the core of TDS as it makes transparent the actual execution environment, either local or distributed. The framework provides the execution container for the agents at Layer 3 and is based on the JADE framework to achieve component integration for the reuse of conventional JADE components. By these features, TDS provides an agent-based formulation of discrete event simulation systems and inherits all the compliance with the

FIPA standard and JADE framework. In addition, TDS operates transparently either in local or in distributed environments, with the latter being implemented on top of Layer 1, by thus obtaining the full transparent use of the distributed simulation standard (HLA in the current implementation). Section 4.2 gives an in-depth description of Layer 2.

Layer 3 deals with the implementation of the agents, the building blocks for the description of simulation scenarios. The agents are domain-specific and can be customarily developed to satisfy the modelling requirements of the specific application. To provide an application example for the TDS framework, Section 5 gives an example of a set of agents that model the movement of human on a space area represented as a graph. This scenario is a common abstraction in several domains that involve motion of individuals in a multi-storey building to simulate operations in normal or emergency situations.

Layer 4 is the top layer, where the simulation model is defined by configuring the simulation scenario, in other words the number and types of the agents involved in the simulation, and the definition of each individual agent. In the current implementation, this is obtained with XML files describing the number and types of agents, in addition to parameters of the Layer 3 individual agents. Currently, the set of agents available at Layer 3 allows the specification of main features such as the world model, the decision model, the motion model, and the health model.

4.2. The core of TDS

The core of the TDS framework is represented by Layer 2. This layer has the objective of making the development of HLA-distributed agent-based simulation systems transparent by raising the abstraction level offered by the underlying Layer 1 to a uniform level for both local and distributed agent-based systems. This is obtained by providing communication and synchronization services that conform to the JADE interfaces (thus making transparent the development of the simulation system) and that are specialized for the local and distributed environments. To this purpose, the TDS framework introduces components such as [Gianni08b]:

- a simulation ontology;
- a simulation agent society and a set of simulation agents (SAs in Fig. 1);
- an interaction protocol;
- a set of simulation behaviours;
- a set of simulation event handlers.

The simulation ontology, named *DES-Ontology* and illustrated in Section 4.2.1, defines the semantic base for the communications among the simulation agents. The ontology consists of DES *concepts* (simulation time) and *actions* (DES and simulation life cycle management services), and allows the incorporation of any other JADE ontology, thus enabling the reuse of standard agent-based components.

The *simulation agent society*, illustrated in Section 4.2.2, is structured hierarchically and is based on two types of simulation agents, the *simulation entity agent* and the *simulation engine agent*, with the former encapsulating the simulation logic, i.e. the sequence of states and DES service requests, and the latter managing the agents. The society defines which agents (types and names) can be part of the simulation execution. The TDS defines *local societies*, which are composed of a specified number of simulation entity agents and are managed by a locally running simulation engine agent, and a *global society*, which interconnects the local societies. A local society can be run in isolation, in the case of local simulation executions, or can be interconnected with other societies, in the case of distributed simulation executions.

The *interaction protocol*, illustrated in Section 4.2.3, defines the communication rules between agents belonging to the same society. Due to the hierarchical structure of the society, the communication takes place only between the entity agents and the engine. The distributed execution extends the interaction protocol for the local version by transparently masking the synchronization and communication issues behind SimArch and HLA services, which are not visible to the entity agents.

The *simulation behaviours* define the actions taken by both types of agents in response to the reception of any of the DES-Ontology actions, by implementing the interaction protocols. These behaviours conform to the JADE interfaces and can encapsulate standard JADE behaviours. The reader can find details of this in [Gianni08b].

The *simulation event handlers* define the routines that must be locally processed by the engine agent to deal with the scheduled requests, such as wake up or event notification. The handlers can be considered as support components that are visible to the engine only. The reader can refer to [D'Ambrogio06] for further details.

4.2.1 DES-Ontology

The *DES-Ontology* extends the JADE standard ontology [Bellifemmine] introducing concepts and actions that characterize the simulation domain. The *concepts* are related to the simulation time, while the *actions* are related to the interaction between simulation entities and simulation engines.

As regards *concepts*, the DES-ontology defines two different representations of the simulation time: *Absolute Simulation Time*, for absolute values of the simulation time; and *Relative Simulation Time*, for relative values of the simulation time, with "relative" to be intended as "with respect to the current time". The two concepts are related by the fact that the Absolute Simulation Time is given by adding up the current Absolute Simulation Time and the Relative Simulation Time. Nevertheless, the definition of a relative time concept is included in the ontology, being a parameter required by several DES services.

As regards *actions*, the ontology defines *simulation management services* and *DES services*.

A *simulation management service* defines actions to manage the simulation life cycle [Gianni08b], namely:

- *register agent*: to request joining a simulation society;
- *registration successful*: to acknowledge the acceptance of a registration request;
- *remove agent*: to resign from a society;
- *move agent*: to move the agent to another society;
- *simulation end*: to notify that the society objective has been reached.

The actions *register agent* and *remove agent*, which are both of performative type REQUEST, have no attributes because the action object, i.e. the name of the agent requesting the action, can be inferred from the message envelope. The *move agent* action is of performative type REQUEST and is characterized by the name of the recipient engine in which the agent is to be started with the initial state (also provided). The actions *registration successful* and *simulation end*, which are both of performative type INFORM, include an instance of *Absolute Simulation Time* that specifies either the simulation start time (in case of *registration successful* action) or the simulation end time (in case of *simulation end* action).

The *DES services* define actions of the following types:

- *conditional hold time*: to request an hold for a given simulated time, under the condition that no event notifications are received;
- *hold time*: to request an unconditional hold for a specified simulated time;
- *move agent*: to request the transfer of the agent to a different simulation engine
- *notify time*: to inform that the specified time has been reached;
- *notify message*: to inform that the specified event was requested to be scheduled for the receiving agent, at the current time;
- *send message*: to request the delivery of the specified event at the specified time to another simulation entity agent;
- *wait message*: to request a wake up when a simulation message is to be notified.

The *conditional hold time* and *hold time* actions, which are both of performative type REQUEST, are characterized by a relative simulation time that specifies the simulation sleep time. The *move agent* action represents a performative type REQUEST that a simulation entity agent can submit to a simulation engine. The *notify time* action, which is of performative type INFORM, informs the receiving agent of the absolute simulation time reached. The *notify message* action, which instead notifies a message, is described by the following four attributes: sender agent, recipient agent, message and time. The first three attributes are of type *String*, while the fourth is of type *Absolute Simulation Time*. The *send message* action is the complement of the *notify message* action. This action is described by the same attributes, but it is of performative type REQUEST. In the specific case, to maintain a logical uniformity with the common practice in DES, the time is of type *Relative Simulation Time*. Finally, the *wait message* action, which is of performative type REQUEST, informs the engine that the sender agent is blocked and waiting for new messages.

All the actions are indifferently used by the entity agents either with a local or a distributed engine agent, with the exception of the *move agent* action, which is accepted and processed only by an engine operating in a distributed environment.

4.2.2 Simulation Agents

A society of simulation agents is populated by two types of agents: *simulation entity agents* and *simulation engine agents*. The entity agents incorporate the simulation logic by use of custom simulation behaviours, while the engine agent is in charge of coordinating the society, and therefore includes the list of simulation events and the record of the society composition, as detailed below.

Simulation entity agent

Fig. 2 illustrates the state diagram that defines the lifecycle of a simulation entity agent. The states are simulation states built on top of the standard states of a JADE agent [Bellifemmine] and are transparently integrated with them. The state diagram of a simulation entity agent looks similar to the state diagram of a conventional DES simulation entity, and therefore we only focuses on the differences between the two diagram - additional details can be found in [D'Ambrogio06]. Such differences concern the *Waiting for Registration Acknowledgement* state and the *Mobility* state. In the former, the simulation engine collects the registration requests and checks whether the society is ready to execute the simulation. In the latter, the agent forwards the request to the engine and terminates the life cycle. The introduction of these states is due to the decentralised and dynamic nature of the agent-based simulation framework, which differently from a conventional DES framework allows the creation and termination of logical processes.

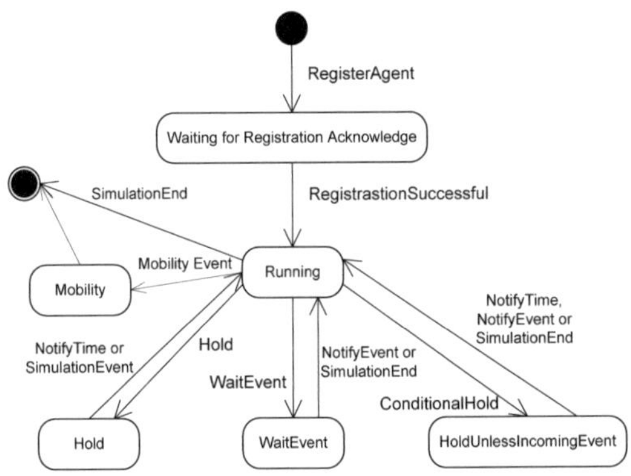

Fig. 2. State diagram of the simulation entity agent [Gianni09]

To implement such dynamics, the entity's behaviour is configured as a serial composition of the *Register Agent Behaviour* and the *Entity Main Cycle Behaviour*, with the latter to be configured according to the model specifications.
In order to allow the easy plug-in of any conventional JADE behaviour into the *Entity Main Cycle Behaviour*, the *simulation entity agent* interface must be consistent with the JADE agent standard interface. To achieve this, the *simulation entity agent* must invoke the simulation actions *conditional hold time, hold time, send event*, and *wait event* by use of the JADE standard methods *blockingReceive(millisecs), doWait(), send()*, and *blockingReceive()*, respectively.

Simulation engine agent
The *simulation engine agent* can be similarly described both for local and distributed engines. The local engine has already been described in [Gianni08], which the interested reader may refer to for further details. The distributed engine is built extending the local one, and by adding the following functionalities:

1. synchronization and communication between local and distributed environment;
2. agent mobility between simulators;
3. handling of distributed events in the framework.

The synchronization and communication concern the consistency between the local and distributed environments with the addition of event delivery to agents running on remote simulators. The agent mobility allows simulation time-stamped transfer of an agent between two different societies.

The distributed simulation engine agent makes use of the JADE framework for the local interactions and uses *SimArch Layer 1* and *HLA* for the synchronization and communications among distributed entities, as illustrated in Fig. 1. By this, the TDS framework transitively makes the implementation of HLA- and agent-based DS systems transparent because no details of the distributed computing infrastructure, HLA in particular, are to be known in order to develop such systems. Besides from that, however, the following additional advantages can be obtained:

- SimArch and its HLA-based implementation allow the integration with other simulation systems developed by use of such technologies, such as SimJ [D'Ambrogio06];
- the integration with SimArch allows to obtain a multi-paradigm (e.g. agent-based, process interaction, event scheduling, etc.) distributed simulation environment;
- HLA proves to perform better in terms of simulation workload compared to RMI-based communications between the JADE nodes [Bellifemmine];
- the implementation remains extremely simplified and conforms to a general reuse and integration trend currently observed in the software and simulation industry.

Fig. 3 shows the state diagram of the *simulation distributed engine agent*. This diagram defines a lifecycle that consists of five phases, denoted as Phase 0 through Phase 4. Phase 0 is the initialization of the distributed environment and proceeds as illustrated in [Gianni07, D'Ambrogio06a]. *Phase 1* is the registration phase and cares of synchronizing the start-up phase through the *Waiting for Registration Requests* and *Confirm Registration Successful* states. In this phase, the engine accepts incoming *register agent* requests while checking whether the simulation society becomes complete. Once the society is completed, the engine notifies the *registration successful* to all the registered agents. After completing this phase, the engine proceeds to the *Phase 2,* which represents the *Engine Main – Cycle Behaviour* and consists of the states *Waiting for Simulation Requests, Advancing Distributed Simulation Time,* and *Processing Internal Event.* In the first state, the engine waits for simulation requests from the agents, which are executing the associated simulation logic. These requests can be: *hold for a time, wait message, send message,* and *move to another engine.* The hold and the wait involve the scheduling of a local event, to which an event processing routine is associated. The sending of a message, differently, requires some processing to determine whether the recipient agent is local or remote. In the case of local agent, the request is dealt with the scheduling of a local event as for the hold and wait services. Conversely, in the case of remote recipient, the message is passed to the underlying layer 1 using the data interfaces provided by the SimArch architecture. Layer 1 in turns delivers the message to the specified remote engine. Finally, the mobility request is dealt with removing the agent from the society composition, and by conventionally invoking the send event service of layer 1 with a special tag that discriminates the type of service invocation on the recipient engine side. When all the agents have sent their requests and entered a blocking state, the engine proceeds to the *Advancing Distributed Simulation Time* state. In this state, the engine invokes layer 1 services to advance

the simulation time to the time of the next internal event. This is needed to guarantee that no incoming events from other engines are being delivered at a lesser simulation time than the time of the next internal event. The transition from this state to the next state only occurs when either a distributed event has been received or the time has been granted. In the latter case, the distributed event is transparently scheduled as a local event by SimArch Layer 1, and becomes the next internal event. In both cases, the next event is retrieved from the list and processed. If this event is a send message event, it is delivered and the execution of the relevant recipient agent is resumed. Differently, if the event is of type mobility event of an incoming agent in the engine, the simulation temporarily blocks until the agent is loaded up and joins the local simulation society. This is obtained by updating the society composition so that the society complete condition is no longer satisfied. This corresponds to the transition from the *processing next internal event* state to the *waiting for registration requests* state of Phase 1 in Fig. 3.
Phase 3 is activated by Phase 2 when receiving the corresponding event from the distributed environment, and consists in notifying the simulation end event to all the local agents.
Finally, *phase 4* concludes the engine life cycle and restores the distributed environment set up. This phase consists in the operations specified in [Gianni07, D'Ambrogio06a].

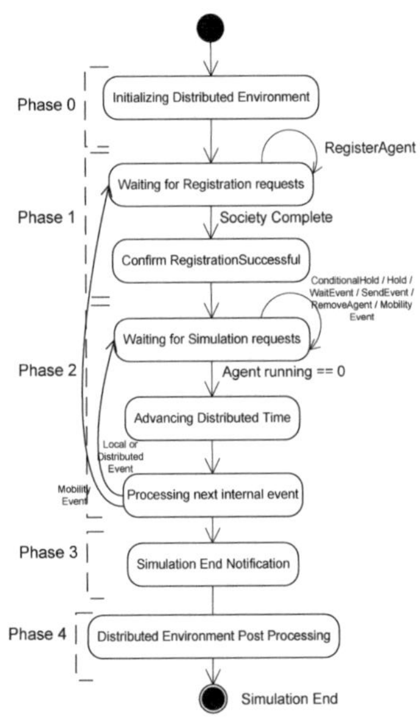

Fig. 3 State diagram of the simulation distributed engine agent

4.3 Interaction Protocol

The interaction protocol defines the rules upon which the conversation between the agents occurs, e.g. which agent talks, which listens, which expects what. The protocol can be distinguished in *intra-society* protocol and *inter-society* protocol. The former takes place for the communications in a local environment, both in the case of local and distributed simulation. Differently, the latter is used in the distributed environment only and involves agents, either engines or entities, which are running within different societies.

The *intra-society protocol* is used between the entity agents and the engine agent of a given society to request and acknowledge the simulation actions defined in the *DES-Ontology*. This protocol is based on the blocking and non-blocking properties of the simulation services. On the entity agent side, the action requests such as *register agent*, *wait time* or *hold time* require the agent to interrupt its execution until given proper conditions are met. Such conditions are monitored by the *engine agent*, which has the entire view of the society and the agents' requests and which activates the individual agents by responding to their requests. For the correct execution of the simulation it is fundamental that the entity agents are aware of and comply with such protocol.

The *inter-society protocol* complements the intra-society rules when operating in a distributed environment. The distributed engine implements this protocol in addition to the intra-society one, and therefore can immediately replace the local engine without modifying the simulation entity agents. The inter-society protocol defines two types of interactions: the sending of an event to a remote entity agent, and the mobility of an agent on a remote society.

The *sending of an event to a remote entity agent* occurs when a local entity agent requests the delivery of a message to a specified entity agent. The engine collects the request and verifies whether the recipient is running locally or on a remote society. In both cases, the intra-society protocol is applied for the interaction between the engine and the entity agent. In the case of a distributed recipient, the protocol assumes that the engine forwards the request to the remote agent before continuing the local processing. The communication between the two engines is obtained by SimArch and by HLA, and therefore is not compliant with the FIPA standard. However, such an approach brings several advantages - as shown above, and does not affect the peculiarities of the local interactions, which are still FIPA compliant.

The *agent mobility* is based on a similar approach but is more complex. Fig. 4 shows an example of agent mobility with the actors of this interaction and the sequence of steps. A *resource manager* agent is needed on the remote site to start the moved agent. The presence of this agent is essential to guarantee the proper application specific initialization typical of an agent start-up.

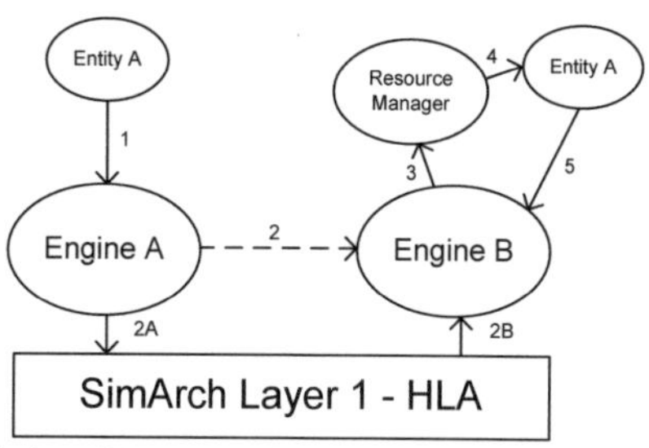

Fig. 4. Example of agent mobility [Gianni09]

Shall we assume that Agent Entity A in Fig. 4 wants to move from Society (Engine) A to Society (Engine) B at simulation time *t*. Entity A first sends a JADE-compliant *mobility request* to Engine A (step 1). The request consists of a simulation event to be delivered to the remote Resource Manager and an attached serialization of agent state. Engine A sends the event to Engine B by specifying that the event is of type mobility (step 2). At the specified time t, SimArch and HLA deliver the event to Engine B (steps 2A and 2B), which in turn processes the event by updating the society composition and by delivering the event to the Resource Manager (step 3), as initially specified by Entity A. Differently from a conventional event, the delivery and the processing of the mobility event does not allow Engine B to continue. The local society on site B is now incomplete and Engine B cannot proceed until it receives the request of joining the society from the locally running Entity A. After having operated the initialization of the agent parameters, the Resource Manager activates Entity A agent with the attached state (step 4). Once running, the agent first requests to join the local society and, after having received the respective acknowledgement, this starts its simulation cycle as at it was a first activation (step 5). Such mechanism guarantees that the mobility is operated transparently and in synchronization with the simulation clock, local and distributed.

5. TDS application example

The TDS framework serves as a general container for domain-specific agents, which are to be developed for the particular application. In this Section, we consider a scenario that involves the motion of individuals in a multi-storey factory building to simulate operations in a normal or emergency situation.
For the sake of conciseness, we consider a simplified manufacturing system where workers move around the factory premises in order to reach the machines they need to use or to reach building evacuation points. The modelling of the system includes the modelling of the space and of the worker agents. A possible space modelling for this system is represented by a *graph* whose *nodes* identify the possible positions, and whose *edges* represent the possible movements of workers between two positions. The *nodes* also represent physical resources that can exclusively be used by only one worker at a time, whereas the *edges* can simultaneously be traversed by more workers at the same time. The worker agents are autonomous entities, each characterized by a set of objectives, a decision model and a motion model.

The reasons for the investigation of such a system can be multiple. For example, the optimization of the factory resources, such as mechanical machines, or the validation of architectural design choices in the factory plan or the assessment of the evacuation capabilities of the factory building in presence of emergency situations. These studies, however, are not in the scope of this chapter and the example is here used to illustrate a TDS framework application only.

The agent-based modeling approach consists of a world model and a set of agents. The *world model* represents the simulated world within which the agents move and interact with each other. The world model consists of a graph representing the physical space, plus a description of the world status for each element of the physical world. The nodes of the graph represent the physical positions reachable by the agents, while the edges define the walking access between two points, as fully described in [Gianni08c]. The *agents*, including their dynamics and the parameterisation, are defined at Layer 3 of the TDS architecture. Their design is based on the key principle of *Separation of Concerns* [Mens] that suggests designing components with a maximized cohesion. Each agent is defined by a behavioural logic, which specifies the interaction with the external world, and a set of parameters that do not affect the pattern of the logic, according to the design outlines [Mernik]. Adopting this approach, the cohesion of each agent is maximised to make it reusable across the several values the parameters might assume. A straightforward, but effective, methodology to identify the candidate parameters comes from the analogy with the physical agents. A *Resource Manager* manages the world model, and the active actors, *human agents*, use and affect the conditions the world model resources. The in-depth description of the behavioural logic and the parameters of both the Resource Manager and the human agents is given in [Gianni08c].

The next subsection presents the design details of the scenario configuration.

5.1 Configuration of the scenario

The development of the distributed agent-based simulation system proceeds with the definition of the simulation scenario at Layer 4 of the TDS framework. In the specific case of the factory scenario, this includes: 1) the definition of the world model upon which the workers operate; 2) the partitioning of the simulated world and, 3) the definition of the number and the characteristics of the workers.

Point 1 can be achieved by first deciding the simulated world, and then by deriving the graph for each of its segments. In our application we considered a two storey factory, whose plan is shown in Fig. 5 for floor 1 and 2, respectively, and whose graph schematization is illustrated in Fig. 6.

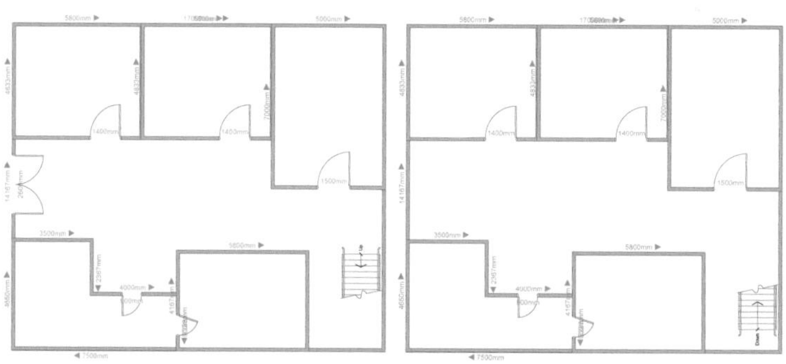

Fig. 5. Factory plan, floor 1 (left) and floor 2 (right)

Point 2 can be straightforwardly obtained by choosing floor 1 and floor 2 as segments of the simulated world to be allocated on independent hosts. The graphs of such floors were adapted for the distributed simulation and finally coded as XML files using GraphML [Brandes]. Each node and each edge are characterized by the relevant properties concerning the point in the physical world (e.g. type of room, type of machine, exit node, stairwell node, and the name of agent - resource manager - in charge of the nodes management). In particular, the nodes corresponding to the exit and the stairwell have a different semantics for the worker agents. The former specifies that the life cycle of the agent must terminate, as it reaches the main exit. Differently, a worker agent that approaches the stairwell knows that it must pass the management of its simulation requests to another resource manager, which is likely to be running on another host. It is also important to note that these graphs are not augmented with a condensed view of the remaining remote world. To simplify the prototypal implementation of this demo, the worker agents are specifically provided with the intermediate objective of reaching the stairwell node before directing towards any of the node being managed in the remote resource manager container.

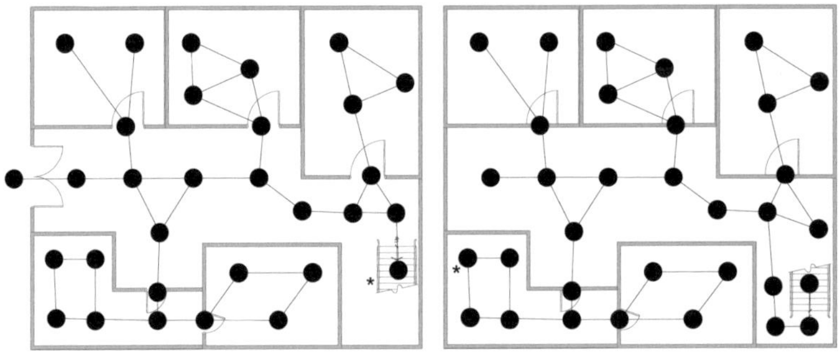

Fig. 6. World model for floor 1 (left) and floor 2 (right)

The number of worker agents is arbitrarily defined to be 40, more specifically 20 per each floor. Each agent is provided with an initial instance of the local graph and with an assigned set of objectives to accomplish before exiting the factory premises. An example of agent state model is reported below:

```
<agentWorker>
    <name>Worker 1</name>
    <initialNode>20</initialNode>
    <initialFloor>1</initialFloor>
    <motionModel>
        <UniformGenerator> <!-- motion over the edges -->
                <lowerBound>45</lowerBound>
                <upperBound>55</upperBound>
                <offset>15</offset>
        </UniformGenerator>
        <Constant>
                <value>0.3</value> <!-- motion over the nodes -->
        </Constant>
    </motionModel>
    <objectives class="SequenceOfObjectives">
        <objective class="SimpleObjective">
                <destination class="LocalDestination">
                <nodeId>34</nodeId>
                <groupId>0</groupId>
                <resourceManager>ResourceManager1</resourceManager>
                <areaName>Floor1</areaName>
        </objective>
        <objective class="SimpleObjective">
                <destination class="LocalDestination">
                <nodeId>62</nodeId>
                <resourceManager>ResourceManager2</resourceManager>
                <areaName>Floor2</areaName>
        </objective>
    </objectives>
</agentWorker>
```

The agent model specifies the agent name, the initial position, the motion model and the objectives that the agent must achieve before leaving the factory premises form the main

exit. The motion model consists in two components: the motion over the edges, which is the first parameter, and the motion over the nodes, which is the second parameter. In this specific case, the objective is of type composite and consists of a sequence of objectives. Particularly, the first objective is reaching the stairwell node 34 of floor 1 and the second one is reaching node 62 on second floor, both denoted with a *star* in Fig. 6. When the worker agent reaches the node 34, it recognizes that this node is of type stairwell and then automatically performs the mobility action to the floor 2 resource manager, which is running on a different host. Once in the new segment of the simulated world, the worker agent is loaded with the local world map, which also includes node 62. The agent finally uses the new map to compute the best path towards the assigned objective node 62.
In the simulated scenario, the 40 worker agents are similarly defined and activated in the HLA federation execution. The whole process proceeds activating first the Runtime Infrastructure, then the Federation Manager federate, and finally the two TDS engines. Each engine is provided with a local *Resource Manager* (Resource Manager 1 for Floor 1 and Resource Manager 2 for Floor 2) which eventually uses the XStream library [XStream] to first load the agent state of the agents, and then activates each of them. These agents register into the simulation society, and then the simulation cycle starts as described above.

6. Conclusion

The development of an agent-based distributed simulation system requires considerable effort in terms of HLA code and knowledge, compared to conventional local simulation systems. In this chapter, we have presented a simulation framework, named TDS, which reduces such an effort by making the development of agent-based distributed simulation systems HLA-transparent. This is achieved by introducing several abstraction layers on top of the distributed environment so that the simulation system developers deal with the same uniform interface when developing either local or distributed simulation systems. Moreover, this interface is uniform with conventional Multi-Agent System (MAS) framework, such as JADE, and therefore this reduces the development of such simulation systems to the one of conventional MAS. By such an approach, any HLA-based agent-based distributed simulation system can practically be developed as a conventional local MAS one, with no extra effort and no extra knowledge. An example development of a simulation system has also been presented to illustrate the application of the proposed framework in a domain that involves the motion of individuals in a multi-storey factory building to simulate operations in normal or emergency situations.

7. Acknowledgments

This work has been partially supported by the FIRB Project "Performance Evaluation of Complex Systems", funded by the Italian Ministry of Research and by the University of Roma TorVergata; by the FIRB Project "Software frameworks and technologies for the development of open-source distributed simulation code", funded by the Italian Ministry of Research; by CERTIA Research Center of the University of Roma TorVergata; and by the FP7 euHeart Project, funded by the European Commission (FP7-ICT-2007-224495).

8. References

[Bellifemine] Bellifemine, F.; Caire, G.; and Greenwood, D.; "Developing Multi-Agent Systems with JADE", Wiley (2007).

[Brandes] Brandes, U.; Eiglsperger, M.; Herman, I.; Himsolt, M.; and Marshall, M.S.; "GraphML Progress Report: Structural Layer Proposal," *Proceedings of the 9th Intl. Symp. Graph Drawing (GD '01)*, LNCS 2265, Springer-Verlag, pp. 501-512.

[D'Ambrogio06] D'Ambrogio, A.; Gianni, D.; and Iazeolla, G.; "SimJ: a Framework to Distributed Simulators", *Proceedings of the 2006 Summer Computer Simulation Conference (SCSC06)*, Calgary, Canada, July, 2006, pp. 149 - 156.

[D'Ambrogio06a] D'Ambrogio, A.; Gianni, D.; and Iazeolla, G.; "jEQN: a Java-based Language for the Distributed Simulation of Queueing Networks", LNCS vol. 4263/2006, *Proceedings of the 21st International Symposium on Computer and Information Sciences (ISCIS'06)*, Istanbul, Turkey, Nov, 2006.

[D'Ambrogio08] D'Ambrogio, A.; Gianni, D.; Iazeolla, G.; and Pieroni, A.; "Distributed simulation of complex systems by use of an HLA-transparent simulation language", *Proceedings of the 7th International Conference on System Simulation and Scientific Computing*, ICSC 2008, Asia Simulation Conference, Oct, 2008, Beijing, China, pp. 460 - 467.

[FIPA] FIPA Specification, http://www.fipa.org.

[Fujimoto] Fujimoto, R.; Parallel and Distributed Simulation Systems, Wiley (2000).

[Gianni07] Gianni, D.; and D'Ambrogio, A.; "A Language to Enable Distributed Simulation of Extended Queueing Networks", *Journal of Computer*, Vol. 2, N. 4, July, 2007, Academy Publisher, pp. 76 - 86.

[Gianni08] Gianni, D.; and D'Ambrogio, A.; "A Domain Specific Language for the Definition of Extended Queueing Networks Models", *Proceedings of the 2008 IASTED Software Engineering Conference (SE08)*, Innsbruck, Austria, February, 2008.

[Gianni08a] Gianni, D.; D'Ambrogio, A.; and Iazeolla, G.; "A Layered Architecture for the Model-driven Development of Distributed Simulators", *The First International Conference on Simulation Tools and Technologies (SIMUTOOLS08)*, Marseille, March, 2008.

[Gianni08b] Gianni, D.; "Bringing Discrete Event Simulation Into Multi Agent System", *10th International Conference on Computer Modelling and Simulation*, EuroSIM/UKSIM, Cambridge, April, 2008.

[Gianni08c] Gianni, D.; Loukas, G.; and Gelenbe, E.; "A Simulation Framework for the Investigation of Adaptive Behaviours in Largely Populated Building Evacuation Scenarios", *International Workshop on Organised Adaptation in Multi-Agent Systems (OAMAS) in the 7th International Conference on Autonomous Agents and Multi-Agent System (AAMAS)*, Estoril, Portugal, May, 2008.

[Gianni09] Gianni, D.; D'Ambrogio, A.; and Iazeolla, G., "DisSimJADE: A JADE-based framework for the Distributed Simulation of Multi-Agent Systems", *The Second International Conference on Simulation Tools and Techniques for Communications* (SIMUTOOLS09), March, 2009.

[Grable] Grable, R.; Jernigan, J.; Pogue, C.; and Divis, D.; "Metrics for Small Projects: Experiences at the SED", *IEEE Software*, March-April 1999, pp 21-29.

[IEEE-HLA] IEEE 1516, Standard for Modeling and Simulation (M&S) High Level Architecture (HLA) - Framework and Rules.

[IEEE-HLA1] IEEE: Standard for modeling and simulation (M&S) High Level Architecture (HLA) - federate interface specification. Technical Report 1516.1, IEEE (2000).

[IEEE-HLA2] IEEE: Standard for modeling and simulation (M&S) High Level Architecture (HLA) - object model template (OMT) specification. Technical Report 1516.2, IEEE (2000).

[IEEE-HLA3] IEEE: Recommended practice for High Level Architecture (HLA) federation development and execution process (FEDEP). Technical Report 1516.3, IEEE (2003).

[JADE] JADE project home; http://jade.tilab.it,Telecom Italia.

[Jennings] Jennings, N.R.; and Wooldridge, M.; "Application of Intelligent Agents", *Agent technology: foundations, applications, and markets*, Springer-Verlag, 1998, pp. 3 - 28.

[Jess] Jess Project; http://www.jessrules.com.

[Kuhl] Kuhl, F.; Weatherly, R.; and Dahmann, J.; Creating Computer Simulation Systems: An Introduction to the High Level Architecture, Prentice Hall (1999).

[Lees] Lees, M.; Logan, B.; and Theodoropoulos, G.; "Distributed Simulation of Agent-based Systems with HLA," *ACM Transaction on Modeling and Computer Simulation*, Vol. 17, N. 8, Jul, 2007.

[Mens] Mens, T.; and Wermelinger, M.; "Separation of concerns for software evolution", *Journal of Software Maintenance*, vol. 14, n. 5, Sept, 2002, pp. 311 - 315.

[Mernik] Mernik, M.; Heering, J.; and Sloane, A.M.; "When and how to develop domain-specific languages", *ACM Computing Surveys*, 37(4):316–344, 2005.

[Ontology-Bean] Ontology Bean Generator, http://hcs.science.uva.nl/usr/aart/beangenerator/index25.html

[Pokahr] Pokahr, A.; Braubach, L.; and Lamersdorf, W.; "JADEx: Implementing a BDI-Infrastructure for JADE Agents", *EXP - In Search of Innovation (Special Issue on JADE)*, vol 3, n. 3, Telecom Italia Lab, Turin, Italy, 2003, pp. 76-85.

[Sarjoughian] Sarjoughian, H.S.; Zeigler, B.P.; and Hali, S.B.; "A Layered Modeling and Simulation Architecture for Agent-Based System Development," *Proceedings of the IEEE*, Vol. 89, N. 2, Feb, 2001, pp. 201 - 213.

[Sloman] Sloman, A.;and Logan, B.; "Building cognitively rich agents using the SIM_Agent toolkit", *Communication of the ACM*, vol. 42, n. 3, 1999, pp. 71 - 77.

[Uhrmacher] Uhrmacher, A.M.; and Schattenberg, B.; "Agents in Discrete Event Simulation," *European Simulation Symposium (ESS98)*, 1998, pp. 129 - 136.

[Wang] Wang, F.; Turner, S.J.; and Wang, L.; "Agent Communication in Distributed Simulations", *Proceedings of the Multi-Agent and Multi-Agent-Based Simulation* (MABS 2004), Springer-Verlag, LNAI 3415, 2005, pp. 11–24.

[XStream] XStream project home page, http://xstream.codehaus.org/.

14

A Survey on the Need and Use of AI in Game Agents

Sule Yildirim and Sindre Berg Stene
Hedmark University College
Norway

1. Introduction

This chapter firstly seeks an answer to the question of whether Non Player Characters (NPCs) in Computer Games can also be viewed as game agents where reactivity, autonomy, being temporally continuous and having goal-oriented behavior are taken as the features of being a game agent. Within this scope, we will try to assess whether naming NPCs as agents point to a desire that one day they will fulfill the requirements of being an agent or whether NPCs actually already fulfill these requirements. Secondly, the chapter looks into the AI needs of video games. We present the AI methodologies that are either being used or under research for use in Game AI. The same methodologies are also likely to contribute to the increasing levels of autonomy and goal-directed behavior of NPCs and help them become more agent-like.

2. Background

In game development and game AI research, terms such as game agents and NPCs are often used interchangeably. However, considering the many years of agent research, are NPCs really game agents? In order to answer this question, we look at different definitions of being an agent from agent research and point out the features that would possibly separate an ordinary NPC from a game agent. Autonomy and goal-directed behavior are features that lie at the heart of being an agent and for that reason we look into the details of what it means to be autonomous and goal-oriented for an agent.

In agent research and applications, having its own agenda and being able to select its own actions are essential parts of being autonomous (Franklin & Graesser 1997). For that reason, the more the NPCs are able to carry out own agenda the more agent-like they are. If an NPC responds to certain conditions with predefined actions scripted in a certain programming language, it would have much less autonomy compared to an agent which can plan its future actions. Furthermore, the actions that NPCs execute cause changes in the environment. NPCs can then select further actions based on the consequences of an applied action, or they can ignore the consequences of their actions. An NPC which can consider the consequences of its actions can plan.

On the other hand, we look into the purpose of game AI and present the capabilities (reasoning, decision making, learning, prediction, goal-oriented behavior) that are expected from NPCs endowed with game AI. We also present a list of AI methodologies (e.g. path finding, Finite State Machines) which are in use or are proposed for use to achieve those capabilities. We summarize different kinds of game genres, the AI status and challenges of these games in order to be able to be more specific about the behaviors (e.g. create an army, form alliances, and so on) which would be expected from NPCs.
Another relevant definition is the definition of "intelligence". Intelligence is the ability to acquire and apply knowledge. The way in which the NPCs acquire knowledge and reason upon it will provide agents with different levels of intelligence.
Then, section 3 investigates the aspects of being a game agent. Section 4 gives the purpose and methods of game AI and the capabilities that NPCs become equipped with through game AI. It also explains what is meant by game AI for different game genres. Section 5 gives an evaluation of games for their agent characteristics. Section 6 gives the conclusions.

3. Agent Perspective: Being an NPC vs. Being a Game Agent

A definition of agents is as follows:

An autonomous agent is a system situated within and part of an environment that senses that environment and acts on it, over time, in pursuit of its own agenda and so as to reflect what it senses in the future (Franklin & Graesser, 1997).

Another definition of agent is given as follows:

Agents can be defined to be autonomous, problem solving computational entities capable of solving effective operations in dynamic and open environments (Luck et al., 2003).

On the other hand, an agent is stated to be autonomous if its behavior is determined by its own experience (with ability to learn and adapt) (Russell & Norvig, 2003).
In robotics, autonomy means independence of control. This characterization implies that autonomy is a property of the relation between the designer and the autonomous robot.
Self-sufficiency, situatedness, learning or development, and evolution increase an agent's degree of autonomy (Pfeifer & Scheier, 1999).
A list of properties is listed at the end of page 5 in (Franklin & Graesser, 1997). The authors state that the first four properties should exist in a program to name it as an agent and these four properties are as follows:

Reactive: Most of the NPCs in existing games have reactive responses, e.g. First Person Shooter NPCs.

Autonomous: Are there any NPCs that have their own agenda and that exercise control over its actions in any of the existing games? Such an NPC would not need to be told what to do but would be able to decide which action(s) to take under what conditions.

Goal-oriented: Does not simply act in response to the environment. Are there any agents in existing games which can pursue its goals?

Temporally continuous: This feature seems to be true in all agents.

In this chapter, we use these four properties to assess whether an NPC can be named as an agent. In existing games, most NPCs are reactive and temporally continuous. However, are they also autonomous and goal-oriented? Which AI methods can be employed to help achieve these properties?

On the other hand, we classify NPCs as software agents (Franklin & Graesser, 1997). This classification allows us further to classify NPCs according to their control mechanisms. In this way, game agents can be algorithmic, rule based, planning based, or otherwise primarily oriented around fuzzy logic, neural networks, machine learning, etc. This kind of classification is also important since it forms a natural bridge between the agent terminology such as being reactive, goal-oriented, autonomous, temporally continuous and the AI methodologies that can be employed to achieve them.

The type of control mechanism to employ depends on the kind of intelligence that is required to build into an NPC and the game genre that an NPC belongs to. For that reason, one of the coming sections will also give an overview of different game types (genres). Next we will look at what is meant by goal-based agents.

3.1 Goal-based Agents

"A game is a form of art in which participants, termed players, make decisions in order to manage resources through game tokens in the pursuit of a goal."

Greg Costikyan - Game designer and science fiction writer

A goal-based agent not only considers the consequences of its actions (See Fig. 1: What it will be like if I do action A) but also considers how much those actions are in line with its goals (See Fig. 1: What action I should do now given certain goals). As an example, F.E.A.R (Yue & de-Byl, 2006; Hubbard, 2005) is a game with goal-oriented behavior.

In (Yue & de-Byl, 2006), an example is presented for goal-directed behavior which is given in Fig. 2. In the figure, blue boxes represent keys and the current and goal values of a key. A key is a state that an agent wants to get into. For example, the topmost box holds a key which is "EnemyIsDead". This key has a current value of "False" and a goal value of "True" as the AI-controlled agent wants to have its enemy dead. In order to achieve that goal value, the enemy can choose to apply the action "fire weapon". The white boxes indicate the preconditions and effects of the action that they are bound to. The precondition of the "fire weapon" action requires that the key "HealthRecovered" has a value of "True" before the action can be applied. The effect of the action is to have the key "EnemyIsDead" have a value of "True" after the action is applied. It can be seen in Fig. 2 that the current value of the key "HealthRecovered" is "False". In order to have a value of "True" for the key "HealthRecovered", the action "take cover" is selected for application before the "fire weapon" action. The "take cover" action does not have any preconditions and for that reason, the goal state is achieved by the application of the "take cover" action first and the "fire weapon" action second.

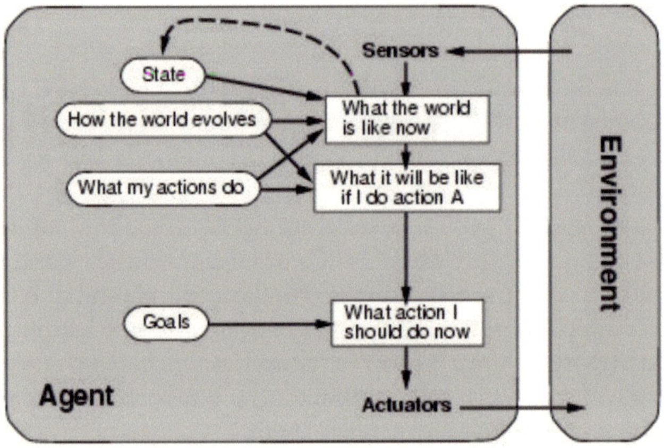

Fig. 1. Goal-based Agents (adapted from (Russell & Norvig, 2003)).

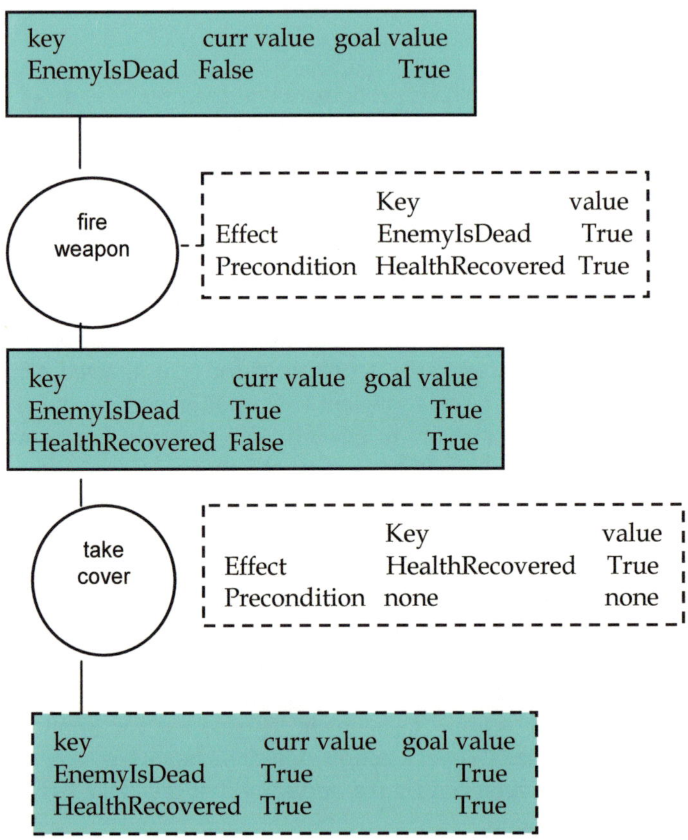

Fig. 2. Taken from (Yue & de-Byl, 2006) - F.E.A.R. © Monolith Productions 2005.

On the other hand, planning is a more complicated goal-directed behavior and more on planning will be given in Section 4. The benefits of a goal-oriented planning behavior are stated as follows in (Yue & de-Byl, 2006).

- There are no hard-coded plans
- Code maintenance is minimized
- Bugs are minimized when planning
- Code is reusable

The drawbacks of a goal-oriented planning behavior are as stated as follows in (Yue & de-Byl, 2006):

- Real-time planning requires processing time
- More complex plans require more time

Different aspects of goal-directed behavior and planning such as representation of world, architectures and applications can be found in (Orkin, 2005), (Orkin, 2004), (Narayek, 2002), (IGDA, 2005) and (Namee & Cunningham, 2001).

4. Game AI in General

One of the aims of Game AI is to increase the difficulty of the game to challenge the human players. The game AI should lead to a fulfilling game experience. On the other hand, games take place in dynamic complex worlds in which complex decisions must be made, often based on partial knowledge (Fairclough et al., 2001).
It is usual to state that Non Player Characters are AI-controlled characters that can only interact with PCs (Player Characters) through scripted events or artificial intelligence (AI). However, what is it that is called Artificial Intelligence in an NPC? For example, World of Warcraft is one of the most popular games and its NPCs are stated to be AI controlled (Blizzard, 2005). Even though it is so popular, it actually has very little AI composed of reactive agents and a great deal of scripted events. For example, a player is tasked with escorting an NPC so that he can walk around and look for his lost backpack or something similar (where you meet monsters and assassins on the way, also scripted NPCs, and everything woven into a storyline about this man's misfortune). On the other hand, even though it is "low AI", this is something which adds to the game experience in terms of AI.

What kind of intelligent behaviors are expected from NPCs? In general, an NPC is expected to maximize goal achievement by choosing the most optimal actions given the available information. An exception to the rule could be when more human-like actions may be a better choice than the most optimal action, for the sake of realism.
The most commonly used AI methodologies to achieve game AI can be stated as follows (McGee, 2005):

- Decision trees: can be realized by If-Then statements..
- Finite state machines
- Command hierarchies

- Manager task assignment
- Path finding (A*)
- Terrain analysis
- Influence mapping
- Formations
- Flocking
- Emergent behaviour

Influence mapping is a technique for terrain analysis to identify boundaries of control or otherwise interesting points/areas/features of a map.
Other possibilities are:

- Artificial Neural Networks
- Genetic Algorithms
- Fuzzy logic

Scripting is the most common means of control in Game AI. Path finding is another common use for AI, widely seen in RTS (Real Time Strategy) games. Emergent AI has been explored in Black & White.
In addition to the methodologies stated above, cheating is also considered a valid technique in game AI. The position of an unforeseen object can simply be looked up in the game's scene graph (Fairclough et al., 2001). This kind of cheating can cause a feeling of unfairness on the player character's behalf and too much of it might not be appropriate for that reason.
As human beings, what is important for us when selecting an action in a certain situation is to behave in a way that we believe is the right way in the particular situation. For that reason, we have certain action formats which tell us what to do or how to act under various circumstances. Such behavior can be implemented using rules, and Finite State Machines model this by combining sets of such rules into "states" where each state also contains rules for which conditions would cause an agent to change state.
FSMs are very rigid and behave poorly when confronted by situations not dreamed of by the game designer (Fairclough et al., 2001). The behavior of the NPC is governed by a set of rules, each rule having a condition and some action(s) to execute when this condition is satisfied by the state of the world (Fairclough et al., 2001). Therefore, as a player interacts with an NPC he gets to know the behavior of the NPC and can predict what it will do next and can develop a plan to despatch the NPC (Fairclough et al., 2001). Non-deterministic FSMs are also employed to increase the unpredictability of NPCs so that the "fun" side of a game increases (Brownlee).
On the other hand, we as humans learn from our mistakes. In (Scott, 2002), it is stated that in general, game AI lacks the learning and reasoning capabilities of humans and that game AI could address the fields of machine learning, decision making based on arbitrary data input, reasoning etc. However, in several games, game AI encompasses some amount of learning and reasoning capabilities (e.g. learning capability of creatures in Black and White). An NPC which executes FSMs to mimic human behavior can learn from its mistakes and build up its own experience to be able to act smarter in time. Equipped with an FSM, an NPC should be able to find out which of its actions has been beneficial, which of them have not been beneficial and what other action types it could employ under given circumstances. Learning

actions which is not in its repertoire and learning them on its own would be a real challenge for an NPC especially when it would obviously lack the observational and mimicking by imitation or natural language understanding capacities of a human player. The research in AI towards this direction can also find its application for developing NPCs.

In (Evans, 2001), learning is stated to cover the following characteristics, specifically for the game Black and White:

- Learning that (e.g. learning that there is a town nearby with plenty of food)
- Learning how (e.g. learning how to throw things, improving your skill over time)
- Learning how sensitive to be to different desires (e.g. learning how low your energy must be before you should start to feel hungry)
- Learning which types of object you should be nice to, which types of object you should eat, etc. (e.g. learning to only be nice to big creatures who know spells).
- Learning which methods to apply in which situations (e.g. if you want to attack somebody, should you use magic or a more straightforward approach?)

Learning can be initiated in a number of very different ways (Evans, 2001):

- From player feedback, stroking or slapping the creature (NPC).
- From being given a command: when the creature is told to attack a town, the creature learns that that sort of town should be attacked.
- From the creature observing others: observing the player, other creatures, or villagers.
- From the creature reflecting on his experience: after performing an action to satisfy a motive, seeing how well that motive was satisfied, and adjusting the weights representing how sensible it is to use that action in that sort of situation.

Reasoning is about finding out why something has happened while showing an awareness of goals and assessing the relative importance of different goals (Hawes, 2000). If the game AI reasons better, the NPCs would become more agent-like.
(Wintermute, 2007) presents the use of SOAR architecture to meet the demands on the AI in RTS games. A discussion of the CogAff architecture as the basis for an agent that can display goal-oriented behavior is given in (Hawes, 2000).
Planning in real-time is an alternative to the more common techniques of modeling character behavior with scripts or finite state machines (FSMs). Rather than traversing a predefined graph of state transitions, a planning Non Player Character (NPC) searches for a sequence of actions to satisfy some goal. Considerations for developing an agent architecture for real-time planning in games is given in (Orkin, 2005).

One project regarding saving the NPCs from being predictable and even allowing them to make predictions about the human player is the TCD Game AI project (Fairclough et al., 2001). On the other hand, Case-Based Plan Recognition is proposed as a prediction mechanism for NPCs to predict a player's actions (Kerkez & Cox, 2001).

4.1 Game AI Specific to Different Genres: NPC Behaviors, AI Methodologies in Use, Expected AI Challenges

Games can be grouped under different types: according to their nature: Real Time Strategy (RTS), First Person Shooter (FPS), Role Playing Game (RPG), God Games etc. This section will present a mixture of the need for AI, the methods of AI and the behaviors that can be obtained by AI for different kind of games.

Role Playing Games

In RPG games, a team is built up to reach a common goal. Some fine examples of RPG's are Secret of Mana, the games in the Final Fantasy series and other many varieties. The intelligence required from a team or from individual characters (collaborating or cooperating) depends on how complex behavior is required to reach the common goal, what kind of resources the team or individuals in the team have and whether the team members have primitive or advanced collaboration strategies. There is a need for more realistic and engaging NPCs in these games (Fairclough et al., 2001).

First Person Shooter Games

First-person shooter games (FPS games), emphasize shooting and combat from the perspective of the character controlled by the player. FPS-type games usually implement the layered structure of the artificial intelligence system. Layers at the lower levels handle the most elementary tasks, such as determining the optimal path to the target or playing appropriate sequences of character animation. The higher levels are responsible for tactical reasoning and selecting the behavior which an AI agent should assume in accordance with its present strategy. The examples for tasks of higher layers are whether the agent should patrol the area, enter combat or run through the map searching for an opponent (Grzyb, 2005).

Some fine examples of FPS games would be Half-Life 1, Half-Life 2, Counter-Strike, Doom III and Quake IV.

The NPCs in the original Half-Life 1 released in 1998 had AI behaviors which were not present in previous games. For example, AI comrades and enemies had different reactions for getting shot, spotting grenades and even a realistic awareness of the actions of the human player. As a result of displaying this intelligent behavior, Half-Life 1 quickly asserted itself as having the best AI of any game at the time. After Half-Life 1, more and more games started to focus on the AI aspect of game design instead of just graphics. Today, combat AI can be seen ducking around corners or behind boxes and tossing the player's grenades back. In many cases, AI controlled NPCs are even standing in for real players in multiplayer games. Even though combat AI can dodge incoming fire and shoot like a skilled player, there are four major things that human combatants offer over AI: knowledge of their environment, efficient use of teamwork, the ability to "hunt", and survival instincts (Schreiner). However, some progress has since been made to address each of these issues.

Real Time Strategy Games

Strategy games require that the human player displays skillful and planned behavior in order to play efficiently and hence achieve victory. Real-time strategy games are strategy games which are played in a real-time environment. In the RTS game environment, the human and computer controlled players compete for resources. The most common setting for RTS games is the war-game setting, where in addition to resource management the player engages in war. The resource management in RTS games encompasses obtaining resources and utilizing those resources to gain an advantage. Resources are valuable minerals, energy, or other materials. Building an army and attacking strategic objectives, such as locations with access to resources, are aspects which make an RTS game a "war game".

Fine examples of RTS games would be Starcraft 1 and 2, Warcraft 1-3, Supreme Commander, the different games in the Command and Conquer series, and many other varieties of games as well.

At the low levels of AI, path planning is important whereas at higher levels, there are modules responsible for economy, development or, very importantly, a module to analyse the game map (Grzyb, 2005).

In Warcraft 3, users are called upon to create an army to defeat one or more computer-controlled villages with armies of their own. Computer controlled villages form alliances, scout surrounding areas and devise appropriate battle plans to do their best to be the last village standing (Wexler, 2002).

God Games

The focus of a god game tends to be control over the lives of people, anywhere from micromanaging a family to overseeing the rise of a civilization as in Spore (Maxis, 2008). Also, Black and White is a god game developed by Lionhead Studios and it was implemented through a variety of AI algorithms and techniques in 2002. What sets "Black and White" apart from any other game before it is its advanced use of AI. There are two types of intelligent agents in "Black and White". The first type is the community of villagers. The villagers have their knowledge, desires and beliefs represented in large tables and situation calculus. The other intelligent agent is the creature. AI in the creature allows the creature to learn how to satisfy its master and know how to correctly act based upon its beliefs and perceptions (Funge, 1999). Symbolic attribute-value pairs are used to represent a creature's belief about any individual object. This type of representation is used with rule-based AI to give creatures basic intelligence about objects (Wexler, 2002). Decision trees are used to represent agents' beliefs about general type of objects (Wexler, 2002). Neural networks are used to represent desires (Wexler, 2002). The creatures also learn facts about its surroundings, how to do certain tasks, how sensitive to be to its desires, how to behave to or around certain objects, and which methods to apply in certain situations. The user can help the creature to learn or it can learn to please its user by differentiating the tasks that please the user versus the tasks that do not.

More advanced AI in terms of a partial-planner with which a creature can satisfy its desires and goals is foreseen to be included in "Black and White". This way a user can create a list of goals that it wishes for the creature to complete (Bandi et al., 1999).

Action-Adventure Games

Action-adventure games focus on exploration and usually involve item gathering, simple puzzle solving, and combat, e.g. Tomb Raider (Core Design, 1996). In action games, having the player as a member of a squad or a team provides an opportunity for the further use of more complex AI.

Also there is need for more realistic and engaging NPCs in Adventure Games (Fairclough et al., 2001).

The other types of games are sport games, racing games and puzzles. There are also games which do not fit squarely in any category.

5. Evaluation of Games for Their Agent Characteristics

In Table 1 and Table 2, we use the agent definition given in (Franklin & Graesser, 1997) to evaluate the agent characteristics of individual NPCs in a diverse selection of popular games.

In reactive agents, a program is just a set of percept → action rules, commonly termed a production-rule system. In each step of the control cycle a rule is selected whose left hand side matches the agent's current percept, and the action on that rule's right hand side is then effected. The first column of Table 1 shows our evaluation of the reactive capabilities of the selected games. The value for reactivity can be High, Low or None in the table, indicating the ability of acting out useful reactive responses in rapidly changing situations. For example, an NPC is unexpectedly attacked on the way to a distant destination, and temporarily stops in order to respond to the attack.

An agent is a temporally continuous software process that senses the environment and acts on it over time, in pursuit of its own agenda and so as to effect what it senses in the future. The corresponding column in Table 1 lists the extent to which an agent's behavior is influenced over time by what it senses in the environment.

In goal-oriented agents, an agent applies actions in pursuit of a goal. A goal-oriented agent is different from an agent where the agent does not necessarily try to achieve a goal, but it applies an action just because it is right to do that action in a given situation (Table 1).

Autonomy characteristic of an agent is split further into following aspects: Self-sufficiency, Complexity of decision making, Variety of action repertoire, Learning and Situatedness (Table 2). These are the aspects of autonomy that we deemed to be relevant for game AI agents.

Self-sufficiency is a property of autonomy in agents. It has three aspects:

1. Supervision by higher level agents where there is a hierarchy of agents and each level of the hierarchy can have various amounts of complexity.

2. Visible inter-agent communication.

3. Being capable of supporting an agent's own life without help, food, shelter etc. This aspect does not apply in game environments.

	Reactivity	Temporally continuous	Goal-oriented
World of Warcraft	Low	Low	Yes
Half Life 2 (Single player mode)	High	Low	Yes
Supreme Commander	Low	High	Yes
Warcraft 3	Low	High	Yes
Black & White 2	Low	High	Yes
Tomb Raider: Anniversary	Low	Low	Yes
Unreal Tournament 2004 (bots)	High	High	Yes

Table 1. Evaluation of different games for their agent aspects related to reactivity, being temporally continuous and goal-oriented.

Visible inter-agent communication is an aspect that influences an agent's autonomy level. More agent interaction might mean higher autonomy, e.g. one NPC informs another that there is a danger.
The complexity of an agent's decision-making mechanism influences the quality of decisions. For example, an agent that uses non-deterministic finite-state machines is better at considering alternative actions for a given situation compared to an agent that uses a deterministic finite state machine. An NPC with a controller of the former type is more likely to survive compared to the latter.
Having a variety of action repertoire will increase an agent's levels of autonomy, by enabling it to choose between more actions.
Being able to learn would mean an agent is likely to become informed about what to do in situations it is not currently able to take an action or take the most suitable action. From the games referred to in Table 2, learning is a feature only present in Black & White 2.
Being situated and hence being informed about the environmental state is a property that exists in all the selected games of Table 2 and is a property of being autonomous for agents.

	Supervision by higher level agents	Visible inter-agent communication	Complexity of decision making	Variety of action repertoire	Learning	Situatedness
World of Warcraft	None	Low	Low	Low	No	Yes
Half Life 2 (Single player mode)	None	High	Low	High	No	Yes
Supreme Commander	High	Low	Low	High	No	Yes
Warcraft 3	High	Low	Low	High	No	Yes
Black & White 2	Low	Low	High	High	Yes	Yes
Tomb Raider: Anniversary	None	High	Low	Low	No	Yes
Unreal Tournament 2004 (bots)	None	High	High	High	No	Yes

Table 2. Evaluation of different games for their agent aspects related to autonomy

6. Conclusion

In this chapter, we investigated whether it is possible to view NPCs in games as game agents. We used the qualities of reactivity, being temporally continuous, autonomy and being goal-oriented for evaluating a representative set of popular commercial games on how much agent-like they are. Our evaluations show that some games have NPCs that achieve more agent-like behavior than others.

Also, we give a survey on the use of various AI methodologies in commercial games and in game research. We indicate that the need for AI in games is centered around maximizing goal achievement by choosing the most optimal actions given the available information. NPCs can challenge human players and add to the quality of experience if they can become better at achieving optimal behavior.

Furthermore, we postulate that further investigation is required before conclusions can be made about whether the given methodologies (especially those that are not commonly used in commercial games at the moment) are really applicable in commercial games. Regarding this point, the use of learning in games is relatively low in commercial arena as can be observed from Table 2 even though learning is an important aspect in achieving artificial intelligence. Another relevant point is that the non player characters are required to make real-time decisions and that it does not seem practical to add time consuming and complicated intelligence control mechanisms in them.

7. References

Bandi, S., Cavazza, M. et al. (1999). Situated AI in Video Games, University of Branford

Blizzard (2005). World of Warcraft, Blizzard. www.worldofwarcraft.com

Brownlee, J. Finite State Machines (FSM), Artificial Intelligence Depot http://ai-depot.com/FiniteStateMachines/FSM.html.

Core Design (1996). Tomb Raider, http://www.tombraider.com/, Eidos Interactive

Evans, R. (2001). The Future of AI in Games: A Personal View, Game Developer Magazine.

Fairclough, C.; Fagan, M. et al.(2001). Research Directions for AI in Computer Games, *Proceedings of the Twelfth Irish Conference on Artificial Intelligence and Cognitive Science*, pp. 333 - 344.

Franklin, S. & Graesser, A (1996). Is it an Agent, or just a Program?: A Taxonomy for Autonomous Agents, *Proceedings of the Workshop Intelligent Agents III, Agent Theories, Architectures, and Languages*, pp. 21–35, ISBN:3-540-I-0 Springer Verlag, London.

Funge, J. (1999). AI for *Computer Games and Animation: A Cognitive Modeling Approach*, AK Peters Ltd, ISBN: 1-56881-103.9, Natick, MA

Grzyb, J. (2005). Artificial Intelligence in Games, *The Software Developer's Journal*

Hawes, N. (2000). Real-Time Goal-Oriented Behavior for Computer Game Agents. *Proceedings of the 1st International Conference on Intelligent Games and Simulation*, London, November, 2000

Hubbard, V. (2005) F.E.A.R First Encounter Assault Recon, Monolith Productions, Vivendi Universal

IGDA (2005). The AIISC Report

Kerkez, B. & Cox M. T. (2001). Incremental Case-Based Plan Recognition Using State Indices, *Proceedings of the 4th International Conference on Case-Based Reasoning: Case-Based Reasoning Research and Development*, pp. 291–305, ISBN: 978-3-540-42358-4, Springer-Verlag, Berlin

Luck, M. & McBurney, P. et al. (2003). Agent Technology: Enabling Next Generation Computing A Roadmap for Agent Based Computing, AgentLink 2.

Maxis (2008). Spore, Electronic Arts. http://www.spore.com/

McGee, K. (2005). Advanced Game Programming: AI Session 2: Genres, Roles, Techniques, http://www.ida.liu.se/~kevmc/courses/2005-ht02/tsbk10-session-2.pdf

Namee, B. M. & Cunningham, P. (2001). Proposal for an Agent Architecture for Proactive Persistent Non Player Characters, Proceedings of the 12th Irish Conference on Artificial Intelligence and Cognitive Science: 221 - 232

Narayek, A. (2002). Intelligent Agents for Computer Games. Computers and Games, *Proceedings of Second International Conference, CG 2000*, pp. 414-422, Springer

Orkin, J. (2004). Symbolic Representation of Game World State: Toward Real-Time Planning in Games, *Proceedings of the Workshop Challenges in Game AI*, AAAI

Orkin, J. (2005). Agent Architecture Considerations for Real-Time Planning in Games, *Proceedings of AIIDE*

Pfeifer, R. & Scheier ,C. (1999). *Understanding Intelligence*, MIT Press.

Russell, S. & Norvig, P. (2003). *Artificial Intelligence: A Modern Approach*, Prentice Hall

Schreiner, Artificial Intelligence in Game Design, http://ai-depot.com/GameAI/Design.html

Scott, B. (2002). The Illusion of Intelligence, In: *AI Game Programming Wisdom*, Rabin, Steve (Eds), 19-20, Charles River Media

Wexler, J. (2002). Artificial Intelligence in Games: A look at the smarts behind Lionhead Studio's "Black and White" and where it can go and will go in the future, University of Rochester.

Wintermute, S., Xu, J., & Laird, J.E. (2007). SORTS: A Human-Level Approach to Real-Time Strategy AI, *Proceedings of the Third Artificial Intelligence and Interactive Digital Entertainment Conference (AIIDE-07)*, Stanford, California.

Yue, B. & de-Byl, P. (2006). The state of the art in game AI standardisation, *Proceedings of ACM International Conference*

Acknowledgement

This chapter is a revised version of a paper by the authors published in the Proceedings of Agent Directed Simulation (ADS'08) within the Conference SpringSim'08, pp. 124-131, ISBN: 1-56555-319-5, Ottawa, Canada, April 2008, The Society for Computer Simulation International, San Diego.

We would like to thank Arild Jacobsen from Gjøvik University College for sharing his ideas about different parts of this chapter with us and his valuable help with the proof-reading of the chapter.

15

A Hierarchical Petri Net Model for SMIL Documents

Samia Bouyakoub and Abdelkader Belkhir
USTHB University
Algeria

1. Introduction

The increasing number of services and products proposed on the Web is mainly marked by the proliferating use of rich media to transmit information. The static Web as it was known during the glorious years of HTML is disappearing to let place to a more dynamic and interactive Web. Synchronized Multimedia Integration Language (SMIL) (SMIL1.0,1998) was developed by the World Wide Web Consortium (W3C) to address the lack of HTML for multimedia over the Web. It provides an easy way to compose multimedia presentations. With the W3C efforts, SMIL is becoming the most popular language in authoring multimedia presentations and it is supported by the newest versions of browsers.

In authoring a SMIL multimedia presentation, the author always wants to guarantee the correctness of the SMIL script, not only syntactically but also semantically. However, the complexity of the SMIL synchronization model is such that it is difficult to guarantee the validity of a scenario using non formal methods. On the other hand, the formal techniques based on mathematical models offer a complete formal semantics and propose formal techniques for consistency checking, but are in general time consuming. In order to respect the interactivity constraint in an authoring environment, a formal model for SMIL documents must offer the best compromise between formal verification capabilities and efficiency in terms of computation time.

Although many research studies were dedicated to multimedia documents authoring, only few of them has addressed temporal consistency checking problems. Yet, it is clear that the temporal consistency of a document has a direct impact on the quality of the presentation and consequently on the client satisfaction (consider the case of a presentation that stops playing before its end, a part of its semantic is lost).

In order to address the lack in SMIL modelling and verification solutions, we have defined a hierarchical temporal extension of Petri Nets, named H-SMIL-Net (Hierarchical SMIL-Petri Net) (Bouyakoub & Belkhir, 2008), for the incremental authoring of SMIL multimedia documents. The H-SMIL-Net model is mapped on the SMIL hierarchical temporal structure to better fit with the modelling needs of this language. The H-SMIL-Net model is based on the SMIL-Net model defined in (Bouyakoub & Belkhir, 2007). In order to better fit with SMIL authoring requirements, we have implemented the H-SMIL-Net model within an interactive authoring environment for SMIL documents.

2. Overview of SMIL

We give a brief overview of the SMIL synchronization elements. A more detailed definition can be found at (SMIL 1.0,1998;SMIL 2.0,2001; SMIL 2.0,2005;SMIL 2.1,2005;SMIL 3.0,2008).
SMIL is an XML-Based language for the specification of multimedia presentations. Using SMIL, an author can describe the temporal behaviour of a presentation, associate hyperlinks with media objects and describe the layout of the presentation on the screen. The latest version of the language is SMIL 3.0 (SMIL 3.0,2008), but the temporal model remains unchanged since the second version.
In this study, we focus on the most used temporal elements of SMIL, including:

- The time containers <seq> and <par>,
- The set of media object elements such as <img>, <video>, <audio> and <text>... etc.
- The time attributes *begin, end* and *dur.*

The <seq> and <par> elements, defined since the first version SMIL 1.0, are the basis of the SMIL temporal model. The <seq> element defines a sequence of elements played one after the other (Figure 1); whereas the <par> element defines a parallel grouping in which multiple elements can be played at the same time (Figure 2).

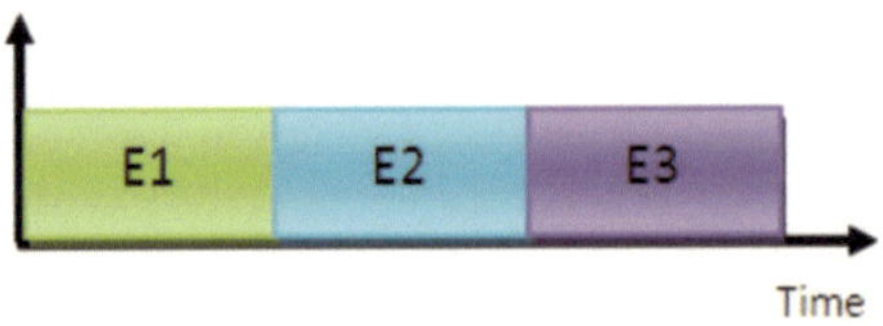

Fig. 1. The Seq element

Three semantics are defined for the termination of a <par> element, according to the value of the "*endsync*" attribute:
- *Last*: the <par> finishes when all its child elements finish,
- *First*: the <par> finishes since one of its child elements finishes,
- *Master*: the <par> finishes when the master element (defined by the ID attribute) finishes.

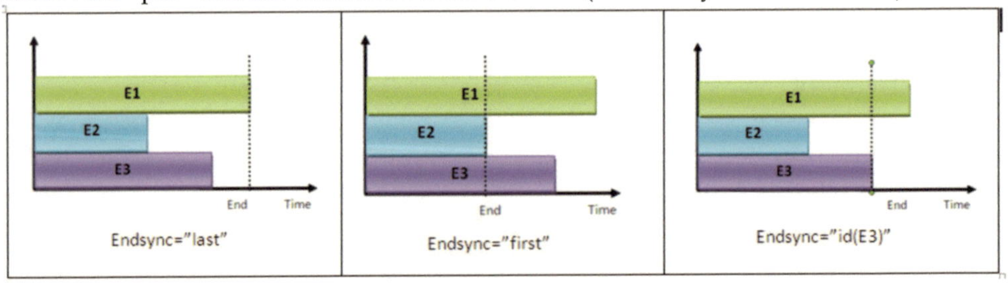

Fig. 2. The Par element

The media object elements allow the integration of media objects into a SMIL presentation, by reference to their URI (Uniform Resource Identifiers).
Besides, the synchronization attributes *begin, dur* and *end* could be associated with these synchronization elements:

- The begin attribute specifies the explicit begin of an element.
- The end attribute specifies the explicit end of an element.

- The dur attribute specifies the explicit duration of an element.

The effect of these time attributes is illustrated in Figure 3.

Since any temporal relationship among multimedia objects could be represented by the combination of parallel and the sequential elements with proper attribute values, it is easy to see that SMIL could be used to specify all synchronization relationships (Yang, 2000).

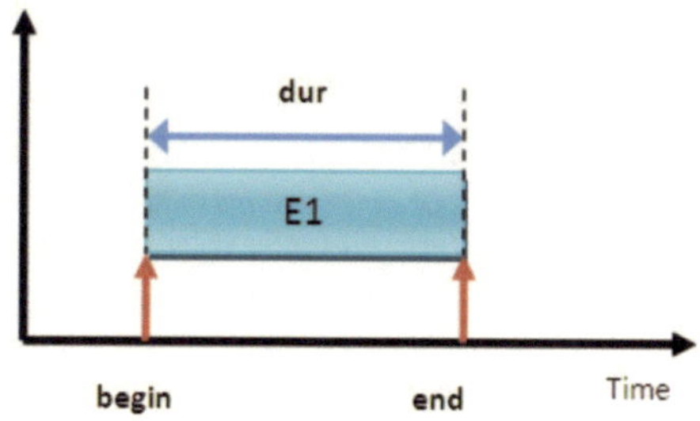

Fig. 3. The time attributes

The complexity of the SMIL temporal specification can lead authors, in some cases, to specify synchronization relations which could not be satisfied during the presentation of the document, thus characterizing the occurrence of temporal inconsistencies. The time conflict is one type of temporal inconsistency, it is defined in (yang,2000) as the case of conflicting values of attributes in the SMIL specification. Two types of conflicts are defined: The intra-element time conflict which is the case of conflicting attributes within a single element and the inter-elements time conflict which is the case of conflicting attributes among different elements. The SMIL specification defines some conventions to ignore one of the conflicting attributes, but the obtained behaviour can be different from the author's specification; besides, the obtained temporal behaviour depends on the implementation of the SMIL player. A detection mechanism for time conflicts is then necessary.

3. Related works

Several models have been used for the specification of the temporal behaviour of SMIL documents.

In (Jourdan et al, 1999), the SMIL temporal relationships are modelled as a CSP (Constraint Satisfaction Problem). The temporal elements are modelled by variables and the temporal relationships are represented by constraints. The obtained constraints system can be analyzed using a constraints solver in order to find a formatting solution and to detect temporal inconsistencies. However, the computation time of the solvers constitutes a limitation to the use of this approach.

In (Sampaio et al, 2004), RT-LOTOS (Real Time LOTOS) formal technique is applied to the modelling of SMIL documents. The RT-LOTOS specification is automatically derived from the SMIL document. The verification of the temporal properties is made on the reachability graph derived from RT-LOTOS. Then, model checking techniques are applied to detect temporal inconsistencies. This approach presents two issues: First, the verification of the temporal properties requires the use of an intermediate model: the reachability graph. Secondly, the number of states of the reachability graph can grow rapidly when the complexity of the SMIL file increases.

In (Newman et al, 2003), the process algebra π-calculus (an event-based formalism derived from CCS: Calculus of Communicating Systems) is used to model the temporal synchronization of SMIL documents. The SMIL relations are represented graphically using a "storyboard". The storyboard is then translated to π-calculus formulas and the obtained system can be analyzed mathematically (using the algebraic laws of π-calculus) to study some safety properties of the system. However, no mechanism for temporal verification has been defined in this study.

In (Bossi et al, 2007) the authors propose a formal semantic for the verification of SMIL documents using a formal system based on the Hoare Logic. A set of inference rules is defined to describe how the execution of a piece of SMIL code changes the state of the playback. Media items definitions are evaluated through axioms, while for <par> and <seq> compositions more complex rules are needed. This complexity increases when adding temporal attributes, or when dealing with composite elements imbrications. Although this approach offers a formal semantic for SMIL timing, it seems too complex to comply with authoring requirements, even though the author says few words about an authoring environment based on the defined semantic.

Many temporal models for SMIL documents are based on temporal extensions of Petri Nets. Petri Net-based models provide a good method to specify temporal relationships (Ramchandani, 1974).

A modified Petri Net model, object composition Petri Net (OCPN) (Little et al, 1990), has been proved to have the ability to specify any arbitrary temporal relationship among media elements. However, when dealing with the real time issues and the complex synchronization constraints of SMIL, this model is not powerful enough to capture all the timing and synchronization semantics of SMIL documents.

(Chung et al, 2003) proposes a new model which is an enhancement of OCPN by adding typed tokens and a new set of firing rules. This model can capture the timing and synchronization semantics of the SMIL presentation. However, no verification techniques are proposed to check the consistency of the SMIL specification.

The RTSM model (Real Time Synchronization Model) proposed by (Yang, 2000) is also based on the OCPN model. In RTSM, two types of places are defined and new firing rules are proposed. The RTSM model can capture temporal semantics of SMIL scripts and detects the temporal conflicts within the same model. However, the verification is not incremental and requires the parsing of the whole RTSM. Moreover, the translation from SMIL to RTSM results on a loss of the SMIL temporal structure (parallel and sequential activities).

The SAM model (Software Architecture Model) used by (Yu et al, 2002) is a combination of two complementary formal notations: Petri nets and temporal logic. SMIL Synchronization elements are modelled by Petri nets whereas safety and liveness proprieties are specified using logic formulas. Formal techniques such as reachability tree, deductive proof and structural induction are used to check some proprieties of the SMIL specification. However, no mechanism of temporal verification is explicitly defined in this study.

Most of the cited models require the use of an auxiliary model to prove the temporal consistency of the SMIL specification, whereas it is more efficient to work on the same model (time and memory space saving). Besides, none of these models propose a structured and incremental modelling of the SMIL specification; consequently, the modification of a single temporal element requires the verification of the whole specification. Moreover, in order to better fit with the SMIL features, it seems more interesting to define a formal model

mapped on the SMIL temporal model rather than adapting existing approaches to this complex language.
We have proposed in a previous work a temporal extension of Petri Nets, named SMIL-Net (SMIL Petri Net) (Bouyakoub & Belkhir, 2007). This model was proposed to address the lack of existing models in the modelling and the verification of the temporal and hyper-temporal dimensions of SMIL documents. We have adopted a global approach in SMIL-Net: at the end of the editing process, the SMIL temporal specification is first translated to a SMIL-Net and then verification techniques can be applied in order to check the temporal consistency directly on the model.
In order to offer earliest errors detection within the editing process, it seems more efficient to integrate the model within the authoring system for an incremental verification. However, although SMIL-Net answers a large part of the needs for SMIL documents authoring, the model needs to be enhanced in order to respect the time constraints of an interactive edition environment. In particular, the modelling and the verification should be done incrementally and offer a good response time. So, we have proposed a hierarchical extension of the SMIL-Net model for the incremental and structured edition. The enhanced model, named H-SMIL-Net (Bouyakoub & Belkhir, 2008), offers structured modelling possibilities permitting, on the one hand, to facilitate the modifications and on the other hand to support an incremental specification of the document. The model is mapped on the SMIL hierarchical temporal structure to better fit with the modelling needs of this language.
The Hierarchical SMIL-Net (H-SMIL-Net) model inherits most of temporal elements defined in SMIL-Net; so, the presentation of some SMIL-Net principles is necessary before presenting H-SMIL-Net.

4. The SMIL-Net Model

In this section, we give an overview of some SMIL-Net components redefined in H-SMIL-Net. The complete definition of the model can be found in (Bouyakoub & Belkhir, 2007).

4.1 SMIL-Net Components

SMIL-Net is a temporal extension of Petri Nets; it includes a set of places, transitions and arcs.
We focus on two types of SMIL-Net places in this study (Figure 4):
- The *regular place* represents the active entity of the system; it is used to model a media object and its internal duration.
- The *virtual place* represents a time delay, it is used to model the temporal attributes *begin*, *end* and *dur*.

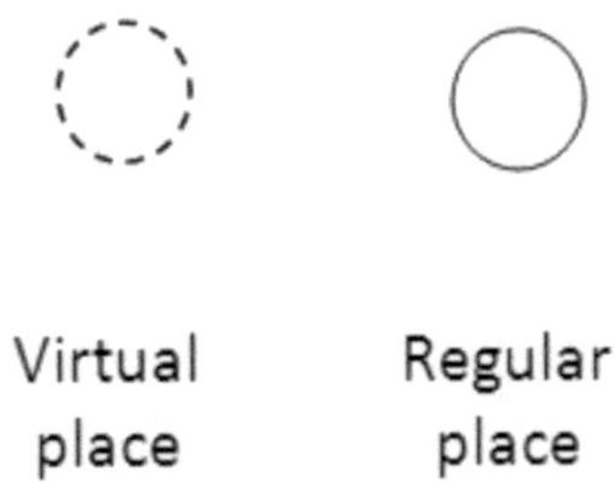

Fig. 4. Graphical representations of Places

The set of transitions defined in SMIL-Net (Figure 5) models the different termination semantics of SMIL elements:

- The *simple transition* fires when the delays associated to all its input places are finished. It models the termination of a simple element, a <seq> element, or a <par> element with a "*last*" semantic.
- The *Master transition* fires when the delay associated to one particular input place, designed by a master arc (designating the Master element), is finished. It represents the termination of the <par> element with a "*Master*" semantic.
- The *First transition* fires since the delay associated to one of its input places is finished. It models the termination of a <par> element with a "*First*" semantic.

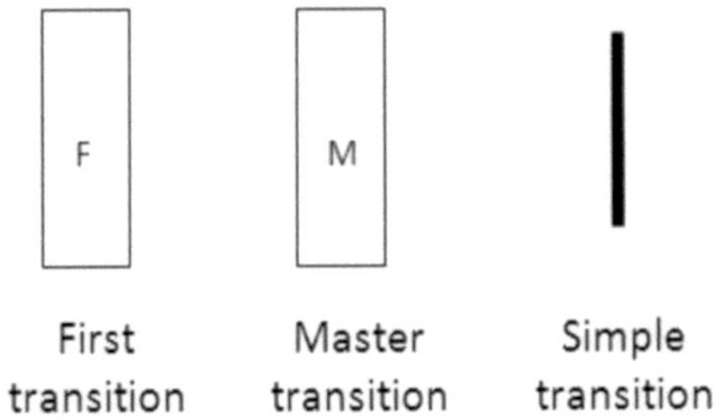

Fig. 5. Graphical representations of transitions

Two kinds of SMIL-Net arcs are used in H-SMIL-Net (Figure 6):

-The *ordinary arc* is used to transport tokens.

-The *master arc* also transports tokens, but in addition it controls the firing of a master transition.

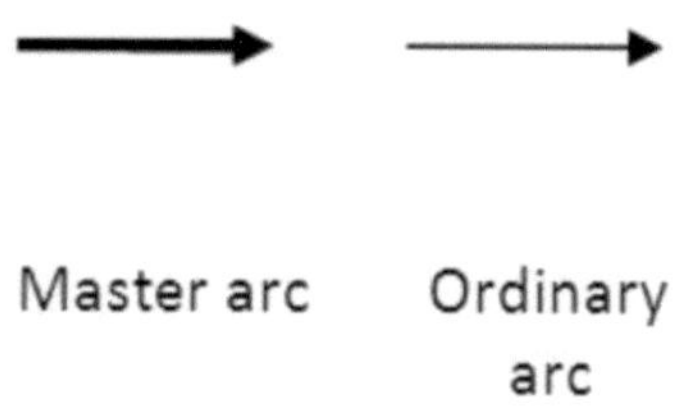

Fig. 6. Graphical representations of arcs

An example of SMIL-Net is shown in Figure 7. The SMIL-Net requires the audio, the video and the text to be played simultaneously. Since the transition T2 is a Master transition, it is fired just after the audio element is finished, no matter video or text elements are finished or not. After firing T2, img is displayed.

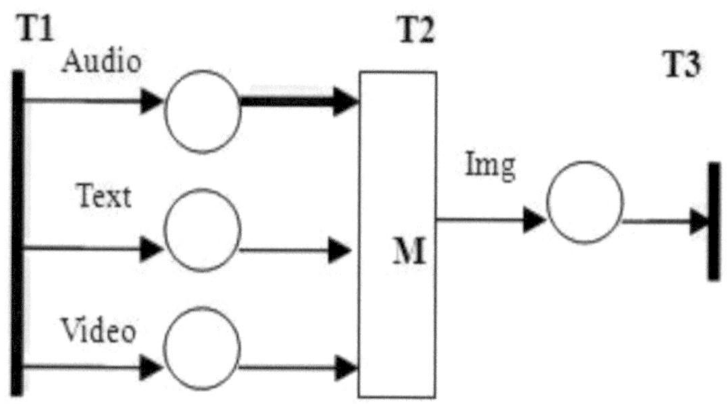

Fig. 7. An example of SMIL-Net

4.2 Calculating the Firing Time of SMIL-Net Transitions

The firing time for each transition is computed by traversing the SMIL-Net transition by transition from the initial state. The computation rule for calculating the firing time of a transition depends on its type:

- ***Simple transition:*** The firing time of the transition is the maximum value of the "firing time of the preceding transition" plus "the nominal duration of the following place of the preceding transition".
- ***First transition:*** The firing time of the transition is the minimum value of the "firing time of the preceding transition" plus "the nominal duration of the following place of the preceding transition".
- ***Master transition:*** The firing time of the transition is the value of the "firing time of the preceding transition" plus "the nominal duration of the place associated with a *master arc*".

4.3 Detection of Time Conflicts

(a) ***The Intra-element time conflict***

The intra-element time conflict is the case of conflicting attributes within the same element. Therefore, to detect the intra-element time conflict, we only need to examine the values of attributes associated to a single element.

Considering the SMIL-Net model for a single element in Figure 8, the respective values of "begin", "dur" and "end" for the element are "B seconds", "D seconds" and 'E seconds". It is easy to see that the case of $B+D \neq E$ results in an unreasonable physical meaning.

The intra-element time conflict is detected in SMIL-Net when a master transition has two master arcs coming from its input places (see Figure 8).

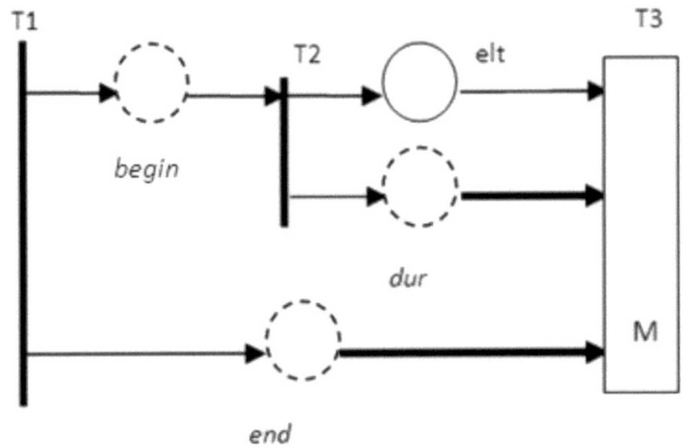

Fig. 8. Detecting the intra-element time conflict

(b) ***The inter-elements time conflict***

The inter-elements time conflict is the case of conflicting attributes among different elements.

There is no easy way to detect the inter-element time conflict directly on the SMIL-Net, since it involves the attributes of more than one element.

In SMIL-Net, the firing time of a transition should be earlier than its following transition (temporal progression criterion). It implies that if the attributes values defined by the author make the firing time of a transition later than the firing time of some following transition, it characterizes an inter-elements time conflict.

The inter-elements time conflict could be detected by traversing the SMIL-Net and comparing the computed firing times of its transitions.

The Figure 9 shows an example of a SMIL script with an inter-elements time conflict and its SMIL-Net representation.

As illustrated in the Figure, the firing time for T2 is 25s whereas the following transition T4 fires at 20s; this situation characterizes a temporal conflict. In the example, two temporal conflicts are identified: (T2, T4) and (T3, T4). It implies that the elements in conflict are (Audio2, <par>) and (text, <par>).

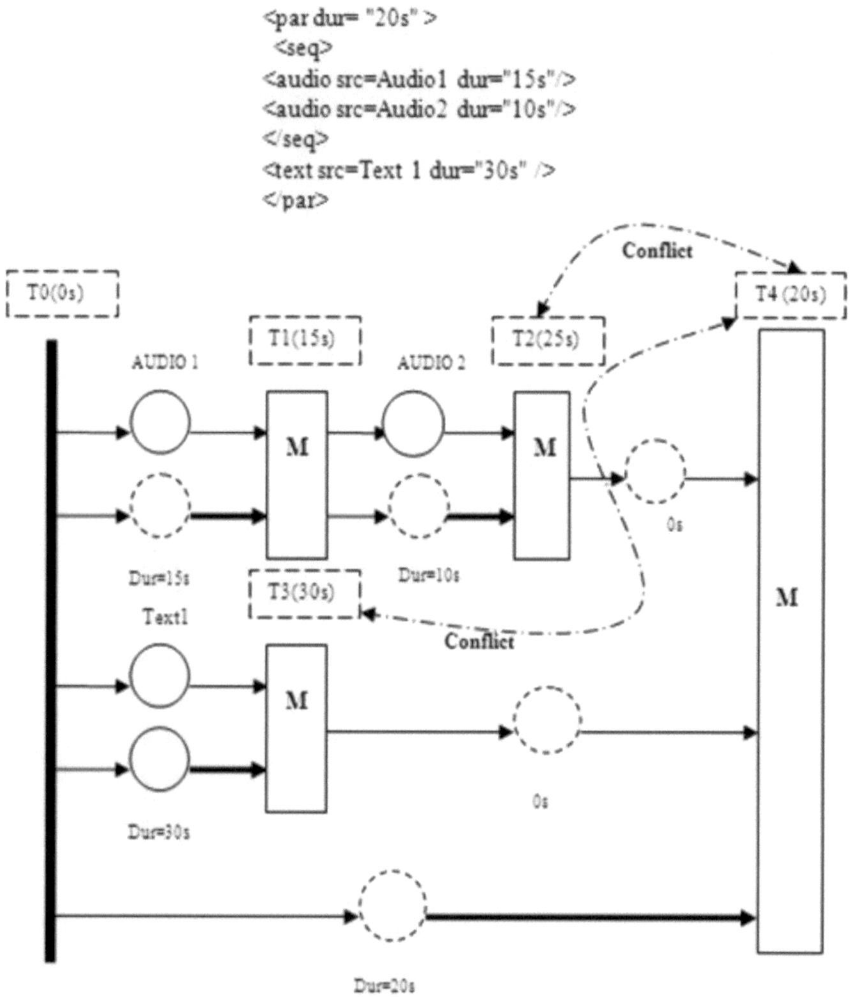

Fig. 9. Detecting the inter-elements time conflict

5. The H-SMIL-Net model

We present in this section the Hierarchical SMIL-Net (H-SMIL-Net) model, a hierarchical extension of the SMIL-Net model for the incremental and structured edition. The H-SMIL-Net model inherits all temporal elements defined in SMIL-Net. It is defined as a two-level tree:

- The atomic level (the leaves) represents the multimedia elements,
- The composite level (the nodes) represents the composite elements <par>, <seq> and the root <body>.

Fig. 10. Graphical representation of composite places

To model the composite elements, we define a new type of places: the composite places are abstract places representing the temporal behaviour of an equivalent H-SMIL-Net. A composite place is defined by its type (*par, seq* or *body*) and the root of the associated H-SMIL-Net. The representation of composite places is shown in Figure 10.

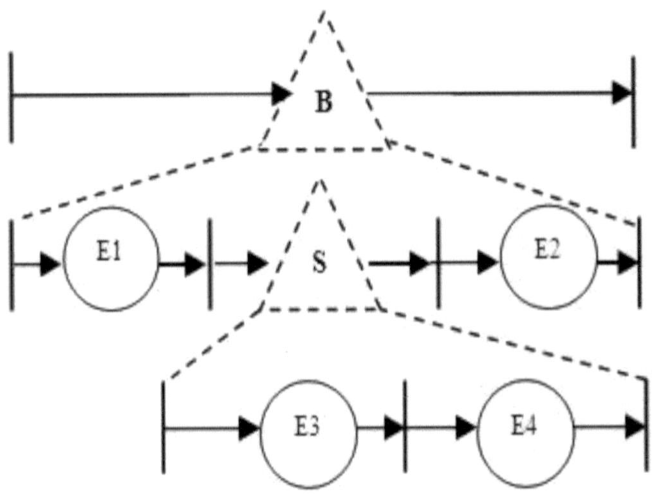

Fig. 11. An example of H-SMIL-Net

An example of H-SMIL-Net is shown in Figure 11. The H-SMIL-Net contains two composite places B (modelling a body element) and S (modelling a seq element). Each composite place is represented by a subnet modelling its child elements.

5.1 Formal definition

An H-SMIL-Net R with a root P_0 is defined as follows:

$R(P_0)=(P_0,(P , T , IN , OUT , M_0) , A , IVT , TT , TP , S , ABS, TA)$, where:

- (P ,T ,IN ,OUT ,M_0) defines a Petri net.
- A is a set of arcs.
- IVT is a mapping from the set of places to a set of time intervals $[X_i, N_i, Y_i]$ defining the temporal interval of the place. X_i, N_i, Y_i represents, respectively, the minimal, the nominal and the maximal duration of the object (or the Petri Net) associated to the place.

IVT:

$P \rightarrow \{ Q+ \cup \{ * \}\} X \{ Q+ \cup \{ * \}\} X \{Q+ \cup \{ * \}\}$

$\forall P_i$, i=1...N$\in$P, IVT (Pi)=[X_i, N_i, Y_i]

The * value represents unknown duration. When X_i= N_i=Y_i we put simply [X_i]

- TT is a mapping which associates a type to each transition of T.

TT: T → {simple, First, Master}

- TP is a mapping which associates a type to each place of P.

TP: P → {regular, virtual, composite}

- S defines the state of the place according to its type and the type of tokens it contains.

S: P → {suspended, active, inactive, #} where # is the state associated to the composite places that are abstract places and don't have a state therefore.

- TA is a mapping which associates a type to each arc of A.

TA: A → {Simple, Virtual, Master}

- ABS is the structural abstraction function that associates an H-SMIL-Net subnet to each composite place:

ABS: $P_{composite}$→ {R / R is an H-SMIL-Net}

P_0→ R(P_0)=(P_0,(P , T , IN , OUT , M0), A, IVT, TT, TP, S, ABS, TA)

Where: $P_{composite}$ = {p$\in$P/TP(p)="composite"}

Besides, we associate to each place a local clock to calculate the internal delays. A global clock is associated to all H-SMIL-Net in order to verify the global synchronization constraints of the model.

5.2 Formal semantic

The H-SMIL-Net semantic enhances the SMIL-Net one (Bouyakoub & Belkhir,2007) by the definition of new firing rules adapted to the composite places.

Definition1. The H-SMIL-Net modelling a composite place is delimited by an input transition and an output transition. An input transition is a transition that doesn't have any input place and an output transition is a transition that doesn't have any output place.

Definition2. When a composite place receives a token, its input transition is immediately fired and the underlying H-SMIL-Net is executed. The firing of the output transition indicates the end of the H-SMIL-Net representing the composite place, the token of the composite place is then unlocked and the following transition can be fired.

Definition3. An input transition is fired as soon as the associated composite place receives a token. Once fired, this transition puts a token in each output place and locks the token of the composite place.

Definition4. An output transition is fired when the firing conditions for the transition are satisfied. The firing of this transition unlocks the token within the composite place.

5.3 Abstraction of composite places

The definition of abstract places implies the definition of structural abstraction techniques. Considering the fundamental role played by time in SMIL, the abstract places must not only offer possibilities of structural abstraction but also temporal abstraction. Thus, we associate to the H-SMIL-Net model the following techniques of structural and temporal abstraction.

(a) Structural abstraction

The structural abstraction defines the techniques allowing the replacement of a composite place by an H-SMIL-Net. The following algorithm explains how to replace a composite place by the underlying H-SMIL-Net:

1) Replace the composite place by the associated H-SMIL-Net, delimited by input and output transitions. *2) Merge the adjacent transitions:* *a) Merge the beginning transition of the composite place with the input transition of the subnet;* *b) Merge the end transition of the composite place with the output transition of the subnet.*

The recursive application of structural abstraction techniques on the set of composite places permits to derive the SMIL-Net model, what allows the hierarchical model to inherit all verification techniques proposed for SMIL-Net.

An example of structural abstraction is shown in Figure 12. The composite place S (Figure 11) is replaced by its equivalent subnet and the adjacent transitions are joined.

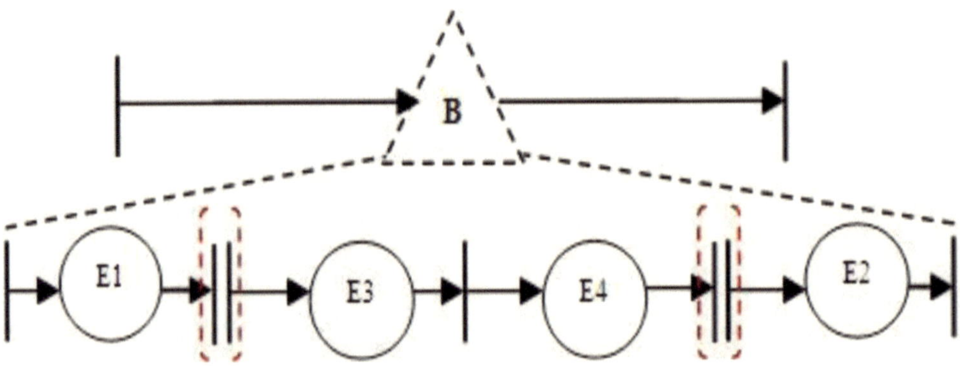

Fig. 12. Structural abstraction

(b) Temporal abstraction

An abstract place should reproduce in an abstract way the temporal behaviour of the underlying H-SMIL-Net. The nominal delay of a composite place C is calculated by the following algorithm:

a) Consider the H-SMIL-Net R(C) modelling the composite place C. If the delays of all elements of C are resolved, go to step c). *b) For each composite child element C' of C whose delay is unresolved go to step a) while considering the H-SMIL-Net R'(C').* *c) If all child elements of C have resolved delays then calculate the nominal duration of R, noted D_r, which is equal to the firing date of the end transition T_e of R while supposing the date of its beginning transition T_b=0.* *d) The delay D_r is the nominal delay associated to the composite place C.*

An example of calculating composite elements delays is shown in Figure 13.

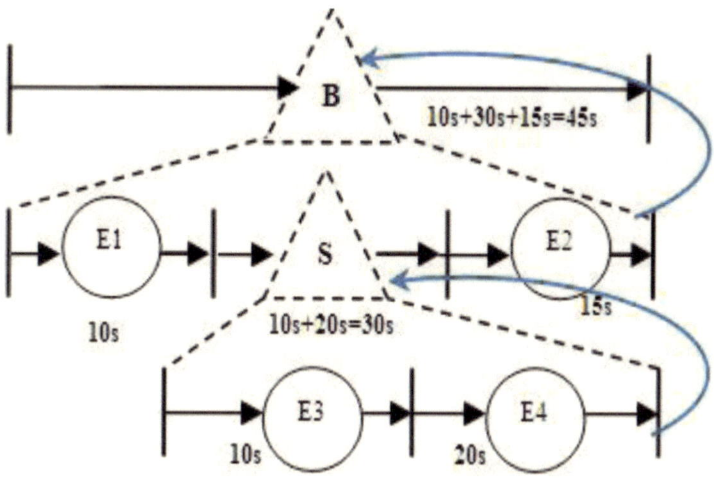

Fig. 13. Temporal abstraction

6. Temporal Verification

We associate to H-SMIL-Net an optimized verification algorithm restricting the verification to the minimal subnet affected by the modification. The verification algorithm is decomposed into two steps:

- Finding the root of the minimal subnet affected by the modification
- Temporal verification of the minimal subnet.

6.1 Research of the minimal subnet

After each editing operation, the H-SMIL-Net model is updated and the modifications are propagated towards the root in order to update the temporal delays of the H-SMIL-Net elements. As soon as the temporal delay of an element is not modified, it is no more necessary to propagate the modifications towards the superior levels, since time values will remain unchanged. So, to find the minimal subnet affected by the modification, we have just to find the first element that remains temporally unchanged after the modification. This element, called *the invariant*, is calculated by the following algorithm:

a) Let C be the composite element containing the modified element and let D_{before} be its initial delay. Calculate the new delay D_{after} associated to the C element. *b) If $D_{before} \neq D_{after}$: consider C' the direct ancestor of C. if C' is the <body>element then go to d); otherwise go to a) while replacing C by C'.* *c) If $D_{before} = D_{after}$ then C is the invariant. Break;* *d) If we arrive to the root <body> without finding an invariant, it means that the modification affects the whole H-SMIL-Net.*

6.2 Temporal verification of the minimal subnet

Once the minimal subnet defined, we have to verify its consistency in order to accept or reject the modification. This verification is done in two steps:

- The transformation of the minimal H-SMIL-Net to an equivalent SMIL-Net by applying recursively the techniques of structural abstraction to the composite places.
- The application of the verification techniques defined for SMIL-Net (detection of conflict situations) on the obtained SMIL-Net.
If no conflict is detected then the modification is accepted, otherwise it is rejected by the system.

7. Modelling SMIL Elements with H-SMIL-Net

The H-SMIL-Net models the most used SMIL temporal elements including the time containers <seq> and <par>, the class of media object elements such as <img>, <video>, <audio>, <text> and the time attributes "begin", "end", "dur". We assume that the syntax of the input SMIL script has been checked before starting the transformation.

(a) Modelling a media object
Media object elements allow the inclusion of media objects into a SMIL presentation. A media object is represented by a regular place and a pair of ordinary transitions (Ts, Te) as shown in Figure 14.

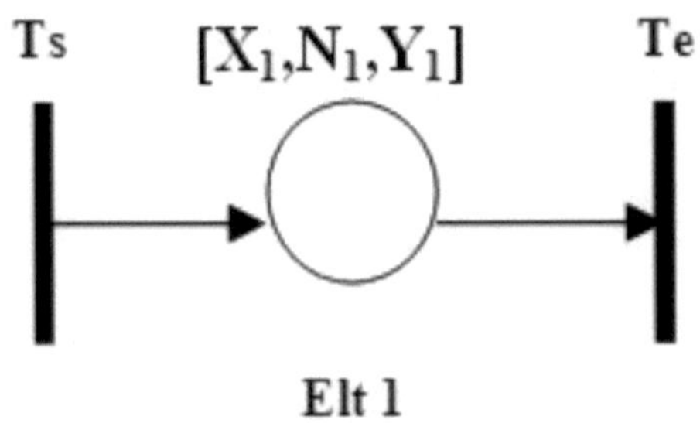

Fig. 14.Modelling a media element

The temporal interval of the element is defined by three time values:
- X_i defines the minimal active duration of the media.
-N_i defines the nominal duration of the media; it takes the value of the internal duration of the media element. When the element has not an internal duration (such as static text or image), $N_i = 0$.
- Y_i defines the maximal active duration of the media.

(b) Modelling time attributes
Time attributes represent time delays, so they are modelled by virtual places with only a nominal duration which takes the value of the attribute (IVT=[N_i])
The *"begin"* attribute specifies the explicit begin time of an element, it is modelled by adding one virtual place representing the begin time with the specified duration before the element starting transition.
The *"end"* attribute specifies the explicit end time of an element, so one virtual place with the end value is added between the original start transition and the end transition. A master transition is added at the end to force the termination of the object at the time specified in the end attribute.

The *"dur"* attribute specifies the explicit duration of an element, thus a virtual place between the start transition and the end transition is added. The end transition is also a master transition. The Figure 15 illustrates the effect of the combination of these attributes.

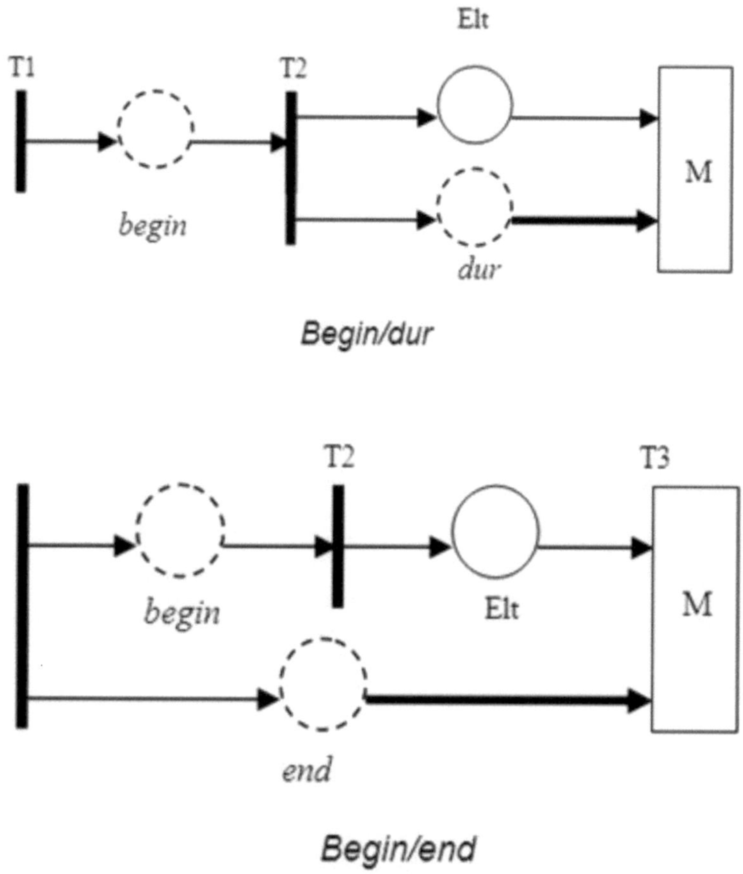

Fig. 15. Modelling time attributes

(c) Modelling the <seq> element

The <seq> element defines a sequence of elements played one after the other.

The children elements of the <seq> element could be any of the synchronization elements such as time containers or media objects, so the conversion is a recursive procedure.

Since the children of a <seq> element form a temporal sequence, we concatenate each child of the <seq>container one by one as illustrated in Figure 16.

Note that the end transition of an element and the start transition of the following element are merged in order to maintain model consistency.

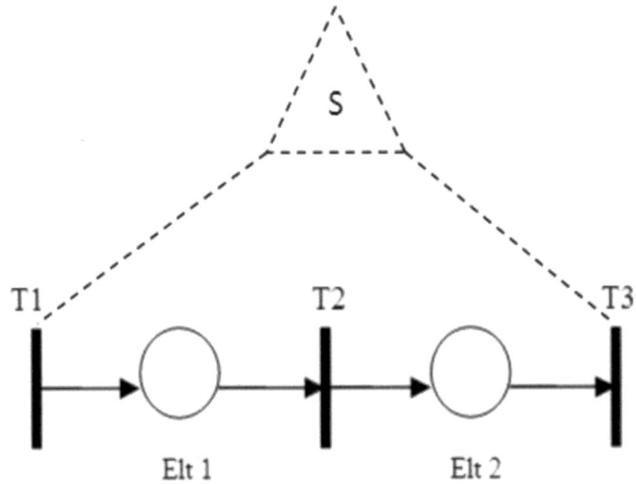

Fig. 16. Modelling the <seq> element

(d) Modelling the <par> element

The <par> element defines a parallel grouping in which multiple elements can be played at the same time. Thus, all children of <par> should be within the same pair of transitions (Ts, Te) as illustrated in Figure 17.

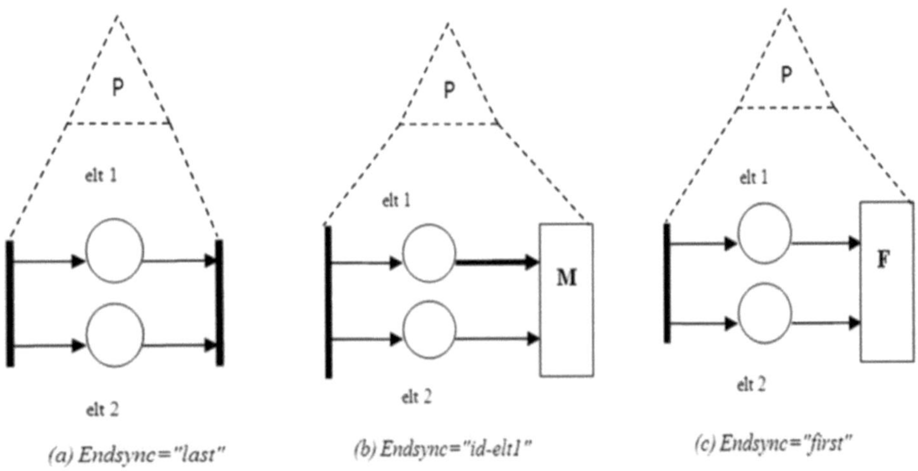

Fig. 17. Modelling the <par> element

The "endsync" attribute controls the end of the <par> element. Legal values for the attribute are "last", "first" and '*id-value*'.

The 'last' value requires <par> to end with the end of all its child elements and the corresponding H-SMIL-Net is shown in Figure 17-(a), where transition **Te** could not be fired until the end of all the <par> children.

The 'id-value' value requires <par> to end with the specified child. So, we change the end transition to a *Master transition* and the arc between the specified child and the transition to a master arc as shown in Figure17-(b).
The 'first' value requires <par> to end with the earliest end of all the child elements. Therefore, we should change the end transition to a *First transition*, as illustrated in Figure 17-(c) so that the child that ends first can fire the transition.
Other synchronization attributes, such as "begin", "end' and "dur", could also be associated with <seq> and <par>, but the conversion is similar to that in the case of media object elements.

8. Implementation: An authoring tool for SMIL documents

Some authoring tools have been proposed for SMIL without imposing themselves to the users, in part because the constraints of the underlying language limit the realization of efficient authoring tools.
Our aim is to propose an easy-to-use temporal environment, with incremental authoring and consistency checking capabilities, based on the H-SMIL-Net model. So, we opted for an interface combining simplicity and ergonomics (see Figure 18)
The architecture is structured on four parts that interact all along an editing session:
- **Opening/saving module:** When opening an existing SMIL file, the system proceeds to lexical and syntactic analysis; before the translation to H-SMIL-Net.
- **Modelling module:** This module translates the document to the H-SMIL-Net model, which is the internal format used in all modules of our authoring tool.
- **Authoring module:** This module provides the functions permitting to create or to modify a SMIL document. In order to maintain the coherence of the specification, the environment doesn't allow the document to enter in an inconsistent state: Each editing operation is first reported on the H-SMIL-Net model and the local verification algorithm is applied. If the author's modification leads to an inconsistency, it is rejected by the system; otherwise it is accepted and the model is updated.
- **The user-interface:** This module offers a number of graphic tools allowing the author to create and modify the document. Four views are proposed:
- The textual view: It displays the source file of the SMIL script.
- The temporal view: This view displays the H-SMIL-Net representation of the SMIL specification. The author can open a composite element by a simple click, which has as effect the application of the structural abstraction algorithm on the selected place.
- The hierarchical view: It represents the document as a tree structure, what permits to visualize and modify the hierarchical structure of the document.
- The attributes view: It allows viewing and modifying the temporal attributes of the object selected in the hierarchical view.

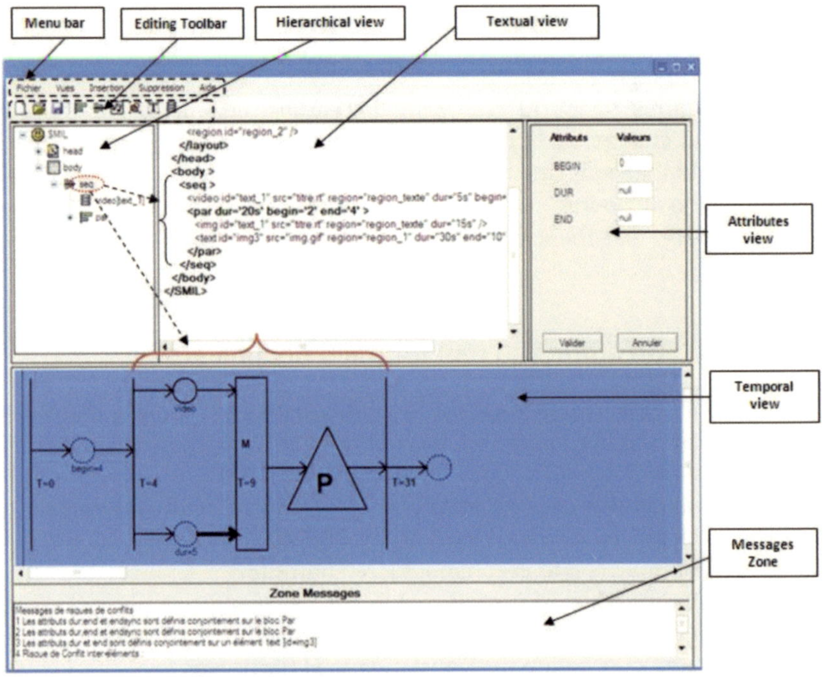

(a) The composite place S is opened

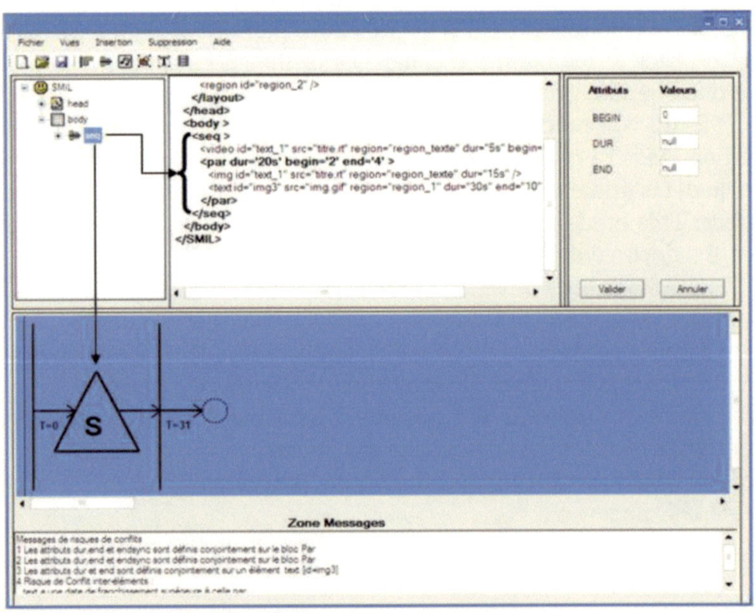

(b) The composite place S is closed

Fig. 18. Interface of the authoring tool

9. Conclusion

We have presented in this chapter a new approach for the modelling and the verification of the temporal consistency of SMIL documents within an interactive authoring environment.
The H-SMIL-Net model offers structured modelling capabilities permitting, on the one hand, to facilitate the modifications of the SMIL script and on the other hand to support an incremental specification of the document.
Moreover, the local approach adopted in H-SMIL-Net guarantees the consistency of the whole presentation through the verification of a minimal part of the model; leading to a considerable time saving.
The editing process followed in this study reflects the methodology followed by most authors: the document is specified in a series of steps going from general definition by components to a more detailed specification. This component-based edition is possible thanks to the hierarchical structure of H-SMIL-Net. Furthermore, the locality of the temporal verification in H-SMIL-Net permits a relative independence between the different components represented by composite elements.
This formal approach has been integrated within an incremental authoring tool for SMIL presentations. Thanks to the use of H-SMIL-Net, the obtained authoring tool offers a good compromise between the power of formal modelling and a reasonable verification response time.
In this first version of H-SMIL-Net, we have modelled the most used SMIL temporal elements. We aim to extend the model so as it can model all the temporal elements of SMIL.
The aim of the editor was to take advantage from the H-SMIL-Net possibilities in the authoring of the SMIL temporal structure. In the second version (which is under construction) we will integrate spatial and hypermedia aspects of SMIL in order to obtain a complete authoring environment for SMIL documents.

10. References

Bossi, A. & Gaggi, O. (2007). Enriching SMIL with assertions for temporal validation. *Proceedings of the 15th international Conference on Multimedia* ,Augsburg, Germany.

Bouyakoub, S., & Belkhir, A. (2007). Formal Design of SMIL Documents . *Proceedings of the 3rd International conference on Web Information Systems and Technologies (WEBIST)*, Barcelona, Spain.

Bouyakoub, S., & Belkhir, A.(2008). H-SMIL-Net: A Hierarchical Petri Net Model for SMIL Documents. *Proceedings of the 10th International Conference on Computer Modeling and Simulation (uksim 2008)*, Cambridge, United Kingdom.

Chung, S. M., & Pereira, A. L. (2003). Timed Petri Net Representation of the Synchronized Multimedia Integration Language (SMIL) of XML. *Proceedings of the 2003 International Symposium on Information Technology (ITCC 2003)*, Las Vegas, USA.

Jourdan, M., Rosin, C., Tardif, L. & Villard, L. (1999). Authoring SMIL documents by direct manipulation during presentation, *World Wide Web journal*, vol.2, No.4, Balzer Science Publishers.

Little, T.D.C., & Ghafor, A. (1990). Synchronization and storage models for multimedia objects. *IEEE journal on selected areas in communications*, Vol. 3, No. 8.

Newman, R. M., & Gaura, E. I.(2003). Formal design of SMIL presentations. *Proceedings of the 21st annual international conference on Documentation SIGDOC'2003*, San Francisco, USA.

Ramchandani, C. 1974.Analysis of Asynchronous Concurrent Systems by Timed Petri Nets. *PhD Thesis*, Cambridge, Mass.: MIT, Dept. Electrical Engineering, United Kingdom.

Sampaio, P., & Courtiat, J-P.(2004). An Approach for the Automatic Generation of RT-LOTOS Specifications from SMIL 2.0 Documents. *Journal of the Brazilian Computer Society*, 39-51.

SMIL 1.0 recommendation. (1998). Synchronized Multimedia Integration Language (SMIL) 1.0. W3C Recommendation. Online at: http://www.w3.org/ TR/REC-smil.

SMIL 2.0 recommendation. (2001). Synchronized Multimedia Integration Language (SMIL 2.0). W3C Recommendation. Online at: http://www.w3.org/ TR/2001/REC-smil20-20010807/,

SMIL 2.0 second edition. (2005).Synchronized Multimedia Integration Language (SMIL 2.0). W3C Recommendation. Online at: http://www.w3.org/TR/2005/REC-SMIL2-20050107/

SMIL 2.1 recommendation. (2005). Synchronized Multimedia Integration Language (SMIL 2.1). W3C Recommendation. Online at: http://www.w3.org/ TR/SMIL/

SMIL 3.0 Recommendation. (2008). Synchronized Multimedia Integration Language (SMIL 3.0). *W3C Recommendation*. Online at: http://www.w3.org/ TR/SMIL3/.

Yang, C.C. (2000). Detection of the Time Conflicts for SMIL-based Multimedia Presentations. *Proceedings of the International Computer Symposium (ICS2000) - Workshop on Computer Networks, Internet and Multimedia*, pp.57- 63, Chiayi, Taiwan,.

Yu, H., Xudong, H., Shu, G., & Yi, D.(2002). Modelling and analyzing SMIL Documents in SAM. *Proceedings of the 4th International Symposium on Multimedia Software Engineering*, Newport Beach, California.

16

A Structural Reliability Business Process Modelling with System Dynamics Simulation

C. Y. Lam, S. L. Chan and W. H. Ip
The Hong Kong Polytechnic University
Hong Kong

1. Introduction

A business process reflects how an organization is organized, and the modelling of it can enable the organization to manage its workflow properly. Business process modelling can systematically map the business activity flow, thus allowing the corresponding analysis and simulation to be carried out.

Business process modelling, analysis, and simulation are recognized as tools that can help an organization to improve their business process from a macro view that help management to work efficiently and to locate problem areas easily (Lam et al., 2009). Moreover, these tools allow the business process to be revolutionized, redesigned or reengineered (Lam et al., 2008). Thus, the better the business process modelling, analysis, and simulation, the better the performance and competitiveness of the organization can achieve.

Business process research falls primarily into two inter-related areas, process modelling and workflow analysis. Process modelling research ranges from process case, task, routing to enactment (Kusiak et al., 1994; Thalhammer et al., 2001; Thorpe and Ke, 2001; Jung et al., 2004; Rosemann et al., 2006; Royce, 2007; Khanli and Analoui, 2008), whereas workflow analysis research includes reachability analysis, structural analysis, performance analysis, sensitivity analysis, and reliability analysis (Bause and Kritzinger, 2002; Haas, 2002; Azgomi and Movaghar, 2005; Cardoso, 2005; Barbosa et al., 2009; Yang and Chen, 2009; Zhao, 2009). All of these approaches have advantages and disadvantages.

System dynamics is a type of modelling and simulation methodology used to investigate and manage complex feedback systems, including business, political and social systems, by gaining an understanding of their structures and dynamics. System dynamics builds on information-feedback theory, which not only provides diagrams and equations for mapping business systems but is also a programming language for computer simulation. Its application provides decision makers with enhanced ability to manage the complex business world by means of visualization and simulation. It also allows them to rehearse business plans and alternative futures through scenario development and strategy modelling, thus providing insight into business situations of dynamic complexity and those characterized by policy resistance. System dynamics is therefore increasingly adopted in business process improvement, managerial problems and organizational policy setting. The literature provides a range of examples (Towill, 1993; Berry et al., 1994; Strohhecker, 2000; Lai et al., 2003; Zhang et al., 2007; Morecroft, 2007; Chan and Ip, 2008).

This chapter provides an alternative structural reliability modelling and optimization approach to the business process by using a communication network of probabilistic graphs, and further simulates and analyzes the business process network model using system dynamics. An example of the proposed modelling and simulation method applied to a customer management process is also presented.

2. Modelling the Business Process

Organizations have many different types of business activities, such as accounting, purchasing, order management, design, manufacturing and so on, which are discrete in nature. That is, each activity has a beginning and an end, and each can be distinguished from every other activity; however, to achieve ultimate business objectives, the interactions between activities must be continuous and interrelated. Within the business process, different activity routing combinations can have different effects on overall organizational performance, and thus numerous researchers and practitioners have attempted to determine the best combinations.

In this structural reliability model, business activities are modelled as the communication network of probabilistic graph $G = \{V, E\}$, which comprises a set of vertices, $V = \{v_i \mid 1 \leq i \leq n\}$, with a number of n nodes and a set of edges, $E = \{e_j \mid 1 \leq j \leq m\}$, with a number of m edges, such that nodes $v_i \in V$ indicate the business activities and edges $e_j \in E$ indicate the connections among business activities.

In modelling the business process, it is assumed that the network and edges have only two states, normal and failure mode, and that all of the nodes are perfectly reliable, with only the edges subject to failure, and the probability of any edge being in a certain mode known. Moreover, in network graph $G = \{V, E\}$, p_i and q_i (or $q_i = 1 - p_i$) represent the normal mode and failure mode probability of edge e_i, respectively, and the in-degree and out-degree processes of the activity are represented as $\lambda_I(v_i)$ and $\lambda_O(v_i)$, respectively. With this notation for the proposed structural reliability modelling approach, the six basic types of business activities can then be modelled, i.e., Start Off Activity (SOA), Serial Activity (SEA), Merge Activity (MEA), Split Activity (SPA), Merge and Split Activity (MSA), and Final Activity (FIA).

Start Off Activity (SOA)

SOA is an initial activity in the business process that leads to the development of subsequent out-degree activities; its nodes in structural reliability modelling can be represented as

$$\{v_i | \lambda_I(v_i) = 0 \ \ and \ \ \lambda_O(v_i) \geq 1\}, \text{ for } i = 1, 2, \ldots, n. \tag{1}$$

Serial Activity (SEA)

SEA is a straightforward serial activity in the business process. It interacts directly with its single previous in-degree activity and single succeeding out-degree activity, and its nodes in the proposed approach can be represented as

$$\{v_i | \lambda_I(v_i)=1 \ \ and \ \ \lambda_O(v_i)=1\}, \text{ for } i = 1, 2, \ldots, n. \tag{2}$$

Merge Activity (MEA)

MEA is a collection of activities in the business process. It combines the activities from the previous in-degree activities and then processes them to the single succeeding out-degree activity. Its nodes can be represented as

$$\{v_i | \lambda_I(v_i)>1 \ \ and \ \ \lambda_O(v_i)=1\}, \text{ for } i = 1, 2, \ldots, n. \tag{3}$$

Split Activity (SPA)

SPA is a splitting activity in the business process; that is, it splits a single previous in-degree activity into its succeeding out-degree activities. Its nodes in the proposed modelling approach can be represented as

$$\{v_i | \lambda_I(v_i)=1 \ \ and \ \ \lambda_O(v_i)>1\}, \text{ for } i = 1, 2, \ldots, n. \tag{4}$$

Merge and Split Activity (MSA)

MSA is a combination of merge and splitting activities. It merges the previous in-degree activities in the business process and then splits them into succeeding out-degree activities. Its nodes can be represented as

$$\{v_i | \lambda_I(v_i)>1 \ \ and \ \ \lambda_O(v_i)>1\}, \text{ for } i = 1, 2, \ldots, n. \tag{5}$$

Final Activity (FIA)

FIA is the concluding activity in the business process, and its nodes in the proposed structural reliability modelling approach can be represented as

$$\{v_i | \lambda_I(v_i)\geq 1 \ \ and \ \ \lambda_O(v_i)=0\}, \text{ for } i = 1, 2, \ldots, n. \tag{6}$$

Key Activities

Among these six basic types of business activities, the key activities can be identified as those that have dense connectivity, i.e.,

$$\{v_i | \lambda_I(v_i)\geq 2 \ \ or \ \ \lambda_O(v_i)\geq 2\}, \text{ for } i = 1, 2, \ldots, n. \tag{7}$$

3. Analyzing the Business Process for Improvement

A map of business activity flow enables an organization to use and manage structured business processes, and analysis of that flow can help it to improve business process performance with regard to completion time, capacity utilization, service level and so on.

For the business activities that are modelled using the approach proposed in Section 2, the reliability analysis of the network can be defined as R, which is the probability of the existence of a minimal set of operational links such that all of the nodes in the network communicate. Because a business process is constructed as a connected sub-graph of $G = \{V, E\}$ that contains all of its nodes without cycling, R can be defined by evaluating the probability of the union of activities that represents the operational state of the spanning trees, i.e.,

$$R = P_r\left((F_1) \cup (F_2) \cup (F_3) \ldots \cup (F_r)\right) \tag{8}$$

$$= P_r\left((e_i \in E|F_1) \cup (e_i \in E|F_2) \cup (e_i \in E|F_3) \ldots \cup (e_i \in E|F_r)\right) \tag{9}$$

$$= (e_i \in E|F_1) \oplus (e_i \in E|F_2) \oplus (e_i \in E|F_3) \ldots \oplus (e_i \in E|F_r) \tag{10}$$

$$= (p_i, q_i \in e_i|F_1) + (p_i, q_i \in e_i|F_2) + (p_i, q_i \in e_i|F_3) \ldots + (p_i, q_i \in e_i|F_r) \tag{11}$$

where P is the probability of possible flow F for activities $1, 2, \ldots r$; p_i and q_i $(or = 1 - p_i)$ represent the normal mode and failure mode probability of edge e_i, respectively; and $\oplus$ represents a disjoint sum operation.

As the business activity flow can be sequential or parallel, in addition to defining the reliability of the business process in terms of probability, that reliability can also be analyzed by the proposed approach of a *k-out-of-n* system with redundancy, i.e., a system that consists of n identical independent components, of which at least $k < n$ of the activities must succeed for the system to succeed. This analysis is carried out under the assumption that some activities will be suspended whenever the system fails, i.e., some failures will occur when the system is down. Formulas are derived from various reliability indices of the system, including mean time between failures, mean working time during a failure, mean downtime, etc.

Probability concepts are also employed in the structural reliability analysis approach to compute the reliability of the business process in terms of the reliability of the network's activities. The success of the business process in a sequential structure depends on the success of all of the activities; therefore, the reliability, R_A, of a process with n number of activities x, in which x_i denotes that the *i-th* activity is successful and $\overline{x_i}$ denotes that it is not, can be further defined as

$$R = P(x_1\, x_2 \ldots x_n) \tag{12}$$

$$= P(x_1)\, P(x_2 \mid x_1)\, P(x_3 \mid x_1 x_2) \ldots P(x_n \mid x_1 x_2 \ldots x_{n-1}) \tag{13}$$

$$= P(x_1)\, P(x_2) \ldots P(x_n) \tag{14}$$

$$= \prod_{i=1}^{n} P(x_i) \tag{15}$$

The success of the business process in a parallel structure depends on at least one successful activity; therefore, the reliability of that process can be defined as

$$R = P(x_1 + x_2 + \ldots + x_n) \tag{16}$$

$$= 1 - P\left(\overline{x_1}\,\overline{x_2} \ldots \overline{x_n}\right) \tag{17}$$

$$= 1 - P(\overline{x_1})\, P(\overline{x_2}|\overline{x_1})\, P(\overline{x_3}|\overline{x_1}\,\overline{x_2}) \ldots P(\overline{x_n}|\overline{x_1}\,\overline{x_2} \ldots \overline{x_{n-1}}) \tag{18}$$

$$= 1 - \prod_{i=1}^{n} P(\overline{x_i}) \tag{19}$$

Compatible with the six basic types of business activities that are proposed in Section 2, the aforementioned *k-out-of-n* structural reliability analysis approach is a network approach that consists of n identical independent activities, of which at least $k < n$ of those activities must be successful to ensure the success of the network. Therefore, if p is the probability of the success of an activity, then the reliability probability, R, of exactly k successes and $(n - k)$ failures in n activities is defined as

$$R = \binom{n}{k} p^k (1-p)^{n-k} \tag{20}$$

4. System Dynamics in Business Processes

System dynamics, which was conceived in the late 1950s, is a system modelling and computer-based simulation method that provides valuable insights into the dynamic behaviour of complex feedback systems and aids in decision making.

Referring to the six basic types of business activity that are proposed in Section 2, business activities are correlated and interacted with one another; while the decisions from one activity also create feedback loops with previous and succeeding activities. These loops react to the decision maker's actions in ways both anticipated and unanticipated. System dynamics can then be used to emphasize the multiloop, multi-state and non-linear characteristics of the feedback system in the business process. The method can also be used to simulate that process.

In system dynamics modelling and simulation, the dynamic feedback loops in the business process need to be determined and represented, along with the stock and flow structures, time delays and nonlinearities. All of the business process dynamics arise from the interaction of the business activities to form feedback loops, in which the feedback may be either positive or negative. Positive feedback loops tend to reinforce or amplify whatever is happening in the system, and generate such feedback as the ambition to achieve certain business objectives or overall excellence to facilitate organizational growth. Negative feedback loops, in contrast, counteract and oppose change. They tend to be self-limiting processes that seek balance and equilibrium, such as the balancing of inventory management or accounting. In addition, system dynamics builds from single events and entities, and takes an aggregate view based on objectives. Then, the system behaviour of a business process's network model, such as the number of interacting feedback loops, balance or reinforcement, the delay structure, the accumulation and movement of resources (including information and materials), and the like, is described in a stock-flow map, thus allowing that network model to be simulated and analyzed.

Constructing a high-level map of an organization's business processes using system dynamics is an extremely useful part of process analysis. A system dynamics model based on business process scenarios can be used to test and analyze alternative policies and strategies through computer-based simulation, followed by a redesign of the system or process to achieve improved efficiency.

4.1 An Illustrative Example of Modelling and Simulation in the Customer Management Process

Maintaining a long-term relationship with customers is one of the critical success factors for an organization, as it is difficult for competitors to understand, copy or displace. An effective customer management process thus not only improves customer service, but also facilitates business growth by enhancing customer retention, increasing the number of referrals and satisfied customers, and improving service flows to allow teams to work efficiently and smoothly.

The customer management process involves information sharing between the organization, its customers and the market. This information is discrete to each party, but the interactions between the parties are continuous and interrelated and together form the customer management process. Such information sharing is also dynamic in nature and often results in unexpected or counterintuitive feedback within that process. Probabilistic graphs are thus useful in the modelling and analysis of communication networks, and system dynamics is often adopted to model and simulate the customer management process within an organization.

The proposed approach benefits the organization by structurally identifying and analyzing the customer management process, as well as the critical factors in managing customer relationships.

As noted in Section 2, despite the differences in the characteristics of activity flows, these flows can be modelled using the aforementioned six basic types of activities. An example of the customer management process with the mapping of business activities is given in Fig. 1.

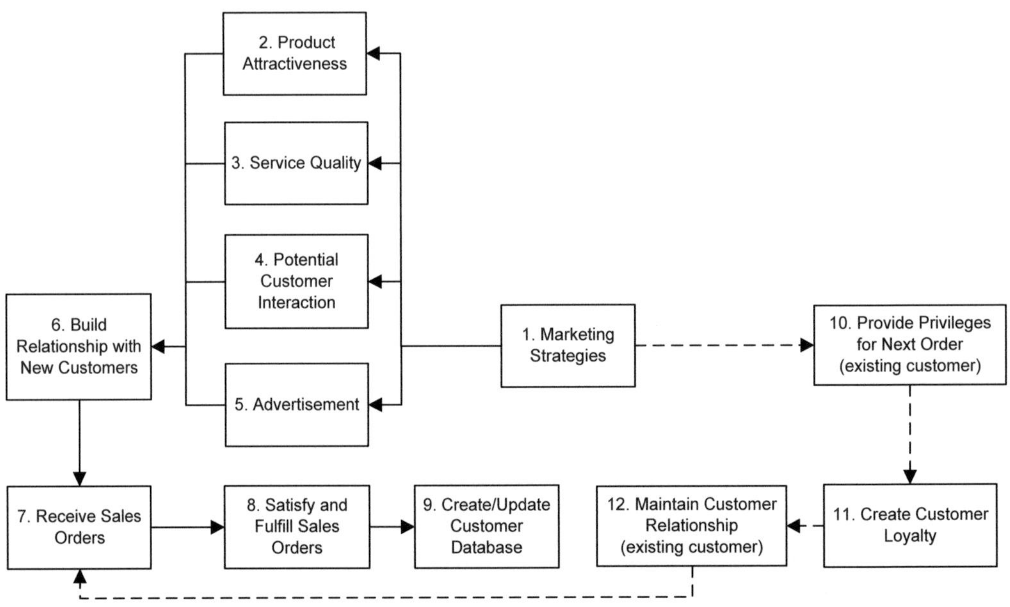

Fig. 1. An example of the customer management process with the mapping of business activities

As noted in Section 2, Activities 1 and 9 are the Start Off Activity and Final Activity, respectively, and Activity 1 is also a Split Activity. Activities 2-5, 8 and 10-12 are Serial Activities, and Activities 6 and 7 are Merge Activities, as well as Key Activities. A system dynamics model is adopted to simulate the customer management process, as illustrated in Fig. 2.

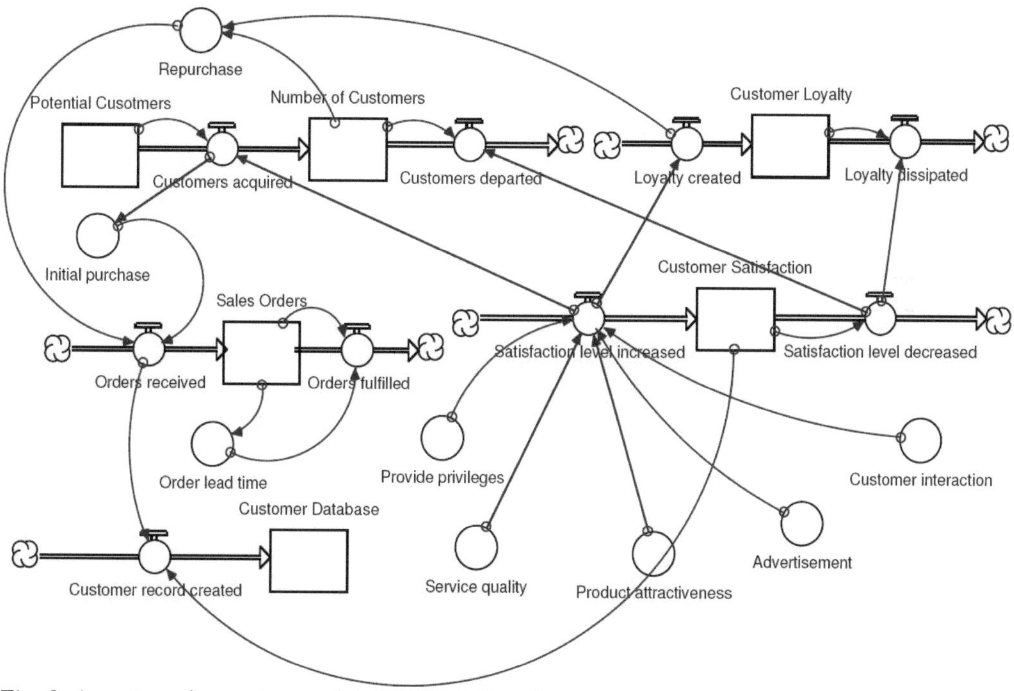

Fig. 2. A system dynamics model for simulating the customer management process

The system dynamics model makes use of a stock and flow diagram to map the customer management process exhibited in Fig. 1, in which a stock is defined as the supply accumulated, and the flow describes the inflow/outflow of stock. After constructing the system dynamics model by defining the inter-relationships and information flow between the variables, the foregoing equations with full explanations and assumptions and the dimensions of each variable must be provided for computer simulation. During the customer management process, customers interact with the company, which serves them in a manner designed to satisfy their needs and establish a good relationship with them. This process is conceptualized by the development of an information feedback system such as that shown in Fig. 2, from which it can be seen that customer satisfaction is affected by four major factors: product attractiveness, service quality, advertisements and customer interaction. Any changes in the value of these four factors lead to changes in the customer satisfaction level. Customer satisfaction plays an important role in customer relationship management, as it is closely associated with customer purchasing behaviour. It not only motivates potential customers to make purchases, but also creates loyalty to the company among existing customers and motivates them to make further purchases. By using the simulation shown in Fig. 2, a company can easily vary the values of any of the variables based on a particular business scenario to test potential strategies. This enables decision makers to execute the most competitive strategies for improving the customer management process and customer relationships.

5. Conclusion

Business activity flow analysis enables organizations to manage structured business processes, and can thus help them to improve performance. The six types of business activities identified here (i.e., SOA, SEA, MEA, SPA, MSA and FIA) are correlated and interact with one another, and the decisions from any business activity form feedback loops with previous and succeeding activities, thus allowing the business process to be modelled and simulated. For instance, for any company that is eager to achieve profitability, a customer-centred orientation, as well as the creation and maintenance of customer relationships and customer loyalty, will be a high priority. The customer management process illustrated herein elucidates the mapping and modelling of the six kinds of business activity based on computer simulation. The proposed system dynamics model helps to evaluate the effectiveness of the customer management process and to examine the factors that affect customer satisfaction, customer loyalty, the number of customers and the number of sales orders received, factors that are essential to company profitability. The proposed structural reliability modelling approach, with the system dynamics simulation of the business process, thus enables decision makers to select the most favourable business strategies and to make the right decisions about policy by simulating the dynamic behaviour of information feedback systems. Sensitivity analysis can also be carried out based on the system dynamics model to determine the optimal value of each variable.

6. References

Azgomi, M. & Movaghar, A. (2005). A Modelling Tool for Hierarchical Stochastic Activity Networks. *Simulation Modelling Practice and Theory*, Vol. 13, 505–524.

Barbosa, V. C., Ferreira, F. M. L., Kling, D. V., Lopes, E., Protti, F. & Schmitz E. A. (2009). Structured Construction and Simulation of Nondeterministic Stochastic Activity Networks. *European Journal of Operational Research*, Vol. 198, No. 1, 266-274.

Bause, F. & Kritzinger, P. (2002). *Stochastic Petri Nets – An Introduction to the Theory (Second edition)*, Vieweg Verlag, Germany.

Berry, D., Towill, D.R. & Wadsley, N. (1994). Supply Chain Management in the Electronics Products Industry. *International Journal of Physical Distribution and Logistics Management*, Vol. 24, No. 10, 20-32.

Cardoso, J. (2005). How to Measure the Control-flow Complexity of Web processes and Workflows. *Workflow Handbook*. Lighthouse Point, FL, 199-212.

Chan, S.L. & Ip, W.H. (2008). A Markov Chains Repurchasing Model for CRM Using System Dynamics. *Proceedings of the 19th IASTED International Conference*, pp. 353-375, May 2008, Quebec, Canada.

Haas, P. (2002). *Stochastic Petri Nets: Modelling, Stability, Simulation*, Springer-Verlag, New York.

Jung, J., Hur, W., Kang, S. & Kim, H. (2004). Business Process Choreography for B2B Collaboration. *IEEE Internet Computing*, Vol. 8, No. 1, 37-45.

Khanli, L. M. & Analoui, M. (2008). An Approach to Grid Resource Selection and Fault Management Based on ECA Rules. *Future Generation Computer Systems*. Vol. 24, No. 4, 296-316.

Kusiak, A., Larson, T.N. & Wang, J. (1994). Reengineering of Design and Manufacturing Processes. *Computer and Industrial Engineering*, Vol. 26, 521-536.

Lai, C.L., Lee, W.B. & Ip, W.H. (2003). A Study of System Dynamics in Just-in-time Logistics. *Journal of Materials Processing Technology*, Vol. 138, No. 1, 265-269.

Lam, C. Y., Chan, S.L., Ip, W.H. & Lau, C.W. (2008). Collaborative Supply Chain Network Using Embedded Genetic Algorithms. *Industrial Management & Data Systems*, Vol. 108, No. 8, 1101-1110.

Lam, C.Y., Ip, W.H. & Lau, C.W. (2009). A Business Process Activity Model and Performance Measurement Using a Time Series ARIMA Intervention Analysis. *Expert Systems with Applications*, Vol. 36, 6986-6994.

Morecroft, J. (2007). *Strategic Modelling and Business Dynamics – A feedback systems approach*. John Wiley & Son Limited, ISBN: 978-0-470-01286-4, UK.

Rosemann, M., Recker, J., Indulska, M. & Green, P. (2006). A Study of the Evolution of the Representational Capabilities of Process Modeling Grammars. *Advanced Information Systems Engineering*, Vol. 4001, 447–461.

Royce, G. K. (2007). Integration of a Business Rules Engine to Manage Frequently Changing Workflow: A Case Study of Insurance Underwriting Workflow. *Proceedings of the 2007 Americas Conference on Information Systems*, Keystone, CO.

Strohhecker, J.G. (2000). Supply Chain Management Software Solutions Versus Policy Design. *Proceedings of the 18th International System Dynamics Conference, August 2000*, Bergen, Norway.

Thalhammer, T., Schrefl, M. & Mohania, M. (2001). Active Data Warehouses: Complementing OLAP with Analysis Rules. *Data & Knowledge Engineering*. Vol. 39, No. 3, 241–269.

Thorpe, M. & Ke, C. (2001). Simple Rule Markup Language (SRML): A General XML Rule Representation for Forward-Chaining Rules, *XML Coverpages*, 1.

Towill, D.R. (1993). System Dynamics - Background, methodology, and applications. *Computer Control Engineering Journal*, Vol. 4, No. 5, 201-208.

Yang, C. & Chen, A. (2009). Sensitivity Analysis of the Combined Travel Demand Model with Applications. *European Journal of Operational Research*, Vol. 198, No. 3, 909-921.

Zhang, D.B., Hu, B., Ma, C.X., Jiang, Y., Hu, X.Y. & Zhang, J.L. (2007). Modelling and Simulation of Corporate Lifecycle Using System Dynamics. *Simulation Modelling Practice and Theory*, Vol. 15, 1259-1267.

Zhao, Y. (2009). Analysis and Evaluation of an Assemble-to-Order System with Batch Ordering Policy and Compound Poisson Demand. *European Journal of Operational Research*, Vol. 198, No. 3, 800-809.

17

Modelling Ethical Decisions

Reggie Davidrajuh
University of Stavanger
Norway

1. Introduction

The collapses of Enron, WorldCom, Arthur Andersen, Martha Stewart's stock sales, etc. have made us aware of the seriousness of ethical implications of business decisions. These days, business decision makers must incorporate ethics in their business decisions. However, confronting ethical dilemmas and making ethical decisions are not easy as:

- There are no magic formulas available to help the decision makers solving ethical dilemmas they confront
- When confronting ethical issues, huge number of variables (from sociology, psychology, economics, business, laws & regulations, etc.) that have to be considered. Hence, without any computing aid, it is not easy for decision makers to make an 'optimal' solution

Thus, this chapter proposes an autonomous system to help decision makers incorporate ethics in their business decisions. In order to develop such a system:

Firstly, it is necessary to make a system model of ethical business decision-making in the networked economy: what are the elements and environments involved in the decision-making process, how the elements are connected or related to each other, how the elements, environments, and the interconnections can influence each other, etc.

Secondly, a validation of the model has to be done; is it possible to realize the model as a computing system, as a set of services; whether suitable enabling technology is available to realize such a system? Will it be possible to program the system? Etc.

2. Why a computing system to assist ethical decision making?

Despite the growing interest in ethical decision-making, there is considerable disagreement about the appropriate way to define business ethics, and business ethical leadership, and the ways to assess the ethical decisions (Yukl, 2006; Heifetz, 1994).

Generally, ethical business decision making is such a difficult process, so much that business leaders use their moral standards to evaluate their ethical decisions as good or bad depending on what extend to which the outcomes of their decisions violate basic laws of society, denies others their rights, endangers the health and lives of other people, or involves attempts to deceive and exploit others for personal benefits. This chapter proposes implementing business ethical decision-making processes as computer software so that it can help solving the following problems associated with ethical decision-making:

Ambiguous process: Ethical decision-making is an ambiguous process that appears to include a huge number of highly interconnected Webs of sub-processes. This is due to the existence of several criteria that are relevant for judging ethical decisions, including the person's values, the person's stage of moral development, conscious intentions, freedom of choice, use of ethical and unethical behavior, and the probable outcomes of the ethical decisions (Yukl, 2006).

Dependency on moral development: Kohlberg (1984) proposed a model to describe how people progress through six sequential stages of cognitive moral development as they grow from child to an adult. With each successive stage, the person develops a broader understanding of the principles of justice, social responsibility, and human rights. Unlike physical maturation, moral development is not inevitable, and some people become fixated at a particular stage. A leader who is at a higher level of development is usually regarded as more ethical than one at a lower level of development; the level of moral development of leaders has an impact on ethical decision-making in business organizations (Trevino, 1986; Trevino and Youngblood, 1990).

Uncertainty in problem identification: An important leadership function is to help frame problems by clarifying key issues, encouraging dissenting views, distinguishing cases from symptoms, and identifying complex interdependencies (Yukl, 2006). In ethical decision-making, identifying and acknowledging key problems and issues is no easy task; a computer program may facilitate leaders systematically identify problems, acknowledge, delegate to followers, and solve problems.

Environmental influences: Ethical behavior occurs in a social context and it can be strongly influenced by aspects of the situation (Trevino, 1986; Trevino et al, 1998). Business leaders' personality and cognitive moral development interact with aspects of the situation in the ethical decision-making. That is, ethical decisions can be explained better by consideration of both the individual and the situation than either variable alone (Yukl, 2006).

Formal Assurance: Burns (1978) and Heifetz (1994) describe leadership as both a dyadic and collective process. Leaders influence individuals, and they also mobilize collective efforts to accomplish adaptive work. The type of influence used by leaders includes not only use of rationality and appeal to values, but also formal authority. Leaders can use their authority to direct attentions to problems, frame issues, structure decision processes, mediate conflicts, allocate resources to support problem solving, and delegate specific responsibilities to individuals or groups. Though formal authority is not necessary as emergent leaders acquire informal authority by taking responsibility for exercising leadership institutions where it is needed, Heifetz (1994) emphasizes that meaningful change requires shared leadership, and it cannot be accomplished by a single, heroic individual. A significant and formal assurance from a computer program could function as a solid backing to leaders to put into practice their decisions.

Empirical research on ethical issue in leadership is relatively new topic, and much still needs to be learned about it (Yukl, 2006). Kahn (1990) proposed an agenda of research questions that would help to bridge the apparent gap between normative concepts (defining ethical behavior) and contextual concepts (the conditions influencing ethical behavior). The objective is to produce knowledge that strengthens both the theory and practice of ethical conduct in Organizations. Examples of relevant research questions include language used to frame and communicate ethical issues, the conditions under which conversations about ethics are likely to occur, the process by which ethical dilemmas and disagreements are resolved, the process by which ethical principles are adapted to changing conditions, and the ways that leaders influence ethical awareness, dialogue, and consensus.

This chapter proposes a natural extension to the line of thought of Kahn (1990); the proposal is to implement the process of ethical business decision-making as a computing system, so that a systematic analysis of the process can be done.

3. Modelling ethical decision making

First, a literature study is given on the existing models for ethical decision-making in the networked economy. From the literature study, a new model for ethical decision-making is developed.

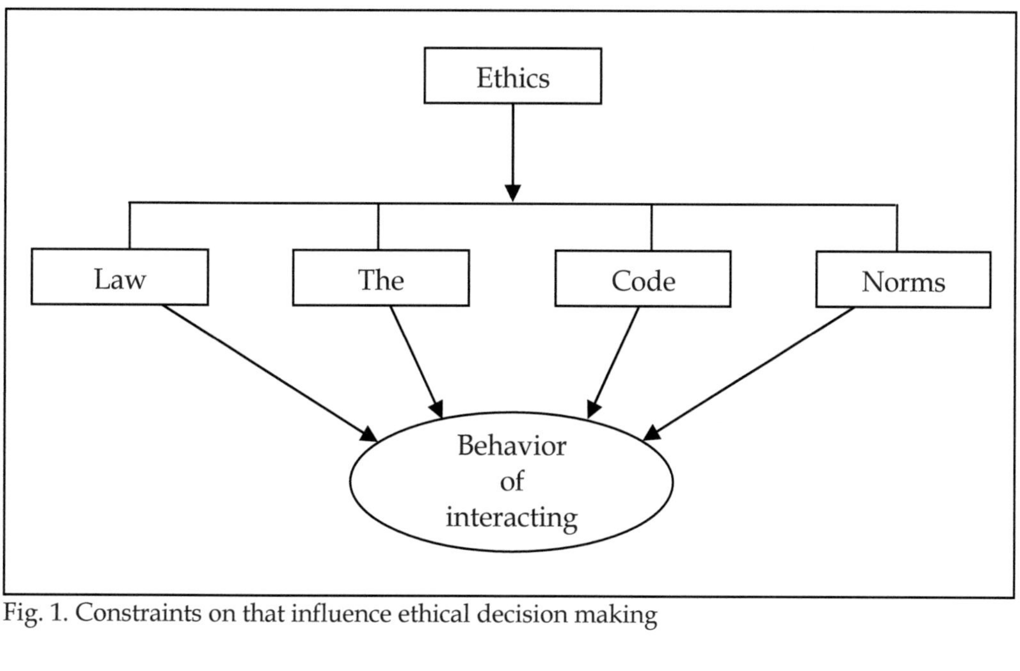

Fig. 1. Constraints on that influence ethical decision making

3.1 Existing models for ethical decision making

A Model based on four constraints:

In business environments, there are many constraints that can guide and shape business transactions. Lessig (1999) presents a model describing four constraints that regulate the ethical behavior of cyberspace activities.

The first constraint is the law. Laws are rules or commands imposed by the government that are enforced through ex post sanctions; ex post sanction means that law retroactively makes criminal conduct not criminal when performed, but increases the punishment for crimes already committed. The second constraint is the market. The market regulates through the price it sets for goods and services.

The third constraint is the code (*aka* architectural constraint). The architectural constraints are physical constraints, natural or man-made, restricts the freedom of business transactions. The fourth constraint is the social norms. Social norms are informal expressions of a community that defines a well-defined sense of normalcy and expects the members of the community to follow. An example for social norm under business context is the dress code.

Modified model by Spinello:

The model by Lessig (1999) incorporated ethics under the broad category of "social norms"; social norms have only cultural or community value. Spinello (2003) argues that the fundamental principles of ethics are metanorms and they have universal validity, and hence should not be classified as social norms. In the modified model by Spinello, ethics is given a directive role, that is, ethics should guide and direct the ways in which the constraints such as laws, the market, code, and social norms, exercise their regulatory power. The modified model is shown in figure 1.

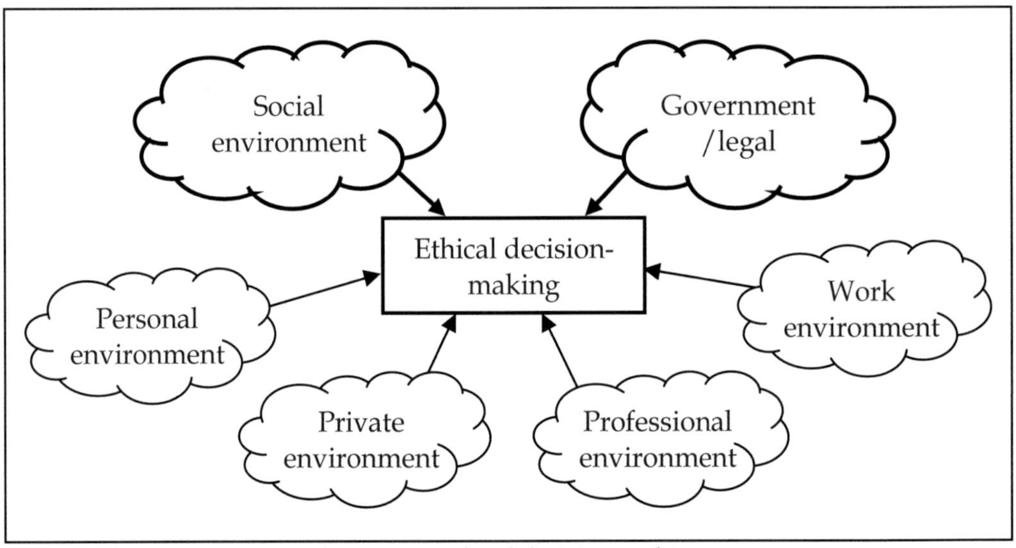

Fig. 2. The six environments that impact ethical decision-making

A model based on six environments:

Walstrom (2006) conducted an empirical study to investigate factors that impact on ethical decision-making processes regarding information ethics. Walstrom (2006) found that the two factors that had predominant impact were:

- The social environment: religious values, cultural values, and social values; and
- The government/legal environment: legislation, administrative agencies, judicial systems, etc.

However, there exist four other factors too that exercise influence on ethical decision-making (Boomer et al, 1987):

- Personal environment: individual attributes including personal goals, motivation, position, demography,
- Private environment: peer group, family, and their influences,
- Professional environment: code of conduct, professional meetings, licensing, and
- Work environment: corporate goals, stated policy, corporate culture.

Figure 2 shows the model in which ethical decision making is impacted by six environments.

A Model Emphasizing Personal Environment:
On contrary to the model by Walstrom (2006) that is based on six environments emphasizing social and legal environments, Haines and Leonard (2007) suggests that the impact of the personal and private environments have a greater influence in certain ethical problems. Figure 3 shows ethical decision making as a process under the influence of the personal and private environments.

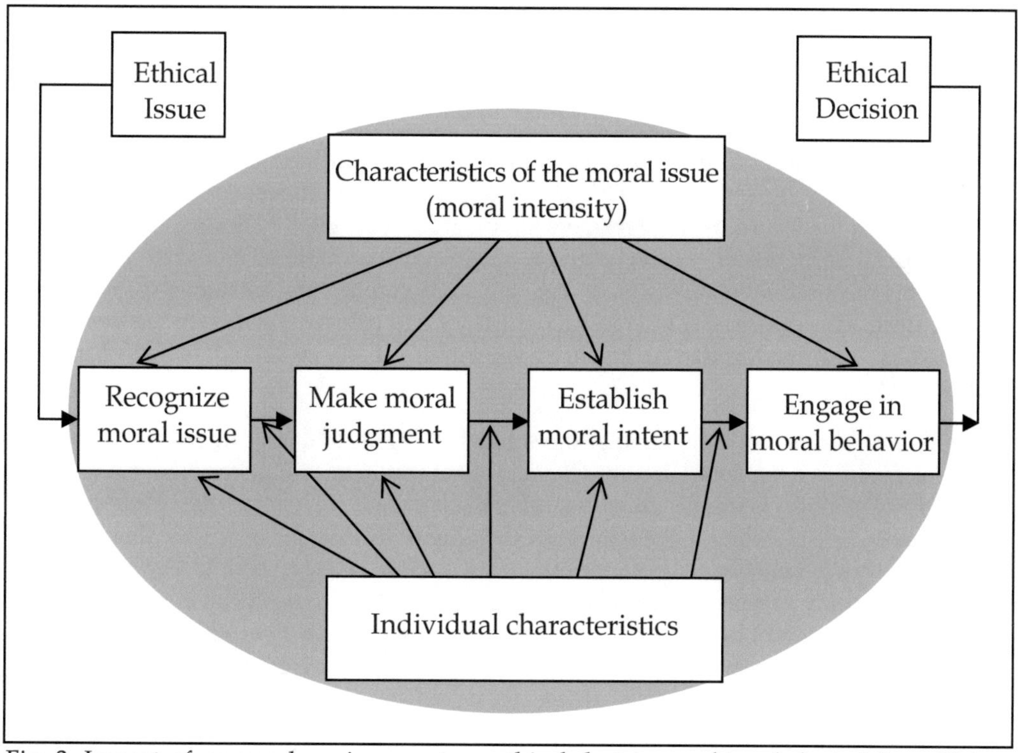

Fig. 3. Impact of personal environment on ethical decision making (adapted from Haines and Leonard (2007)

3.2 Theoretical basis for developing a new model

It is easy to see that the existing models presented in the previous subsection are only for qualitative reasoning; and that these models can not be used towards realization of computer systems that can make autonomous decisions, as the models do not facilitate inclusion of inference engines for decision making. Thus, in this subsection, a new model for ethical decision-making is developed; the main reason for developing the new model is to build a computing system that can autonomously make ethical decisions.

Although there are no magic formulas to start with, it is helpful to have a framework with which the ethical decision-making process can be organized (Silbiger, 2007); stakeholder analysis is a framework that helps us identify various elements involved in the decisions.

Stakeholder analysis:
Under stakeholder analysis, three theories of ethics are applied in business environments. These are stockholder theory, stakeholder theory, and social contract theory. These theories and their interpretations and implications are given below:

Stockholder Theory: According to the stockholder theory, the stockholders contribute capital to the businesses; corporate leaders act as agents in advancing the stockholders interests (Pearlson and Saunders, 2006). According to the originator of this theory, the only social responsibility of business and hence the agents, is to use the resources to engage in business activities designed to increase profits for the stockholders; profit making must be done by open and free competition, without deception or fraud (Friedman, 1962; Pearlson and Saunders, 2006).

Stakeholder Theory: According to the Stakeholder theory, in addition to the obligation to the stockholder, agents are also responsible for taking care of the interests of *all the stakeholders* of the business; the term stakeholder refers to any group that vitally affects the survival and success of the corporation (e.g. employees, suppliers, distributors, customers) or whose interest the corporation vitally affects (e.g. the local community, customers) (Smith and Hasnas, 1999). This means, unlike stockholder theory that primarily look into the interests of stockholders, stakeholder theory balances the rights of all stakeholders (Pearlson and Saunders, 2006).

Social Contract Theory: Both stockholder theory and stakeholder theory do not talk about the society; according to the social contract theory, agents are responsible for taking care of the needs of a society without thinking about corporate or other complex business arrangements. Social contract theory forces the agents to interact in a way that business transactions bring benefits to the members of a society. Hence, society can grant legal recognition ('social contract') to a corporation to allow it to employ social resources toward given ends (Smith and Hasnas, 1999). The social contract allows a corporation to exist and demands that agents create more value to the society than they consume for the business transactions.

Summary of Stakeholder Analysis: By skimming through the three theories of business ethics, one can see that these three theories related. The social contract theory is the most restrictive one, demanding that the whole society should be taken care of by the agents when they conduct business exchanges. The stakeholder theory is lesser restrictive than the social contract theory, as instead it demands that all the stakeholders of the business (not the whole society) should be taken care of. Finally, the stockholder theory is the least restrictive one, as it demands that only the stockholders are to be taken care of by the agents. In summary, stakeholder analysis presented above suggests that first we draw a list of all the elements (stockholders, customers, etc.) potentially effected by an ethical decision; then, we evaluate net economic benefits that the ethical decision will cause on each elements on the list.

3.3 The new model

Based on the stakeholder analysis presented in section 2 and on the literature study on the existing models for ethical decision-making, presented in section 3, we formulate a new model consisting of the following processes:

- Initialization: Identifying the main elements (stakeholders) and the environments involved in the ethical issue.
- Establishing the connected system: Determining the rights and responsibilities of each element and the relative weights of each element, thus establishing the connection between the elements.

The process of measurement: Setting up the governing equations that that combines the elements and the environments, and measuring the harms and benefits to each element, and finally, making decisions based on the net harms and benefits to the elements involved in the issue.

Identifying the primitive elements of the model

There are a number of elements already identified in the literature: Lessig (1999) identifies four elements such as laws, the market, code, and social norms, as the primitive elements of a system for ethical business decision-making. Walstrom (2006) identifies six elements such as social environment, legal (or government) environment, personal environment, private environment, professional environment, and work environment, as the primitive elements. In addition to all these elements, the literature also cites the following primitive elements: interacting agents, leaders, shareholders, etc.

Establishing the connections in the model

Before we start thinking about the internal connections of the system, let us identify the sources (or the external disturbances that agitate the system to produce an output) and the output of the system. Business opportunities are the sources of the system. Obviously, without business opportunities there won't be any ethical business decisions; ethical business decisions are the output of the system. Given below is a step-by-step formulation of the connections between the primitive elements of the system:

When the input (a business opportunity) is fed into the systems, the legal environment and the work environment (business goals and objectives, etc.) must recognize the business opportunity as a valid one. For example, when a company in US receives a business opportunity from a company in Cuba, the legal environment will reject the opportunity. In some other cases, an opportunity may be rejected because the opportunity does not satisfy business goals and objectives (work environment) of a company.

Business relationships evolve from valid business opportunities, to realize business exchanges. The business relationships are formulated by the professional environment (code of conduct, professional meetings, etc.) of the respective companies involved.

Business decisions are made to strengthen profits from the business relationships. A major player that influence formulation of business decisions for business relations is the personal environment (individual attributes including personal goals, motivation, position, etc.) and the private environment (peer group inclusive colleagues and immediate leaders, family and their influences).

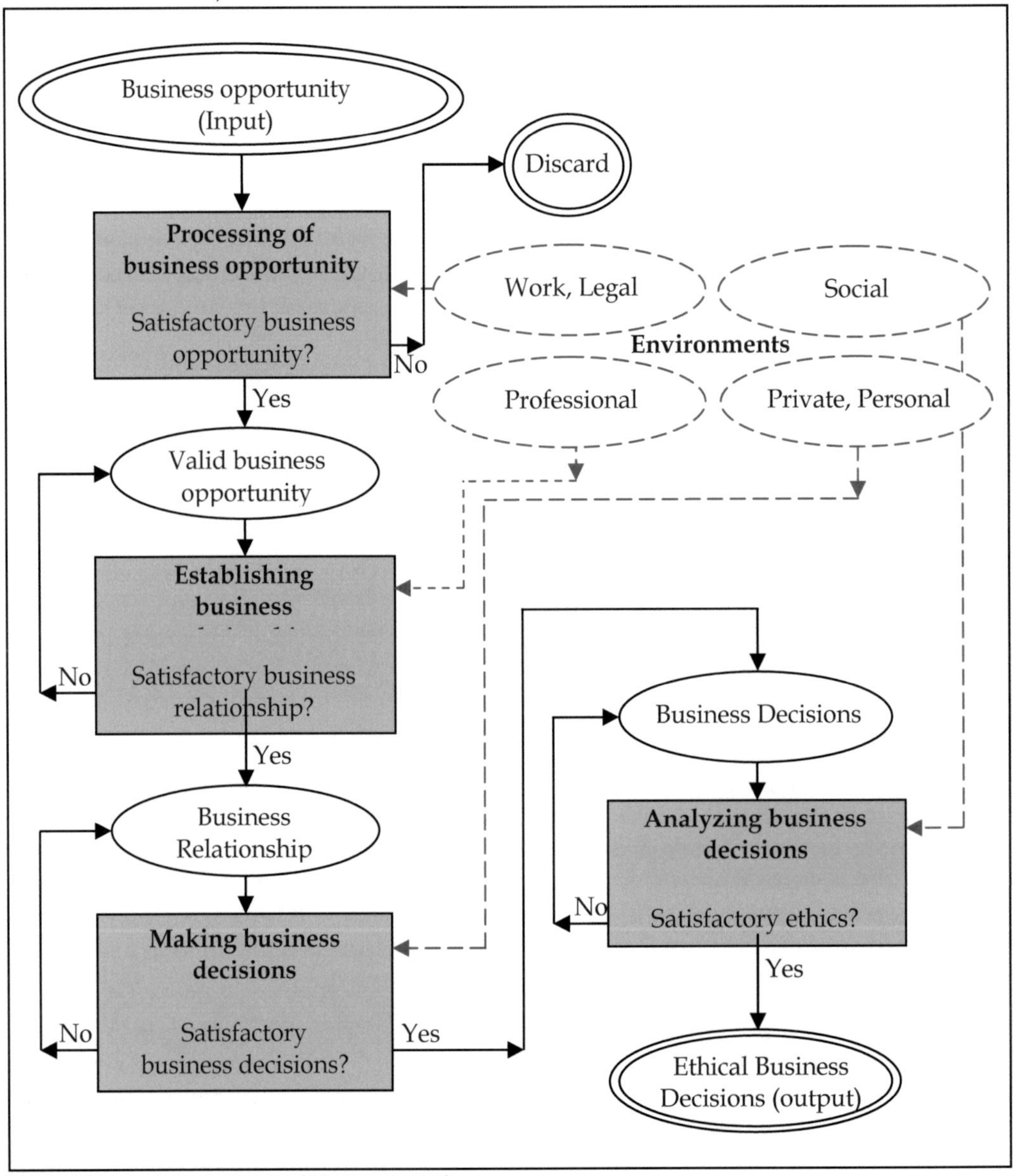

Fig. 4. The model for ethical decision making

Finally, ethical business decisions evolve from business decisions. As Walstrom (2006) states, social environment (religious values, cultural values, and social values) plays the major role in shaping ethical business decisions. In addition, the agent's personal ethics (might also be called morality - the ability to recognize moral issues, make moral judgment, awareness about profit for "all the stakeholders", etc.) play an important role.

Figure 4 shows the model for the ethical business decision-making processes. As figure 4 depicts, business goals and objectives are the driving force of business relationships, which is opened up by business opportunities. The six socio economic environments formulate the business decisions. And finally, it is the agent's moral judgment that shapes the business decisions; the agent's moral judgment depends on his or hers ability to recognize the moral issues, to establish moral intent, engagement in moral behavior, characteristics of the moral issue, and the individual's own characteristics or personality (Haines and Leonard, 2007).

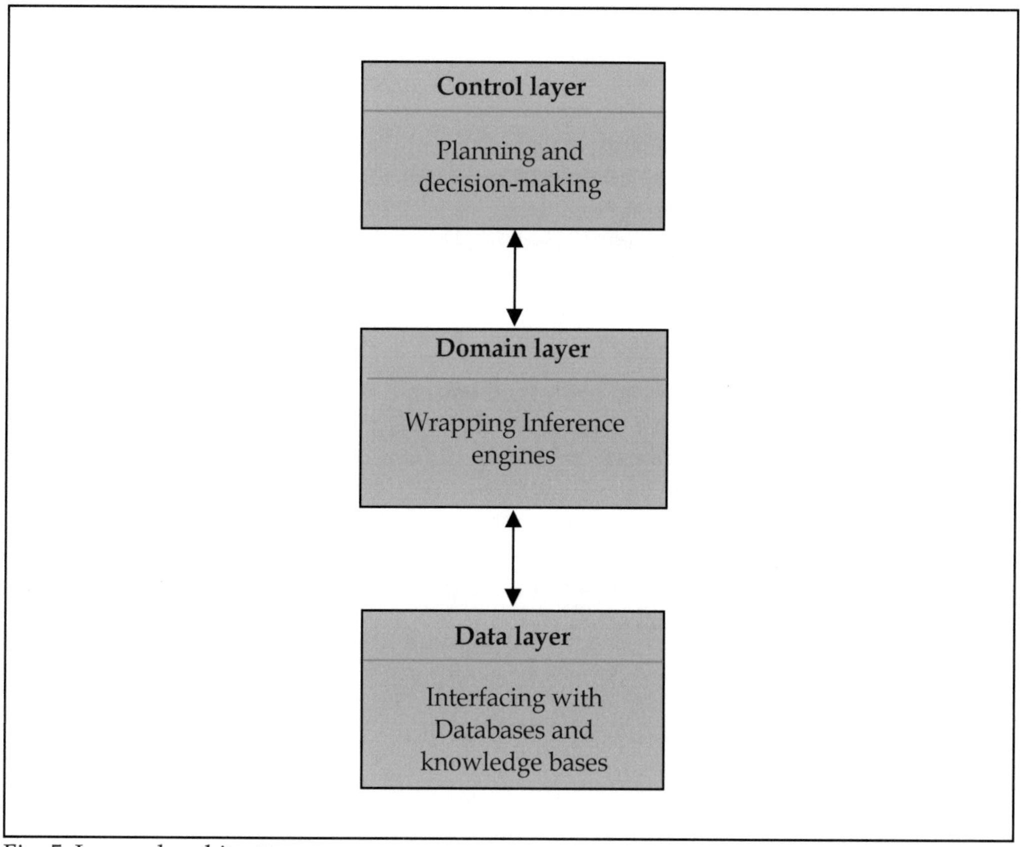

Fig. 5. Layered architecture

4. Utilizing the model for realizing a computing system

This section shows how the model shown in figure 4 can be utilized to develop a computing system. The model clearly shows the environments that influence the system ("data"), decision making points ("control"), and the inference engines ("domain").

The architecture of the computing system is a hybrid architecture based on previous works on autonomous and adaptive business systems; se Muller et al (1995), Fasli (2007), and

Woolridge (1999) for some of the architectures. The architecture consists of three distinguishable layers, such as Control layer, Domain layer, and Data layer. Figure 5 shows the architecture.

4.1 Control layer

The control layer uses the models to predict potential outcome of a scenario. First it checks the overall validity of the business opportunity (see figure 4); it then generates goals which are associated with ethical business strategies. Subsequently, business goals are propagated down to the in domain layer, which uses the data from the data layer to make decisions. The domain layer hosts a number of inference engines. The data layer mainly consists of databases and knowledge bases.

4.2 Domain layer

In figure 4, oval shaped components are passive components (such as input buffers for incoming business opportunities, intermediate buffers for storing intermediate decisions made, and output buffers for storing final decisions, etc). Rectangular components are active components, such as inference engines for decision-making. In figure 4, four inference engines are visible: 1) Processing of business opportunity, 2) Establishing business relationships, 3) Making business decisions, and 4) Analyzing business decisions. These inference engines are the main components of the domain layer.

The inference engines are equipped with mathematical models for decision-making. We believe that it is possible establish mathematical models to measure net economic benefits even for the complex problems like ethical issues, as the necessary enabling technologies are already available. We can utilize fuzzy logic (Ross, 2004; Tsoukalas and Uhrig, 1997) to code the mathematical models; the reason for proposing the use fuzzy logic is that fuzzy logic filters away inaccuracies in the input parameters; in addition, compared to pure mathematical approaches (such as mixed integer programming, linear programming, etc), with fuzzy logic it is easy to model a system.

4.3 Data layer

Figure 6 shows details of the data layer, which consists of several brokers:

- The software agents
- Semantic Web
- Web Services
- Databases

At the bottom of the data layer rests data bases that are frequently updated to synchronize with the changes occurring in the external world. There can be many databases (e.g. as shown in figure 4, a database for storing data from each environment, legal database, work environment database, etc.). Since the databases are geographically distributed (it is less likely that any two databases are kept in the same location), Web services are used to delegate the data whenever needed.

Data from databases through Web services are pieces of data. We need ontologies to integrate the data together to form meaningful information. Finally, when a request comes from inference engine, it is the software agents that identify the needs, locate the Web services and delegate the response back to the inference engine.

The system proposed in figure 6 should not be assumed as a static system as it may looks like. The databases shown in the figure are static databases, but frequently updated by a set of software agents that can learn about the environment, and the changes in the environment. Use of software agents gives the autonomous property to the proposed computing system.

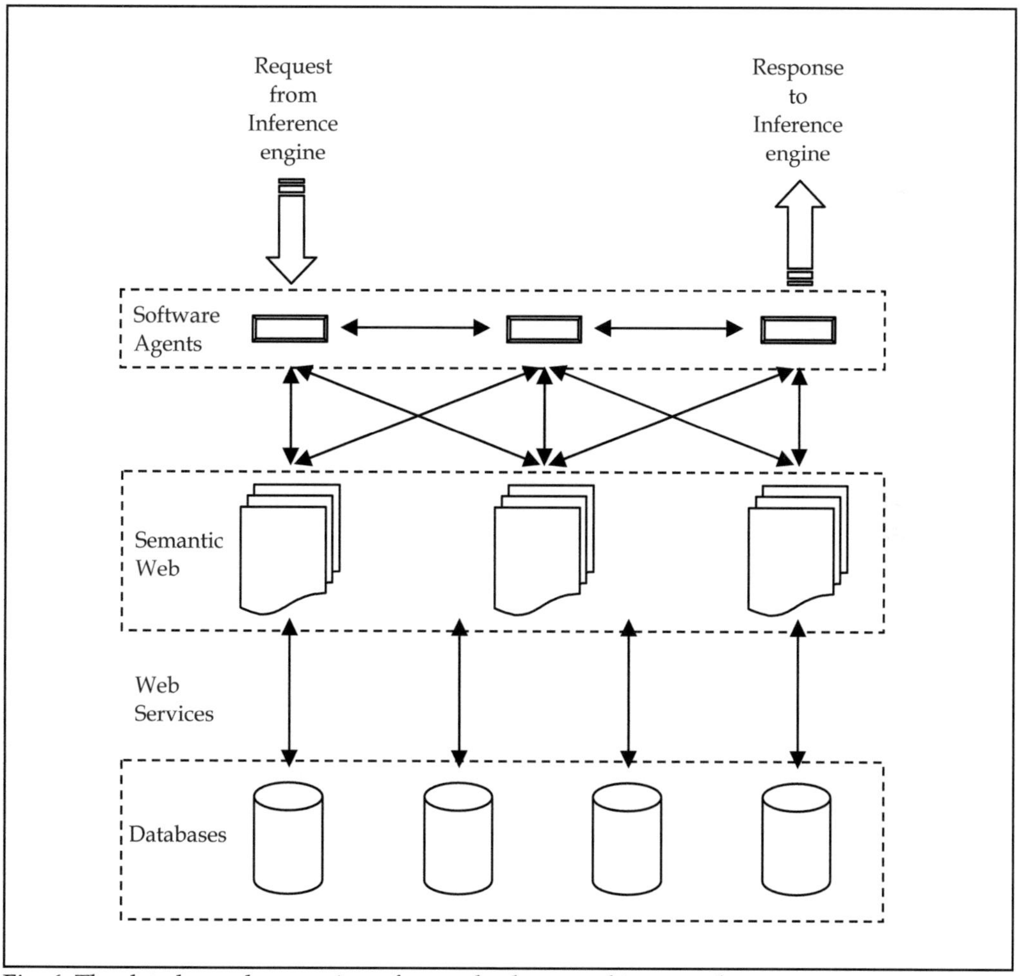

Fig. 6. The data layer that consists of many brokers working together

5. Conclusion

In this chapter, a model is created for ethical decision making. This chapter also shows how the model can be used to develop a computing system for making autonomous ethical decisions.

Why a computing system to assist business leaders in making ethical decisions? Leaders can do many things to promote ethical practices in organizations. The leader's own actions provide an example of ethical behavior to be imitated by people who admire and identify with the leader. Leaders can also set clear standard and guidelines for dealing with ethical issues provide opportunities for people to get advice about dealing with ethical issues, and initiate discussions about ethical issues to make them more salient. However, as the section 2 explained, how can a leader be sure about whether the decisions he or she proposes are ethical or not? There are too many parameters involved, and one man ethically valid decisions is other man's unethical decision. The autonomous computing system proposed in this chapter is to assist leaders making ethical decision.

6. References

Boomer, M., Clarence, G., and Tuttle, M. (1987) A behavioral Model of Ethical and Unethical decision Making. Journal of Business Ethics, 6(4), (May 1987), pp. 265-280

Burns, J. (1978) Leadership. New York: Harper & Row Cassandras, G. and LaFortune, S. (1999). Introduction to Discrete Event Systems. Hague, Kluwer Academic Publications

Dickson, M., Smith, D. Grojean, M., and Ehrhart, M. (2001) An organizational climate regarding ethics: The outcome of leader values and the practices that reflect them. Leadership Quarterly, 12, 197-217

Fasli, M. (2007) Agent Technology for e-commerce. Wiley

Friedman, M. (1962) Capitalism and Freedom. Chicago: University of Chicago Press

Haines, R. and Leonard, L. (2007). Individual characteristics and ethical decision-making in an IT context. Industrial Management & Data Systems, 107 (1), pp. 5-21

Heifetz, R. (1994) Leadership without easy answers. Cambridge, MA: Belnap Press of Harvard University Press

Kahn, W (1990) Toward an agenda for business ethics research. Academy of Management Review, 15, 311-328

Kohlberg, L. (1984) The psychology of moral development. New York: Harper & Row

Lessig, L. (1999) Code and Other Laws of Cyberspace. New York: Basic Books

Muller, J., Pischel, M., and Thiel, M. (1995) Modelling reactive behaviour in vertically layered agent architecture. In Wooldridge, M. and Jennings, N., editors, Intelligent Agents: Agent Theories, Architectures, and Languages (ATAL), LNAI Volume 890, pages 261-276, Springer, Berlin

Pearlson, K. and Saunders, C. (2006) Managing & Using Information Systems: A strategic Approach. 3ed., Wiley

Peterson, J. (1981) Petri Net Theory and the Modeling of Systems. Prentice-Hall, N.J.

Ross, T. (2004). Fuzzy logic with Engineering Applications. 2. ed. John Wiley & Sons

Silbiger, S. (2007). The 10-Day MBA. Piatkus, London.

Smith, H. And Hasnas, J. (1999) Ethics and Information Systems: The Corporate Domain. MIS Quarterly, 23 (1), (Mar. 1999), pp. 109-127

Spinello, R. (2003) CyberEthics: Morality and Law in Cyberspace. 2nd ed. Jones and Bartlett Publishers

Trevino, L. (1986) Ethical decision making in organizations: A person-situation interactionist model. Academy of Management Review, 11, 601-617

Trevino, L. Butterfield, K. and McCabe, D. (1998) The ethical context in organizations: Influences on employee attitudes and behaviors. Business Ethics Quarterly, 8(3), 447-476

Trevino, L. and Youngblood, S. (1990) Bad apples in bad barrels: a casual approach. Journal of Applied Psychology, 75, 378-385

Tsoukalas L. and Uhrig, R. (1997). Fuzzy and Neural Approaches in Engineering. John Wiley and Sons

Walstrom, K (2006) Social and legal impacts on information ethics decision making. Journal of Computer Information Systems, XLVII (2), (Winter 2006-2007), pp. 1-8

Wooldridge, M. (1999) Intelligent Agents. In Weiss, G., editor, Multiagent Systems: A modern approach to Distributed Artificial Intelligence, pages 27-77. The MIT Press, Cambridge, MA

Yukl, G. (2006) Leadership in organizations. 6th Ed. Pearson / Prentice-Hall

18

Education Quality Control Based on System Dynamics and Evolutionary Computation

Sherif Hussein
Mansoura University
Egypt

1. Introduction

Today, virtually all strategic planning involves the identification of indicators that will be used to monitor progress and often the setting of quantitative targets. As part of a results based management approach, some reward or penalty can be attached to achieve the targets. However, rarely is there an attempt to link explicitly the policy actions with the results, tracing through exactly how a given set of policy actions is expected to lead to the final outcome. The ideas regarding what needs to be done and how to proceed are usually implicit and buried within the minds of policy makers.
The quality management principles have varied greatly from the researchers' point of view. According to (Harris & Baggett, 1992), they classified them into three main principles. The first of them focused on the customer by improving the service quality through improving and training workers. The second principle concentrates on the workers themselves through improving their contribution to increase the education effectiveness. The third principle deals with the contracted service and aims to achieve the standards agreed upon. That could be done through the main factors that can be measured in the education process.
In (Williams, 1993), on the other hand, he stressed on the necessity to have quantitative measures for performance. That can help the organization to measure how far is the achieved progress by applying the quality management program from the point of view of the provided service compared to the service expected from customers. He believed that there are another two directions for the quality management. The first direction provides a tool for the management to increase the productivity and provide customer satisfaction while reducing the unnecessary expenses. The second direction provides a tool that can be used to improve the way we are doing our work.
While in (Michael & Sower, 1997), they considered quality as the quality from the point of view of customers especially in higher education. As the product of the higher education institutes is not visible, the end product can't be analyzed or checked against defects. Thus, when customers are happy with the service provided from the education institute, the quality is acceptable.

Based on an extensive review of literature on Total Quality Management (TQM) in higher education, in (Tribus, 1986), it was proposed a specific definition of "customer" and developed a comprehensive TQM model that is comprised of eight steps. The definition of "customer" and the TQM model developed can serve as a basic foundation for colleges and universities to follow when implementing TQM at their respective institutions. He also recommended a list of things to do and problems to look for when implementing a TQM project. While in (Motwani & Kumar, 1997), they looked at the applicability of TQM in education and some of the concerns addressed in the literature. They explored the different approaches used by several educational institutions in implementing TQM. They also suggested a five-step programming model that any university can use for implementing TQM.

Oregon State University implemented TQM in nine phases: exploration; establishing a pilot study team; defining customer needs; adopting the breakthrough planning process; performing breakthrough planning in divisions; forming daily management teams; initiating cross-functional pilot projects; implementing cross-functional total quality management; and setting up reporting, recognition, and awards systems as shown in (Coate, 1991).

On the other hand, in (Taylor & Hill, 1992), they examined the emerging paradigm of TQM and summarized its implications for higher education. Rather than prescribing a set of generic implementation steps, they suggested that there are other, more significant, factors to be considered related to the timing of the initiative rather than where it should begin. They discussed four necessary issues: the removal of abstraction from the concept of quality in higher education; organization-wide understanding of the customer; the importance of assessing the current quality level; and the need for strategic quality planning. Also they cited classical organizational facets such as structure, culture, human resource management and leadership as being among the determinants of TQM success. Concentration on these key matters attenuates the importance of the method of implementation. They argued that to disregard these harbingers of success is to risk long term damage to the organization and considerably reduce the likelihood of sustained and self generating organizational improvement.

In producing indicators of institutional quality in Ontario universities and colleges: options for producing, managing and displaying comparative data, the Educational Policy Institute (EPI) assessed the information needs of Ontario's postsecondary system, what types of comparative quality indicator data are currently available, and how effective common higher education data architecture could be structured. EPI found that a wide variety of potentially comparable data existed in Ontario, though not in a centralized or easily accessible format. Examples of this data include Common University Data Ontario, the National Survey of Student Engagement, and commercial institutional rankings. After reviewing several potential models for common data architecture, EPI suggested that an "Open Access Model" would best serve the needs of Ontario postsecondary stakeholders. Such a model would be collaboratively developed and maintained, striving to meet the informational needs of government, institutions, and students as presented by (Educational Policy Institute, 2008).

Despite many approaches became available, Education Quality Control (EQC) is considered a difficult task, as few policy-makers have adequate tools to aid their understanding of how various policy formulations affect this complex, socio-technical system. The impact of EQC is far-reaching, impacting the regional economy, environment, and society through many interactions. The effect of a policy meant to improve one aspect of education quality is not always known a priori, and the interactions of that policy with other policies are seldom understood well. Additionally, there are not always clearly-defined objectives that all policy planners use as described in (Barski, 2006).

Thus, the goal in this chapter was to develop a proof-of-concept model of the EQC, extended to include the different resources and utilities of the education institute, which can be analyzed to provide insight to policy-makers by comparing the relative effectiveness and interactions across policies.

Once the model was developed and tested, a system optimization was performed. Thus, this chapter aims to better understand the interactions and behaviours of the effect of the resources distribution on the total quality achieved, and to understand and quantify tradeoffs that must be made when choosing a final policy to be implemented.

2. Computer simulation

Simulation is a powerful tool used to study complex systems. It is the development of a model of a complex system and the experimental manipulation of that model to observe the results. Models may be purely physical, such as a wind tunnel; a combination of physical objects under software control, such as flight simulator; or logical, as represented in a computer program.

Computer simulations have been used to help in decision making since the mid-1950s. Building computer models of complex systems has allowed decision makers to develop an understanding of the performance of the systems over time. How many tellers should a bank have? Would the materials flow faster through the manufacturing line if there were more space between stations? What is the weather going to be tomorrow? Where is the optimal place to put the new fire station? We can gain considerable insight into all of these questions through simulation.

Although the definition of systems implies that their objects interact, the more interactions that exist in the system, the better it is as a candidate for simulation as explained in (Pidd, 1994). Thus, the best systems suited for simulation are the dynamic and complex ones. Their characteristics may be understood and captured in mathematical equations, such as the flight of a missile through nonturbulent atmosphere. Alternatively, their characteristics may be partially understood and the best way to simulate them is to use statistical representation, such as the arrival of people at a traffic light.

The keys to construct a good model are to choose the entities to represent the system and correctly determine the rules that define the results of the events. Pareto's law says that in every set of entities, there exist a vital few and trivial many. Approximately 80% of the behaviour of an average system can be explained by the action of 20% of the components. The second part of the definition of simulation gives us a clue where to begin:" and experimenting with that model to observe the results. "Which results are to be observed? The answers to this question give a good starting point to the determination of the entities in the real system that must be present in the model. The entities and the rules that define the interactions of the entities must be sufficient to produce the results to be observed as shown in (Shannon, 1998).

Therefore, the essence of constructing a model is to identify a small subset of characteristics or features that are sufficient to describe the behaviour under investigation. So, a model is an abstraction of a real system; it is not the system itself. Therefore, there is a fine line between having too few characteristics to accurately describe the behaviour of the system and having more characteristics than you need to accurately describe the system. The goal is to build the simplest model that describes the relevant behaviour.

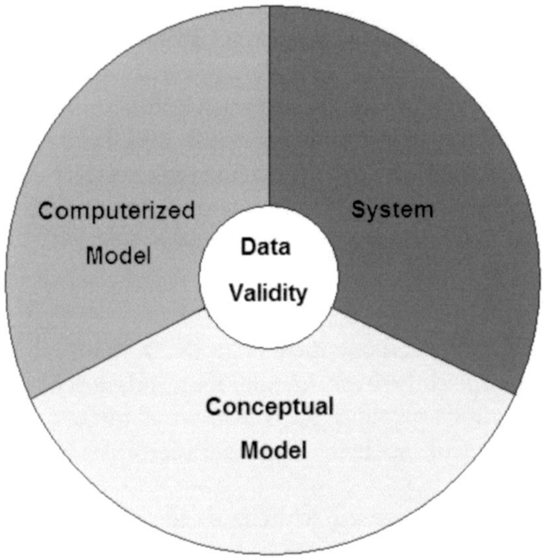

Fig. 1. The modelling process

Because a computer program implements an abstract model, we can consider the simplified version of the model development process as shown in fig. 1. The problem entity is the system, idea, situation, policy, or phenomena to be modelled; the conceptual model is the mathematical/logical/verbal representation of the problem entity developed for a particular study; and the computerized model is the conceptual model implemented on a computer. The conceptual model is developed through an analysis and modelling phase, the computerized model is developed through a computer programming and implementation phase, and inferences about the problem entity are obtained by conducting computer experiments on the computerized model in the experimentation phase. Conceptual model validation is defined as determining that the theories and assumptions underlying the conceptual model are correct and that the model representation of the problem entity is "reasonable" for the intended purpose of the model. Computerized model verification is defined as assuring that the computer programming and implementation of the conceptual model is correct. Operational validation is defined as determining that the model's output behaviour has sufficient accuracy for the model's intended purpose over the domain of the model's intended applicability. Data validity is defined as ensuring that the data necessary for model building, model evaluation and testing, and conducting the model experiments to solve the problem are adequate and correct as explained in (Robert, 2007).

3. System dynamics and model implementation

System dynamics, created during the mid-1950s by Professor Jay Forrester of the Massachusetts Institute of Technology, is considered a way of thinking about the future which focuses on 'stocks' and 'flows' within processes and the relationships between them, the system dynamics approach forces policy-makers to acknowledge upfront if there is uncertainty and to identify where this uncertainty lies as shown in (Zhang et al., 2008). This acknowledgment may make it easier to get people to buy-in to the more systematic approach that is considered in this chapter.

Cutting a system up into bits often destroys the system you are trying to understand. This, of course, is a matter of connectedness: if you break the connectedness of a system, you break the system itself. Rather more subtly, many systems show characteristics that are not properties of any of their constituent parts. It therefore follows that no study, however exhaustive, of any individual constituent part will ever identify the existence of these system-level characteristics, let alone how they behave as explained by (Sherwood, 2002).

It is important to note that the system dynamics approach for monitoring and evaluation does not only consist of the modelling of a complex problem, rather it should be conceived more as a process in which various things occur. First, at the policy-making level, one must specify how a particular target will be reached. That is, one specifies a structural model underlying the achievement of the target. System dynamics tools can help develop such structural models. Second, one must identify exactly what information is needed to ensure that one is on track to achieve the desired results. Third, there should be an on-going review of a program's outcomes, comparing expected outcomes to actual outcomes and, if actual outcomes fell short of expected outcomes, why this occurred. The expected outcomes may not have been achieved because the planned policy actions were not carried out. Or it may be the case that the actions were carried out, but certain key parameter values were mis-estimated. If the actions were carried out and the key parameter values were, indeed, correct, it may be that the underlying structural model was incorrect and needs be reconsidered. With the system dynamics approach, the model is constantly being reconsidered and appropriate modifications and adjustments are expected in the course of one's work as shown in (An et al., 2004).

As one can imagine, taking a more structural approach through system dynamics is much more intensive in the use of information and requires more work than with a reduced-form approach. Although collecting information and allocating the necessary human resources all involve significant burdens, there are certainly ways of reducing these information costs. For example, by identifying the key drivers of desired outcomes within a given system, one can focus efforts on generating the necessary data only for those particular areas. This also helps to reduce the financial costs of collecting information which can be considerable. In doing this, one can thus develop a work program which concentrates work efforts only in certain areas.

It is possible to perform good system dynamics work with many different tools, including spreadsheets and programming languages, though this is not usually practical. There are few software programs that were designed to facilitate the building and use of system dynamics models. DYNAMO was the first system dynamics simulation language, and was originally developed by Jack Pugh at MIT. The language was made commercially available from Pugh-Roberts in the early 1960s. DYNAMO today runs on PC compatibles under

Dos/Windows. It provides an equation based development environment for system dynamics models as shown in (Kasperska et al., 2006).

The Stella software, originally introduced on the Macintosh in 1984, provided a graphically oriented front end for the development of system dynamics models. The stock and flow diagrams, used in the system dynamics literature are directly supported with a series of tools supporting model development. Equation writing is done through dialog boxes accessible from the stock and flow diagrams. Parallel to that, in the mid 1980s the Norwegian government sponsored research aimed at improving the quality of high school education using system dynamics models. This project resulted in the development of Mosaic, an object oriented system aimed primarily at the development of simulation based games for education. Powersim was later developed as a Windows based environment for the development of system dynamics models that also facilitates packaging as interactive games or learning environments. Another language that originally developed in the mid 1980s for use in consulting projects Vensim was made commercially available in 1992. It is an integrated environment for the development and analysis of system dynamics models. Vensim runs on Windows and Macintosh computers as discussed by (Eberlein, 2009). On the other hand, MapSys from Simtegra's flagship systems thinking and system dynamics is another software that allows for the drawing of causal loop diagrams or stock & flow maps using simple drag and drop operations. It can export system diagrams to popular applications such as WORD or simulate it and view the results using a powerful graph editor.

In addition, there are a number of other modelling and simulation environments which provide some support for building system dynamics models and one of these is NetLogo which is a programmable modelling environment for simulating natural and social phenomena. It was authored by Uri Wilensky in 1999 and is in continuous development at the Centre for Connected Learning and Computer-Based Modelling. NetLogo is particularly well suited for modelling complex systems developing over time. Besides being able to use the system dynamics tool integrated into the software, modellers can give instructions to hundreds or thousands of "agents" all operating independently. This makes it possible to explore the connection between the micro-level behaviour of individuals and the macro-level patterns that emerge from the interaction of many individuals as explained in (Wilensky, 1999).

The remainder of this chapter will discuss the proposed methodology to model and assess the education quality system. The model will be further optimised to find the solution that gives recommendations for the best resources distribution that increase the quality.

3.1. Causal loop diagram

Fig. 2. Cause and effect relationship

Casual Loop Diagram (CLD) is considered the first step in system dynamics and it enables complex systems to be described in terms of cause-and-effect relationships. CLD is a visual method of capturing the system complexity providing a powerful means of communication, and its use can ensure that as wide a community as you wish has a genuinely, and deeply, shared view. This is enormously valuable in building high-performing teams and can also help you identify the wisest way of influencing the system of interest. As a result, you can avoid taking poor decisions, for example decisions that look like quick fixes but are likely to backfire.
The way in which real systems evolve over time is often bewilderingly complex. System dynamics enables us to tame that complexity, offering an explanation of why a system behaves as it does, and providing insights into the system's likely behaviour in the future. The key is to understand the chains of causality, the sequence and mutual interactions of the numerous individual cause-and-effect relationships that underlie the system of interest. These chains of causality are captured in a causal loop diagram, in which each cause and effect relationship is expressed by means of a link represented by a curly arrow as shown in fig. 2.
Links are of only two types: positive links and negative links. If an increase in the 'cause' drives an increase in the 'effect', then the link is positive; if an increase in the 'cause' drives a decrease in the 'effect' then the link is negative.

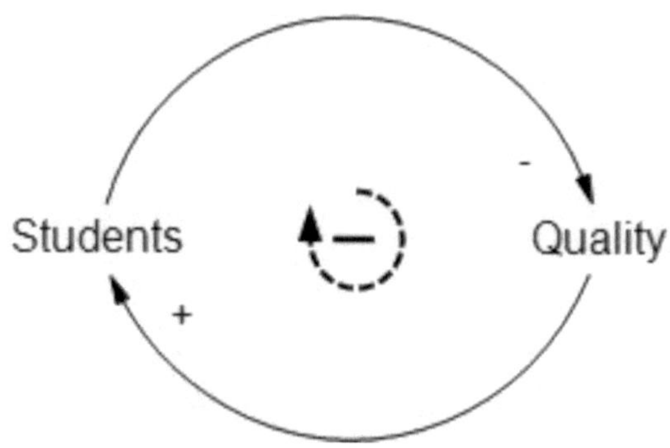

Fig. 3. CLD loop (balancing loop)

CLDs of real systems are composed primarily of closed, continuous chains known as feedback loops. There are only two fundamental types of feedback loop: the reinforcing loop and the balancing loop. Reinforcing loops are characterized by having an even number of minuses around the loop (with zero counting as an even number); balancing loops have an odd number of minuses as shown in fig. 3. The action of a reinforcing loop is, as its name implies, to amplify the original effect on each turn. Reinforcing loops therefore behave as virtuous or vicious circles, depending on the circumstances. The action of a balancing loop is quite different: The system seeks to achieve or maintain a target or a goal. For example, the action of a thermostat in a heating system maintains the ambient temperature at a constant level; likewise, the objective of many budgeting systems is to steer the corporation toward a set of pre-determined goals.
All real systems are composed of interlinked networks of reinforcing loops and balancing loops, often in conjunction with a (usually small) number of dangles, which represent items

that determine the boundary of the system of interest, such as the output of the system or the targets or goals that drive it.

Compiling a good CLD for a real system requires deep knowledge of the system. It also encourages the explicit articulation of relationships that we all know are present but are rarely talked about, and the recognition of fuzzy variables, which are important but difficult to measure, such as the effect of having good staff on attracting and retaining customers.

The original intent for the education quality model was to model large scale regional behaviour and pin point the different factors that affect quality. Some of those factors are naturally the ones set by the standardisation committees responsible for ranking the educational organizations. Other factors are equally important such as students and employees satisfaction and even they are not very tangible, they can definitely guide the optimisation of the budget distribution.

Costs in the quality requirements are attributed to salaries and expenses and include building and facilities, courses, marketing, counselling, libraries and information centres, students' services, legalism and morals, research and environmental services, and scientific evaluation. The total budget is therefore the sum of these costs.

Design factors	Effective weight
Building and facilities	14%
Courses	15%
Marketing	5%
Counselling	5%
Libraries and information centres	8%
Students' services	8%
Research and environmental services	10%
Legalism and morals	5%
Scientific evaluation	5%
Staff level	15%
Management	10%

Table 1. The design factors along with their weights contributing to the university accreditation

The design vector for the model consists of the budget shares for each of the design factors which in turns offer regulatory actions for the education quality. The nine design factors chosen along with another two factors (staff level and management that are not optimized in education quality model) are shown in table 1 (based on the Arabian business schools association), with their percentage contribution to the accreditation quality for each variable as shown in (ARADO, 2009).

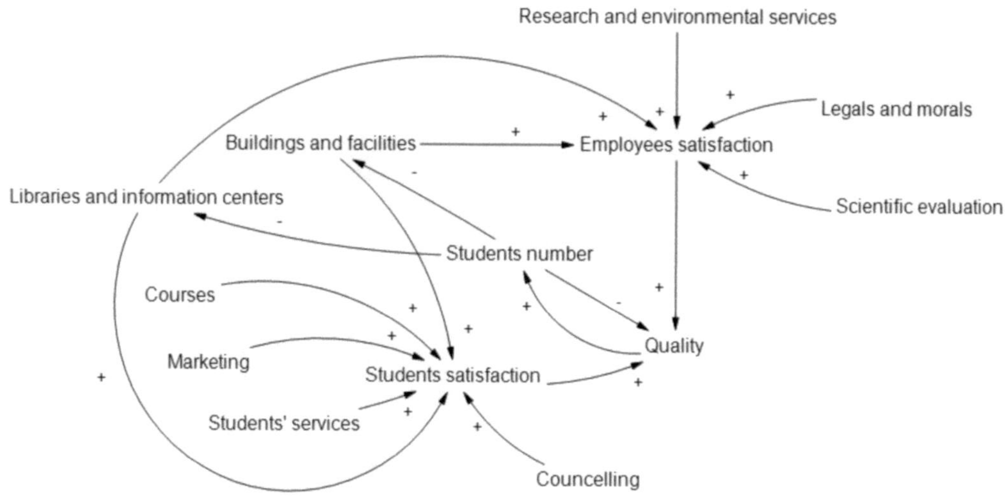

Fig. 4. The education quality control model CLD

The model based on a view of the EQC has been represented and simplified in Fig. 4. In this model the main factors affecting the quality are included for optimization. The quality is mainly affected by both the students' satisfaction and the employee's satisfaction. In addition, the students' number that join the institute can increase or decrease depending indirectly on the education quality. Both the students' satisfaction and the employees' satisfaction are affected by different factors that are improved and maintained by allocating suitable financial resources. The spending can be scheduled on a yearly basis to maximize the total quality of the institute and is based on the effective weight of each factor on the quality improvement. As accreditation is considered another way of evaluating the institute performance, the accreditation criteria plays an important role of weighing the importance of the different institution spending. That spending need to keep the institution facilities within a certain value if not increased. In other words, if some facilities such as libraries and information centres are not improved consistently, they will be obsolete and decrease in value with time. The number of students affects as well the effective value of the libraries and information centres as its increase will definitely decrease their effective value. On the other hand, buildings can increase in market value when lands and building materials goes up. In that sense many institutes directs their initial attention toward buying lands that are suitable for future expansion. The diagram was designed in a way that combines students and employees satisfaction with the accreditation factors in order to improve the over all quality of the institute.

3.2. Stock-flow diagram

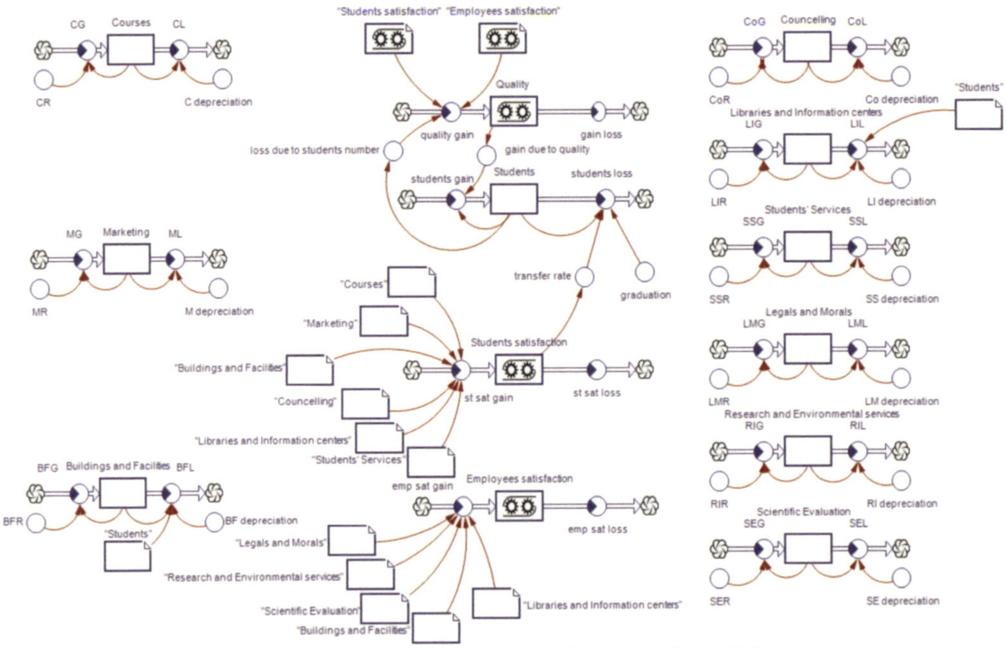

Fig. 5. The stock flow diagram for the education quality control model

As can be seen from the view in fig. 4, the EQC model must encompass many factors in order to provide useful data to policy planners. In addition to the more apparent factors such as students' satisfaction, employees' satisfaction and policy planning, a good model must consider the regional economics, supply chain management, and environmental assessment.

To address these issues, a modular model that encompasses the factors listed above has been implemented into the stock-flow diagram as shown in fig. 5. At the highest level, we have a quality module that contains the direct factors that affect its values, such as the students' satisfaction, the employees' satisfaction, and the students' number. At a lower level, we have multiple modules that model a particular aspect such as the courses, marketing, buildings and facilities, counselling, libraries and information centres, students' services, legal and morals, research and environmental services, and scientific evaluation with their effect on both the students' satisfaction and the employees' satisfaction while additional modules can be added if needed.

The quality, the students' satisfaction and the employees' satisfaction are all treated as conveyers while the students' number and the rest of the factors are treated as stocks. Stocks are accumulations. They collect whatever flows into them, net of whatever flows out of them. While in the conveyor, material gets on and rides for a period of time, and then gets off. The transit time can be either constant or variable. That selection was done to be close to the nature of the system as variables that need to keep track of previous values were modelled with stocks while variables that can change periodically independent on the previous values were modelled with conveyors.

3.3. Model equations

Stock and flow diagram only offers us the connection between variables but the real relations are realised behind the scene with equations. Those equations can be a simple equality or a table that connects two variables. The following figure (fig.6) shows a sample of the equations linking the different variables in the stock and flow diagram.

```
starttime = 0
stoptime = 3
dt = 1; time step
; For the buildings and facilities equations
BFG = max (0, BFR*Buildings_and_Facilities); BFG: Building and facilities gain, BFR:
buildings and facilities resource
BFL = max (0, Buildings_and_Facilities*BF_depreciation/Students); BFL: building and
facilities loss, BF_depreciation: buildings and facilities depreciation
For the courses equations
CG = max (0, Courses*CR); CG: courses gain, CR: courses resource
CL = max (0, C_depreciation*Courses); CL: courses loss, C_depreciation: courses
depreciation
; For the employees satisfaction
emp_sat_gain = max (0, E1*Buildings_and_facilities
+E2*Legals_and_morals+E3*Libraries_and_information_centers+E4*Research_and_envi
ronmental_services+E5*Scientific_evaluation); E1-E5: constants
gain_due_to_quality = table (Quality)
loss_due_to_students_number = table (Students)
quality_gain = max (0, Employees_satisfaction*Q1+Students_satisfaction*Q2-
loss_due_to_students_number); Q1, Q2: constants
; For the students satisfaction
st_sat_gain = max (0,
S1*Buildings_and_facilities+S2*Councelling+S3*Courses+S4*Libraries_and_information
_centers+S5*Marketing+S6*Students_services); S1-S6: constants
students_gain = max (0, Students*gain_due_to_quality)
students_loss = max (0, (graduation+transfer_rate)*Students);
transfer_rate = table (Students_satisfaction)
```

Fig. 6. Sample equations for the education quality model

3.4. Simulation

	Estimated quality	Real quality
Year 1	0.42	0.45
Year 2	0.46	0.51
Year 3	0.52	0.54

Table 2. The estimated qualities of the model along with the real qualities

In order to verify the accuracy of the model, real data that cover three years has been used. That limited duration was chosen as the adoption of new techniques may require a special set of data that is difficult to be obtained in a longer time frame. The model performance is shown in table 2 and illustrates the simulated results for the quality along with the real quality values achieved by the policy makers with traditional methods. It can be derived from the results that the trend of improvement for both the real and the estimated qualities are similar for the three simulated years. That in turns reflects the potential of the model to capture some details that can be of great importance in the planning process.

4. Evolutionary computation and model optimization

Evolutionary computation is a general term for several computation techniques which are all based to some degree on the development of biological life in the natural world. Currently there exist several major evolutionary models. The genetic algorithm, by far the most common application of evolutionary computation, is a model of machine learning taking inspiration from genetics and natural selection. In natural evolution, each species searches for beneficial adaptations (species optimizations), which arise through mutation and the chromosomal exchange and recombination of breeding. The two key axioms underlying the genetic algorithm are that complex nonbiological structures can be described by simple bit strings (analogous to the "genetic code" of chromosomes), and that these strings could be improved, according to a particular measure of fitness, by the application of simple transformation functions (just as living species may be "improved" through mating). Evolutionary strategies simulate natural evolution similarly to the genetic algorithm. Like genetic algorithms, evolutionary strategies are most powerful while comparing populations of data, as opposed to individual samplings. Differences between the two lie in their application; evolutionary strategies were designed to be applied to continuous parameter optimization problems seen in laboratory work, while the genetic algorithm was used originally in integer optimization problems. Evolutionary programming is a stochastic optimization function, similar in many ways to the genetic algorithm. However, evolutionary programming places emphasis on the behavioural link between parent and offspring, as opposed to the genetic algorithms attempt to model the exact code transition as seen in nature. Evolutionary programming follows a general process with obvious similarities to natural evolutionary progression. An initial population of trial solutions is selected at random from a coding scheme. A chosen mutation factor is applied to each solution, generating a new population. Because evolutionary programming resembles biological evolution at the level of reproductive populations of species, and there is no genetic recombination between species, evolutionary programming transformations take place without crossover- combination of two parent member's genetic code. The offspring species' members are weighed for overall fitness; the best are kept while the rest are eliminated, and the algorithm repeats with the new, fitter population. The learning classifier system's purpose is to take in input and produce an output representing a classification of that input. They have undergone and continue to go through multiple minor changes of name and scope, but the enduring foundation originates in J.H. Holland's Adaptation in Natural and Artificial Systems, wherein he envisions a cognitive system capable of classifying and reacting appropriately to the events in its corresponding environment. This most obviously parallels the inherently intelligent behaviour seen in all macro- and microscopic living creatures. Though there are certainly other forms of evolutionary computation, the above offers a brief summary of the most established and useful evolutionary techniques as discussed in (Floreano, 2008).

4.1. Genetic Algorithms

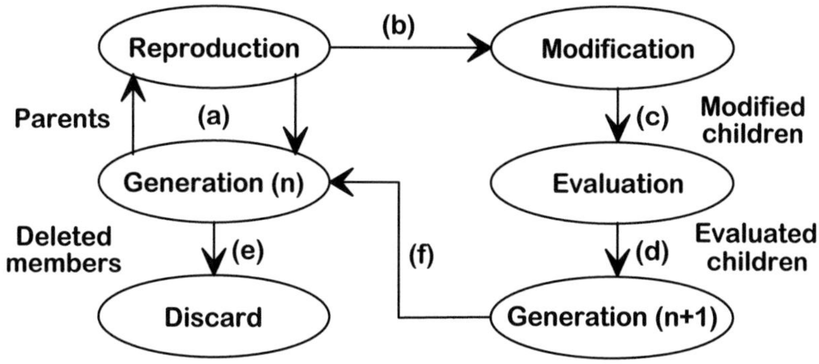

Fig. 7. Genetic algorithm cycle of reproduction. The algorithm uses (a) reproduction to select potential solutions (b) genetic operators to modify the solutions (c) evaluation against the objective function (d) new generation produced, which replaces the old solutions (e) while the other solutions are deleted.

In this research the basic features of genetic algorithms were used to optimize the spending for each of the nine variables that controls the design factors mentioned in table 1 in order to maximize the education quality. Genetic algorithms use the evolutionary process of natural selection as a metaphor for what is essentially a hill-climbing search without backup. Genetic algorithms search for an optimal solution or a global maximum among an enormous set of data. That can be achieved by computationally modelling the alteration, recombination, and propagation of genes that forms the basis of biological evolution. To achieve this, certain complex biological details of evolution must be abstracted in favour of more relevant principles.

Genetic splitting and pairing, as well as phenomena such as crossover and mutation, are modelled probabilistically. Assuming that parameter encoding, population size, propagation iterations, genetic operators, and a fitness function have been chosen. The 'target-size' sets the length of the binary sequence (zeros and ones) that must be found. This sequence can be thought of as the optimal genetic information (genome) for a particular environment. The 'population-size' sets the number of individuals that can try out their own genomes in that environment. The genetic algorithm runs through the following sequence of events that are summarised in fig. 7:

(a) A population of given size is initialized.

(b) For a specified number of generations:

1) Assign each individual node a fitness level according to the fitness function.

2) Probabilistically select a specified number of pairs of individuals according to fitness levels. Higher fitness levels increase an individual's chance of being selected.

3) Apply the specified genetic operators to these chosen pairs to produce new individuals.
4) Randomly select individuals from the population. Replace them with the newly produced individuals.

(c) Return the individual with the highest fitness level as the output.

A careful choice of genetic operators can improve the efficiency of the genetic algorithm or enable it to find otherwise inaccessible solutions. Crossover switches two subsequences of two parent strings; the goal is to place two fit sequences on the same string. Subsequences are selected probabilistically.
Mutation introduces "genetic diversity" into the population by randomly altering one character of an individual string. Mutation provides a way to help the genetic algorithm avoid the situation in which the system fixates on a local maximum after repeatedly propagating a particular character as discussed in (Tian, 2008).
The optimization problem in this research is a maximization problem which aims to maximize the total quality of the institute.

4.2. Variables selection

A single objective has been used for the optimization analysis of the model as the basis of optimization. The objective has been selected to reflect the task of EQC with long-term sustainability in mind: to maximize the quality of the institution as a function of the design vector calculated over a predetermined number of years.
The System Dynamics Modeller in NetLogo allows for drawing a diagram that defines "stocks" and “conveys”, and how they affect each other. The Modeller read the EQC diagram and generated the appropriate NetLogo code: global variables, procedures and reporters. The next step was to optimise the model using genetic algorithm on the proposed model. Genetic algorithm is then implemented in the NetLogo environment to search for a quasi optimal solution (best budget distribution) that increases the model quality. The genetic algorithms implemented here works by generating a random population of solutions to a problem, evaluating those solutions and then using cloning, recombination and mutation to create new solutions to the problem.
The design vector represents the spending on each design factor that in turns affect the education quality. The relationship between each design variable and the corresponding design factor is based on an estimated formula that was derived from either statistical or economical evaluation for the true values of the utilities.
The design vector which is composed of the nine variables that contribute to improve the nine design factors, as explained earlier in table 1, has been constrained to have a total greater or equal to zero and less than or equal to the total budget. Although the limits of the constraints are not necessarily realistic, they give the program the ability to cover all the possible solutions.
It was also chosen to run the model for three years as the basis for optimization. This time period was chosen to minimize the time required for the model evaluation while allowing for enough time for possible effects to take action, such as the impact of increased spending on the different design factors.

4.3. Optimization

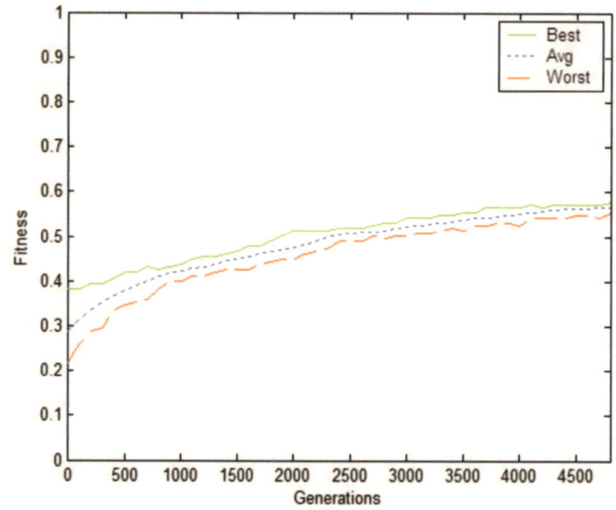

(a)

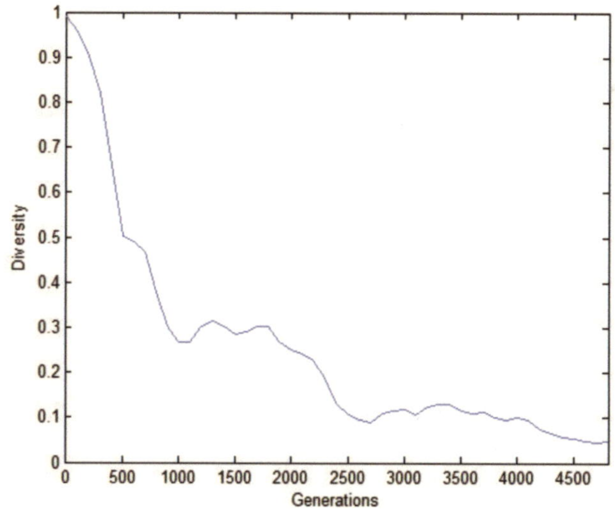

(b)

Fig. 8. Fitness (a) and diversity (b) curves for the optimization process

Initially many individual solutions are randomly generated to form an initial population. The population size is of 300 possible solutions. During each successive generation, a proportion of the existing population is selected to breed a new generation. Individual solutions are selected through a fitness-based process, where fitter solutions are typically more likely to be selected. The used selection method, roulette wheel selection, rates the fitness of each solution, which is based on the average quality over the three years, and preferentially selects the best solution.

The next step is to generate a second generation from population of solutions selected through crossover, and mutation. For each new solution to be produced, a pair of "parent" solutions is selected for breeding from the pool selected previously. By producing a "child" solution using the above methods of crossover and mutation, a new solution is created which typically shares many of the characteristics of its "parents". New parents are selected for each child, and the process continues until a new population of solutions of appropriate size is generated. These processes ultimately result in the next generation population of chromosomes that is different from the initial generation. This generational process is repeated until a termination condition has been reached; the highest ranking solution's fitness has reached a plateau such that successive iterations no longer produce better results fig. 8.a.
Diversity was measured using the Hamming distance between the bit strings representing each structure (ie the number of bits which do not match). So that a large uniqueness value does not preclude search in a small subspace at the end of the search, the uniqueness value of k bits is slowly decreased to one bit as the search proceeds. Thus at the start of the search the space is sampled over a relatively coarse ``grid," and as the search progresses, the grid size is gradually reduced until adjacent points are considered as shown in fig. 8.b.
Table 3 shows how the technique could improve the quality of the institution compared to the estimated quality found from the model over the selected years of simulation.

	Estimated quality	Optimized quality
Year 1	0.42	0.51
Year 2	0.46	0.59
Year 3	0.52	0.63

Table 3. Optimized qualities against estimated qualities from the model

Design factors	First year budget distribution	Second year budget distribution	Third year budget distribution
Building and facilities	25%	26%	28%
Courses	5%	4%	4%
Marketing	8%	6%	4%
Counselling	3%	4%	3%
Libraries and information centres	15%	16%	17%
Students' services	10%	11%	12%
Research and environmental services	27%	28%	26%
Legalism and morals	2%	1%	1%
Scientific evaluation	5%	4%	5%

Table 4. Optimized resources distribution proposed for the three years duration

The best solution is therefore, the best budget distribution over the three years period and aims to give the organization managers an indication for the priority of spending in order to better utilise their resources and provide the best affordable quality of education.
Table 4 summarises the best possible budget distribution which depends on the initial resources of the institution and their financial budgets over the years.

5. Conclusion

In this research, system dynamics has been chosen to capture the complex relations that affect the behaviour of the education quality model. The environment selected for this simulation provides an easy way for integrating different tools and allows for different techniques to be utilized. The modular design also allows for additional modules to capture additional factors that can influence the system.
The modelling of the system itself before it is to be used in optimizing the budget distribution needed a great involvement in the design of the model from different parties to achieve advanced levels of prediction. That involvement proves more useful for the policy makers and helps to integrate them with system formulation and interrelated causalities.
This research provided as well a comparison between the normal quality management for budget distribution and the optimized budget distribution and their effect on the quality. For comparison reasons, it was important to use realistic values which were obtained from the normal management methods and compare the results with the estimated values for the quality. That comparison although it is an estimated one but it can give an idea to the quality management planers of what the outcome can be if they relied on modelling the EQC system and optimizing the solution to achieve maximum education quality.

6. References

An, L.; Jeng, J. J.; Ettl, M. & Chung, J. Y. (2004). A system dynamics framework for sense-and-respond systems, *IEEE International Conference on E-Commerce Technology for Dynamic E-Business*, ISBN: 0-7695-2206-8, pp. 6 - 13

Barski, T. (2006). The Assurance of Quality of Education in Context the Higher Education Reforming Process (Bologna Process), *Microwave & Telecommunication Technology, 16th International Crimean Conference*, ISBN: 966-7968-92-8, Vol. 1, Sept., pp. 65 - 67

Coate L. E. (1991). Implementing total quality management in a university setting. *Total Quality Management in Higher Education*, New-Directions-for- Institutional-Research, ISSN: ISSN-0271-0579, No. 71, Autumn, pp. 27-38

Floreano, D. (2008). *Bio-Inspired Artificial Intelligence: Theories, Methods,* and Technologies, ISBN-13: 978-0262062718, The MIT Press, 2008

Harris, J.W. & Baggett, J.M. (1992). *Quality Quest in the Academic Process*, ISBN: 1879364255, Samford University, Birmingham, AL, and GOAL/QPC, Methuen, MA

Kasperska, E.; Mateja-Losa, E. & Slota, D. (2006). *Comparison of Simulation and Optimization Possibilities for Languages: DYNAMO and COSMIC & COSMOS – on a Base of the Chosen Models*, ISBN: 978-3-540-34379-0, Springer Berlin / Heidelberg

Michael, R. K. & Sower, V. E. (1997). A comprehensive model for implementing total quality management in higher education. *Benchmarking for Quality Management & Technology*, ISSN: ISSN-1351-3036, Vol. 4, No. 2, pp. 104-120.

Motwani, J. & Kumar, A. (1997). The need for implementing total quality management in education. *International Journal of Educational Management*, ISSN-0951-354X, Vol. 11, No. 3, pp. 131–135

Mayo, D. D. & Wichman, K. E. (2003). Tutorial on business and market modeling to aid strategic decision making: system dynamics in perspective and selecting appropriate analysis approaches, *Proceedings of the 2003 Winter Simulation Conference*, ISBN: 0-7803-8131-9, Vol. 2, Dec. 7-10, pp. 1569 – 1577

Producing Indicators of Institutional Quality in Ontario Universities and Colleges: Options for Producing, Managing and Displaying Comparative Data (Educational Policy Institute, July 2008)

Pidd, M. (1994). An introduction to computer simulation, *Proceedings of the 1994 Winter Simulation Conference*, pp. 7 – 14, ISBN: 0-7803-2109-X, Orlando, Florida, United States

Robert, G. S. (2007). Verification and validation of simulation models. Winter Simulation Conference 2007, ISBN : 0-7803-5134-7, pp. 124-137

Shannon, R. E. (1998). Introduction to the art and science of simulation, *Proceedings of the 1998 Winter Simulation Conference*, Vol. 1, pp. 7-14, ISBN: 0-7803-5133-9, Washington, DC, USA

Sherwood, D. (2002). *Seeing the Forest for the Trees: A Manager's Guide to Applying Systems Thinking*, ISBN: 978-1857883114, Nicholas Brealey, 2002

Tribus, M. (1986). TQM in education: the theory and how to put it to work, in Quality Goes to School. Readings on Quality Management in Education, American Association of School, ISSN: ISSN-0954-478X, Vol. 61, No. 5, pp. 404-6

Taylor, W.A. & Hill, F.M. (1992). Implementing TQM in higher education. *International Journal of Educational Management*, ISSN; ISSN-0951-354X, Vol. 5, No. 5, pp. 4-9

Tian, H. (2008). A New Resource Management and Scheduling Model in Grid Computing Based on a Hybrid Genetic Algorithm. *International Colloquium on Computing, ISBN: 978-0-7695-3290-5, Communication, Control, and Management*, pp. 113-117

Williams, P. (1993). Total quality management: some thoughts. *Higher Education*, ISSN: ISSN-0018-1560, Vol. 25 No. 3, pp. 373-5

www.vensim.com/sdmail/sdsoft.html cited on 12th Feb. 2009

www.arado.org.eg cited 12th Feb. 2009

Wilensky, U. (1999). NetLogo. http://ccl.northwestern.edu/netlogo/. Center for Connected Learning and Computer-Based Modeling, Northwestern University. Evanston, IL

Zhang, W.; Xu, H.; Wu, B. & Li, S. (2008). Safety Management of Traffic Accident Scene Based on System Dynamics, *International Conference on Intelligent Computation Technology and Automation*, icicta, vol. 2, pp. 482-485

19

Modeling a Two-Level Formalism for Inflection of Nouns and Verbs in Albanian

Arbana Kadriu
South East European University
Macedonia

1. Introduction

The core task of computational morphology is to take a word as input and produce a morphonological analysis for it. Morphotactics defines the model of morpheme ordering that explains which classes of morphemes can follow other classes of morphemes inside of a word (Jurafsky & Martin, 2000). But there are situations where the word formation process is not just joining of morphemes, such as assimilation, insertion, duplication, etc., and this are the situations where the phonological rules show up. Phonological rules may apply and change the shape of morphs (Mitkov, 2003).

Many linguists have modeled phonological rules, but it is considered that the most successful one is the model called *two-level morphology* (Koskenniemi, 1983). The two-level morphology model has been proved successful for formalizing the morphology of very different languages (English, German, Swedish, French, Spanish, Danish, Norwegian, Finnish, Russian, Turkish, Arab, Aymara, Swahili etc.) (Uibo, 2003). This system is used even for conversion between different writing systems (Maleki & Ahrenberg, 2008).

Thus, we can expect that the model is in fact universal and it may be possible to describe Albanian morphology in this framework as well.

Extensive research is done in this area in widely-used languages. For the Albanian language, to our knowledge, there is no such research that offers two-level formalism for any grammatical category. Initial point of the research presented here is a list of 4200 Albanian verbs in ten different tenses and a list of more than 100 Albanian nouns, where each record of the list holds the noun's form in all possible cases. This input data is used to obtain suffixes and rules that define the phonological alternations during concatenations.

2. Verbs in Albanian

Verbs are the most complex area of Albanian inflection (Trommer, 1997). An Albanian verb can be in one of the 6 possible moods: *indicative, admirative, conjunctive, conditional, optative,* and *imperative.*

The *indicative mood* is used for simple statements, declarations, etc., such as **shkruaj** (*I write*). The *admirative mood* is used to make statements of admirations, especially when surprised or in unexpected situations. *Conditional mood* and *subjunctive mood* are used to express

possibility. *Optative mood* is used for wishes or for curses. The *imperative* is used for orders, commands, or demands.
Verbs are conjugated in six tenses: *present, imperfect, future, past, present perfect, past perfect.* Each mood has *tenses,* and each tense has 6 *persons*: 3 for singular and 3 for plural. Only indicative mood has all six tenses.
Verbs are listed in the vocabulary in the present first person singular of the indicative: **unë shkoj** *(I go)* - **shkoj** *(to go)*. Some other examples are: **shkruaj** *(to write),* **shkoj** *(to go),* **ndihmoj** *(to help),* **pres** *(to wait),* **përsëris** *(to repeat),* **mësoj** *(to learn) etc.*
Verbs in Albanian do not have infinitive. There is a form, so called *paskajore* (translated as *infinitive*), that assumes many functions of the infinitive. Besides this, Albanian verbs have the *participle* and the *gerund*. For the verb **shkoj** (*to go*), participle is **shkuar**, gerund is **duke shkuar**, and infinitive **për të shkuar**.
Table 1 shows the conjugation of the verb **notoj** (*to swim*) in indicative mood, in the first four tenses. The future tense often is formed with the present subjunctive and the particle *do.* Table 2 shows the conjugation of this in indicative mood, in perfect tenses. The present perfect tense and the past perfect tense are formed with the participle form and finite forms of the auxiliaries ***kam*** *(to have*), or ***jam*** (*to be*).

	Present	**Imperfect**	**Past**	**Future**
unë (I)	notoj	notoja	notova	do të notoj
ti (you)	noton	notoje	notove	do të notosh
ai, ajo (he, she)	noton	notonte	notoi	do të notojë
ne (we)	notojmë	notonim	notuam	do të notojmë
ju (you)	notoni	notonit	notuat	do të notoni
ata (they)	notojnë	notonin	notuan	do të notojnë

Table 1. The conjugation of the verb **notoj** (*to swim*) in indicative mood – present, imperfect, past, future

	Present Perfect	**Past Perfect**
unë (I)	kam notuar	kisha notuar
ti (you)	ke notuar	kishe notuar
ai, ajo (he, she)	ka notuar	kishte notuar
ne (we)	kemi notuar	kishim notuar
ju (you)	keni notuar	kishit notuar
ata (they)	kanë notuar	kishin notuar

Table 2. The conjugation of the verb **notoj** (*to swim*) in indicative mood - the perfect tenses

Like in English, verbs in Albanian may be *transitive* or *intransitive,* of *active* or *passive* voice. The intransitive verbs (including reflexive verbs) are called in Albanian grammar *non-active.*

3. Nouns in Albanian

Albanian nouns are inflected by gender (masculine, feminine and neuter) and number (singular and plural). There are 5 declensions with 5 cases (nominative, accusative, genitive,

dative and ablative). The cases apply to both definite and indefinite article. The equivalent of a genitive is formed by using the prepositions *i/e/të/së*. The equivalent of an ablative is formed by using the prepositions *prej*. It should be mentioned that inflection of the Albanian nouns is realized through suffixes and no prefixes are used.
Table 3 shows the declension of the masculine noun *lis* (type of tree). Table 4 shows the declension of the feminine noun *fushë* (field).
The base form is considered the indefinite article nominative (Agalliu et al., 2002). The definite article can be in the form of noun suffixes, which vary with gender, case and number. For example, in singular nominative, masculine nouns often add *-i* or *-u*:

- *lis* (a tree) / *lisi* (the tree);
- *mik* (a friend) / *miku* (the friend).

	Indef. Sing.	**Indef. Pl.**	**Def. Sing.**	**Def. Pl.**
Nom.	lis (tree)	lisa (trees)	lisi (the tree)	lisat (the trees)
Gen.	lisi	lisave	lisit	lisave
Dat.	lisi	lisave	lisit	lisave
Accu.	lis	lisa	lisin	lisat
Abl.	lisi	lisash	lisit	lisave

Table 3. The declension of the masculine noun *lis* (tree)

	Indef. Sing.	**Indef. Pl.**	**Def. Sing.**	**Def. Pl.**
Nom.	fushë (field)	fusha (fields)	fusha (the field)	fushat (the fields)
Gen.	fushe	fushave	fushës	fushave
Dat.	fushe	fushave	fushës	fushave
Accu.	fushë	fusha	fushën	fushat
Abl.	fushe	fushave	fushës	fushave

Table 4. The declension of the feminine noun *fushë* (field)

4. Two-Level Morphology

This model includes two components:

- the phonological rules described through finite state transducers,
- the lexicon, which includes the lexical units and the morphotactics.

The formalism called *two-level phonology* is used in the two-level morphology model. The Koskenniemi's model is two-level in the sense that a word is described as a direct, symbol-to-symbol correspondence between its lexical and surface form (Antworth, 1990).
The two-level rules consist of three components: the correspondence, the operator and the environment.
Every pair lexical symbol-surface symbol is called correspondence pair. The notation for this correspondence is: *lexical symbol : surface symbol.*
For the first character of the previous example, we would write m:m, while for morpheme boundary we have +:0.
The operator defines the relation between the correspondence and the environment, where it appears. There are four operators, illustrated as follows:

- => - the correspondence appears only in this environment, but not always

- <= - the correspondence appears always in this environment, but not only in this one
- <=> - the correspondence appears always and only in this environment
- /<= - the correspondence never appears in this environment

The third component relates to the environment and specifies the phonological context where a specific phenomenon happens. The notation for this component is realized through the underline sign "_", called environment line, and its general form is LC__RC, where LC denotes the left context, while RC denotes the right context.

4.1 Automatic learning of morphotactics and two-level rules

Theron&Cloete used an augmented version of edit distance to align an underlying and surface string and discover morpheme boundaries (Theron & Cloete, 1997). They then look for insertions, deletions, and replacements in the alignment to find the location of a two-level rule, and look for the minimal context surrounding the rule using extensions of the heuristics in Johnson (Johnson, 1984) and Touretzky (Touretzky et al., 1990).
For automatic acquisition of two-level phonological rules for the inflection of the Albanian verbs and nouns, this model is adapted and upgraded.
They use the notion of string edit sequences assuming that only insertions and deletions are applied to a root form to get the inflected form. They determine the root form associated with an inflected form and consequently the suffixes and prefixes by exhaustively matching against all root words (Oflazer & Nirenburg, 1999).
As a first step for this research, a set of pairs base_noun (base_verb) - inflected_noun (inflected_verb) is constructed. The output of this phase is used as input for the second phase of the algorithm. For every pair of this input, according to the Theron&Cloete algorithm, a string edit sequence is constructed, using the insert, delete and replace operations.
With the aim to improve the results, a few string edit distance algorithms are tested and the best results are gained with the Brew string distance (Kadriu & Zdravkova, 2008).
After all the transformations, for all input pairs that are processed, the next step is to deal only with the special pairs. A special pair is every pair that presents deletion, insertion or replacement of a character.
For every special pair, the context in which they appear is constructed as follows: first left neighbour, then the first right neighbour, followed by the second left neighbour, then second right neighbour, and so on. At the end of this sequence a special pair is written, called *marked pair*. Some other special signs are also used, depicting the start of the string (SOS), the end of the string (EOS), and the sign (OOB), which is used when one context (left or right) is longer than the other one.
Using the resulting sequences, a minimal acyclic finite automaton is constructed, and it has only one start and one final state. The edges of this automaton represent the special pairs, while all terminal edges represent the marked pairs. The automata are constructed using xfst tool (Beesly & Karttunen, 2003), considering the constructed contexts as regular expressions.
If for a marked pair all paths go through some shortened path, the new found path is considered as context for that pair.
The next step is for every marked pair *x:y* to answer the question: 1) is this context the only one in which this pair occurs, and 2) is this pair always occurring in this context.

To answer the first question, all the paths that contain the marked pair should be passed. If they all have a common segment, the answer is yes. In other words, this means that for this context the rule => is true.
For the second question, all the terminal edges that have left component x are verified. If they all have right component equivalent to y, the answer for the second question is yes. This means that for this context the rule <= is true.
If the answer is positive for both questions, that means that this marked pair occurs always and only in this environment, i. e. for this context the rule <=> is true.
At the end, from the set of gained rules, the rule <=> with the shortest context is taken. If there is no <=> rule, the shortest context for the <= rule and/or => rule is picked up. If both have a common context, then they are concatenated in a single <=> rule.

5. Acquisition of morphotactics and two-level rules

5.1 The achieved morphotactics for verbs inflection

As it was mentioned, perfect tenses are formed using the participle form and finite forms of the auxiliary verbs. Since the participle is fixed and doesn't suffer phonological changes, these tenses are not covered by the research presented in this paper. Imperative mood has only the present tense and is conjugated only in the second person - singular and plural. For this reason, this mood is also not considered for further processing in this paper.
The input for the automatic acquisition of morphotactics and two-level phonological rules is a list of 70 verbs in ten different tenses: indicative (present, imperfect, past, future), conjunctive (present, past), admirative (present, imperfect), conditional (present), optative (present). Table 5 shows all 60 input forms used in our system for the verb **ftoj** (*to invite*).

Indicative				**Conjunctive**	
Present	*Imperfect*	*Past*	*Future*	*Present*	*Past*
ftoj	ftoja	ftova	do të ftoj	të ftoj	të ftoja
fton	ftoje	ftove	do të ftosh	të ftosh	të ftoje
fton	ftonte	ftoi	do të ftojë	të ftojë	të ftonte
ftojmë	ftonim	ftuam	do të ftojmë	të ftojmë	të ftonim
ftoni	ftonit	ftuat	do të ftoni	të ftoni	të ftonit
ftojnë	ftonin	ftuan	do të ftojnë	të ftojnë	të ftonin
Admirative		**Conditional**	**Optative**		
Present	*Imperfect*	*Present*	*Present*		
ftuakam	ftuakësha	do të ftoja	ftofsha		
ftuake	ftuakëshe	do të ftoje	ftofsh		
ftuaka	ftuakësh	do të ftonte	ftoftë		
ftuakemi	ftuakëshim	do të ftonim	ftofshim		
ftuakeni	ftuakëshit	do të ftonit	ftofshi		
ftuakan	ftuakëshin	do të ftonin	ftofshin		

Table 5. All input forms of the verb **ftoj** (*to invite*)

In view of the fact that each tense has six persons, it indicates that we have 4200 different forms of verbs as input for our system. Some of the tenses are formed with particles such as *do, u, të*. They are fixed and do not change. For this reason, we are interested only on the verb part and will not consider the particles during the morphological analysis of the verbs in those tenses. No particular distinction between transitive and intransitive verbs is made here.

As it was mentioned, verbs are listed in vocabularies in the present first person singular of the indicative. Given this fact, we use this form as a base form for further processing. All other forms as considered as derived forms. So, for each tense and for each verb, a list of 6 pairs base_verb-derived_verb is formed. For the verb **ftoj** (Table 3), imperfect tense, we have the following list of six pairs as an input.

ftoj *ftoja*
ftoj *ftoje*
ftoj *ftonte*
ftoj *ftonim*
ftoj *ftonit*
ftoj *ftonin*

For each tense, there is an input list of 420 such pairs of verbs. The output of the first step of the algorithm is a list of pairs *base_verb+obtained_suffix - derived form*. For the above input, the automatically achieved output is as follows:

ftoj+a *ftoja*
ftoj+e *ftoje*
ftoj+im *ftonim*
ftoj+in *ftonin*
ftoj+it *ftonit*
ftoj+te *ftonte*

So, from this process, the suffixes used for inflection in every particular tense are obtained. Table 6 shows all suffixes obtained.

Mood	Tense	Gained suffixes
Indicative	Present	më, në, m, n, t, i, ni, sh, im, in, o, 0
	Imperfect	a, e, it, te, *ësh,* sha, she, *shim, shin, shit,* j, ja, je
	Past	ëm, ët, ën, va, ve, am, at, an, u, të, ë, m, n, sh, më, në, im, in, ni, a, e, i, *ësh,* 0
	Future	më, ni, në, sh, ë, im, in, i, t, n, 0
Conjunctive	Present	më, ni, në, sh, in, im, i, t, n, ë, *ësh,*0
	Past	a, e, it, im, in, te, *ësh,sha, she,* ja, je, nim, nin, nit
Admirative	Present	*kam, kan,* ka, ke, *kemi, keni*
	Imperfect	kësh, kësha, këshe, këshim, këshin, këshit
Conditional	Present	a, e, it, im, in, te, *sha, she,* ja, je, j
Optative	Present	im, in, sha, shi, sh, të, shim, *shin*

Table 6. Suffixes obtained for every particular tense

It should be mentioned that there are some cases where it is intervened manually (suffixes in italic):

- There are some letters in Albanian that consist of two characters. One such case is the letter **sh**. There were cases where instead of suffixes *sha, she, shim, shin, shit,* the suffixes ha, he, im, in, it were obtained (and the insertion of character s was suggested).
- The suffixes of the admirative mood, except for present tense suffixes *ka* and *ke,* come out without the first character *k*. For example, instead of the suffix *këshim,* the suffix *ëshim* is obtained.

The suffix *ësh* does not appear as a suffix in itself. Instead, it appear as insertion of character *ë* plus suffix *sh*.

5.2 The achieved morphotactics for nouns inflection

List of over 100 Albanian nouns in all cases is used to automatically learn the morphotactics and two-level phonological rules. As base word is considered the indefinite singular of nominative. The following tags are used to describe special cases: S - stays for singular, P - plural, indef - indefinite, def - definite, nom - nominative, gen - genitive, dat - dative, acc - accusative, abl - ablative.

For example, the noun *ditë* (*a day*), corresponds to this input record:

- *ditë (S_indef_nom&acc)*
- *dite (S_indef_gen&dat&rrj)*
- *dita (S_def_nom)*
- *ditën (S_def_acc)*
- *ditës (S_def_gen&dat&rrj)*
- *ditë (P_indef_nom&acc)*
- *ditëve (P_indef-gen&d_def_gen&dat&abl)*
- *ditët (P_def_nom&acc)*
- *ditësh (P_indef_abl)*

From the above list, it can be noticed that the same form can be used for several cases. This is so because, as explained in the second part of this paper, same cases are defined using prepositions, and other cases are defined from the context.

The procedure is applied to all 8 cases in separate (the first case is used as a base form). After applying the first step of the above described algorithm, we obtain all proposed (by the system) segmentations, which are in a form as the one shown below:

- *bukë+e buke* (bread)
- *burrë+i burri* (man)
- *dashuri+e dashurie* (love)
- *dhembje+je dhembjeje* (pain)
- *dhomë+e dhome* (room)
- *diell+i dielli* (sun)

Following inflectional suffixes are automatically obtained:

Case	**Gained suffixes**
S_indef_gen&dat&abl	e, je, i, u, ri
S_def_nom	i, u, a, ja, 0
S_def_gen&dat&abl	t, së, s, it, rit, ut
S_def_acc	n, në, in, un
P_indef_nom&acc	a, e, em, ëz, j, ë, arë, ra, 0
P_indef-gen&d_def_gen&dat&abl	ve, ave
P_def_nom&acc	të, ët, at, et, t
P_indef_abl	sh

The learned suffixes are implemented in the lexicon used for defining two-level model of Albanian nouns.

5.3 The achieved phonological rules

The segmentations achieved in the previous phase are used as input for the second phase, where the morpho-phonological alternations are learned. Taking into consideration the fact that we want to create a model that will include all verbs/nouns, and not distinct models for each tense/case, we automatically reduce the rules so that they will not conflict with each other.

For each special pair, merge left-arrow rules with right-arrow rules into a double-arrow rule with intersecting context. If several contexts are available for some rule, the new rule will have the intersected context. If for some special pair same-arrow rules have several contexts with an empty intersection, make a new rule with disjunctive contexts. Finally, resolve conflicts as explained in any two-level literature.

For example, for all cases we got the special pair ë:0, but in different context:

- ë:0 <=> _ +:0
- ë:0 <=> _ +:0 i:i t:t EOS
- ë:0 => _ +:0 i:i n:n EOS
- ë:0 => _ +:0
- ë:0 => _ +:0
- ë:0 => _ +:0
- ë:0 => _ +:0
- ë:0 => _ +:0

After the reduction, we got only a single rule for the above obtained rules: ë:0 =>_ +:0.

The automatically learned rules were used as a base for further extension, testing them and manually improving the "holes" in the system:

- The rules that involve insertion of characters *k, s, ë* or replacement of some characters to *k, s, ë* are removed (for reasons explained in the previous section).
- The rules with a too long context are removed, as it is for example the following rule:

0:e => SOS r:r ë:ë n:n k:k ë:ë s:s h:h +:0 +:0 _ EOS OOB OOB OOB OOB OOB OOB OOB OOB[1]

- For some of the marked pairs the context is too short to describe the environment where they appear. For example, rule "0:n => +:0 _ " is extended to the rule "0:n => +:0 _ t:t e:e".

[1] EOS, OOB, SOS are special signs used in the algorithm for machine learning of rules

- Some special pairs appear in the context of some rules, but they never appear as marked pair. For example, in the rule *"o:u => _ 0:a +:0"* we have the special pair *0:a*, but this never appears on the left side of any rule (as marked pair).

After improving these gaps, there are twelve two-level rules implemented for the verb inflection:

1. 0:o => _ n:n i:i #:#
2. u:0 => _ a:0 +:0
3. a:0 => u:0 _ +:0
4. m:0 => [e:e | e:0] _ +:0
5. j:0 => _ +:0
6. 0:n => +:0 _ t:t e:e
7. t:s <=> _ +:0 t:t e:e #:#
8. h:0 => [o:o | o:u] _ e:0 m:0
9. e:0 => _ [m:0 +:0 | +:0]
10. o:u => _ [h:0 e:0 m:0 | j:0]
11. 0:f => +:0 _ [s:s h:h | t:t ë:ë]
12. 0:a <=> o:u [h:0 e:0 m:0 | j:0] +:0 _ k:k

For the noun inflection, the following rules were implemented:

1. *ë*:0 => _ +:0 | _ r:r +:0
2. e:0 => _ +:0
3. 0:[a | e | ë] => _ +:0 v:v e:e
4. u:0 => _ a:a +:0
5. 0:r => +:0 _

6. Evaluation of the implemented system

The Albanian alphabet has 36 letters: a, e, i, o, u, ë, b, c, d, f, g, h, j, k, l, m, n, p, q, r, s, t, v, x, y, z, ç, dh, gj, ll, nj, rr, sh, th, xh, zh. The last nine letters are concatenation of two characters. Since there are no phonological alternations obtained for these letters, they are dropped out when defining the alphabet used in the system - when they show up in the words, they are considered as distinct characters.

The system is implemented using PC-KIMMO environment (Antworth, 1995). It includes a lexicon file, a rules file and a file that contains list of verbs in their base form - the present first person singular of the indicative. The lexicon file includes the list of suffixes and the defined morphotactics for creating inflectional form of verbs and nouns. The rules file consists of several finite state automata that describe the defined rules.

6.1 Verbs system

An aspect that we considered while implementing the rules is the fact that there are cases where verbs ending in *em*, follow two segmentations, where one is semantically incorrect. For example, for the verb **ankohem** (*to complain*) both a semantically correct (1) and a semantically not correct (2) segmentation will be produced:

1. ankohem+ [V(ankohem)+AGENT-zero]
2. ankohem+m [V(ankohem)+AGENT-m]

The same situation is with verbs ending in *j*, when adding the suffix *j* or suffix that starts with the character *j*. That is why we added two disallowing rules, that is, rules that define that these correspondences never occur in this context:

1. m:0 /<= e:e _ +:0 m:m #:#
2. j:0 /<= _ +:0 j:j

After all the phonological and morphotactical rules are implemented, the system is tested on 4200 different forms of verbs. The result obtained is that all verbs are correctly segmented for the indicative present, indicative imperfect, indicative past. For the other tenses, in total 84 verbs are not segmented. Twelve of them (two verbs in six different cases) are result of situations where the rules with a too long context are removed.
In Albanian, there are cases of so-called irregular verbs, or verbs that in conjunctive past, admirative (present and imperfect), conditional and optative are derived from the participle and not from the present first person singular in the indicative mood. Since we used the present first person as a base form in input data, these occurrences are not modeled in our system. This case would be a subject of further research. Even with this "weakness" of the system, it has successfully segmented 98% of the verbs.

6.2 Nouns system

An aspect that we considered while implementing the rules is the fact that some gained rules produced morphologically correct, but semantically non-correct segmentations. It is the case when a suffix that corresponds to a masculine noun adds to a feminine noun. For example, if we consider the noun *britaniku* (*the Britain* – masculine). The system produces the semantically correct segmentation – *britanik+u* (a Britain masculine + suffix u), but also the semantically incorrect segmentation – *britanike+u* (a Britain feminine + suffix u). This is the case with some feminine nouns that end in *e* or *ë*. That is why we added two disallowing rules, that is, rules that define that these correspondences never occur in this context.

- *ë:0 /<= _ +:0 ë:ë [s:s | n:n | t:t | #:#]*
- *e:0 /<= _ +:0 [u:u | i:i | e:e | ë:ë]*

After all the phonological and morphotactical rules are implemented, the system is tested on 856 nouns that were not in their base form. These are seen verbs (verbs that were used for training). Table 7 gives a picture for the "negative" results when testing the system. All others are correctly segmented and produced only a single segmentation.

Case	**No segmentation**	**Two segmentations**
S_indef_gen&dat&abl	0	3
S_def_nom	0	5
S_def_gen&dat&abl	2	0
S_def_acc	2	0
P_indef_nom&acc	8	4
P_indef-gen&d_def_gen&dat&abl	8	0
P_def_nom&acc	8	0
P_indef_abl	8	0

Table 7. All "error" occurrences

All cases that contain two segmentations are situations when the fifth rule is applied (the insertion of character *r*).
For example, for the noun *syri* (*the eye*), we get the segmentation *sy+ri* (the suffix *ri* is added), but also the segmentation *sy+i* (here the character r is inserted).
The gained no-segmentation situations for cases: S_def_gen&dat&abl and S_def_acc are as a result of the fact that suffixes *-ës* and *-ën* are not obtained automatically from the first part of the algorithm. These suffixes are added to the lexicon and after that we did not have any no-segmentation situation for these two cases. Thus, we are left with only eight non-segmented nouns in four cases in plural. These are situations with so-called irregular nouns or nouns that undergo more complicated phonological alternations. In fact, as it was mentioned in section 6, rules are also produced for these alternations, but they were not considered for implementation, having in mind that a longer input list of "irregular" nouns would produce better results. Below is the list of pairs *S_indef_nom - P_indef_nom* of all those nouns:

- *babë - baballarë (a father – fathers)*
- *diell - diej (a sun – suns)*
- *djalë - djem (a boy – boys)*
- *dorë - duar (a hand – hands)*
- *natë - net (a night – nights)*
- *njeri - njerëz (a person – persons)*
- *vëlla - vëllezër (a brother – brothers)*
- *vit - vjet (a year – years)*

It should be mentioned that the other three cases are similar to the case *P_indef_nom*. It means that if the rules will be implemented for one of the cases, it will work for all other three cases.
The next step was testing of the system on unseen nouns. We used 416 nouns, extracted from a tagged text - the initial part of a novel (Trommer & Kallulli, 2004). To our knowledge, this is the only tagged text in Albanian. From these nouns, 405 nouns were correctly segmented. The remaining 9 nouns were irregular nouns, mentioned above (on seen nouns).

- *duar (hands) – twice*
- *miqve (to the friends)*
- *motrës (to the sister)*
- *njerëz (persons) – three times*
- *njerëzit (the persons)*
- *njerëzve (to the persons)*

This means that the system successfully segmented 98% of unseen nouns.

7. Conclusions

The research presented here is of a great significance as an already known methodology has been extended and put in another linguistic framework - Albanian verbs and nouns. It also describes a methodology for defining two-level formalism for a specific grammatical category. This approach can be used for other grammatical categories, in Albanian or in any other language.
Except this contribution, it shows that a machine learning algorithm can be applied to completely define the two-level morphology for this language.

8. References

Agalliu, F.; Angoni, E.; Demiraj, S.; Dhrimo, A.; Hysa, E.; Lafe, E. & Likaj, E. (2002). *Gramatika e gjuhës shqipe 1*, ISBN: 99927-761-6-1, BASH, Tirana

Antworth, E. L. (1990). PC-KIMMO: A Two-level Processor for Morphological Analysis, *Summer Institute of Linguistics*, Dallas

Antworth, E. L. (1995). Introduction to PC-KIMMO, *North Texas Natural Language Processing Workshop*, University of Texas

Beesly, K. R. & Karttunen, L. (2003). *Finite state morphology*, CSLI Publications, Leland Stanford Junior University, USA

Johnson, M. (1984). A discovery procedure for certain phonological rules, *Proceedings of COLING-84*, pp. 344 - 347, ISBN: 9991746080, Stanford, CA, July 1984, ACL

Jurafsky, D. & Martin, J. H. (2000). *Speech and Language Processing*, Prentice Hall, ISBN: 0-13-095069-6, Pearson Higher Education, New Jersey

Kadriu, A. & Zdravkova, K. (2008). Semi-Automatic Learning Of Two-Level Phonological Rules For Agentive Nouns, *Proceedings of EUROSIM/UKSim 2008*, pp. 307-312, ISBN: 9781424431922, Cambridge, England, April 2008, IEEE

Koskenniemi, K. (1983). Two-level Morphology: A General Computational Model for Word-Form Recognition and Production, *PhD Dissertation*, Department of General Linguistics, University of Helsinki

Maleki, J. & Ahrenberg, L. (2008). Converting Romanized Persian to the Arabic Writing System, *Proceedings of LREC 2008*, pp. 2904-2908, ISBN: 2-9517408-4-0, Marrakesh, Morocco, May 2008, ELRA

Mitkov, R. (2003). *The Oxford handbook of computational Linguistics*, Oxford University Press Inc., ISBN: 978-0-19-823882-9, New York

Oflazer, K. & Nirenburg, S. (1999). Practical Bootstrapping of Morphological Analyzers, *Proceedings of CoNLL-99, Workshop at EACL'99*, pp. 143-146, Bergen, Norway, June 1999, Springer Verlag

Theron, P. & Cloete, I. (1997). Automatic Acquisition of Two-Level Morphological Rules, *Proceedings of ANLP*, pp. 103 - 110, Washington, USA, April 1997, ACL

Touretzky, D. S.; Elvgren, G. & Wheeler, D. W. (1990). Phonological rule induction: An architectural solution, *Proceedings of COGSCI-90*, pp. 348–355, Hillsdale, New Jersey, August 1990, Lawrence Erlbaum Associates

Trommer, J. (1997). Eine Theorie der albanischenVerbflexion in mo_lex, *M.A. thesis*, University of Osnabruck

Trommer, J. & D. Kallulli (2004). A Morphological Tagger for Standard Albanian, *Proceedings of the LREC 2004*, pp. 201-225, ISBN: 2-9517408-1-6, Lisbon, Portugal, May 2004, ELRA

Uibo, H. (2003). Experimental Two-Level Morphology of Estonian, *8th Estonian Winter School in Computer Science (EWSCS)*, Palmse